Praise for *A Mad Catastrophe*

"*A Mad Catastrophe* finally brings some clarity to how the death of one Archduke, while admittedly tragic, could lead to the deaths of millions. . . . Wawro's excellently written book, in chilling detail, explains all the frustrating and infuriating blundering. The war was completely senseless, the insane war-lust of a failing state; this book gives Austria-Hungary its rightful, starring role as cause of the conflict."

—*San Francisco Book Review*

"Wawro writes about the Austro-Hungarian Empire's role in the start and unfolding of the Great War with verve, inescapable black humour and a certain note of there-but-for-the-grace of God."

—*Macleans* (CAN)

"Wawro is a historian of the US military, but his damning portrait of the neurotic empire . . . well reflects the surreal fiction of Hasek and Musil."

—*Literary Review* (UK)

"*A Mad Catastrophe* is a welcome contribution to the small but growing number of scholarly studies of the eastern front that have appeared in English over the last few years."

—*BBC History Magazine*

"2014 marks the centennial of the outbreak of World War I, and Geoffrey Wawro's *A Mad Catastrophe* is a welcome addition to the growing list of books covering the causes and development of the horrific war. Even in a crowded field, however, Wawro's study will, I think, stand out, thanks to its focus on the much-neglected eastern front. . . . Battle by battle, Wawro catalogs the collapse. Accompanied by detailed maps, his descriptions are blow-by-blow accounts, all written in lively prose. His is a sad story of carnage and destruction that drives home, yet again, the futility and stupidity of this 'Great War.'"

—*Providence Journal*

"An engaging case study in the disaster that can happen when interests and capabilities get greatly out of kilter. . . . Readable and entertaining."

—*Army Magazine*

"*A Mad Catastrophe* is a highly readable and cogently argued book that, once again, shows the level of sheer idiocy that lay behind this pivotal period of history."

—*History of War* (UK)

"A fascinating addition to the military and diplomatic scholarship surrounding Austria-Hungary's inept move toward war and its incompetent execution of the conflict. . . . Wawro's book is an excellent account of where plunging over a cliff will land you: in pieces."

—*MHQ: The Quarterly Journal of Military History*

"Wawro's authoritative account is a damning analysis of an empire and a people unready for war."

—*Publishers Weekly*

"Wawro offers a crucial insight into the Eastern Front. . . . On this centennial of the Great War's beginning, Wawro has composed a thoroughly researched and well-written account, mercilessly debunking any nostalgia for the old monarch and the deeply dysfunctional empire over which he presided."

—*Kirkus*

"Wawro's contribution lies in his focus on how the overall decline of Austria-Hungary broke relations with the Balkan states and Russia and how its military blundering caused its ultimate destruction. A worthwhile read."

—*Library Journal*

"*A Mad Catastrophe* is an absorbing and shocking look at a now neglected aspect of the origins of the First World War. The author—a master military historian, whose works are standard accounts of late-nineteenth-century Austro-Prussian wars—shows just how reckless Viennese policy before and after the outbreak of hostilities was. Wawro's book should be on every reading list and in the hands of every policymaker."

—Brendan Simms, author of *Europe: The Struggle for Supremacy from 1453 to the Present*

"This is not just a story of the part played by the Habsburg Empire in precipitating the First World War, and of the truly lamentable performance of its armies once the war began. It is a devastating indictment of a whole regime, whose slovenly incompetence resulted in a military catastrophe of which Geoff Wawro gives a truly horrifying account. Of all the histories of 1914 that are now pouring from the press, this will rank among the very best."

—Sir Michael Howard

"Considering the central role played by the Dual Monarchy in the outbreak of First World War, it is astonishing that so little is known to this day about the fighting on the Austro-Hungarian fronts. Geoffrey Wawro's *A Mad Catastrophe* triumphantly fills this gaping hole in our knowledge. The most important study of the Eastern Front in decades, Wawro's brilliant and thoroughly researched narrative easily replaces existing books on the subject. Eschewing the Radetzky March nostalgia which so often suffuses books on the last years of the Dual Monarchy, Wawro summons forth a searing indictment of the lethal Austro-Hungarian blundering which helped unleash the First World War and brought all the horrors of the modern age to Eastern Europe."

—Sean McMeekin, author of *July 1914: Countdown to War*

"*A Mad Catastrophe* systematically eviscerates Austria-Hungary's final, fatal efforts to play the role of a great power. Wawro presents a case study of culpable, comprehensive, synergistic incompetence at every level of policy-making, strategic planning, and operational effectiveness. A decaying empire went to war fecklessly, conducted war haphazardly, and pulled Europe down into its final vortex. Brilliantly acerbic and comprehensively researched, this is a book difficult to put down."

—Dennis Showalter, author of *Patton and Rommel: Men of War in the 20th Century*

"A distinctly unique and long overdue contribution to the historiography of early WWI. The aficionados of Barbara Tuchman's *Guns of August* and Istvan Szabo's film *Colonel Redl* will find this a marvelous, engrossing and distinctly well-written read that gives necessary balance to the already well-covered narrative of WWI's Western Front. Understanding the challenges and ultimate fate of the creaky, polyglot, decrepit yet also curiously progressive Austrian-Hungarian Empire is essential for comprehending the furies that erupted and boiled over the subsequent century within the vast, complicated, multi-ethnic expanse it spanned. Master historian Geoff Wawro does a tour de force job in colorfully bringing this to light."

—Brigadier General Peter Zwack, US Army

"Geoffrey Wawro has done a superb job in explaining and describing how the Habsburg Empire, in trying to save itself, provoked a great war and then destroyed its army through a combination of incompetence and pretentiousness."

—Norman Stone, author of *World War One: A Short History*

"Professor Wawro has produced a gripping and highly recommended account of Austria-Hungary's descent into the carnage of the First World War's first year. Unprepared but self-confident, divided by nationality, religion, and interest, the Habsburg armies got an unexpected thrashing that anticipated the demise of the rickety monarchy. This is a very instructive primer on imperial overreach, political irresponsibility, and the dreadful cost in human lives that was the epitaph for old Central Europe."

—Ivo Banac, Bradford Durfee Emeritus Professor
of History, Yale University

A MAD CATASTROPHE

Also by Geoffrey Wawro:

The Austro-Prussian War: Austria's War with Prussia and Italy in 1866

Warfare and Society in Europe, 1792–1914

The Franco-Prussian War: The German Conquest of France in 1870–71

Quicksand: America's Pursuit of Power in the Middle East

A MAD CATASTROPHE

The Outbreak of World War I and the Collapse
of the Habsburg Empire

GEOFFREY WAWRO

BASIC BOOKS
A Member of the Perseus Books Group
New York

Books published by Basic Books are available at special discounts for bulk purchases in the United States by corporations, institutions, and other organizations. For more information, please contact the Special Markets Department at the Perseus Books Group, 2300 Chestnut Street, Suite 200, Philadelphia, PA 19103, or call (800) 810-4145, ext. 5000, or e-mail special.markets@perseusbooks.com.

Designed by Jack Lenzo

The Library of Congress has cataloged the hardcover edition as follows:
Wawro, Geoffrey.
A mad catastrophe : the outbreak of World War I and the collapse of the Habsburg Empire / Geoffrey Wawro.
p. cm.
Includes bibliographical references and index.
ISBN 978-0-465-02835-1 (hardback)—ISBN 978-0-465-08081-6 (e-book)
1. World War, 1914–1918—Causes. 2. World War, 1914–1918—Campaigns—Balkan Peninsula. 3. World War, 1914–1918—Campaigns—Galicia (Poland and Ukraine) 4. Habsburg, House of. 5. Austria—History—Franz Joseph I, 1848–1916. I. Title.
D512.W38 2014
940.4'14—dc23
2013039393
ISBN 978-0465-05795-5 (paperback)

10 9 8 7 6 5 4 3 2 1

To Judith Aileen Winslow Stoughton Wawro

Contents

List of Illustrations

List of Maps

Acknowledgments

A CENTURY AGO my Austro-Hungarian grandparents landed on Ellis Island from a dusty little village in Galicia near Tarnopol. It was just the sort of enervating outpost—I've been there—that would have driven one of Roth or Zweig's Viennese cavaliers to drink, dice, despair, or all three. Had my grandparents chosen to shake the dust of Galicia from their boots any later, those hard-working Ukrainian peasants—Vasil and Anna Wawro—would almost certainly have been consumed by the Great War. Mobilized in 1914 with his Austro-Hungarian 15th Regiment, Vasil would have plunged immediately into the cauldron of Lemberg. Reading this book, it's hard to imagine that he would have survived, for his outflung III Corps bore the brunt of the Russian onslaught. Anna would have been occupied by the Russians, whose Third and Eighth Armies passed on either side of her village in August 1914. Food was always scarce in Galicia, the age-old "kingdom of the naked and the starving," and it became even scarcer in wartime. Anna might have starved, or died of the camp diseases that stalked civilians near armies in the field. This book draws much of its inspiration from the memory of my paternal grandparents and of their great American son, my father N. William Wawro. They have all rested for years in a peaceful cemetery in Connecticut, having created so much by their flight and hard work in America.

A Mad Catastrophe is dedicated to my mother, Judith Stoughton Wawro, on the occasion of her ninetieth birthday. She's been a tremendous source of love and help to me over the years, most recently throwing open the doors in New England whenever the Texas summer bites and looking after me and my two sons, Winslow and Matias, with stupefying cheerfulness, efficiency, and grace. I've visited the villages of my father's parents in eastern Galicia thanks to my mother, who gamely rented a car in Vienna and drove with me all the way to Zbaraz, sharing the potholes, watery beer, bribes, thefts, and other tribulations (including being struck and nearly obliterated by an army jeep at an intersection in Bukovina). Together, we found the villages, just as they'd been described, and a cemetery filled with Wawros: the quick (all looking exactly like my father) and the dead (Wawro in Cyrillic, *Babpo*, etched on the headstones).

Readers of my acknowledgments in previous books will recall my picaresque drive as a grad student with my mother through Bohemia and Moravia to view the battlefields of 1866. On later trips, we also toured some of the battlefields described in this book, from Tannenberg down to Przemysl and Lemberg. I have an indelible memory of her in the passenger seat of our rented Opel, peering at grainy photocopies of old Habsburg general staff maps, patiently cross-referencing them with modern maps, and affecting not to notice as I slewed around country lanes roaring things like: "Mother, for the hundredth time, Hradec Králové *is* Königgrätz!"

These, of course, are just the most immediate of her contributions. Mother took total responsibility for a large and challenging family after my father's early death in 1978 (an accident that she barely survived herself) and shepherded all seven of us into adulthood. Like some wise Ottoman vizier ruling over brawling tribes, she did this with ineffable fairness and decency, and now presides over a vast, generally contented family of children and grandchildren. We've just celebrated her ninetieth birthday at a family reunion and the outpourings of love, admiration, and respect from every quarter were a striking testimony to her goodness, acuity, and leadership. As the youngest of seven, I probably leaned hardest on her over the years, and she's been a stalwart to me, providing emotional support, but also the sort of logistical assistance—described above—that military historians can only dream of. Her love for travel and adventure is infectious. There's not one Ruritanian corner that I've had to visit in the course of my research that she wasn't eager to see as well.

I finished the research for this book two summers ago in Vienna. It was not nearly as much fun as earlier research trips; I was older; I had children back in the States; I was living alone (not with the Falstaffian roommate the Fulbright Commission had arranged for me twenty years earlier), and I was working daily in the grimy suburban seat of the new Vienna archives, quite unlike the stately old Baroque venue in the heart of the city. I'd return every day to my apartment, jog morosely around the Augarten, prepare some insipid dinner on my single-burner stove, and then stare at the walls. One evening—as I drained this cup of bitterness while shuffling notes around my desk—the laptop rang and it was . . . Mother. She had read between the lines of my e-mails, installed Skype (no mean feat for a woman who still calls computers "word processors"), and called me, a kindness she would perform almost every evening until my return.

Marianne Cook has been my best friend for many years. As I was making final revisions to this manuscript—and chuckling over General Conrad von Hötzendorf's overreaction to the flu—I contracted the flu myself, and within hours of the first symptoms Marianne was at my bedside with vitamin C, zinc, DayQuil, Gatorade, and even a dog, her lab Abby, who she kindly gave me for a week to take the edge off my quarantined loneliness. That's the sort of person she is, and she's made me very happy over the years. Marianne also shared many of the travels involved in this book. Though she has a clear preference for the islands and vineyards of Croatia, she joined me for an unforgettable climb to the summit of Montenegro and a hair-raising descent (on the slender Austrian military road) to the great Bay of Kotor. It's hard for me to imagine life in Dallas without Marianne.

My two sons, Winslow and Matias, have also been a great help to me. They are so full of energy, life, and quicksilver passions, and their onrushing, competitive adolescence always puts me in mind of a quarrelsome Austro-Hungarian headquarters and makes me cringe and laugh by turns. As they've matured, Win and Mati have become good friends as well, able to discuss my work and theirs, and the many mysteries of life. I feel certain that my occasional outbreaks of ennui—traceable to that bleak Galician root—are as helpful to them as their raw joy and enthusiasm are to me.

Research assistance from the University of North Texas enabled me to research in European archives and tour the battlefields described in this book in Poland, Ukraine, and Serbia. Many years ago, I won a research prize and travel grant from Oakland University, which also paid for some of the research in this book. Ukraine—today's Galicia—always was and still is the land of broken roads, and so there I relied on the car and guide services of Jarek Vitiv and Igor Holyboroda, who patiently drove me (at the speed of a loping peasant) around all of the battlefields of Lemberg and Rawa-Ruska. Ivo Banac (of Yale and Zagreb) and his wife Andrea Feldman were very good to Marianne and me in Dubrovnik, Ston, and the Peljesac Peninsula, enlarging our knowledge of Balkan history and Croatian wine.

Lothar Höbelt at the University of Vienna let me stay with him during an early research trip, and more recently, was very helpful to me in the archives. Lothar was also kind enough to introduce me to Christian Ortner, the director of the Austrian Military History Museum. Christian, in turn, connected me with Peter Enne and Werner Scherhaufer in the museum's excellent photo archive. These two gentlemen let me use their office for days on end to choose many of the photographs for this book. I must collectively thank the many archivists in Kew, Vincennes, Vienna, and College Park, who facilitated the research for this book.

David and Caroline Noble were kind enough to let me stay with them in London for some of the research for this book, as did Jun Hiraga. In Paris, my nephew Marc Bataillon was a generous host during the Vincennes research. Closer to home, Michael Leggiere, my good friend and deputy at UNT's Military History Center, has helped me more than he knows with his hard work at the center and his good cheer and friendship. Thanks also to my brothers and sisters: Peter, David, Mark, Jill, George, and the memory of Robin. Growing up in a large family is a blessing, a statement I know that certain of my siblings will stare at in (feigned) amazement.

My agent Tina Bennett at William Morris Endeavor helped me pull the book proposal together and has been a wise reader and consigliere as always. Simon Winder, author of *Danubia,* also helped shape the proposal in the early days, especially by his insistence that I return to the archives to delve deeper into the Eastern Front. My editor, Lara Heimert of Basic Books, has made this a far better volume by stemming my lust for illustrative anecdotes. The book would be twice as long but half as good without Lara's astute intervention. I must also thank Alex Littlefield, Katy O'Donnell, and Melissa Veronesi at Basic for their excellent work editing and producing the book. Phil Schwartzberg made the excellent maps for this book and bore up patiently under the barrage of obscure place names. Finally, thanks to the great scholars who volunteered to read galleys of the book: Sir Michael Howard, Ivo Banac, Niall Ferguson, Dennis Showalter, Norman Stone, Christopher Clark, Brendan Simms, and Sean McMeekin. Thanks to Brigadier General Peter B. Zwack, US Defense Attaché to the Russian Federation, who gave the book a good read in Moscow and—with his own distinguished Austro-Hungarian ancestry— has been an informed and careful reader of my work since we first met many years ago at the Naval War College.

Foreword

IN THE FALL OF 1866, the aide to an Austrian general assaulted a Russian diplomat in the delicatessen of the Hotel Sacher in central Vienna. The Russian had been snickering about Austria's defeat that year in the Austro-Prussian War, a seven-week-long conflict between the two historical allies that had effectively ended that July with Prussia's decisive victory over the Austrians at the Battle of Königgrätz. Throughout the short war, Russia had watched from the sidelines as its two great-power rivals bloodied each other. Now, annoyed by the Russian official amusing himself at Austria's expense, the aide took a swing at him.

That scuffle at the Hotel Sacher flared into an international incident and fired speculation that a war between Russia and Austria was in the offing. While these rumors proved false, they suggested that despite the Austrian Empire's crushing defeat at Königgrätz, it was still possible for the empire and its Habsburg rulers to contemplate a war with Russia unassisted.

By 1914, that was no longer the case. Austria—by then part of a Dual Monarchy with neighboring Hungary—had been reduced to a Balkan power, vying with Italy for the epithet "Least of the Great Powers," and, like the Ottoman Empire, in danger of slipping out of the great-power club altogether. The story of how this stunning and rapid transformation came about is as interesting as that of Austria's last war—a bloody, reckless disaster from beginning to end.

Vienna is the essential starting point for any inquiry into the origins of the First World War. There the fires that consumed

Europe and the world were lit, then fanned into a blaze. Both the long- and short-term causes of the ruinous conflict can be traced back to the Habsburgs' peculiar worldview and fractious central European holdings. The short-term cause of the conflict, all agree, was the July Crisis of 1914, which followed the assassination of Habsburg archduke Franz Ferdinand in June by a Bosnian Serb named Gavrilo Princip. The escalating tensions in July, driven by the suspicion that the Russian-backed Serbian government had aided the assassination plot, exploded into war in August. The war's long-term causes included imperialism: the competition among the European great powers, the United States, and Japan for new markets, raw materials, and naval bases, chiefly in Africa and Asia. Another long-term cause of the Great War was the existence of contending alliance systems: the Anglo-French-Russian Triple Entente and the German-Austrian-Italian Triple Alliance.

Those alliance systems, dangerous enough in themselves, became far more explosive when outfitted with aggressive war plans, mass conscripted armies, and modern armaments: dreadnought battleships, quick-firing field artillery, high-explosive shells, and machine guns. Indeed, the European arms races that began in the 1890s were themselves another powerful spur to war. The German Schlieffen Plan of 1905, which called for the rapid mobilization and offensive use of the German and Austro-Hungarian armies, was answered by equally aggressive French and Russian war plans. All of the plans were given force with massive military and naval buildups that had begun in the 1890s and made the mood of 1914, already dark and dangerous, even more so.

The generally reactionary attitude that prevailed in Europe during this period also contributed to the outbreak of war. The heart of Europe was commanded by moody, conservative monarchies: Russia, Germany, Austria-Hungary, and Italy. Without the safety valve of liberal governments, those regimes looked queasily at the new politics, culture, and manners of their time. Socialists, pledged to the abolition of monarchy, became the biggest party in the German Reichstag in 1906, prompting at least one German general to call for a "brisk merry war against the reigning confusion." Conservatives in Russia, Austria-Hungary, and Italy had similar views—as did British and French conservatives, for that matter. War would permit martial law, union-bashing, and crackdowns on "subversive" parties; it would also harden a nation's muscles, flush out the riffraff, devalue materialism and eroticism, and revive patriotism. This colossal naivete in the face of the looming bloodbath, which would leave sixteen million dead and twenty-one million wounded, still beggars explanation.

Austria-Hungary played an unlikely role in sparking the conflagration. It is often argued that Germany deliberately and paradoxically hastened the war's outbreak because of the *weakness* of its Austro-Hungarian ally. As both statesman and historian, Churchill noted the dangerous absurdity that "the glory and safety of Europe hung upon its weakest link."[1] Austria was disintegrating in the modern "age of nationalism." An essentially feudal power whose crown lands with their dozen nationalities were botched together in the sixteenth century, Austria-Hungary limped into the twentieth century under attack from its own peoples, who wanted federalism, home rule, or independence.

Germany's nervousness about the future of Austria-Hungary was a major cause of the Great War. Churchill, in his own history of the Eastern Front in World War I, cited it as perhaps *the* cause: "This vicious, fatal degeneration made the peace and civilization of mankind dependent upon the processes of disintegration and spasms of recovery which alternately racked the Habsburg Monarchy."[2] Having gone to the brink of war with France and Britain in 1905 and 1911 over the issue of Morocco only to see the Austrians back out, the Germans seized on the July Crisis of 1914 as their last, best chance to push the Austro-Hungarians into a reinvigorating world war before the monarchy collapsed from its internal divisions or was swallowed up by the surrounding pan-Slav powers of Russia and Serbia.

A Mad Catastrophe is about Austria-Hungary's fatal degeneration and its impact on European civilization. This is one area of the First World War that has been largely overlooked by historians. Most allude to Austro-Hungarian weakness but don't plumb it in depth. Other historians have treated Austria-Hungary as a genuine great power and analyzed its military and foreign relations as if nothing extraordinary were amiss. *A Mad Catastrophe* fills in this neglected area by charting the decline of Austria-Hungary in the decades after 1866—when it had fought (and lost) its last great European war—and its stumbling course through the crucial years 1912–1914, when the Balkans were in an uproar and Vienna looked, hesitated, looked again, and then madly leaped into a great war that it had no hope of winning.

Austria-Hungary's decision to enter the war in the first place was exceeded in its recklessness only by the Austro-Hungarian offensives of 1914, another neglected area amid all the scholarship on World War I. The Austro-Hungarian invasions of Serbia and Russia in 1914 had been planned for years, and their bloody, disastrous failure confirmed Austria-Hungary's impotence, which had only been suspected before the war. Those guns of August in Serbia and Russia established the pattern for the rest of the war: an overextended Germany, a winded Russia, and a demoralized Austria-Hungary with its hands in the air.

Central to the origins of the war, Austria-Hungary played a no less crucial role in the war's outcome. War plans in 1914 had been fixed for a decade. Germany was to destroy the French and British armies with a massive, enveloping "right hook" through Belgium (the first phase of the Schlieffen Plan), while Austria was to blunt and unhinge the Russian "steamroller"—an army of six million—with a quick, efficient mobilization and brutal jabs by four Austro-Hungarian field armies deployed in southern Poland and western Ukraine, a borderland the Habsburgs named Galicia. Austria's exertions would, it was hoped, throw the slow-moving Russians back and buy time for Germany to win on the Western Front, then transport three million troops east to join two million Austrians for a final reckoning with Russia. Russia was not expected to survive such a contest. Its army was huge but hamstrung by a low level of education and shortages of everything from coats, boots, and medicine to rifles and shells. The Serbs were not even supposed to be a factor. The Austro-Hungarians would parry them with a "Minimal Balkan Group" of eight divisions while Austria's forty other divisions dealt with Russia. Only then would Belgrade be beaten and carved up.

We know why the Germans failed to win in the west. We have books on the Marne and Ypres, as well as analysis of the Schlieffen Plan and its application by General Helmuth von Moltke the Younger, one of the chief architects and overseers of Germany's war plans. But what happened in the east in 1914? We have only the foggiest view of the war there. How could the Austrians—still clinging to great-power status—have sent twenty divisions (not eight) against the Serbs and still have been defeated? And what happened against the Russians on the Eastern Front? History speaks of stirring Austro-Hungarian victories at Krásnik and Komarów in August 1914—but then, on the very next page, puzzlingly describes a chaotic Austrian *retreat* from those places, leaving all of Poland and Ukraine to the Russians and requiring a massive German rescue effort that doomed whatever hope the Germans had of winning the war in the west.

Austria-Hungary's anxieties and pretensions as a fading great power were a chief cause of the war, and these same qualities were also the source of its defeat. The war began with gunshots in Sarajevo that struck down the Habsburg heir apparent and his wife. These murders should not have triggered a world war. Why they did had much to do not just with German aggressiveness but also with the same Austro-Hungarian blundering that was so much in evidence during the war itself. Even as Habsburg diplomats drafted the deliberately hard-edged ultimatum that would make war unavoidable, the Austrian military was making no preparations for hostilities. In fact, Austria's generals and statesmen took vacations during the height of the July Crisis of 1914—hardly the behavior one would expect from the indignant leaders of a wounded great power. When war came, due to Vienna's prodding, the Austrians marched with the same lack of resolve, and deployed an army that was feeble in every important area: transport, artillery, shells, machine guns, rifles, and tactics.

The deficit in Austro-Hungarian leadership was at least as bad. Emperor Franz Joseph I, the darling of the Austrian tourist industry today, with his benevolent gaze and white mutton-chop whiskers, was an altogether malevolent force in 1914. Although not as senile as the Czech writer Jaroslav Hašek suggested in his novel *The Good Soldier Svejk* ("two wet nurses, breast fed three times a day and so gaga he probably doesn't know there's a war on"), the emperor had been in an alarming state of dotage for years. He proudly refused to abdicate in favor of his nephew, the fifty-year-old Archduke Franz Ferdinand, but he also refused to take his job seriously. An old man who had lost his way, he stranded the Habsburg monarchy in the middle of every vital crossroads it encountered in the years leading up to 1914.

Compared with the eighty-four-year-old emperor, the sixty-one-year-old general staff chief, General Franz Conrad von Hötzendorf, was a Young Turk. Conrad was regarded as a brilliant strategist who would deliver victory against the big, ungainly Russians and then smack down the Serbs as well. Why he didn't is another fascinating, neglected story. The Great War in the east was so unrelievedly ungreat because of Conrad. Even by loosened 1914 standards, his leadership and decisions were appalling, wrecking the Austro-Hungarian army in a matter of weeks.

Austria-Hungary's spectacular self-destruction also doomed its German ally. Whatever hope Germany had of winning the Great War ended with the humiliating Austrian defeats of 1914. The smoldering residue of those defeats—a contested Poland, Galicia, and Serbia—piled up on Germany's plate and made victory on any major front far more difficult than it would have been with even a mediocre Austro-Hungarian performance at the start of the war. *A Mad Catastrophe* adds the eastern face to a war generally regarded from the west, and helps explain the slide of Vienna and Berlin into unwinnable wars of attrition and eventual defeat.

Introduction

NEVER HAD AN EMPIRE SWOONED so quickly. In 1866, the mighty Austrian Empire—the anvil on which British subsidies and seapower had hammered Napoleon into dust—was decisively beaten in the Austro-Prussian War. On the eve of this crushing defeat at the hands of Germany's junior power, the Austrians had seemed practically invincible. Austria's Habsburg dynasty ruled the second-largest empire in Europe (after Russia), encompassing an array of peoples from varying backgrounds and nationalities. For years the Habsburgs had also presided over the German Confederation, a league of thirty-six independent states, ranging from Protestant Prussia in the north to Catholic Bavaria in the south and bonded by a common culture and tongue. When the Kingdom of Prussia, the most industrialized and ambitious of these Habsburg subsidiaries, attempted to carve out the heart of the confederation and bring it under its own leadership with the backing of Italy, which coveted the last Austrian footholds south of the Alps, Austria rallied its loyal retainers—the majority of the German states—and declared war.

No one saw Austria's defeat coming. Pundits like Friedrich Engels (who made a living analyzing armies before he turned to economies) had predicted an Austrian victory. War correspondents gaped in disbelief at the ineptitude of the Austrians, who saw their once magnificent army beaten at Königgrätz in July, driven from Italy in August, and forced to capitulate on the banks of the Danube as the Prussian statesman Count Otto von Bismarck and general staff chief Helmuth von Moltke the Elder dissolved the

1

Austrian-led German Confederation, attached most of its states to Prussia, and prepared to besiege Vienna.

It would be hard to understate the psychological trauma of 1866. A whole idea was lost, the "Austrian idea," which held (with a straight face) that the nationalities under the Habsburg scepter, whether German, Italian, Polish, Czech, or Hungarian, were as happy to be there as under any other arrangement, including a nation-state. Vienna had been fighting a rearguard action against the nation-state since the French Revolution of the 1790s, which had grouped nations like Italy and Poland—previously partitioned and occupied by alien great powers (including Austria)—into new states administered by their own peoples. The Congress of Vienna of 1815, which had terminated the Napoleonic Wars, restored those new nation-states, including the Kingdom of Italy and the Duchy of Warsaw, to Austrian, Russian, or Prussian rule. Thereafter, Vienna regarded the breakaway of any part of its empire—Germans to Germany, Italians to Italy, or Hungarians to Hungary—as nothing less than treason that threatened the survival and legitimacy of Austria.

That risk of dissolution was what made the defeats of 1866 so dangerous. Habsburg emperor Franz Joseph I had derived much of his prestige from his control of the great Italian port and hinterland of Venice and his presidency of the German Confederation. The exotic Italian outpost and the industrious German dependencies validated the multinational character of Austria. If the Habsburgs could hold here, they could hold anywhere. Once the emperor lost Venetia to the Kingdom of Italy in 1866 and the German states to an expanded Prussia (which renamed itself Germany in 1871), he was forced back on the largely Slavic, Hungarian, and Rumanian crown lands of the empire, where only trouble awaited in an increasingly assertive "age of nationalism."

The nations of Austria—Germans, Czechs, Croats, Hungarians, Rumanians, Poles, and a half dozen others—began to question more vigorously the "Austrian idea" after Königgrätz. "I was born a German," Austrian poet Franz Grillparzer mused, "but am I *still* one?" What use was there for a little German rump in multinational Austria when a vast German great power had formed just across the border? *Anschluss*—the idea of merging Austria with Germany, a cause that would gain traction and ultimately infamy in the first half of the twentieth century—already beckoned. The soul-searching was just as intense in the other, non-German nations of east-central Europe, which had been taught to trade their independence and national development for union under German Austrian tutelage in what one Austrian official called "a saucepan of the nations." But the saucepan burned through at Königgrätz, and the small nations began to reconsider their options in view of Austria's defeats and waning power.

None reconsidered with quite the daring of the Hungarians. A Turkic people, who had ridden out of the Ural Mountains with the Huns and settled the plains of the middle Danube in the ninth century, Hungary's dominant Magyar ethnic group had always been insecure about its place in a largely Slavic and Rumanian land. The Magyars now seized on the weakness of Austria to magnify their power. Leading Hungarian politicians appeared in Vienna after Königgrätz to press a Faustian pact on the thirty-six-year-old Habsburg emperor Franz Joseph I. If he would recognize a Kingdom of Hungary, embracing not just the Magyars but the surrounding Croats, Slovaks, Germans, Ukrainians, and Rumanians as well, then Hungary—which had rebelled against Vienna as recently as 1848—would put those expanded resources at the service of the Habsburg monarchy.

Emperor Franz Joseph was a punctilious man who famously spurned the featherbeds of his palaces and slept on an iron army cot instead, rising each morning at first light to visit (briefly) his mistress of twenty years before beavering away at the mountains of paperwork thrown up by his German-speaking officialdom. Impelled by his beautiful (and untouchable) wife, Elisabeth, whose strong sympathy for the Hungarians may have had something to do with the fact that they were as keen to escape the clutches of her husband as she was, Franz Joseph duly conceded all of the Hungarian political demands. He had been nudged into the decision by his new foreign minister, Count Friedrich von Beust, who was a Saxon expat with little understanding of Austrian history or culture. Beust, who also held the post of Austrian prime minister, pressed the emperor to meet all of Hungary's demands on the assumption that a quick resolution of the Hungarian problem would solve all of the other ones: "You manage your hordes," Beust winked to Hungarian prime minister Gyula Andrássy in 1867, "and we'll manage ours."

Contemporaries expressed surprise at this Habsburg eagerness to please, for the Hungarians, despite their vast pretensions, accounted for just one-seventh of the monarchy's population, and their demands might have been easily dismissed. But Franz Joseph wanted a quick fix after the defeat of 1866, and he thought he was securing the monarchy's future by agreeing to split its administration between two capitals (Vienna and Budapest), two "peoples of state" (the Germans and the Hungarians), and two monarchs (himself as emperor of Austria and himself as king of Hungary).

On paper, at least, the creation of Austria-Hungary from Austria contained a certain logic. The Hungarians would no longer seek to secede from the monarchy and would put their Hunnish talents to work repressing any who would. The division of the empire into a German-run "Cisleithania" and a Hungarian-run "Transleithania"—separated by the muddy Leitha River, which curled between Vienna and the Hungarian city of Sopron—superficially simplified the monarchy's nationality problems by subcontracting the eastern ones to the Hungarians so that the German Austrians could focus on the western ones in a system of "dualism."

But whereas the German Austrians had a relatively soft touch, officiousness tempered by irresolution, the Hungarians were officious, hard-nosed, and resolute. After the 1867 *Ausgleich* or compromise, which created Austria-Hungary, they pressed ahead with a hard campaign of "Magyarization." Their saucepan of the nations had a single flavor: paprika. Whereas the Germans viewed the "people of state" label as license merely to patronize Cisleithania's Slavs by requiring them to interact with Habsburg officialdom in the German language, the Hungarians viewed theirs as license to *abolish* Transleithania's other nationalities: Slavs and Rumanians would be "de-nationalized" by prohibitions on their churches, schools, languages, and cultures. It became a treasonable offense to refer to Franz Joseph as "emperor" inside the borders of royal Hungary. "King" was preferred; "monarch," "sovereign," and "crown" were acceptable.

A French visitor to Austria-Hungary in 1902 observed that everything was "dualist" in the empire, including the banknotes. One side of an Austro-Hungarian crown note was Austrian, with the denomination spelled out in German as well as the eight other languages of Cisleithania: Polish, Italian, Czech, Serbian, Croatian, Slovenian, Rumanian, and Ukrainian. The flip side of the note was Hungarian, with the denomination spelled out in Magyar alone. "Astonishing," the French visitor commented; "for official Hungary, the nationalities here do not even *exist*." Such ethnic arrogance naturally commanded nothing more than a sullen obedience. "Faced with this internal campaign of national annihilation, non-Hungarians here are reduced to silence and immobility, even though they are the majority!" the Frenchman concluded.[1]

Desperate to hit upon some new, invigorating mission for his aging empire, Franz Joseph began to repent very quickly of the great sellout of 1867.[2] It sharpened, not diminished, the national rivalries in the monarchy as Hungarian Liberals jailed any priests, leaders, writers, or politicians in eastern Austria who resisted Magyarization. Having declared in 1867 that "the Slavs are not fit to govern; they must be ruled," Hungarian prime minister Gyula Andrássy and each of his successors until 1918 enforced that rule with a hard hand.[3] By the 1880s, millions of Austro-Hungarians were emigrating to America. Those who remained looked beyond Austria-Hungary for rescue—the Slavs to Russia or Serbia, the Rumanians to Rumania.

Conceived as a solution to Austria's problems, the *Ausgleich* had only made the dire strategic predicament of 1866 worse, for Austria's foreign enemies were now joined by an incorrigible domestic one. By 1900, Habsburg officials were referring to Hungary as the "internal enemy," *der innere Feind*. By 1905, Emperor Franz Joseph and his nephew and heir apparent Archduke Franz Ferdinand were actually drafting secret plans to invade Hungary, shutter its parliament, and bring the Hungarians back under Vienna's control.

Invading Hungary would not be easy. Until 1867, Hungarian regiments had been scattered across the empire in the usual extraterritorial way, to dampen national sentiment and prevent the junction of political and military power in Budapest. But the *Ausgleich* authorized the Hungarians to raise their own army, the Honvéd. Technically, the Honvéd was just a national guard like the Austrian Landwehr, and the Hungarians were still required to furnish regiments of conscripts to the Austro-Hungarian "imperial and royal" joint army with its German language of command and culture. But Franz Joseph never stipulated the ratios of conscripts that would be directed to the regular army and the Honvéd, so in the decades after 1867, the Hungarian parliament opportunistically bulked up the Hungarian-speaking Honvéd and starved the German-speaking army.

The Austro-Hungarian War Ministry would try to redirect recruits from the Honvéd to the regular army on the perfectly reasonable argument that fewer than 45 percent of the troops recruited east of the Leitha in any given year were actually Hungarian, but they were unfailingly thwarted by the Hungarian parliament.[4] Since Austro-Hungarian budgets had to be approved by both parliaments, the Hungarians got in the habit of slashing or vetoing army bills that would expand or modernize the regular army, which they viewed as a threat: German-drilled "Mamelukes" who might invade Hungary and tear up the *Ausgleich*. Not content merely to bankrupt the joint army, the Hungarians aimed to demoralize it as well; politicians in Budapest demanded a steady campaign to "nationalize the Hungarian component of the regular army," by which they meant wean it from German commands and culture and make it speak Hungarian.[5]

The Austro-Hungarian army withered away amid this infighting. In 1900, the joint army received a niggardly budget of 439 million crowns, which represented just 35 percent of Britain's defense expenditures, 40 percent of Russia's, 41 percent of Germany's and 45 percent of France's. Britain, which plowed most of its resources into the Royal Navy, still managed to spend more on the six divisions of its regular army than Austria-Hungary spent on its forty-eight divisions.[6] For an empire that valued its great-power standing, this paucity of military funding was astonishing.

The Germans might have been expected to object to this withering away on military and political grounds. The Hungarians, after all, were *their* men in Vienna, mentored by Berlin since 1866 to ensure a pro-German policy in Vienna. This was another conspicuous problem after 1867: the Hungarians got dualism in large part because of German support. Fearing an Austro-French "revenge coalition" after the Prussian victories in 1866 and 1870–1871, Bismarck spent the 1870s doubling down in his support for the Hungarians inside Austria. Berlin and Budapest agreed that it would be a bad thing for the Habsburgs to try to reverse the verdict of 1866 and reenter German politics as the tribune of a "Catholic League" determined to weaken (Protestant) Bismarck's hold on Germany's Catholic regions.[7] The Hungarians needed German support for the *Ausgleich*—without it Vienna might have cracked down on Budapest—and Bismarck gave that support because the Austro-Hungarian compromise seemed to kill two birds with one stone. It set an internal barrier against Austrian resurgence by cleaving the empire in half, yet it ensured that Austria-Hungary, at least in its western half, would retain its German character and culture, thus preserving Vienna as a German ally. Worried that the weakened Austria beaten in 1866 might adopt anti-Prussian policies or fall prey to pan-Slavs agitating among Austria's Czechs, Poles, Croats, and other Slavs, Bismarck backed Budapest to the hilt and thus created the fruitless politics of dualism. Bad for Austria, it was good for Germany (in the short term), and that was all that mattered to Bismarck in the tense years after Königgrätz.[8]

Hungarian loyalty to the Germans was always expressed negatively: the Hungarians campaigned against any return to "Old Austrian" (i.e., independent) policy in the foreign ministry, and undercut all efforts at Austro-Russian rapprochement. The Hungarians also stymied every attempt by the Austrians to wriggle out of the Austro-German-Italian Triple Alliance, created in 1882. Although the Italians openly coveted Austrian South Tyrol, Trieste, and Dalmatia, the Hungarians vetoed every army bill that included fortifications or troops for Austria's threatened crown lands. The Austrians, a French official concluded, were trapped in the pact by dualism, by "a Prusso-Magyar clique in the foreign ministry" that served German interests more than Austrian ones.[9]

The once vaunted Austrian army faded away after 1900. One of the biggest armies in 1866, it had become one of the smallest by 1914. It had just 355,000 troops and embarrassingly small quantities of field artillery, shells, and machine guns, which were the new coin of modern warfare.

These depressing data points acquired more than statistical significance during the Balkan Wars of 1912–1913. Evicted from Germany and Italy in 1866, Austria-Hungary had embraced a new, hopefully revivifying role as *Balkanmacht* or Balkan power. Turning his gaze south after Königgrätz, Emperor Franz Joseph planned to open an Austrian corridor across Serbia and Macedonia to Salonika and the Aegean. A refurbished Austria-Hungary would inherit the European provinces of the Ottoman Empire and radiate power and influence from new ports on the Mediterranean. To this end, Vienna had occupied Bosnia-Herzegovina in 1878 and annexed it in 1908, risking a war with Russia and Serbia to enforce its sphere of influence. Now, in 1912–1913, Franz Joseph watched aghast as the Serbs, who saw themselves as more logical heirs to Turkey-in-Europe than Austria was, hunted the Turks (and then the Bulgarians) out of the formerly Ottoman provinces of Kosovo and Macedonia, both of which lay athwart the route to Salonika. Vienna was expected to intervene forcefully in the wars to ensure that Belgrade did not convert the rout of the Turks into a vast accretion of Serbian power; it tried but failed. Incensed by the Serbian freelancing, which raked in Macedonia and thrust impudently across the Austrian-administered Sanjak of Novipazar to seize the Albanian ports of Scutari (Shkodër) and Durazzo (Durrës), Emperor Franz Joseph ordered the mobilization of five corps to terrify the Serbs and make them retreat. Nothing happened: the Hungarian parliament refused funds for the venture, and the Austrian parliament—filled with Serbophile Slavs—enacted a month-long filibuster to deny funds there as well.

Desperate, the emperor turned to Wall Street's Kuhn Loeb and Co. for a $25 million loan that paid for the spectacle of Austro-Hungarian regiments reporting to their depots singing Serbian anthems and cursing their own monarch. In Austria's Czech provinces, mothers and wives of reservists lay across the rails to prevent their men from entraining for the front. The Czechs, who had one of the most sophisticated cultures of the empire, had become the monarchy's weakest link. Political privileges revoked in the seventeenth century had never been restored, and the Czechs nursed a deep resentment of this as well as their subordination to ethnic Germans in the provinces of Bohemia and Moravia. While two hundred thousand Serbian troops overran the western Balkans, twelve thousand demoralized Austrians filtered into Bosnia—hardly a fearsome deterrent. Problems in Vienna further undercut the effort. The general staff chief was forced to resign at the peak of the crisis (for being insufficiently aggressive), and the Austro-Hungarian war minister's resignation promptly followed: he was accused of speculating on the shares of firms to which he intended to award military contracts. No sooner were replacements named than the monarchy was racked by the Redl Affair—news that forty-seven-year-old Colonel Alfred Redl had been selling German and Austrian military secrets to the Russians since 1905.

Austria's planned intervention to arrest Serbia fizzled and the empire seemed to teeter on the brink. The Austro-Hungarian general staff studied Serbia's annexations in the two Balkan Wars and concluded that the new territories would shortly furnish Belgrade with the men and resources to double the strength of the Serbian army, from two hundred thousand to four hundred thousand—bigger, in other words, than the peacetime establishment of the Habsburg army. General Blasius Schemua, the outgoing general staff chief, direly concluded that Austria-Hungary would no longer be able even to contemplate a war with Russia and Serbia—"our forces will no longer be sufficient for both," surely the greatest understatement of 1913.[10]

The rhetoric in Vienna on the eve of 1914 recalled 1859 and 1866, when the Habsburgs had reviled the threats from Piedmont

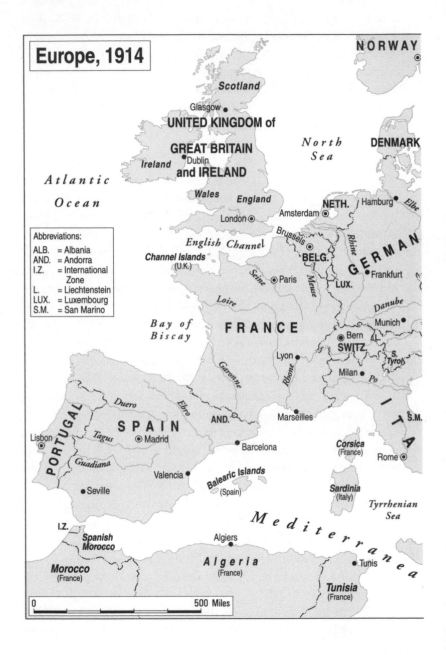

and Prussia. Serbia was now described as the "Prussia" or the "Piedmont" of the Slav South, a rising regional power committed to its manifest destiny in the Balkans, just as Piedmont had unified Italy and Prussia had done with Germany. Serbian nationalists wanted nothing less than the Austro-Hungarian provinces of Bosnia-Herzegovina, Croatia, Dalmatia, Slovenia, and southern Hungary—everywhere, in short, where Serbo-Croatian was spoken. Worse, there was widespread sympathy *inside* Austria-Hungary for the Serbs. Treated as second-class citizens by the Germans and Hungarians, Austria-Hungary's Slavs viewed Serbian national unification as a harbinger of their own. "Our monarchy," Archduke Franz Ferdinand growled, "must awake from its lethargy and proceed forcefully. Should it not do so, its role is played out."

By 1913, no one wanted a forceful Austria-Hungary more than Germany. Flanked by the modernizing armies and navies of Britain, France, and Russia—which had allied in the anti-German Triple Entente in 1907—the Germans had been reduced to a single real ally: Austria-Hungary. Berlin could not imagine a world without Austria, and it began planning a great European war to smash Serbia and Russia and shore up Vienna. At a council of war in Potsdam in December 1912, the German kaiser had recommended an immediate war with Serbia, Russia, and France, using the pretext of Serbia's gains in the Balkans. "Germany's sword lies loose in the scabbard," the kaiser assured Austria-Hungary's military attaché before the Potsdam meeting. "You can count on us."

As usual, however, the Austrians could not count on the Hungarians. Pressed by Vienna in 1913 to vote for increases in the army and navy, to expand the strategic railways toward Russia and the Balkans, and to add batteries of field artillery, the Hungarians again demurred. They would vote for nothing that would benefit the joint army or, with regard to new railways, anything that might benefit the *Austrian* as opposed to the Hungarian economy.

Despite Hungary's obstinacy—or perhaps because of it— Berlin by 1914 was ready to risk all. Scheduled French and Russian military buildups would not be completed until after 1916. Germany's was nearly complete. Austria-Hungary, which had shrunk from war during the Moroccan Crises of 1905 and 1911, needed somehow to be forced into the breach at Germany's side. The Balkans *had* to be the place. The press in Austria was helpfully lamenting the impotence exhibited during the Balkan Wars. In mid-June 1914, the *Österreichische Rundschau* judged Serbian expansion "a second Königgrätz," direly noting that "in 1866, we were expelled from the German Confederation and Italy; this time we were chased out of the Balkans."[11]

The running had to stop, and when the fateful pistol shots rang out in Sarajevo two weeks later, killing the Habsburg crown prince and his wife, German leaders were secretly pleased. They felt certain that the murder of the Habsburg heir apparent and the arrest of a Bosnian Serb assassin would propel even the timid Austrians to war.

CHAPTER 1

The Sick Man of Europe

"AUSTRIA IS THE LOSER—the *Schlemihl*—of Europe," a Vienna newspaper scoffed in February 1913. "No one likes us and every disaster befalls us." Only the "Sick Man of Europe," the decrepit Ottoman Empire, which had just lost provinces in North Africa and the Balkans to hungry new powers, could compete with Austria for the title of "world's biggest loser."[1] Indeed, the Habsburgs and the Ottomans were engaged in a race to the bottom for the title of Europe's Sick Man, the great power most likely to wither and die in everyone's lifetime.

Austria's weakness emanated from its quarreling, disaffected nationalities. The name "Austria" connoted Germanic uniformity, but the sprawling empire was far more than its German-speaking core around Vienna, Graz, Salzburg, and Innsbruck. In 1913, Austria was Europe's second-largest country (after Russia), with Europe's third-largest population (after Russia and Germany). But only 12 million of those 52 million Austrians were Germans, and therein lay the problem. The average "Austrian" in 1913 was a Slav. The monarchy, which ran from the Swiss border in the west all the way to Russia in the east, included 8.5 million Czechs and Slovaks, 5.5 million Croats and Serbs, 5 million Poles, 4 million Ukrainians, and 1.3 million Slovenes. Slavs constituted 50 percent of the Austrian population. Plus there were nearly as many

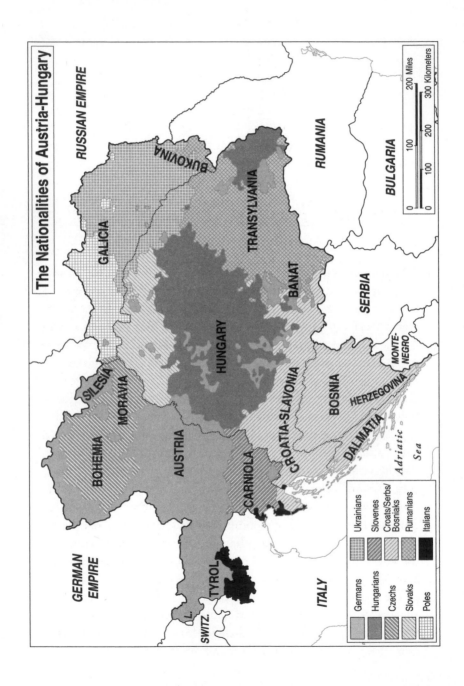

The Nationalities of Austria-Hungary

Hungarians as Germans in the monarchy—10 million, or 19 percent.

These Hungarians, who had arrived from Central Asia in the ninth century, were a unique racial islet, speaking a unique language, Magyar. Their existence was defined by fear: the fear of being mastered by the Germans or swallowed up by the Slavs. This gave the Hungarians a bullying spirit, a determination to "Magyarize" everyone around them in order to augment their own small numbers and nip ethnic competition in the bud. The most immediately affected were the Rumanians of Austria. Three million strong—6 percent of the imperial population—they lived cheek by jowl with the Hungarians in the Carpathian basin and were under constant pressure to give up their language and culture and speak Magyar instead.

Strong leadership and a spirit of fair play in Vienna might have tempered these problems, but Emperor Franz Joseph had always come across as a weakling and a temporizer. He'd lost the only war he led personally, to the French in 1859, and then lost the next war, to the Prussians in 1866, after entrusting command to a general who seemed brilliant but turned out to be incompetent. This made Franz Joseph fundamentally pessimistic and unsure of himself. To keep critics and issues requiring hard choices at bay, he surrounded himself after 1866 with a few trusted yes-men and gatekeepers, like his long-serving friend and general staff chief General Friedrich Beck. This group implemented the emperor's only fixed policy, which was to postpone but never attack problems. They were, as Winston Churchill put it, "a curious small coterie . . . an ancient band of survivors, eminently Victorian, unswervingly faithful," but woefully out of touch.[2] Lest anyone try to get in touch with modern times, Franz Joseph made sure they couldn't: he clapped Europe's most rigid protocol on the Habsburg courts in Vienna and Budapest, leaving no opening for anyone to speak to the emperor unless spoken to first. "It's like a musical comedy without the music," an American traveler observed.[3]

The wars against the French in 1859 and the Prussians in 1866 had redefined the Habsburg monarchy. It had been a bona fide great power until then, regarded as the equal of England,

Loser of two wars in his youth, Emperor Franz Joseph I—seen here at the Hofburg in Vienna—was an unimaginative pessimist in old age, the worst sort of leader for a fragile multinational empire adapting uneasily to the twentieth century.
CREDIT: Heeresgeschichtliches Museum, Wien

France, and Russia and greater than Prussia or Italy. After those wars—in which the Austrian generals had squandered opportunities and lost every battle—the monarchy wasn't quite a laughing-stock, but almost.

The defeat of 1859 triggered soul-searching in Vienna. Franz Joseph's confidence was shaken. He conceded a parliament for the first time—the Reichsrat in 1860—and then wavered between forms of government. In the 1860s, Austria began to grapple seriously with the problem of nationalism (how much power and representation to give the non-German peoples of the monarchy), which would dog it until the end in 1918. One method of coping was "centralizing," which involved concentrating imperial powers in the capital and exercising them in the provinces through a repressive, German-speaking bureaucracy. The other method was "federalism," relaxing the hold of the emperor and the bureaucrats in Vienna and letting the provinces govern themselves through their own peoples and languages. In the 1860s, this generally meant through aristocrats—the "hundred families" of the monarchy, such as the Windischgrätz clan of Austria, the Esterházys of Hungary, and the Schwarzenbergs of Bohemia—but also local diets or assemblies and their national clubs, including Czechs in Bohemia and Moravia, Magyars in Hungary, Croats in Zagreb, Poles in Galicia, Italians in Trieste, and Slovenes in Ljubljana.

Over the years, the emperor and his ruling clique shifted anxiously between the federalist and centralizing methods, but neither method worked. Centralization provoked the wrath of non-Germans. Federalism could no longer be exercised through aristocrats in the modern age of industrialization and liberalism, and if exercised through middle-class national clubs like the "Young Czechs," it led inexorably to secession and dissolution. It didn't help that of Austria-Hungary's seventeen principal regions, only six were ethnically homogeneous; the rest were tinderboxes like Bohemia, where Czechs and Germans scuffled in the towns and villages over language, jobs, and status.[4] By the time Franz Joseph was thirty—he would live and reign to eighty-six—Austria was already unworkable, a veritable dodo bird, too fat and unwieldy to fly, too slow and helpless to live on the ground.

Count Otto von Bismarck, minister president of Prussia in the 1860s, noticed this immediately. He had resented Austria since the 1850s, when he remarked that "the two powers could no longer breathe each other's breath in Central Europe." He took aim at Franz Joseph in 1866, demanding Prussian control of the German states that had been loosely led by Vienna since the end of the Napoleonic Wars. In the haphazard way that was his style, Franz Joseph weighed compromise and war and then chose war to "save Austria's honor." He was never much of a strategist, always fighting for intangible "honor" instead of tangible interests— something he would do again in 1914. Imperial interest in 1859 and 1866, as in 1914, would have been far better served by some face-saving deal short of war, which would have preserved the appearance of Austrian power while preventing a ruinous clash between the two historic allies.

In a lightning campaign, the Prussian army of General Helmuth von Moltke invaded Austria in June 1866 and defeated the Austrian army in a sequence of battles culminating at Königgrätz, a fortress on the Elbe River in Bohemia, on July 3. An Italian army invaded Venetia as the Prussians thrust into Bohemia, took the province, and marched nearly to Trieste. The defeat was total: Austrian diplomats had failed to buy off either the Prussians or the Italians with concessions, and the Austrian generals had failed to exploit good chances to win on both fronts.

This was an army that had been a stalwart in the wars against Napoleon, and its defeat in 1866 was earthshaking. Indeed, the pope's foreign minister gasped, "Casca il mondo" (the world has turned upside down) when he heard of the Prussian victory at Königgrätz and the rout of the Austrian army. The political developments that followed were even more astonishing; British Conservative leader Benjamin Disraeli spoke for the rest of Europe when he judged in a speech to the House of Commons in February 1871 that Bismarck's unification of the three dozen German states under Prussian rule had "entirely destroyed the balance of power" in what amounted to a "German Revolution, a greater political event than the French Revolution of the last century." The Austrian-led German Confederation had been established at the close of the Napoleonic Wars to deny the wealth, industry, and fast-growing population of Germany to a single power. With those resources suddenly in Prussian hands, the effect on the equilibrium of Europe was revolutionary. An ambitious new power, centered in Berlin, filled up the previously fragmented space between Russia and France and resolved to assert itself.[5]

Austria grappled with the fallout from the German Revolution of 1871 more than any other European power. "There is not a diplomatic tradition which has not been swept away," Disraeli had declared after the Prussian triumph. "You have a new world, new influences at work, new and unknown objects and dangers with which to cope." But the new world did not favor Austria. Respect for Vienna—an ancient diplomatic reflex—withered away as the other powers registered Austria's defeat at Königgrätz as well as its inexplicable failure to intervene in the Franco-Prussian War to recover the ground lost in 1866. "We have sunk to the level of Turkey," an Austrian general muttered, confirming that the Habsburg and Ottoman Empires were the twinned Sick Men of Europe.[6]

Taking stock of Austria-Hungary in 1878, the French embassy concluded that only the regions around Vienna and Graz remained "reliably German." Everywhere else was under siege by national parties—Hungary by the Magyars, Trieste by the Italians, Croatia and Dalmatia by the Croats, Carinthia and Carniola by the Slovenes, Bohemia and Moravia by the Czechs, and Galicia and Bukovina by the Poles, Ukrainians, and Rumanians. In this "mosaic of peoples," the French observed, Jews emerged as "the only reliable class in Austria." Tolerated better in Austria than they were in Russia, where they were subject to intense discrimination and lacerating pogroms, Jews were one of the few groups in the empire that rallied enthusiastically to the Habsburgs. "They are multiplying in the East out of all proportion to the other peoples," the French embassy noted in 1878, "and plundering the peasantry through usury; in the cities they control the press, professions, and banks." Jewish moneylending in the country and commercial success in the towns spurred waves of Russian-style anti-Semitism in Austria, but the emperor, not yet fifty, didn't give much thought to these attacks on his most loyal subjects. "He's sympathetic and well-liked," the French reported, "but he has no character to speak of; he's a drifter, floating from one system to the next; he has no real friends or confidants; he trusts no one, and inspires confidence in no one, nor does he even believe in himself."[7]

That was as fair a summary of Emperor Franz Joseph I as any, and the monarch did not ponder long after the defeat of 1866 before deciding on a "fix" to the crisis unleashed by German and Italian unification. Militarily, he adopted—superficially—the Prussian style. The Austrian army defeated in 1866 had relied on aristocratic officers and long-service peasant soldiers, and thus found itself without intelligent, trained reserve troops or officers after the initial battlefield defeats. The emperor's new war minister, General Franz Kuhn, introduced compulsory three-year service for all Austro-Hungarian males and competitive exams for officer aspirants. Within five years, most of the monarchy's military aristocracy had left the army, never to return, to protest Kuhn's cancellation of their privileges (chiefly immunity from competitive exams or any other "merit process"), a step that the snobbish and traditionalist emperor never would have authorized had he not been so discredited by the defeats of 1859 and 1866. Unfortunately, within five years most of the best middle-class officers had left the army too, for the 1870s were the Gilded Age, and the brightest men would leave the miserly military to seek their fortune in finance. Increasingly the Habsburg officer corps became what it would be in 1914: the preserve of lower-middle-class men of slender means who were packed off to the army by their fathers for the free education offered at good military schools like the Technical Academy in Vienna or the war college at Wiener Neustadt.[8]

Organizationally, the Habsburg army after 1866 adopted a territorial structure like Prussia's. The monarchy was carved into fifteen corps districts, from Innsbruck east to Lemberg (Lviv) and from Prague south to Ragusa (Dubrovnik), with every regiment drawing its four battalions locally and joining them to the nearest corps, a perfectly logical system that had never been attempted in Austria because the multinational peoples were not judged reliable in the age of nationalism. Had they been left in their home districts, they might have fraternized with unhappy locals and turned their guns on the emperor, so until the defeat of 1866 Austrian regiments had bounced around the monarchy every three years—Czechs to Budapest, Hungarians to Prague, Croats to Venice, Germans to Cracow, Ukrainians to Vienna, and so on. This "extraterritoriality" in peacetime, maintained as a counterrevolutionary measure, had so complicated Austrian mobilizations in wartime that it was largely abolished in the 1880s. But the new territorial system was not without its own problems. "Please replace my staff company with one made up of more intelligent human material," one Austrian general wrote another in February 1914, only to be told: "Denied, do what you can with your men of lower intelligence." The general had wanted Germans for his staff company, and was ordered to make do with Serbs instead.[9]

Tactically, the Habsburg army also attempted to mimic the Prussians. Austrian planners abandoned shock tactics—the massed charges in company columns that had been shredded by Prussian fire in 1866—and introduced Prussian fire tactics in their place. A French officer invited in 1875 to an Austrian exercise on the old battlefield of Trautenau reported that the Austrian instructor opened the exercise thus: "You all know what happened here in 1866; our task is to purge and forget forever the sentiments and tactics that cost us so much blood and delivered so little success. For the old methods, we substitute this: rapid fire by dispersed units."[10]

The new method of warfare made perfect sense but was never really implemented. The Habsburgs would always be slow to procure the latest technologies and to train sufficient numbers of men in the effective use of them. If men were not drafted in large numbers and trained to estimate ranges and aim fire, they could not actually deliver rapid, dispersed fire; they would have to be massed together under the supervision of their officers and NCOs, presenting easy targets to the enemy, as they had in 1866. Even before the technological revolutions of the 1890s—repeater rifles, machine guns, and quick-firing artillery—Emperor Franz Joseph was showing a distressing tendency always to do the wrong thing, or at least to fail to follow through on the right thing. Under his long-serving general staff chief General Friedrich Beck, he authorized largely ceremonial maneuvers, and for years after 1866 he became the advocate of his cavalry mafia—the last preserve of aristocrats in the army—opposing every effort by his most effective cavalry commander in 1866, General Leopold Edelsheim, to abolish the lance and saber and replace them with the carbine and pistol.[11]

Politically, the emperor was no less retrograde. To solve the political crisis thrown up by the defeat of 1866, he sat down with his most fiery domestic opponents, the Hungarians, and offered them the deal of a lifetime. In return for their loyalty to the Habsburg crown, the Hungarians, who constituted just 19 percent of the monarchy's population, were offered control of 52 percent of Austrian territory and 40 percent of its population. For this half share of Austria, they would remit just 30 percent of Austrian taxes.[12]

The Magyars effectively seceded from the unitary Austrian Empire in 1867 and revived a "Kingdom of Hungary" in Transleithania that was to have no direct connection with Vienna. The Austrian emperor's actual title allowed that he was king of Hungary (as well as king of Bohemia, Croatia, Galicia, and other regions of the empire), but these titles had always been regarded as purely ceremonial and the domains they spanned merely provinces. Now the emperor was made to understand that the Hungarian crown trumped all others, including even the Austrian one. Budapest could make all manner of demands on Vienna, but Vienna must make none on Budapest. The Austrian emperor had been king of Hungary since Vienna's acquisition of the land in 1526, but his control had been expressed on Austrian buildings and stationery thus: *k.k.*, which stood for *kaiserlich königlich,* or imperial royal. No more: in 1889, the Hungarians demanded that a *u* be inserted between the *k*s, so that they would no longer rub companionably alongside each other. *Kaiserlich und königlich*— imperial *and* royal—was deemed more pleasingly divisive than *kaiserlich königlich.*[13]

Hair-splitting such as this was greeted with shock in Vienna. The emperor had supposed that by his Compromise of 1867 he had traded Hungarian home rule for a unified Austrian great power. The Hungarians were supposed to participate wholeheartedly in "common" or "joint" *k.u.k.* ministries of war, foreign affairs, trade, and finance in exchange for the unique power to direct their domestic affairs. The Hungarians now appeared to be reneging on the deal; although they spun good profits from the joint monarchy—two-fifths of the population of Austria-Hungary paying just one-third of its taxes every year—their continuous obstruction of the single state for war, foreign policy, finance, and trade amounted to sabotage, to say nothing of ingratitude. From his perch in Vienna's Belvedere Palace, Archduke Franz Ferdinand growled that Austria was falling not to rival powers but to an "internal enemy—Jews, Freemasons, Socialists and *Hungarians*."[14]

Franz Joseph's work increasingly became ensuring the survival and relevance of the Habsburg dynasty by juggling the contending capitals of Vienna and Budapest. This was an uphill battle, for the dynasty was unimposing even by the loosened standards of a more permissive age. In 1889, Franz Joseph's only child and heir, the thirty-year-old Archduke Rudolf, fell in love with a teenage baroness and then shot her and himself in Mayerling, his hunting lodge in the Vienna Woods. That murder-suicide, which shortly made the unsmiling Archduke Franz Ferdinand the new crown prince, also severed what little connection there was between the emperor and the empress, who now embarked on her endless travels away from Vienna, a routine that ended with her own assassination in 1898.

Dynastic damage control was the order of the day. Although everyone knew the emperor kept a mistress for three decades— the actress Katharina Schratt—no one talked about it in the press. When the emperor's brother Archduke Ludwig Viktor was twice arrested with male companions in public baths in 1904 (first in Vienna, then in Italy), the scandal was hushed up. No Austro-Hungarian newspaper even mentioned it; those that tried were fined and confiscated. Ludwig Viktor himself was given a diagnosis of "depression" and confined to his country house.[15] After the debacle of Königgrätz, where middle-class generals had failed as spectacularly as aristocratic ones, Franz Joseph began placing archdukes—princes of the Habsburg house—in every important command to underscore the imperial prerogative, but none of them impressed. Taking stock of the two leading archdukes in 1897, the French embassy commented: "Friedrich: lacks the essential qualities of a general. Eugen: a hard worker, but not gifted in any way." And these two Habsburgs were the cream of the crop.[16] While the dynasty unquestionably survived, the monarchy as a great power began to die.

Hungary was the virus that was killing the Habsburgs. Hungarian obstruction after 1867 gnawed at the roots of Habsburg power and administration. In 1878, uprisings burned through

Ottoman Bosnia and Herzegovina, and Vienna saw the opportunity to wrest the provinces from Turkey, attach them to Austria, and thus ensure Austrian preeminence in the Balkans, which had become the new mission for the empire after its ouster from Italy and Germany in 1866. Unfortunately, the Hungarians opposed even occupation of the territories, let alone annexation, fearing that the million or so Slavs in Bosnia-Herzegovina would further dilute the monarchy's Hungarian minority. Bismarck, who was trying to *give* Austria-Hungary the two Turkish provinces at the Congress of Berlin in order to rebalance power after Russian gains in their war with Turkey in 1877–1878, found the situation ludicrous: "I've heard of people refusing to eat their pigeon unless it was shot and roasted for them, but I've never heard of anyone refusing to eat it unless his jaws were forced open and it was pushed down his throat."[17]

Nor was there a unified pro-Habsburg bloc in Cisleithania to array against the Magyars. Throughout his reign, Franz Joseph had swerved between German liberal centralizers and Slavic feudal federalists. From 1879 until 1897, the emperor turned politics in Cisleithania over to Count Eduard Taaffe's "Iron Ring," a cabinet whose highest aim was to keep the empire's various nationalities in a "balanced state of mild dissatisfaction."[18] But that dodge, which gave the emperor a degree of control, became less effective in the modern age of nationalism and mass communication. By the end of the nineteenth century, Austrian cabinets rose and fell over minor issues—trumpeted in the national clubs and press—like the language of instruction in a small-town elementary school, a situation that would have been unthinkable at the beginning of the century. In the seventeen provinces of Austria, German had always been the required language of school instruction and the local language had been offered only as an elective subject; accepted in the past, this arrangement now enraged increasingly assertive Czechs, Slovenes, and others. Czech historian Frantisek Palacký had famously argued in 1848 that "if the Austrian Empire had not existed, it would have had to be invented" to forestall Russian domination. That imperial talking point had become a thing of ridicule fifty years later. The peoples of Austria did not want Austria or Russia; they wanted freedom.

In Austria-Hungary, 1897 was a year of existential crisis. The Czechs—who had been stewing for years over the dualist concessions to the Hungarians—finally rebelled against the official German culture of Cisleithania and demanded parity for the Czech language. The new Austrian prime minister, Count Casimir Badeni, sought to mollify the Czechs (and fortify Taaffe's old "Iron Ring") by placing the Czech and German languages on an equal footing in the Czech-speaking provinces of Bohemia and Moravia. Officeholders would be forced to know both languages, but since Czechs already knew German from school, the reform really only affected Germans, few of whom had ever bothered to learn Czech. The result was a veritable civil war, as furious Germans disrupted the functioning of the Reichsrat in Vienna, overturning benches and hurling inkpots, and resorted to violence in Prague and the other towns of Bohemia and Moravia.[19] German nationalists crossed the border from Saxony singing *"Wacht am Rhein"* and *"Deutschland über Alles"* and vowing to prevent the eclipse of their "Austrian brothers."

One diplomat jotted down the startling observation that "the German element, always the strongest glue in Austria, has now become the most powerful element of its decomposition."[20] The Germans, fearing their eclipse in Austria, hotly defended their language and culture and abandoned traditional liberal parties in favor of *völkisch* ones like Georg von Schönerer's Pan-Germans, who asserted that nationalism "is more important than dynastic patriotism."[21] For the first time, even German Austrians began to argue for the partition of the Habsburg monarchy into national states. Schönerer spoke of his "German heart" and called the German (not the Austrian) kaiser "our emperor." German deputies in Badeni's Reichsrat cheered every time the name Hohenzollern was mentioned, support for the ascendant Prussian dynasty being a pointed rebuke to the Habsburgs. Subversive ideas such as this strangled the old multinational ethos of the Habsburgs.

The growth of Vienna mayor Karl Lueger's Christian Social Party reflected the new tone.[22] Austria's Pan-Germans, who had weakened after the fall of Bismarck in 1890 and the indictment of Schönerer in various scandals, rebounded under Lueger during

Badeni's tenure as prime minister. With all of his adoring references to the German Reich, Schönerer had been an alien on the Austrian scene. Lueger threw all that out, expressing loyalty to the Habsburgs, but kept the popular bits: anti-Semitism and contempt for Austria's majority Slavs. Where the cosmopolitan flavor of Vienna had previously been a point of pride, with Viennese dropping words from around the empire into their daily speech, it now suggested mongrel decadence to German chauvinists. Could a real German still refer to the waiter who brought drinks in the café as *piccolo,* the Italian word for "boy"? And casually use a Polish word, *chai,* to order tea? Could the Hungarian word for "other" still be dropped into everyday speech, as in *"Geh'n wir auf die maschik Seite"* (let's cross to the other side)? Could a German still describe a sour business deal as *meschuge,* Yiddish for "crazy"?[23] Austria's vibrant Jewish culture, in particular, found itself under attack. Yiddish receded as anti-Semitism—"the socialism of fools"—expanded. Books such as *Die Judenfrage* (The Jewish Question) pointed to a Jewish plot to subvert and destroy the monarchy: two-thirds of the newspapers in Cisleithania were in the hands of Jewish editors, and according to the anti-Semites the situation was worse in Hungary, where "Judeo-Magyars" dominated the press, professions, art, commerce, and industry, serving as "staff officers of public opinion."[24]

Tolerance and even admiration for diversity became passé as bigoted German nationalism developed into a pulsing force in Austrian politics. Feeling this German pressure, the Slavs—with the Czechs in the forefront—asserted their own interests, threatening to dismantle the German administration and ambience of Cisleithania. Austria's leaders wrung their hands but did little else, Badeni making the obvious but overlooked connection between these internal hatreds and the military security of the empire: "A country of nationalities cannot wage war without danger to *itself."*[25]

Archduke Franz Ferdinand, who bulked larger as the emperor aged, worried most about Austria's Hungarian nationality. He was appalled by Franz Joseph's massive new round of "national concessions" to the Hungarians in 1903, which the archduke interpreted as nothing less than a death blow to the monarchy's already impaired military.

The Habsburg army served a social and political function in Austria-Hungary as nowhere else. With every male in the monarchy liable for military service, it was potentially a "school of the state" that would de-nationalize the empire's dozen nationalities, teaching them to speak German, revere the emperor (whose portrait hung everywhere), and value their status as multinational "Austrians." It was precisely that unifying function that the Hungarians attacked, by slashing military budgets—even in times of crisis and rapid technological change—and creaming off as many recruits as they could for the Magyar-speaking Honvéd or national guard instead of the regular army.[26] The *k.u.k.* army had been withering away for years because of Hungary's boorish refusal since 1889 to permit the synchronization of the empire's annual recruit contingent with population growth on either side of the Leitha. Thus, even as the empire's population exceeded 50 million, the army still recruited based on a census of 37 million. In 1900, only 1 man out of every 132 was a soldier in Austria, compared with 1 in 65 in France, 1 in 94 in Germany, and 1 in 98 in Russia. This yielded an army half the size of France's or Germany's and one-quarter the size of Russia's. Even Italy drafted and trained more men per 100,000 inhabitants than Austria.

Hungary's refusal to allow increases in the recruit contingent or budget meant that artillery—the new queen of the battlefield in an age of quick-firing guns and chemical explosives—could not be increased. Here too the Austrians lagged, with just one (obsolete) gun per 338 troops compared with one gun per 195 troops in Germany and France.[27] This shortfall would have massive repercussions in 1914, when the Dual Monarchy would find itself outgunned and outclassed by its rivals.

Finally, in 1903, the Hungarians made a great show of granting an additional twenty-four thousand recruits per annum, but at a breathtaking price. Hungarian emblems would now be affixed to Austro-Hungarian units raised in Hungary, a blow to the notion of the "joint army"; Austrian officers serving in Hungarian staffs and regiments would be "repatriated" to Austria, as if it were a foreign land; Hungarian would now be the official language of Austro-Hungarian military schools and tribunals located in Hungary; and the Honvéd would finally be permitted to have its own artillery. That last privilege had been scrupulously withheld by Vienna since 1867 so that Austrians would have the upper hand in any civil war with Hungarians. Adding insult to injury, Austrian taxpayers would henceforth have the privilege of paying not only for their own Austro-Hungarian regiments but for one-fourth of Hungary's as well—52 of 196 Hungarian infantry battalions, 28 of 108 Hungarian batteries, and 28 of 108 squadrons of Hungarian cavalry—at an annual cost to Austrians of 40 million crowns, a sum that surely would rise every year. This insult was only compounded by the fact that Hungary shouldered so little of the Dual Empire's military burden; with three times the population of the little Balkan kingdom of Rumania, Hungary paid about the same to the Austro-Hungarian common army every year as Rumania did for its own.[28]

All objective observers laid the decline of the Austro-Hungarian military at Hungary's door. The rulers in Vienna were no exception, and following the 1903 concessions those outside the emperor's drowsy and rather credulous inner circle began planning to do something about the Hungarian impediment. Quietly, the forty-two-year-old Archduke Franz Ferdinand added a Plan U—as in Ungarn (Hungary)—to the raft of Austrian war plans in 1905. If the Hungarians continued their obstruction of every Austrian effort to revive the monarchy, a large Austrian army would stream into Hungary by rail and the Danube, seize Budapest, and install a Habsburg military governor. Of the five Austro-Hungarian corps situated in Transleithania, only one—IV Corps, recruited around Budapest—was expected to fight for Hungary in a civil war. The rest were manned with Croats, Rumanians, Slovaks, Ukrainians, and Serbs and were expected to fight for the emperor. According to the French embassy, a civil war "like 1848," when Austrian troops had invaded Hungary and crushed a revolution there, was avoided in the early 1900s only because the Hungarians knew that they would lose a military contest and the Austrians feared that the Italians would seize the opportunity presented by an Austro-Hungarian civil war to invade contested Habsburg territories like Trieste, Trentino, and South Tyrol.[29]

The humiliation of the 1903 army concessions was such that Franz Joseph's prime minister, war minister, and general staff chief all submitted their resignations (all were refused). The French embassy spoke of the "emperor's utterly inert, stupid and despairing soul": how else could the "disastrous arrangement" with Hungary be explained? "The emperor treats the biggest, richest, most populous half of his monarchy as if it were nonexistent," the embassy marveled. "Unless this measure is repealed, the consequences will be enormous."[30] The language and flag concessions—which everyone assumed the Hungarians would deploy as precedents to finish off German altogether the next time around—emboldened the Czechs to demand their own Bohemian flags as well as the Czech language of command, which the emperor—illogically—refused even to discuss. Czech nationalists pretended not to notice; now Czech recruits defiantly answered *zde* (here) instead of *hier* when officers called the roll.

The collapse of the multinational army, traditionally held together by the German language, was accelerating. Fluency in German had previously been demanded from all officers, with all recruits obliged to memorize eighty German words of command. Supplementing this agreement to give the Hungarian language pride of place in Hungary's military schools and tribunals, the emperor had made the most stunning concession of all: freeing Hungarian officers from the obligation to learn and speak German. Henceforth they could palm that job off onto their NCOs. Franz Ferdinand's military secretary wrote a withering (anonymous) critique of this appeasement—this *Militärpolitik*—and the archduke applauded from his Bohemian country house at Konopischt: "Outstanding! Publish immediately. I will bear all of the costs."[31] Now military leaders in Vienna spoke of an *Armeefrage*, a wide-open "army question," since everything seemed to be in play: language, flag, hymns, and even armament, the Hungarians having finally won the right to procure their own artillery. Worse, as Colonel Karl Bardolff—one of Franz Ferdinand's closest advisors—noted, each of these exhausting negotiations with the

Hungarians revealed just how far the Austrians were falling behind the other European armies: their trained companies of infantry were smaller, they had fewer machine guns per battalion, and they possessed less artillery.[32] Funds and men were so short that a new Austro-Hungarian corps district, the XVI in Dubrovnik, was manned not with fresh battalions but with cooks, musicians, clerks, and scrapings from the other fifteen corps. In 1910, the Hungarians tried to block construction of two Austro-Hungarian dreadnoughts, relenting only when the emperor promised to build a third battleship in the Hungarian shipyard at Fiume (Rijeka).[33]

In 1907, Emperor Franz Joseph finally discovered a way to pressure the Hungarians, or thought he had. He would grant universal male suffrage in both halves of the monarchy with an edict from the throne, thus empowering—at last—the non-Hungarian, potentially pro-Austrian elements in Transleithania. But the Hungarians would simply ignore the emperor's edict for three years and then, in their 1910 parliamentary elections, refuse to implement it, confining Transleithania's vote to wealthy, educated Magyars. Cisleithania introduced universal male suffrage immediately, and the results were an unexpected disaster for the throne. Social Democrats took 86 of the Reichsrat's 516 seats, and petulant blocs of Slavs and Germans took the rest, paralyzing the parliament with their quarrels. The Reichsrat, previously divided between centralizers and federalists, now divided along class and ethnic lines. Social Democrats attacked the privileges of the crown, the rich, and the church. Most deputies joined one of more than twenty "national clubs" inside the chamber. By 1913, the Austrian Delegation that met annually with a Hungarian Delegation to coordinate policy and ratify budgets had degenerated into a spoils system, with seven Germans, seven Poles, four Czechs, five Social Democrats, seven from the Christian Social Party, three Croats, three Slovenes, two Ukrainians, two Italians, and so on, until the forty seats were filled.[34] On the Hungarian side of the Leitha, the delegation was not so diverse, as the dominant Magyars stamped out every effort by the Rumanians and other subject nationalities to speak their own languages in school or public offices as "contradicting the cardinal principles of Hungarian national policy."

The more chauvinistic among the Magyars, such as Count Albert Apponyi, spoke proudly of a cultural "policy of colonization."[35]

Opening the first Reichsrat elected with expanded suffrage in 1907, Franz Joseph implored the deputies to "be more conscious of their duties to the imperial state" than to their various peoples, but there was little hope of that in the age of nationalism.[36] Under pressure from Austria's Germans, the emperor had repealed Badeni's enlightened language law in 1899, and a new outbreak of German-Slav violence forced the mass resignation of the emperor's cabinet in November 1908. Martial law followed in Prague, where twenty thousand Czech and German rioters pummeled each other for two days, the Czechs swarming out of the Czech-speaking departments at the essentially segregated Charles University, the Germans from the German ones. Three hundred were killed and six hundred wounded—breathtaking carnage in peacetime.[37] Similar outbreaks over the education issue followed in Laibach (Ljubljana), Troppau (Opava), Vienna, and Brünn (Brno), where furious crowds of Austrian Slavs tore down Habsburg flags and bellowed Russian and Serbian anthems. The American embassy in Vienna judged this latest internal crisis "of interest from the international standpoint, as showing the extremes that racial feeling has reached in various parts of Austria." The empire was imploding, and the emperor was forced to quarter his most reliable troops—Bosnian Muslims—in the streets and squares of towns like Ljubljana to stop the attacks on German schools, theaters, and clubs. As the Austrian novelist Robert Musil put it, German institutions in non-German areas had come to annoy everyone: the towns "had a past and even had a face, but the eyes did not go with the mouth, or the chin with the hair."[38]

And so the fabled Austro-Hungarian bureaucracy supplanted representative institutions to govern the monarchy.[39] To absorb the growing numbers of college graduates, revenue-depleting jobs abounded in the state service. Debarking in his hometown of Klagenfurt, Robert Musil took in "the provincial headquarters, schools and universities, barracks, courthouses, prisons, bishops' palace, assembly rooms and theater, together with the people needed to run them." It was "a vast apparatus of imperial administration," consisting mainly of "German burgher stock transplanted centuries ago to Slavic soil," and the transplants bloomed from one end of the monarchy to the other.[40] The costs of this patronage—2 billion crowns per year on bureaucrats, about five times what the emperor spent on the military—utterly overwhelmed the state budget, the Habsburg civil service alone consuming more than a quarter of total state revenues in 1913. Addressing the Austro-Hungarian delegations in December 1911, Franz Joseph's war minister revealed that Hungary alone (which was forever protesting the size of the Habsburg army) employed 320,000 civil servants—more Hungarian bureaucrats, in other words, than there were soldiers in the entire Austro-Hungarian army.[41] The coming mass war would require effective mass administration, and Austria-Hungary was ill equipped for the challenge. General Franz Conrad von Hötzendorf, who would direct the Austrian war effort in 1914, raged before the war against Austria-Hungary's self-defeating culture of "memos, permission slips, stamps, petitions, minutes and reports."[42] Position, title, rank, and form were always cherished above efficiency, leading to the empire's legendary bumbling, which was bad enough in peace and would be ruinous in war.

The Habsburg army was supposed to operate more efficiently and bridge the empire's increasingly virulent national differences. It didn't. A polyglot like Conrad, who became chief of the general staff in 1906 and spoke seven of Austria-Hungary's fifteen languages, was the exception and not the rule in an army that historically had prided itself on its "supranational" tolerance and élan. In Hungary, languages other than Magyar were simply banned. In Austria, foreign military attachés noticed that the multilingual ideal was rarely attained in practice; theoretically, the men in a Slovenian regiment, for example, would speak Slovenian among themselves but be commanded in German. The troops therefore learned a few dozen phrases in German, but officers in such a regiment were expected to be fluent in Slovenian in order to explain complicated matters and build esprit de corps with their men. In reality, the largely German officer corps would lean hard on cheat sheets like *Military Slovenian: A Handbook,* which contained useful phrases including "Shut your mouth," "Don't speak unless spoken to," "Wait for me in my office," "No smoking in the stables," and "Do you *still* not understand?" Regimental officers had to know the language of their men, or at least these fragments of it, but staff officers didn't. This led to comical scenes at maneuvers—not so comical in war—when staff officers would gallop up to line troops and bawl questions in German ("Where is the enemy, in what strength?") and the line troops would stare back uncomprehendingly.[43]

These linguistic controversies augured badly for an empire founded on the idea of regional and ethnic cooperation. With most Austro-Hungarian officers really just knowing their native languages plus German—the army's own statistics revealed that fewer than 10 percent of them could speak languages like Slovenian, Ukrainian, or Rumanian—the notion that they were eager citizens of their Ruritanian world was a myth. At least as disturbing as the lack of fluency in so many important languages were the demoralizing politics involved in the ones they *did* speak. Hungarian officers in the common army, for example, were unofficially exempted from the requirement to attain fluency in other languages, so desperate was the emperor to have proofs of "loyalism" from the Magyars. This enraged Austrian officers, who were not released from the obligation and who hated having to wrestle in their spare time with Czech or Polish grammar or the Ukrainian alphabet.[44] Czechs furnished a high proportion of officers in the army but rarely made general; they were also routinely denounced for speaking Czech among themselves, or even to ladies in the café. An army that would punish an officer for writing a postcard in Czech had clearly lost whatever supranational élan had characterized it in the past.[45]

Language was just another of the many problems facing the Habsburg military. The Hungarians, determined to curb the power of Vienna, had kept the army so small since 1867 that it was ludicrously over-officered. With 20,000 officers for an army of 335,000 in 1913, it had the highest ratio of officers to troops of any great power, and these officers were changing. In the first place, they were graying, which meant senescent commanders and a huge apparatus of well-paid retirees who drained funds from the active-duty army. *Pensionopolis* was Habsburg army slang for that bloated corps of retirees.[46] In 1910, for example, there were thirty-three active three-star generals and three times as many living in retirement. Among two-stars, the situation was just as bad: 91 active, 311 retired. Among one-stars, the retiree-to-active ratio was four to one.

The rump of actually active officers was no less alarming, as General Moritz von Auffenberg's 1910 report on the Austro-Hungarian officer corps made clear. The army until 1866 had been officered at the highest levels by aristocrats and at the junior levels by gentry and upwardly mobile sons of rich peasants—what Auffenberg called "conservative, calm, and safe social elements." Those were the sort of men who could bond platoons of peasant infantry and persuade them to endure hard marches and take casualties. The new officers of the twentieth century, however, were changing along with the rest of society; the aristocrats, Auffenberg discovered, had "almost entirely abandoned the military career," and the gentry and rich peasant sons were also declining—down to 40 percent or less, by Auffenberg's reckoning. Now most officers descended from "railway personnel, innkeepers, clerks, petty officials, teachers and shopkeepers." They lacked the "toughness, spirit, and panache [*Schwung*]" of the old breed, who had commanded a largely peasant army as if they had been born to it, which, of course, they had. Now the army mingled rural and urban troops and put them under plebeian officers who were susceptible to the very national politics that were tearing the monarchy apart, and who would probably not hold up well under fire. It didn't help that 80 percent of these officers and the great majority of NCOs were Germans, in general decidedly mediocre men who had judged the army's notoriously low pay and slow promotion acceptable. Dionysus Gablenz, the son of the only Austrian general to wring a victory from the Prussians in 1866, found himself a sixty-year-old major in 1914, still active, if you could call it that, in the fortress administration of Theresienstadt (Terezin).

Austria-Hungary's enlisted men were largely non-German and would not obey these officers for long in war or peace.[47] Much was made of the facility of Austro-Hungarian officers with the languages of their men, but here too Auffenberg was unimpressed, observing that the "national chauvinism" of the age required far more than a German officer with a smattering of Czech or Slovenian. It required German-speaking Czech or Slovene officers, who would be able to inspire their men, but such men had long since left the professional army for other opportunities.

Auffenberg also rued the absence of educated officers of the well-situated middle class. Those candidates were all flocking to finance and the professions "in pursuit of riches and status." The army had lost and never recovered its social prestige after the twin blows of 1859 and 1866, and it was fighting a losing battle with the "easy money" and "materialist spirit" of the modern age. In the peacetime army it took on average sixteen years to rise from lieutenant to captain, the rank at which the *Durchschnittsoffizier*— average officer—would probably retire, single and unloved (no ambitious woman would marry such a man), and on a meager pension, with most of his savings squandered on horses, uniforms, gambling, prostitutes, balls, and the debts contracted to pay for them. A man lucky enough to make major after a plodding twenty-five-year career would be earning just 3,600 crowns ($500) a year: less than a schoolteacher, a trolley conductor, or even a plumber. And those were the lucky ones, who had to cope only with the slow promotion and niggardly salaries that had been frozen (by the Hungarian Delegation) at 1860s levels to discourage an army career. The unlucky were forced out earlier with an injury, an illness, or some disciplinary infraction and forced to live out their lives in grinding poverty.

The result of these social changes in the Austro-Hungarian officer corps, Auffenberg reported in 1910, was a "deep and dangerous complacency that one finds in greater measure only among officers of the Turkish army." There was also a joylessness about the Austrian mess. "Walk into one," Auffenberg noted, having visited dozens of them as army inspector, "and you won't even find wine on the table." Everyone present fretted about the cost of it. The old "happy warrior spirit" or *Landsknechtsgeist* that had united drunken, guffawing Austrian officers in the evening had become a relic of the past.[48]

There was also a tendency toward corruption in the penny-pinching Habsburg army, which Auffenberg revealed in 1910 (and which he was punished for in 1915, after his own insider trading on the shares of defense contractors). "Strivers will do *anything* to raise their social standing, improve their finances, and escape their little border posts. . . . Gloominess, rage, doubt, and sick brains drive our officers to criminal acts," he observed. Auffenberg spoke scathingly of the poor education of army officers, "most of whom lack even the ability to carry on a decent conversation."[49] Those who were socially gifted waged ferocious turf wars to place themselves closer to Vienna and its circles of wealth and influence.

The defeat at the hands of Prussia in 1866 had also changed the status of the general staff in Austria. Until 1866, the staff—which was responsible for intelligence collection, mobilization, and war plans—had been regarded as a despised backwater; service with it had impeded careers, not accelerated them. But the brilliant victories wrought by the great general staff of Prussia's General Helmuth von Moltke in the German Wars of Unification had persuaded all armies—including Austria's—to increase and empower their general staffs. It was never an easy transition, not even for Prussia. Moltke had famously issued an order to a corps commander at the Battle of Königgrätz in 1866, and the general had replied, "This is all fine, but *who* is General Moltke?" He had known, of course, but he hadn't wanted to know, lest the general staff try to micromanage his affairs.

The same personnel politics *(Personalpolitik)* that had once bedeviled the Prussian army now rooted themselves in Austria-Hungary. Staff officers warred with regimental officers, infighting that was only encouraged by the military's new proclivities. On the pretext of making the army smarter and "more Prussian," the Habsburg general staff had continually increased the number of staff officers serving with every regiment, so by 1910 there were ten or more, two per battalion. But this was viewed in the field army more as a way to extend the reach and patronage of the reigning general staff chief than to make the field troops more effective. Cliques were notorious. General Friedrich Beck, who had been Emperor Franz Joseph's general staff chief for twenty-five years, from 1881 to 1906, was the only man in the world whom the old emperor called "mein Freund" (my friend). The old fox Beck had accumulated so much wealth and power through that friendship that he was fearfully known as the *Vizekaiser* (vice emperor).[50] An increasingly idle bon vivant, Beck stubbornly refused to retire, relying on subordinates to do his work. The most reliable of these, known as "Beck's crown prince," was General Oskar Potiorek, who would play a ruinous role in 1914. When the sagging Beck was finally forced out—by Archduke Franz Ferdinand in 1906, the sad emperor compensating Beck with a lucrative sinecure—the cliques intensified, as new factions jockeyed for the powers Beck had accumulated over a quarter century.[51]

As army inspector and heir to the throne, Archduke Franz Ferdinand ran a potent clique, but Emperor Franz Joseph and his adjutant, General Arthur Bolfras, had their own. Beck had been the emperor's confidant since 1866, and so the emperor and Bolfras naturally intended to make Beck's crown prince, Potiorek, the next general staff chief. But Franz Ferdinand had no desire to see Beck's tenure continued by other means and thus hit upon General Franz Conrad von Hötzendorf, whom he had met at imperial maneuvers in Hungary in 1901.[52] Bewildering alliances formed and dissolved. General Franz Schönaich, the Austro-Hungarian war minister from 1906 to 1911, used the war ministry as a mafia, pushing his protégés up the ladder. He allied with the emperor and Bolfras against Conrad, but also against the archduke and his über-efficient military secretary, Captain (then Major, then Colonel—promotion was not slow in these charmed circles) Alexander Brosch von Aarenau.

The Schönaich Crisis of 1911 exposed these rivalries to the public eye. A grand bargain was hatched that year: the emperor, who loathed Conrad for his war-mongering and anti-Hungarian rhetoric, would secure the archduke's assent to Conrad's dismissal in return for the emperor's assent to Schönaich's dismissal. The archduke despised Schönaich for his softness and readiness to appease the Hungarians. Potiorek, "cold, dry, always nervous and brittle," in the judgment of the French embassy, had the seniority and gravitas to ally with this "Schönaich circle" against Conrad in Potiorek's fierce quest for the general staff chair. "He *craves* the fauteuil of the general staff," the French noted. This time Potiorek's craving was unappeased, but he would keep intriguing until the outbreak of war in 1914, and indeed into the war itself.[53]

To keep the encroaching archduke at bay and underscore his own continuing relevance, the aging emperor insisted that he, not Franz Ferdinand, hand promotions and assignments down from the throne each year. Austro-Hungarian officers waited jealously to see who got "the best garrisons" and offices and who was exiled to the backwaters. Field officers were reviled by staff officers as *Frontbestien*, "beasts of the front," and the "beasts" in turn reviled the nonstop intrigues of the staff officers in *das graue Haus*—the gray house, which was the general staff headquarters in Vienna. Under Beck and Conrad, the neglected "beasts of the front" got older and the coddled staff younger, one officer in 1912 deploring what he called the "disturbing asymmetry" of an army that blended Europe's oldest field officers with its youngest general staff.[54] Auffenberg recommended in 1910 that the windows of the gray house be thrown open so that "light, air, and fresh breezes [could] be let in to blow away the Vienna cliques, the coffeehouse crowd, and the office-bound dynasts."[55] Colonel Brosch warned in 1913 that Conrad—an early protégé of the archduke— had founded his own clique in the general staff operations bureau, which now was known as the *Feldherrngestüt*, the stud farm for generals. If Conrad never rotated an officer through it, the man would never get a corps or an army. Like Beck before him, "Conrad had become too powerful, overshadowing the whole officer corps, and filling the best jobs with his creatures, which had devastated morale." Invidious rumors "born in the coffeehouse, the nest of all gossip," divided one faction from another.

Colonel Brosch, with his protective connections to the archduke, whispered nonstop against Conrad in the years before the war, and also complained about money. The contrast between a (well-placed) officer's social status and the poverty those without independent means were forced to endure both during and after their service made the entire officer corps nervous. General Urban, a war ministry section chief, retired with a full pension in 1911 only to return to active duty in the ministry in 1913 "because he found that he could not make a good living on the outside."[56]

Moneygrubbing and corruption flourished in this atmosphere. Writing to Auffenberg from Bozen (Bolzano), where Franz Ferdinand had arranged for him to command the prestigious 2nd *Kaiserjäger* Regiment after his long tour in the Belvedere, Colonel Brosch sighed that "even though I am in a spa town, I cannot relax." He fretted about a planned cruise to Greece and Sicily with his wife: "How will I make my little money go a long way?" They were cruising in the winter, "not the best time for a sea voyage," because "it will be cheaper to sail then and to live on a ship." Since safe and comfortable liners such as those of Hamburg-Amerika or the Austrian Lloyd were expensive, he had chosen a cheap tub— "it is small and cramped and heaves around sickeningly in a heavy sea"—to save yet more money. Brosch proudly observed that he had chiseled the price down to 95 crowns, as "officers and their families receive a 50 percent discount!" This was a double savings, since the cruise would remove him from Bozen and the obligation to attend the various Carnival balls for officers, NCOs, and veterans, all of which were a drain on his paltry salary. Regimental command was essential to his career—and Brosch owed his illustrious regiment and salubrious garrison to his contacts—but he clearly missed access to what he called "the well-endowed positions" of Vienna.[57]

While the Habsburg army thus scrounged around for the means of subsistence, the Habsburg Empire teetered on the brink of extinction. The economic and military terms of the *Ausgleich* or Compromise of 1867 had to be renewed every ten years, and the renewal debates in 1907 were more furious than ever. They had become intertwined with the fraught question of universal male suffrage. To give the wheezing empire a new lease on life, the emperor had conceded the vote to all adult males in both halves of his monarchy, but only the Austrian half implemented it. Accustomed to ignoring inconvenient directives from Vienna, the Hungarians ignored this one as well, continuing to enfranchise just 7 percent of their population in a pointed snub to their peoples

and monarch. Only the emperor's belated threat to force—as opposed to merely order—implementation of universal male suffrage in Hungary persuaded the Magyars in 1907 to renew the
Ausgleich and give the constitution another decade of life. The
survival of Magyar supremacy in Hungary depended on keeping
the kingdom's Slavs and Rumanians cowed in a system that gave
the Hungarians, with only 55 percent of Hungary's population,
98 percent of its 405 parliamentary deputies. By now, this me-
dieval arrangement had become an international embarrassment
even for the thick-skinned emperor. Franz Joseph recoiled at the
publication (and international sensation) of Oxford scholar R. W.
Seton-Watson's 1908 book *Racial Problems in Hungary,* which
detailed Budapest's myriad abuses of non-Hungarians in Transleithania. To end the scandal and persuade Hungarian lawmakers
to do what the Austrians had already done—and what they had
expected Hungary to do as well—the emperor took the highly un-
usual step of transferring his court to Budapest in the fall of 1908
to implement electoral reform.

After enduring a jolting ten-hour train ride from Ischl to Budapest to settle the issue of male suffrage, the seventy-eight-year-
old emperor-king was jilted instead. Magyar supremacy rested
on rigged elections, and Hungarian "Liberals" saw no reason to
change this state of affairs, even at the emperor-king's orders. Actual Hungarian suffrage "reform" in 1908 amounted to this: one
out of every ten illiterates—more than 25 percent of the population—was conceded one vote in elections (the other nine could
not vote at all); high school graduates, all of whom were educated
in Magyar, received two votes each; university graduates and
wealthy taxpayers could vote three times. Nor was voting secret;
ballots had to be cast publicly so that "voters would not break
their promises under the veil of secrecy." With rules such as these,
Magyar-speaking gentry and professionals would have little trouble ruling the roost in Hungary forever against the wishes of less
privileged Hungarians, Slavs, and Rumanians.[58]

Hungary, in short, was dragging the Habsburg Empire over
a cliff. The only hope for the monarchy in an era of expanding
literacy, liberalization, and national consciousness was a softening

of the grip of the "master nationalities." The Austrians were willing; the Hungarians weren't. They shunned manhood suffrage and even extorted lower tax rates in return for nothing more than renewing the *Ausgleich*, leaving the Austrians with 64 percent of the "common" tax bill, the Hungarians with just 34 percent. Austrian taxpayers—already deeply resentful of Hungarian privileges—increasingly found themselves paying for Hungarian projects. No less than a quarter of the military units raised in Hungary ended up being paid for by Austrian taxpayers. Artillery that had always been manufactured in Austria by the Skoda works would now be made at a new Hungarian facility in Diosgyör.

In the last years before World War I, the Hungarians gave only lip service to the joint monarchy. Head of the National Liberals and prime minister from 1903 to 1905, István Tisza gave the old party a face lift in 1910, renamed it the National Party of Work, and resumed the premiership in 1910. Tisza superficially supported the *Ausgleich*, but he resisted every effort by Vienna to tighten or even equitably share the costs of the Austro-Hungarian union.[59] Not without reason, Italian commentators jocularly referred to Franz Joseph as *"il Kaiser d'Ungaria,"* the emperor of Hungary—a reference to the way real power in the monarchy was wielded from Budapest.[60]

The growing disparity between Austrian and Hungarian influence came into sharp focus during the suffrage and renewal debates, when Austria attempted to close its grip around the small eastern region of Bosnia-Herzegovina. In 1908, with the Young Turk revolution shaking Constantinople and a pro-Russian Serbian dynasty hungrily eyeing Bosnia-Herzegovina, which lay between Austria-Hungary and the tottering Ottoman Empire, Vienna felt bound to annex the territories it had merely occupied thirty years earlier at the Congress of Berlin. This led to another, revealing round of Hungarian obstruction. Budapest would not agree to incorporate Bosnia-Herzegovina into either part of the monarchy. Instead, the Hungarians insisted on yet another half measure. Though the new provinces would be treated as a "hereditary possession of the Habsburg house," they would actually be ruled not by the emperor but by the Austro-Hungarian finance minister.[61]

That minister would spend most of his time trying to figure out how to communicate with his subordinates, the emperor having agreed that all Bosnian correspondence with Austro-Hungarian ministries would be in German, with Hungarian offices in Hungarian, and with Croatian officials in Croatian.[62] These absurd arrangements were calculated to leave the new Balkan crown lands in permanent limbo as a "special administrative territory"; Budapest feared strengthening Cisleithania, yet also feared adding more Slavs to Transleithania, especially South Slavs, who might ally with the Croats and Serbs of Hungary against the Magyars.[63]

The fatuity of all of this military and political floundering was not lost on someone as dry and methodical as Archduke Franz Ferdinand. In 1913, the fifty-year-old heir apparent vowed that when he became emperor, Bosnia-Herzegovina would become Austrian; he noted the strategic absurdity that Hungary, by its continual manipulation of the provinces (and the weak emperor), was effectively "cutting Austria off from the Balkans," which, the archduke continued, were "Austria's future." The monarchy would thrust down to Salonika, absorb abandoned Turkish territory, open new ports on the Mediterranean, and became the engine of trade and development for the new Balkan kingdoms of Rumania, Bulgaria, Greece, and even Serbia.[64]

But in this plan, as in all others, Hungarian cooperation was required, and by 1913 the Hungarians had all but dropped out of the imperial system. They were refusing even to sing the words to the Austro-Hungarian national anthem—Haydn's *Gott erhalte*—because it contained the hated word *Kaiser*. They would hum, fall silent, or even hiss. Government efficiency, always a weak spot in Austria, plummeted, as the Hungarians insisted on ever-increasing paperwork and protocol to connect the two capitals, the two parliaments (one in Vienna, the other in Budapest), and the delegations that bridged the two governments. At best, this system was, as a foreign observer put it, "an incomplete federalism," with no ultimate authority.[65] At worst, the system was, as another foreign observer put it, one of Hungarian-administered "terror and blackmail . . . Franz Joseph has always given in to the Hungarians; a stronger and more intelligent monarch would have struck back by now against this little nation that is no more numerous than the people of Belgium."[66]

The stronger man who *wanted* to strike back was Franz Joseph's nephew: Archduke Franz Ferdinand. After the suicide of Archduke Rudolf in 1889, the twenty-six-year-old Franz Ferdinand had survived tuberculosis and then been named Austria-Hungary's crown prince and heir apparent in 1898. His energy, independence, and pugnacity were legendary; he was an obsessive hunter who shot 275,000 beasts in his lifetime; he chose as his wife not the Habsburg cousin selected for him but her lady-in-waiting, Countess Sophie Chotek, which caused a scandal and a "morganatic marriage," which meant that the archduke's children would be barred from the throne.[67] Few liked this humorless, churchy son of a Habsburg archduke and a Neapolitan princess, least of all the emperor. Indeed, everyone assumed—until 1898, when they gave up assuming—that the emperor would simply remarry and produce another son, rendering his nephew irrelevant. But the emperor, besotted with Frau Schratt, never bothered remarrying, and so the monarchy was stuck with Franz Ferdinand.

Whereas Franz Joseph viewed the *Ausgleich* as the unassailable basis of the monarchy, Franz Ferdinand viewed it as a cancer that had to be cut out. Like a puppy harrying an old dog, Franz Ferdinand established his own military chancery in the Lower Belvedere Palace in 1904 and ran it as a shadow government, with his own de facto ministers of war, foreign affairs, and domestic policy, most of whom had run afoul of Franz Joseph at one time or another.[68] Whereas Franz Joseph was content to cling to the dissolving structure of the Habsburg monarchy, Franz Ferdinand wanted to tear the monarchy down to the foundation and rebuild it. The contrast between his youth and the emperor's age had everyone speculating about abdication: the drowsy old emperor stepping down to make way for, as the French embassy put it, "the primordial solution—the resolute, energetic crown prince, who might save the monarchy, if it's not already too late."[69] Ordered by the emperor to go to Budapest in 1907 to celebrate the fortieth anniversary of the *Ausgleich,* Franz Ferdinand had only grudgingly complied: "I must tell Your Majesty the truth—this celebration is

Like a puppy harrying an old dog, Archduke Franz Ferdinand created a shadow govern-ment in the Belvedere Palace that openly competed with Emperor Franz Joseph's gov-ernment in the Hofburg for control of the empire. "We not only have two parliaments, we have two emperors," a senior Austrian official complained as the competition intensified.

CREDIT: National Archives

really a *confusion of concepts*, this 40 years Jubilee of the *Ausgleich* at a moment when *these people* rule, people whom I can only describe as traitors and who constantly *agitate* against *everything*: Dynasty, Empire, Army, etc. etc."[70]

Officers and bureaucrats loyal to Franz Joseph increasingly had to hedge their bets in view of the emperor's advanced age as well as the archduke's ambitions and the deft office politics of his chief aide, Colonel Brosch von Aarenau, who was Franz Ferdinand's adjutant from 1906 to 1911 and who began organizing the *Thronwechsel* or imperial succession in 1911, five years before the emperor's death. Brosch's program vowed to introduce Austrian voting rights into Hungary, end the abuses of Magyarization, solve the question of administrative languages everywhere, normalize the status of Bosnia-Herzegovina, put the joint army on a solid footing, and rename Austria-Hungary the "Austrian Monarchy," with a single flag: the Habsburg double eagle on a black-and-yellow field. Most of all, Franz Ferdinand promised to obliterate the impression of "muddling through" *(fortwursteln)* that was Vienna's hallmark.[71] Overall, he would implement "a policy of even-handed repression" to replace the thankless pro-Hungarian policies of Franz Joseph. The Viennese satirist Karl Kraus was no friend of the Habsburgs but nevertheless had a grudging respect for Franz Ferdinand, who, unlike Franz Joseph, "never pandered to the fickle, tacky *(kitschig)*, and smarmy *(gemütlich)* instincts of the Viennese, and never even tried to be popular." The archduke was a "Fortinbras, not a Hamlet," and the monarchy's last best hope for "an orderly country and an end to chaos."[72]

Franz Ferdinand may have been the monarchy's best hope—there were no imposing alternatives—but he was unlikely to succeed: the national problems were too intractable, and the archduke himself was a muddle of contradictions. He was more competent and focused than Franz Joseph—who wasn't?—but he had no plan to harmonize the quarreling nationalities, and he was hemmed in by an alarmingly religious wife, who vetted generals and ministers on their Catholic piety, as well as by a coterie of sycophants. He was a bully, enabled by the obsequious Austrian system, and his oafish prejudices became his policy, as his analysis in 1909 of a conversation between an Austrian ambassador (Count Mensdorff) and a British official (Noel Buxton) made clear: "Mensdorff is totally incompetent. He's married to a Hungarian and has forgotten that he's an Austrian. Buxton, like all Englishmen, is blind and stupid. You may share these impressions with General Conrad."[73]

With supervision like this, it was no wonder that the Austro-Hungarian general staff chief, General Franz Conrad von Hötzendorf, had a reputation for bluster and recklessness. Still, in the land of the blind the one-eyed man is king. Made general inspector of the Habsburg armed forces in 1913, Franz Ferdinand poached more and more on the emperor's last preserve. He and Conrad replaced every one of Austria-Hungary's sixteen corps commanders that year, removing the emperor's men and inserting their own.[74] The press referred to the archduke guardedly and obliquely as "the Competent Office," "the Very High Position," or "the Alternate Factor." Every great-power embassy had informants inside Schönbrunn and the Hofburg, telling them what medications the emperor was on, what his weight was, and how severe his regular illnesses were. Increasingly, the emperor avoided the Hofburg altogether, remaining in the summer palace at Schönbrunn year-round to spare himself the strain of a move.[75] Most observers expected his death any day.

Franz Ferdinand's rise and the emperor's eclipse divided the already fragmented empire further. "We not only have two parliaments, we have two emperors," a senior official grimaced.[76] The archduke—"the Sphinx of the Belvedere"—was instrumental in the appointment of Austro-Hungarian foreign minister Count Alois Lexa von Aerenthal in 1906, as well as Aerenthal's successor in 1912, Count Leopold von Berchtold.[77] General Moritz von Auffenberg, made war minister in 1911 at the archduke's urging, deplored the emperor's unwillingness to "solve the Hungarian question" and stop the erosion of army morale.[78] General Franz Conrad von Hötzendorf had also rallied to the archduke's policies, winning promotion to general staff chief in 1906 at the age of fifty-four.[79]

Conrad never concealed his frustration that ten million Hungarians had achieved a headlock on the fifty-million-man monarchy's foreign, fiscal, and military affairs. Like Franz Ferdinand—who had said that "the army's main task is not defense of the fatherland against an external enemy but against all internal enemies"—Conrad believed that the monarchy's mission was to "unite Europe's western and southern Slavs" against Russian, German, or Hungarian domination.[80] Like Aerenthal, he believed that a forward policy in the Balkans was needed to inspire Austria-Hungary's demoralized peoples and deter the monarchy's enemies.

To give teeth to the empire's Balkan strategy, Conrad reworked Austro-Hungarian war plans after 1906. Plan U, to invade Hungary, was supplemented with three additional scenarios: Plan I (Italy), Plan B (Balkans), and Plan R (Russia). The first of these plans targeted a nominal partner of Austria's, but the fact that Italy had technically been an Austrian ally in the Triple Alliance of Germany, Austria, and Italy since 1882 fooled no one. The Italians had joined the alliance only to get diplomatic cover in their regular spats with the French over North African colonies. They coveted Austrian Trieste, Dalmatia, and the Tyrolean region around Trento far more than Libya or Tunis. This made war between the "allied enemies"—as Austria and Italy were known in diplomatic circles—likely.

The existence of Russian and Balkan war plans in Vienna was anything but surprising. Since war with Russia would almost certainly flow from an Austro-Hungarian clash with Serbia, Conrad's Plans B and R kept to the defensive on both fronts, with a potentially decisive Echelon or *Staffel* of four corps held in reserve to intervene on either front as needed. If the Russians backed down, Serbia would be crushed; if they didn't, they would be fought to a standstill in Galicia and then enveloped in Poland by allied Austrian and German armies. This, at least, was the idea.[81]

CHAPTER 2

Between Blunder and Stupidity

THE RUSSIANS SMELLED THE DECAY of Austria-Hungary more acutely than most. Having themselves been crushed in the Russo-Japanese War of 1904–1905, the Russians knew a thing or two about decay. Earlier focused on expansion into East Asia—hence the war with Japan—the Russians now swerved opportunistically back to Europe. Inspired by pan-Slavism, which held that all Slavs were a single family best led by Russia, Tsar Nicholas II vowed to push into the Balkan space, nurture Slavic kingdoms like Serbia, and annex a land bridge to Constantinople and the Dardanelles, reclaiming the old Eastern Orthodox capital and linking the Black Sea and the Mediterranean through the Turkish Straits. In this way, the Russians would expunge the shame of their Asian defeat, escape the "prison" of the Black Sea, and proclaim their arrival as Europe's dominant power.[1]

Russia's selection of Serbia as a key ally in this strategic re-orientation was a disastrous development for Austria-Hungary. In 1903, the pliable, pro-Austrian Obrenovic dynasty in Serbia had been overthrown by the pro-Russian, aggressively nationalistic Peter Karageorgevic. King Peter and his prime minister, Nikola Pasic, detected weakness in both Sick Men of Europe: the Ottoman and Habsburg Empires. The 1878 Congress of Berlin—a tortured compromise between the old policy of propping up the Ottomans and the new policy of recognizing new nations (like Greece, Rumania, Serbia, and Bulgaria) cut from "Turkey-in-Europe," as the Balkan provinces of the Ottoman Empire were called—had opened the door to all kinds of changes by its inconsistencies. Serbia felt free to nibble at surrounding (still Ottoman) provinces including Macedonia, the Sanjak of Novipazar, Kosovo, and Albania, and even to claim the 2.1 million Serbs living under Austrian rule in Bosnia-Herzegovina, Hungary, Croatia, and Dalmatia.[2] The Serbs resolved to use the heft of a Russian alliance to expand into Macedonia and Albania, open a corridor across the Sanjak to Montenegro and the sea, and begin the demolition of the Habsburg monarchy, which the Serbs derided as "a gaudy bird made of borrowed feathers."[3]

Many of those borrowed feathers had been plucked from Serbia's historic dominions. The Serbia that had wrung independence from the Turks in 1867, with its capital in Belgrade, encompassed barely half the landmass of the old Serbian Empire shattered by the Turks in the fourteenth century. The Serbs were determined to reconstitute that empire in the twentieth, by retaking Macedonia (seat of the ancient Serbian capital at Skopje), Kosovo (site of the mythic Field of the Blackbirds, where Serbia had lost an epic battle and its independence to Turkey in the fourteenth century), and as much of Austria-Hungary as they could grab.[4] Serbia now styled itself the "Prussia of the Balkans," planning to unite all of the South Slavs in an enlarged Kingdom of Serbia, just as Bismarck had united the Germans. There were ten million South Slavs on the Balkan Peninsula in 1903, but only three and a half million of them lived within the borders of Serbia or Montenegro. The rest were in the Ottoman and Austro-Hungarian Empires. Serbia wanted them all, and was prepared to fight to get them.[5]

Franz Joseph and Franz Ferdinand perceived the danger: if the Serbs succeeded in uniting all of the southern Slavs under a single crown, they would shoulder Austria-Hungary out of the Balkans by creating a Serb-run "Yugoslavia." This "Slav South," governed from Belgrade, would unite Austria's military occupation zones and Turkey's dying *vilayets* or provinces in a single, Slavic, Christian hand.[6] The situation was analogous to the 1860s, when the

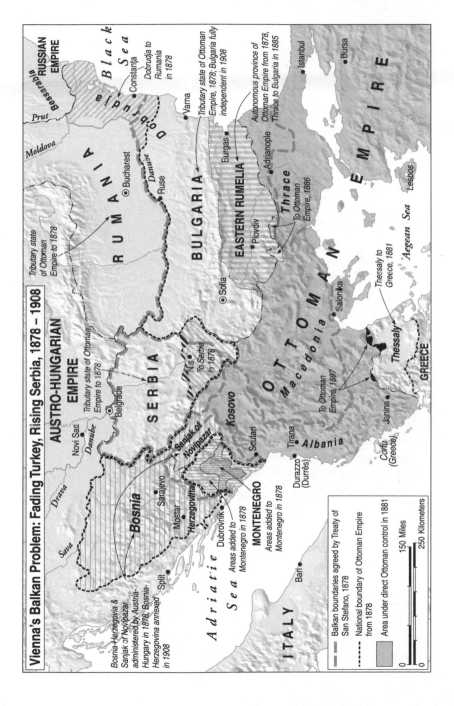

Vienna's Balkan Problem: Fading Turkey, Rising Serbia, 1878 – 1908

RUSSIAN EMPIRE

Bessarabia

Prut

Moldova

Black Sea

Constanța

Dobrudja to Rumania in 1878

Varna

Tributary state of Ottoman Empire, 1878; Bulgaria fully independent in 1908

Istanbul

Bursa

E M P I R E

Autonomous province of Ottoman Empire from 1878, Thrace to Bulgaria in 1885

AUSTRO-HUNGARIAN EMPIRE

Tributary state of Ottoman Empire to 1878

R U M A N I A

Bucharest

Danube

Ruse

Burgas

Adrianople

Thrace

To Ottoman Empire, 1886

Tributary state of Ottoman Empire to 1878

B U L G A R I A

EASTERN RUMELIA

Plovdiv

To Ottoman Empire, 1885

Sofia

Salonika

Aegean Sea

Lesbos

Novi Sad

Danube

Belgrade

S E R B I A

Niš

To Serbia in 1878

Drava

Bosnia-Herzegovia & Sanjak of Novipazar administered by Austria-Hungary in 1878; Bosnia-Herzegovina annexed in 1908

Sava

Bosnia

Sarajevo

Mostar

Herzegovina

Sanjak of Novipazar

Herzegovina

Dubrovnik

Kosovo

Scutari

Tirana

Albania

Durazzo (Durrës)

O T T O M A N

Macedonia

To Ottoman Empire, 1897

Janina

Thessaly

Thessaly to Greece, 1881

GREECE

Corfu (Greece)

Split

MONTENEGRO

Areas added to Montenegro in 1878

Areas added to Montenegro in 1878

Areas added to Montenegro in 1878

Adriatic Sea

Bari

I T A L Y

Balkan boundaries agreed by Treaty of San Stefano, 1878

National boundary of Ottoman Empire from 1878

Area under direct Ottoman control in 1881

150 Miles

250 Kilometers

0

0

Piedmontese had pushed the Austrians out of Italy and the Prussians had pushed them out of Germany. Now Archduke Franz Ferdinand began referring to the Serbs as the *Donaupiemont*—the Danubian Piedmont—and he persuaded the emperor to appoint Count Alois Lexa von Aerenthal foreign minister in 1906 to energize the Habsburg foreign office, which had stagnated under his two unimaginative predecessors.[7] Whereas Aerenthal's predecessors had dully promoted an Austro-Russian entente in the Balkans, the new foreign minister wanted to wipe the slate clean and start fresh. That Austria-Hungary lacked the power to reorganize the Balkans did not trouble him. As the Viennese wit Karl Kraus jotted, "Policy is what you do in order to conceal what you are."[8] Austria was weak, but it would pretend to be strong.

Having served as ambassador in St. Petersburg during the Russo-Japanese War, Aerenthal assumed that the Russians would be unable to oppose a newly aggressive Austrian policy in the Balkans. It never occurred to him that the opposite might be true: that, having lost in East Asia, the Russians could not afford to lose in Europe as well. Blissfully secure in assumptions that took no account of Austria-Hungary's military weakness, Aerenthal embarked on a strong policy in the Balkans, determined to push back the Russians, rally the Habsburg peoples to a revived dynasty, intimidate the Serbs, and remind the Germans that Austria-Hungary was still capable of managing its (shrunken) sphere of influence. It was time, Aerenthal argued, to convert the hesitant, thirty-year occupation of Bosnia-Herzegovina into a bold annexation. Annexation of Bosnia would open the door to a wider Austrian aim: Salonika. Once the greatest city of Macedon, then a rich Roman and Byzantine port, Salonika in the twentieth century remained the greatest strategic prize in the Balkans. Aerenthal planned to seize it, link it to the Habsburg Empire by a corridor through Macedonia and the Sanjak, command the Aegean port's trade routes to the Middle East and Asia, and use it to spring open Austria's Adriatic "backwaters" of Trieste and Fiume (Rijeka).

Aerenthal and his mentor, Archduke Franz Ferdinand, envisioned using these new annexations, from Bosnia down to Salonika, as a means to reshape the monarchy. Externally, the Turks and Serbs, who had prevented construction of an Eastern Railway *(Ostbahn)* from Vienna to Salonika, would be brushed aside. Austria would become, as Franz Ferdinand's mouthpiece put it, "Europe's bridge to the Levant and the Middle East."[9] Internally, Hungary would be shorn of Croatia, which would be beefed up with the new Balkan conquests and used, in league with Austria, to cut Hungary and its colossal pretensions down to size in a refashioned system. The hugely inefficient Dual Monarchy would become a (hopefully) more efficient Triple Monarchy, with capitals at Vienna, Budapest, and Zagreb. If the Hungarians continued to obstruct, they would simply be outvoted, two against one, by the Austrians and Croats.[10]

Little Serbia blocked all of these soaring plans. In the past, the Serbs had kowtowed to Austria. But with firm Russian backing, they now could assert their national interests with little fear of a crushing Austro-Hungarian invasion. Historically restrained by republican France and imperial Britain, the Russians by 1907 had allied with both of those powers in the Triple Entente. The effect of that diplomatic revolution was to bolster Serbia and push Austria-Hungary deep into the pocket of what Vienna considered its only reliable ally, Germany. But Germany was hardly reliable. Berlin had adopted a new strategy of *Weltpolitik*—world policy— and begun to build a high-seas fleet at the turn of the century to challenge the British and French overseas empires. Even Germany's impressive population (sixty-eight million), army (eight hundred thousand men in peacetime, three million in war), and industry (the biggest in Europe) would probably be insufficient to defeat Britain and France and still have enough force left over to aid the Austrians against the Russians. Unless Austria-Hungary built an army big enough to deter the Serbs and the Russians, it might find itself alone on the Eastern and Balkan Fronts facing vast numbers of enemy troops.

Despite the obvious urgency, Vienna was in no mood to contemplate the massive military expenditures that the twentieth century demanded. Warfare and technology had advanced in giant bounds since 1866, and every European military would have to either adapt or face ruin. The first stride forward—universal conscription—all but ensured financial ruin, as armies that had never exceeded three hundred thousand in the past now ballooned to nearly a million in peacetime, and several million in the event of war. Whether one followed the French doctrine of a massed army on a narrow front aiming at a breakthrough or the German doctrine of a dispersed army on a broad front aiming to outflank, huge troop numbers were required to attack the mass conscript armies and extensive fortifications of the modern age. But the Austrians lacked the funds and political will to draft and arm the masses; on the eve of war in 1914, they were still training just 0.29 percent of their population, compared with 0.75 percent in France, 0.47 percent in Germany, 0.37 percent in Italy, and 0.35 percent in Russia. This fact alone should have persuaded Vienna *never* to go to war with another great power. After mobilizing all of its reserves, it would have fewer than 2.3 million trained troops for a major war, whereas Russia alone would have three or four times as many, and France, with ten million fewer citizens than Austria-Hungary, would have twice as many.[11]

What men the Austrians had would have to be armed at tremendous expense. In the hotly competitive European military arena, artillery had been massively upgraded. New steel casting and rifling techniques meant that cannon and howitzers could hurl shells farther and more accurately than ever before. Whereas guns had fired a maximum range of two thousand yards (a little over a mile) during the American Civil War, standard pieces (such as the British eighteen-pounder) were now firing shells out to seven thousand yards (four miles). They were also firing more quickly thanks to spring and hydraulic recoil systems that absorbed the kick of the gun and held it in position for the next round. France's legendary 75 mm cannon could fire fifteen to thirty aimed rounds of shell or shrapnel every sixty seconds. Chemical high explosives like trinitrotoluene (TNT) replaced the old black-powder shells of the 1860s, with devastating results. Armed with better fuses, these rounds killed masses of men with splinters, balls, and shock waves.

Lighter weapons too had undergone massive improvements in recent decades. Magazine-fed repeating rifles, firing a dozen aimed rounds a minute, saturated the field with fire and forced all riflemen to become "walking arsenals," as the Austrian army's handbook put it, lugging up to two hundred cartridges in their haversacks at all times. Machine guns, self-loaded by the action of gas pressure, followed in the 1880s, spewing six hundred rounds per minute. They were a terrific force multiplier. A single six-man machine gun team could deliver a division's worth of rifle fire, and with two machine guns per battalion and twelve battalions to a division, the impact on rate of fire was astonishing.

Investment in these new quick-firing weapons (rifles, machine guns, and field artillery) required unprecedented investment in supply services as well. Prussian musketeers at Leipzig in 1813 had fired an average of twenty rounds in the battle; in the battles of the Russo-Japanese War, infantrymen were routinely firing two hundred rounds or more. Since a soldier could carry no more than two hundred rounds and since even this number of cartridges would not last longer than fifteen minutes in a hot fight—armies needed expanded supply services. Battalion and company ammunition wagons, bearing an additional three hundred rounds per man, now had to push into the firing line to feed the slaughter.[12] Every infantry division had to be followed into battle by 120 of these ammunition wagons, carrying six hundred thousand additional rifle rounds and fifty thousand machine gun rounds.

The new quick-firing artillery, which shot shells as fast as riflemen shot bullets, posed identical cost and logistical problems. Whereas nineteenth-century armies had manufactured no more than seven thousand shells a week in times of war, the armies in World War I would have to manufacture ten or even twenty times that number every *day*. It was easy to see why: a Prussian cannon at Leipzig in 1813 fired an average of 61 rounds per day, but a Russian cannon at Mukden in 1905 fired 504 rounds per day, causing the French to allot 600 rounds per gun per day by 1914. Had all of these shells been carried to the front, the guns would have disappeared under a stack of crates, so every artillery battery—there were fourteen batteries of six guns in a typical field artillery regiment—required a dozen ammunition wagons, half of which crowded around the guns themselves, the other half trailing behind in the ever-lengthening train that threatened to swallow up the twentieth-century army.[13] Nor were ammunition wagons the only piece of the modern military's new entourage; devastating fire from the new guns forced divisions to add yet more wagons for countermeasures, which included sandbags (seven thousand per division), lumber, ladders, and shovels.[14]

In order to compete with these fearsome new technologies, perennially improvident Austria-Hungary would have to replace its outmoded equipment—black-powder rifles and bronze-barreled artillery from the 1870s—and buy more of everything, at terrific cost. Vienna would also have to upgrade its railways and roads to move troops faster to the front. Mobilization of a relatively small army in Austria's last major war (in 1866) had taken an agonizing fifty-five days.[15] In the next war, Germany planned to mobilize, deploy, smash France and Britain, and then move its entire army east to defeat Russia in a mere forty-two days. Austria was expected to move just as briskly.

Emperor Franz Joseph feared the size and cost of everything. Whereas General Franz Conrad von Hötzendorf exulted over all of the new inventions—"Napoleon wouldn't recognize this world of railways, turnpikes, telegraphs, telephones, automobiles, balloons and canned food"—Franz Joseph loathed them. When an experimental armored car sputtered past his suite at maneuvers in 1906, the emperor, a man of the Victorian age, reacted angrily, vowing that "such a thing would *never* be of any military value."[16]

In 1908, Franz Joseph, prodded by the hyperactive Aerenthal, wobbled uncertainly toward annexation of Bosnia-Herzegovina. Even clad in Aerenthal's new strategy of Balkan and Mediterranean dominance, the task seemed thankless; there were now 674,000 Serbs, 548,000 Muslims, and 334,000 Croats in the territories, all administered by an eye-popping 9,500 Austrian bureaucrats. (The Turks had made do with 180 officials.) Few of these people saw much gain for themselves under Austrian rule, for the simple reason that the Hungarians had insisted that no common Austro-Hungarian funds could be disbursed for the development of the backward provinces. All funds for the upkeep of the region would have to be raised locally, on the backs of the already poor populace, virtually ensuring their hostility to Vienna.

The Austrians were also slow to introduce land reform in the new provinces; Muslim landlords essentially imprisoned Christian serfs *(kmets)* on their big estates, but the Austrians hesitated to reform the system lest they alienate the wealthy Muslims and empower the Serbian *kmets,* whom they assumed would gravitate to Belgrade, not Vienna. Vienna's refusal to help the *kmets* ensured that they would do just that.[17]

The Young Turk revolution in Constantinople in July 1908 made some Austro-Hungarian reply essential. Faced with an aggressive new Turkish regime, not the slack sultanate of the past, Vienna knew that its continued hold on the occupied area and any future grabs at Macedonia and Salonika would be contested by the Young Turks. The reform party was led by a pair of twenty-nine-year-old Turkish army officers, Mustafa Kemal and Enver Pasha. Kemal (the future Atatürk) had been born in Salonika; Enver's father had worked in Macedonia, and his mother was Albanian. Neither officer regarded the Balkans as anything other than a Turkish space, and both were committed to the consolidation of Turkey, not its withering away. This new Turkey, the American diplomat Robert Lansing observed, was "reborn and tingling with national ambition." It could be expected to demand the immediate return of Bosnia-Herzegovina with its half a million Muslims (who were already calling for the Young Turk constitution) as well as its other European *vilayets,* not let them fall to a Christian power like Austria.[18] To Aerenthal, annexation of Bosnia-Herzegovina seemed the best "palliative" not just against the Turkish threat but also against sharpening Serbian attacks on the legitimacy of Austro-Hungarian rule in Sarajevo and elsewhere.[19] Still, the proposed *Palliativmittel* harmed relations with Great Britain, which wanted no weakening of the promising Young Turk regime. It also threatened war with Russia, which now firmly backed the Great Serbian program of King Peter Karageorgevic.[20]

As they pondered annexation, Austro-Hungarian leaders took another nervous glance at their somnolent military. In a major war, Austria-Hungary would be able to eke out just forty-eight infantry divisions against ninety-three Russian divisions, eighty-eight French, forty-six Italian, and eleven Serbian. A Habsburg army of four hundred thousand men, a French officer drawled in 1913, "is really not much at all for an empire of 50 million." A German officer agreed: "Adequate for a campaign against Serbia, but inadequate for a major European war."[21]

Austria-Hungary's artillery establishment was even more inadequate, with just forty-two guns per division, compared with forty-eight in a Russian division and eighty in a German one. When General Moritz von Auffenberg became war minister in 1911, he discovered that Austria had the lowest proportion of artillery to infantry among the great powers. Auffenberg called artillery the army's "Achilles' heel," and he would shrink from intervention in the looming Balkan Wars because of this and other shortcomings.[22] Although the Franco-Prussian War of 1870–1871 had furnished conclusive proof of the superiority of steel to bronze cannon, the Austrians were still procuring bronze guns in 1914 because they *lasted* longer, which suited Hungarian accountants more than Austrian generals.

With new artillery regiments priced at a quarter million dollars for sixteen new field guns, the straitened Austro-Hungarians clung to the old ones, which meant that their gun batteries blended forty-five different gun types, requiring dozens of different munitions. This made the mass production of shell even more difficult than usual and virtually guaranteed a "shell crisis" in the event of a long war.[23] In terms of heavy artillery, the entire Habsburg army possessed just fifty-six heavy howitzers. "The army's undergunned," the British military attaché wrote from Vienna in 1913, "but guns are expensive." Everyone, by then, being so familiar with Austrian penury, no further explanation was required. At the most recent Austrian maneuvers, the British attaché had been struck by "the low proportion of artillery," concluding prophetically, "If they are going to attempt to do in real war what they often attempted to do in these maneuvers, they are going to suffer very severely indeed." Taking it all in, Auffenberg commented: "Favorable is not a word you would use to describe our state of affairs."[24]

Nor did the Austrians do their best with what they had. Conrad paid lip service to the new fire tactics—"*moderne Kampf ist Feuerkampf,*" modern battle is fire battle—but his operational art remained stubbornly pre-fire. As in all things, Conrad in this area was a dilettante. He analyzed the Anglo-Boer War in 1903, which had featured quick-firing Boers decimating their British attackers from trenches, and decided that such modern tactics could not reasonably be taught to the "schoolboys, peasants, shopkeepers, factory and office workers and artisans" likely to fill the Austro-Hungarian ranks in a general mobilization. Conrad preferred older tactics—the very ones that would result in the slaughter of the entire Austro-Hungarian army in just four months of combat once war broke out. The fact that these tactics probably wouldn't work didn't trouble him. He was looking for a way to present the increasingly undergunned and undertrained Austro-Hungarian army as an army. Foreign attachés were beginning to comment on its feebleness.

Shock tactics approximating those that had destroyed the Habsburg army in 1866 seemed to offer a solution of sorts.[25] Austrian troops, Conrad argued, must be forced to attack. Camouflage, new pike-gray uniforms to replace the old blue ones, would provide some security against fire, but to really achieve it, the men would have to maneuver briskly (despite the clutter of wagons and other impediments), achieve numerical superiority at the critical point (despite the enemy's defensive fire), and turn the enemy's flank (despite the difficulty of even finding the flank of a million-man army). It was that simple, or so it seemed to Conrad. Foreign attachés were not so sure. Attending Austro-Hungarian maneuvers in 1905—after the carnage of the Boer and Russo-Japanese Wars—Prince Karl Schwarzenberg had been surprised to witness an attack by massed Austrian "red" troops on standing Austrian "blue" troops, neither making any use of the shovel. The red troops charged with the bayonet; the blue troops stood erect in neatly dressed lines. Schwarzenberg turned to the Japanese military attaché beside him, who was a veteran of the recent war with Russia, and asked: "What do you make of this?" The Japanese pondered for a moment, then said: *"Wer nicht grabt, ist tot"* (he who doesn't dig in is dead).[26]

One Austrian general ascribed these failings to Austria's lack of military experience. The monarchy had not fought a real war since 1866 and had essentially lost touch with reality. Habsburg maneuvers never tested the ability of officers to combine cavalry, infantry, and artillery to take positions by fire and movement. Rather, they involved identifying key points on a map—heights, woods, villages—and then attempting to take them first, which invariably meant a wild steeplechase by gaily adorned squadrons of cavalry and sprinting columns of infantry, without any pause to reconnoiter and fire.[27] In 1912, the British attaché confirmed this total lack of "war conditions." Skirmishes were choreographed, with troops delivered to each unfolding "scene." A bridgehead was taken by Austrian cavalry in a "shock attack"—a wall of horsemen swinging their sabers as if this were 1812, not 1912. The Austrian infantry attacked in massed company columns, running 150 yards with fixed bayonets at an enemy who, in the real world, would have annihilated them before they covered half that distance.

"The underlying principle in the Austrian army appears to be to get as close to the enemy as possible without firing at all," the British attaché marveled. The Austrian artillery committed the opposite sin, "blazing off rounds without waiting for range or even for targets," and was unable to cooperate with friendly infantry without accidentally killing them. The two arms fought a parallel, disconnected battle, not least because the army simply did not have enough guns to bombard the enemy from long range and then take him under fire from closer range to support the infantry assault "without running the risk of depriving the infantry of support during the process of movement of the guns," as the British officer put it. Nor was any effort made to simulate the friction of battle and the trade-offs it imposed. In real war, officers would have to choose between various objectives and ration the energy of their troops to attain them.[28]

In the fall of 1908, with their military still stagnating, the Austro-Hungarians finally annexed Bosnia and Herzegovina. The Turks were paid off with $11 million and the return of the Sanjak, but the ensuing crisis with Russia, which objected to the absence of compensations for itself and Serbia, nearly led to war.[29] Aerenthal had promised to help secure Russian naval access to the Dardanelles—closed to the Russians since the Crimean War—in return for Russian acceptance of the annexation, but then he reneged, inflicting a brutal diplomatic double cross and defeat on the Russians. Aerenthal inflicted a similar defeat on the Serbs, asserting that the 1878 Treaty of Berlin, which had authorized nothing more than Austrian occupation of Bosnia, was a dead letter, Greece and Bulgaria having already violated the treaty by annexing Crete and declaring independence, respectively. Now, Aerenthal insisted, outright annexation was necessary to "suppress political unrest in Bosnia-Herzegovina."[30] For Austria to achieve its "high cultural and political purposes," Belgrade was forced to disband the regular troops and irregulars *(komitadjis)* it had mobilized for operations in Bosnia and—adding insult to injury—avow "friendly relations" with Vienna "without compensation or reserve."[31] Following the crisis from Bucharest, an American diplomat judged it "a remarkable political game." The Serbs had imagined that a Habsburg annexation, violating the treaty of 1878, would so outrage the international community that Austria would, as the American put it, "lose all sympathy of the powers" and even find itself at war with a coalition eager to defend the rights of "weak yet valiant Serbia."[32]

Aerenthal had squirmed out of the trap, but not without cost. Sir Edward Grey, the British foreign secretary, deplored Aerenthal's "disruptive course," and the American embassy in Vienna worriedly noted that in his personal quest for "greatness," Aerenthal was "playing with fire to run so close to plunging Europe in a war, the final spread of which cannot be foreseen."[33] Seeking that wider war, Serbia had appealed to Russia for help. But Russia was still rebuilding after its defeat in the Russo-Japanese War, and Russia's principal ally, France, had no stomach for a great war over the Balkans.[34]

A German note to Russia in March 1909 insisting that St. Petersburg give Vienna a free hand against Serbia "or matters would have to take their course" sufficed to terminate the crisis.[35] The Russians were again deeply humiliated as a great power, but also as the standard-bearer of pan-Slavism, which seemed to have lost a test of wills with the German powers. Conrad foolishly believed that it was his partial mobilization, not German intervention, that had turned the tide. "He represented," Churchill drawled, "that most dangerous of combinations, a Chief of the General Staff absorbed in Foreign Policy."[36] In Sarajevo, General Michael Appel—as fervent a war-monger as Conrad—insisted that a punitive campaign against Serbia and Montenegro would pay a double dividend, removing Austria's most pressing external threat and then permitting an invigorating crackdown on the internal one: "Once we've defeated and disarmed the gentlemen in Belgrade, Nis and Cetinje, we'll march on Budapest and Prague, and make *them* obey too."[37] But Appel, like Conrad, was overreaching. Vigor required resources, and Auffenberg judged the army too weak in every department to fight a war. Government accountants gaped at the cost of just the partial mobilization in 1908: 180 million crowns ($36 million), a sum that amounted to half the year's military budget and was equal to the cost of four new dreadnought battleships.

Conrad, for his part, merely gaped at Aerenthal's failure to use the cover of the German ultimatum to invade and partition Serbia without the risk of a Russian second front. But Aerenthal—who was made a count by a grateful emperor for his hand in the venture—was wise enough to grasp the one signal fact that emerged from this crisis: that the Russians had backed down only because of German threats, not Austrian ones. They would accept Austrian annexation of Bosnia-Herzegovina (under German duress) but would not permit an invasion of Serbia. As an American diplomat put it, Aerenthal "owed his success primarily to bluffing and to the favor and influence of Germany." But the Germans would not write a blank check for Austrian adventures in the Balkans yet.[38]

The blank check was being prepared, however. The kaiser and Franz Joseph met in November 1908 to tighten the alliance. In 1909, the Austro-Hungarian and German militaries held their first staff talks since 1896. The last time the general staffs had convened, Russia had been the main order of business; at the new staff talks, Moltke told Conrad that he wished war *had* come in 1908, when "the conditions for Austria and Germany would have been better than they would be in a few years' time."[39] The new conditions—and the plans intended to exploit them—were certainly different. Following the 1896 staff talks, the Germans had planned merely to hold off the French in the west and launch a crushing offensive with the Austrians against the Russians in the east. Everything had changed under the influence of the Schlieffen Plan—named for German general staff chief Alfred von Schlieffen—in 1905. Now the Germans planned the opposite: they would hold off the slow-mobilizing Russians with a skeleton force of their own and most of the Austrian army while massing 90 percent of their strength against the French. Within six weeks, the Germans, having beaten the French, would shift their troops to the Eastern Front to finish off the Russians as well.[40]

To say that this change of plan was worrisome to Austria-Hungary—which at full wartime strength would be outnumbered four to one by the Russians—would be an understatement. Yet Conrad accepted the change with surprising equanimity. The tactical writings that had brought him fame before his appointment in 1906, *Studies on Tactics* and *The Battle Education of Infantry,* argued that combat was more psychological than physical. "Tough and brave" troops conditioned to press forward and sacrifice themselves would prevail against even more numerous entrenched infantry and artillery, Conrad insisted.[41] Most Austrian officers agreed with him; as in the other European armies, confidence in bayonet charges survived deflating evidence from the Boer, Russo-Japanese, and Balkan Wars. "The moral role of this primitive instrument must not be understated," an Austrian officer wrote in May 1914. "The bayonet is the supreme expression of the offensive spirit; it bonds the soldier's confidence to his desire to defeat the enemy."[42]

The probability that politically disaffected Austro-Hungarian troops would be among the least likely in Europe to sacrifice themselves did not worry Conrad. Worse, he never pressed the Germans for details of their operational plans or shared his own. Both armies merely sketched their strategic aims—a defeated France, Britain, and Russia and a subjugated Balkans—without agreeing on how to achieve those aims. Eager to guard their operational independence, both sides merely agreed that the Austrians would hurl themselves at the Russians before the Russian mobilization was complete and that the Germans would deploy an unspecified number of troops to the east to buy time for the Austrians to get their troops to the Eastern Front.

Conrad knew he would need time because he planned to destroy Serbia en route to Russia, a plan that he never shared with the Germans. Conrad calculated that twenty Austro-Hungarian divisions thrusting out of Bosnia and southern Hungary would suffice to destroy the Serbs. He merely assumed that the remaining Austro-Hungarian divisions and a German army of indeterminate size would hold the line in Poland and Galicia until he had paraded victoriously through Belgrade and turned his attention to the east. This studied vagueness would be fatal to the Austrians. Even in peacetime, the Russian army counted a million and a half troops; when mobilized for war, it would grow to six million or more. The Austrians, with four hundred thousand under arms in peacetime and a maximum force of two million in wartime, none of them well-equipped, would drown under the Russian flood.[43]

Aerenthal had always assumed that a forceful Austrian policy in the Balkans would deter Russia, intimidate Belgrade, and persuade the Croats, Serbs, and Slovenes of Austria-Hungary to stop agitating for a South Slav kingdom. Just the opposite happened: enraged by the annexation of Bosnia-Herzegovina, the Serbian press launched daily attacks on the Habsburgs and the Serbian government encouraged the formation of patriotic societies like Narodna Odbrana, which counted 220 branches in Serbia and Bosnia-Herzegovina.[44] In 1909, Aerenthal's foreign ministry brought suit against fifty-three Croats, accusing them of treasonous ties to Belgrade. In this sensational "Friedjung Trial"—named after the Austrian historian Heinrich Friedjung, who was the prosecution's key witness—the documents Friedjung, Aerenthal, and then Conrad certified as evidence of the treason proved to be forgeries concocted inside Aerenthal's foreign ministry. This embarrassing fiasco offered a glimpse of the panic that was beginning to engulf the Danube monarchy. Karl Kraus's satirical newspaper Die Fackel sputtered in disbelief: "This is Austrian history in a nutshell: so much happens and yet nothing actually happened." The trial was an "earthquake, and yet not a leaf fell from a tree";

it represented "a battle between blunder and stupidity." Aerenthal was "not making policy, he was compromising it." Friedjung's role was pathetic: "He spoke in the best *Burgtheaterdeutsch,* sonorous, rolling; he sounded like Ottokar—'This Austria, it is a good land.'" Referring to the jolly music played in the Viennese wine bars, Kraus concluded that *"Heurigenmusik* will not deceive the world as to the actual meaning of this trial."[45]

The Friedjung trial had been part of a broader strategy to undergird Aerenthal's forward policy in the Balkans, yet the Serbs were having none of it. In June 1910, a Serbian assassin shot at the Habsburg governor of Bosnia and missed. To improve their aim, Serbian army officers grouped around Colonel Dragutin Dimitrijevic—alias "Apis"—founded a secret society called Union or Death. Better known as the Black Hand (*Crna Ruka*), Union or Death called for the gathering in of all Serbs in the Balkans, including those living inside the borders of Austria-Hungary.[46] Apis, who had orchestrated the murder of the last Obrenovic king in 1903 and now called for "revolutionary, not cultural, action" against the Austrians, was a proven threat that Vienna could not discount.

Inside Bosnia-Herzegovina, the mood was even darker. The emperor had conceded the annexed population a *Landtag* or assembly, to consist of Orthodox Serbs, Muslim Bosniaks, and Catholic Croats based on their relative numbers in the provinces. He promised that the assembly would be a "true copy" of actual population numbers—43 percent Serbs, 35 percent Bosniaks, 22 percent Croats—but promptly reneged. Surprising no one, the assembly turned against Austria, the Serbs preferring Serbia and the Bosniaks the Young Turks, so Vienna resorted to gerrymandering (to sideline Serbian voters) and a vast church-building program to win converts to Catholicism. There had been just one Roman Catholic church in Bosnia-Herzegovina in 1878. Thirty years later, there were 179 of them, as well as dozens of new monasteries, convents, and schools. Young Serbs and Muslims were removed from the provinces in disproportionate numbers to man Habsburg army regiments in the far corners of the monarchy. The Habsburgs called this "de-nationalization."[47] But nationalism couldn't be defeated unless the Austrians pulled up its roots. When General

Oskar Potiorek arrived in Sarajevo in 1911 to command the XV Corps and serve as Bosnian military governor, he too embraced Conrad's view that only war and victory against Serbia would slow the spread of Serbian nationalism inside Austria-Hungary.[48]

The deterioration of Austria's position in the Balkans despite the annexation of Bosnia-Herzegovina, which had been intended to buttress the monarchy, depressed Conrad. Aerenthal's "bold stroke" looked increasingly fruitless as Bosnia-Herzegovina crumbled internally. Serbia and its allies, meanwhile, were growing stronger. The appointment of a violently anti-Austrian Russian ambassador to Belgrade in 1909, followed by a state visit of the Russian tsar to Italy (and a Russo-Italian agreement to consult on all future changes in the Balkans), convinced Conrad that the monarchy had to lash out singly at its various enemies before they all combined against Vienna. All the hopeful premises of the Schlieffen (and Conrad) war plans were coming undone. French-financed railways would now convey the Russians to the Austrian border in weeks, not months.

Efforts to bind Serbia to Austria economically failed miserably, as Austrian agrarians and industrialists battled over commercial treaties with Serbia and agreed only to leave trade relations with Belgrade in a mutually destructive mess. One "pig war" followed another in the early 1900s as Austro-Hungarian governments were forced by parliamentary obstruction to appease Austro-Hungarian landowners by raising the tariffs on pigs, cattle, plums, wheat, barley, and corn, effectively sundering their most promising link to the Serbian state.[49] Belgrade, which had routinely taken 60 percent of its imports from Austria before 1906, was down to 24 percent on the eve of World War I. The American ambassador in Vienna could not believe that the Austrians were missing the opportunity "to separate Serbia's conservative business element from its radical war party." The British embassy was equally incredulous: instead of "rendering Serbia innocuous by mutually profitable trade," the Austrians "were creating ill-will with the Serbs, without any solution of their underlying differences."[50]

Indeed, rather than driving a wedge between Belgrade's business and war parties, Vienna's policies pushed them closer

together. In 1908, Austro-Hungarian agrarians succeeded in limiting imports of Serbian food to 1.6 percent of annual consump-
tion (with a 400 percent increase in tariffs even on that niggardly
amount), to which the Serbs reacted with devastating tariffs on
Austrian manufactures: 70 percent on textiles, 100 percent on cutlery, and so on. Ominously, the Serbs also cancelled a big artillery
order with Austria's Skoda and gave it instead to France's Creusot,
which tightened Belgrade's military links to the Triple Entente.[51]
Serbian governments rose and fell over this annual humiliation
at Vienna's hand, Aerenthal declaring that "if Serbia only learns
how to take the right road, she can always reckon upon benevolent
treatment by us."[52]

Relations between the two states iced over, as the Austrians
not only demanded access to the Serbian market (without compensation) but also insisted that Belgrade abrogate its trade treaties
with neighbors like Bulgaria.[53] In Serbia, hatred for the Magyars
and *Schwabas*—the "Swabians" of Austria—mounted, and Serbian merchants quietly redirected their trade elsewhere: to Germany, Britain, and France. Conrad took little interest in these
portents. He constantly pressed Aerenthal and the emperor to
strike preemptively at the Serbs or the Italians (who bought every
Serbian pig boycotted by Austria), and went hog wild after Italy's
invasion of Turkish Libya in September 1911. Conrad *demanded*
war over Aerenthal's protests, vowing that he would "cut off his
arm" rather than back down. Austro-Hungarian fall maneuvers
for 1912 were scheduled in the Alföld, the flat plain of Hungary,
because it "resembled Upper Italy."[54]

In a rare—and fleeting—display of decisiveness, the emperor
briefly fired Conrad in 1911, insisting on a "policy of peace" for
Austria. Franz Joseph wasn't the only one who had become fed up
with Conrad's bellicosity. Having secretly promised Italy Libya in
exchange for Rome's acceptance of the Bosnian annexation three
years earlier, Aerenthal rolled his eyes at Conrad's bluster. Even
Conrad's mentor, Archduke Franz Ferdinand, saw that the general had gone too far, and agreed to his removal. Conrad had lost
his grip, deeming his "responsibilities greater than [those of] the
foreign minister" and warning Aerenthal never to let "diplomatic

considerations" override "military preparations." Auffenberg, war minister at the time, summarized Conrad thus: "He believed that the empire had to prove that it was willing to lash out, or it would be dragged into war." The best defense, in other words, was a good offense. But this essentially theoretical demand for a demonstrative war with Italy could not be made to fit reality; simply put, it made no sense at any time after 1882, when Italy became an Austrian ally. There was no way for the Austrians to initiate a war with Italy over Libya, for as Auffenberg observed, an Austrian invasion of Italy would almost certainly "trigger a general European war" and cast Austria in the worst possible light.[55] With Conrad now regarded as a liability in every quarter, the emperor replaced him with General Blasius Schemua in December 1911. Franz Ferdinand arranged a soft landing for Conrad in one of the army's many well-paid inspectorates. "This," Conrad grumbled after being dismissed by the emperor in an audience at Schönbrunn, is the same policy "which led us to Königgrätz."[56]

The decision to dump Conrad was comically untimely, for the Balkans were on the verge of explosion when Conrad stepped down and Schemua stepped up. "I've been trying to get some information on just who General Schemua is," the French military attaché wrote from Vienna. "No one seems to know much about him. He's an introvert, and he's never seen at the officers' club; he lived in Persia for a time and has adopted aspects of their religion. . . . The chief of military intelligence says that Schemua is completely out of the loop and will need months to learn the intricacies of this new job."[57] In fact, Schemua had been sent to Persia in 1878 as part of an unsuccessful military mission to sell Austro-Hungarian advice and arms to the Qajar shahs; they had chosen German advisors and arms instead, leaving Schemua little to do but study with various fakirs and then, on his return to Austria, join a secret cult of anti-Semites, the New Templar Order of Jörg Lanz von Liebenfels, which held occult meetings in a castle on the Danube flying the swastika flag.[58]

Schemua's latest task seemed as hopeless as his mission to Persia or his New Templars, and he wouldn't have months to get up to speed. The swift convergence of the Young Turk Revolution, the Bosnian annexation crisis, and the growing assertiveness of the Balkan states—all of which had security relationships of some kind with Russia and France—meant that no international consensus remained on how to preserve "Turkey-in-Europe." "The Balkans are the battlefield of nations," Robert Lansing wrote from the US State Department, "a land of blazing villages, a land of sudden death. . . . 'Peace' is a forgotten word. Slavs, Albanians, Greeks and Turks have deluged the land with their blood and buried it beneath ashes in their struggles to possess it."[59] Bismarck had famously declared that the region was "not worth the bones of a single Pomeranian grenadier," but that declaration looked increasingly tenuous. Austria-Hungary and the other powers would not be able to evade the slaughter much longer.

CHAPTER 3

The Balkan Wars

THE SLAUGHTER IN THE BALKANS was about to get much worse. In March 1912, the Russian ambassador in Belgrade successfully forged a Serb-Bulgarian alliance that aimed to block the Young Turks' recovery of lost ground in the Balkans and roll back Austro-Hungarian inroads. Russia then helped broker an agreement among the Greeks, Bulgarians, and Serbs to partition Macedonia. Austria had always assumed that the disputed past of Macedonia—which had belonged at various times to the Bulgarian, Serbian, and Byzantine empires—and its ethnic and religious complexity would prevent any of the Balkan states from expanding there. The Turks, after all, had ruled Macedonia in the twentieth century in part by encouraging the inhabitants—Bulgarians, Serbs, Greeks, Rumanians, and Albanians—to persecute each other, periodically forcing the great powers to insist on reforms and even to send international commissions to enact them.[1]

But Russia's intervention threatened the plans of Turkey and Austria far beyond Macedonia. Thanks to Russian ministrations, Belgrade and Sofia made common cause, roped in Greece and Montenegro, and declared war on the Ottoman Empire in October 1912. The nations of this Balkan League would shortly fight over the spoils of the war, but they all had an immediate interest in defeating the Turks before the vigorous new government in

73

Constantinople could consolidate its power at home and in its few remaining European *vilayets* like Macedonia and Albania.

The war that followed ripped big chunks from the Ottoman Empire and devastated its army. In just three weeks of fighting, half a million Turks—an army of 220,000 in Thrace and a second army of 330,000 in Macedonia—were beaten by a Balkan coalition that totaled 715,000. The Greeks took Salonika; the Bulgarians advanced to the gates of Constantinople; the Montenegrins advanced into Kosovo and Scutari (Shkodër); the Serbs plunged south into Macedonia as far as Monastir (Bitola) and then marched west to the sea in November. With the Greeks and Bulgarians lodged on Turkey's Aegean coast, the Serbs helped themselves to the Ottoman Empire's four Adriatic ports in Albania: San Giovanni di Medua (Shëngjin), Alessio (Lezhë), Durazzo (Durrës), and Valona (Vlorë). The Treaty of London, signed in May 1913, sounded the death knell of Turkey-in-Europe, as the Ottoman Empire's Balkan provinces were mostly made over to the Balkan League. Austria-Hungary, Europe's Balkan power, got nothing. Vienna's *Die Zeit* goggled in disbelief: "This Balkan crisis is an 1866 for our diplomacy."[2]

Indeed, Austria-Hungary did not cut a dashing figure in the crisis. Aerenthal—who died in the midst of it, in February 1912— had been content to leave Macedonia in Turkish hands until Vienna was ready to renew its advance to the Aegean and absorb the province en route; suddenly the Greeks were in Salonika and the Serbs were in Skopje, Kosovo, and the Albanian ports. Economically, the episode was no less of a disaster. Austrian manufactures that had sold briskly under a Turkish tariff of 11 percent would never penetrate the new markets, which were walled off with tariffs on imports ranging from Bulgaria's 33 percent to Greece's 150 percent. Bohemian woolen mills that had supplied virtually every fez worn in the Ottoman Empire would shortly lose this lucrative business.[3] "The first casualty of these flying Balkan bullets is the status quo," an Austrian general bitterly noted. A status quo that had benefited Vienna suddenly lay "dead as a mouse," *Mausetot.*[4] Within Austrian military circles, the solution to the Balkan crisis seemed clear. "Let's let this thing explode into

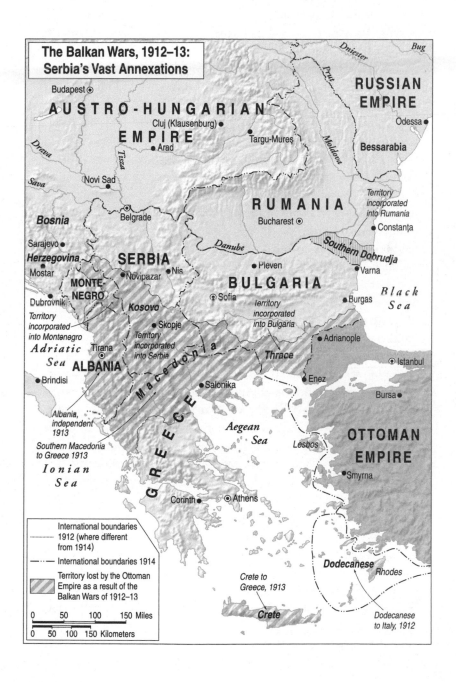

The Balkan Wars, 1912–13:
Serbia's Vast Annexations

Budapest ⊙

AUSTRO-HUNGARIAN

Cluj (Klausenburg) ●

EMPIRE
● Arad

Targu-Mureş

RUSSIAN
EMPIRE

Odessa ●

Bessarabia

Drava

Tisza

Sava

● Novi Sad

Moldova

RUMANIA

Territory
incorporated
into Rumania

Bosnia

Belgrade ⊙

Bucharest ⊙

● Constanţa

Sarajevo ●

Herzegovina

Mostar ●

MONTE-
NEGRO

Dubrovnik ●

Territory
incorporated
into Montenegro

Adriatic
Sea

SERBIA

Novipazar ●

● Nis

Kosovo

Danube

● Skopje

Territory
incorporated
into Serbia

● Pleven

BULGARIA

⊕ Sofia

Territory
incorporated
into Bulgaria

Southern Dobrudja

● Varna

● Burgas

Black
Sea

Tirana ⊙

ALBANIA

● Brindisi

Albania,
independent
1913

Southern Macedonia
to Greece 1913

Ionian
Sea

Macedonia

● Salonika

G R E E C E

Thrace

● Adrianople

● Enez

Aegean
Sea

Lesbos

● Istanbul

Bursa ●

OTTOMAN
EMPIRE

● Smyrna

Corinth ●   ⊙ Athens

.... International boundaries
1912 (where different
from 1914)

—··—··— International boundaries 1914

Territory lost by the Ottoman
Empire as a result of the
Balkan Wars of 1912–13

0   50   100   150 Miles

0   50   100   150 Kilometers

Crete to
Greece, 1913

Crete

Dodecanese

Rhodes

Dodecanese
to Italy, 1912

Dniester

Bug

Prut

war," General Appel scribbled from Sarajevo. "What do we have to fear? Russia? They won't do anything, and we need to smash the Serbs once and for all."[5]

But the Russians probably *would* do something, and neither Franz Joseph nor Franz Ferdinand had the stomach for war, even though war was precisely what had allowed Serbia to make vast annexations in Austria-Hungary's prime sphere of influence. Aerenthal's successor, Count Leopold von Berchtold—who had secured the backing of the emperor and the archduke to be the new foreign minister because of his determination to stop the war escalation and forge an Austro-Russian entente instead—now insisted that Austria-Hungary take no military action lest it remind the powers of its "aggressive role" in 1908.[6] With no saber to rattle, Berchtold fell back on a limp diplomacy that impressed no one. He organized a visit by a "Macedonian delegation" (two professors from Sofia and a retired Turkish administrator from Skopje) to the British embassy in Vienna, where they pleaded for independence instead of partition. "Macedonia deserves autonomy and should not be handed over to the Greeks and Serbs," they argued, to no avail.[7]

But what realistically could the Austrians do to enforce their shrinking writ in the Balkans? In Berlin, the kaiser—who would have to backstop any major Austrian war effort—scoffed that he would not go to war "for a few Albanian goat-pastures."[8] Knowing that any war for Albanian goat pastures would expand to the fields of Galicia, General Schemua reacted with horror to the crisis, especially to Russian trial mobilizations in the Warsaw and Kiev districts in the fall of 1912. Schemua stoically ordered his own partial mobilization, half a million Austrians in Bosnia and Galicia, but had no intention of using them.[9] Emperor Franz Joseph worriedly convened a military conference in Budapest that Conrad attended, along with Schemua and Franz Ferdinand, and they all agreed to do nothing. The situation was almost identical to the one the empire would face in July 1914: Serbia was challenging Vienna, and Russia and France were taking Serbia's side. In 1912, however, the Austrian decision was markedly more sensible than it would be two years later. The Budapest conference concluded that there simply were no viable military options for an army as weak as Austria's.

The superficial suppleness of War Plan R + B—forces for Russia (R) and the Balkans (B) with a floating reserve between them—concealed glaring shortages of the coin of modern warfare: transport, artillery, and trained infantry. Berchtold thus focused on limiting Austria's losses and containing the embarrassment, promulgating a modest, barely face-saving list of demands: that the enlarged Balkan states must "respect Austria's economic interests, negotiate trade agreements with Vienna, and leave the roads and rails to the [Aegean and Adriatic] seas open."[10] Berchtold also became the unlikely father of independent Albania—to keep the land and its four Ottoman ports out of Serbia's hands—and he insisted that Serbia remain landlocked, barred from direct access to Montenegro and the Adriatic by the Sanjak of Novipazar. The Austrians had controlled the fifty-mile-wide strip for years but had returned it to Turkey in 1908 as partial compensation for the Bosnian annexation. They now found themselves in the slightly absurd position of trying to defend the sovereignty of a vanishing Turkey-in-Europe. "I know the 'old saw' had it that at the moment the Ottoman Empire dissolved, Austria must grab the Sanjak to prevent a great Serbian state," Berchtold explained to the Austrian Delegation, "but we find that such a course today would be too costly."[11] Serbia, flush with a heady sense of its own destiny, had just reconquered all of the territory it had lost to the Turks on the Field of the Blackbirds in 1389, and this was the best that Vienna could do, demanding an independent Albania?[12] Traveling in Bosnia, General Appel detected contempt: "Even stupid villagers around here are starting to mutter 'trula Austria'—'rotten old Austria'—as is the press; everyone thinks the monarchy is weak and quaking in fear."[13]

Archduke Franz Ferdinand, who had always dismissed Serbia as a meager "land of pigs and pigherds," now traveled to Berlin with Schemua to secure German pledges of support in case of war with the pigherds. The Berlin press studied these worried Austro-Hungarian allies with interest: "In theory, the six European great powers are all equal; in practice, there are vast differences in national traits, financial and economic strength, the ability to mobilize quickly and the quality of armed forces on land and sea."[14] Traits were the only item on the list that the Hofburg could change on short notice and so, in December 1912, Conrad—whose blustering traits were legendary—was recalled at Franz Ferdinand's urging to replace Schemua. It now emerged that Conrad had been fired during the "Schönaich Crisis" as part of a deal between the Belvedere and the Hofburg. Franz Ferdinand had wanted to fire Aerenthal and War Minister Schönaich, but the emperor had insisted on a quid pro quo, to retain his grip on the army. Thus Franz Ferdinand had agreed to dump Conrad for Schemua if the emperor would let the archduke replace Schönaich with Auffenberg. But Auffenberg became too hot to handle, even for the archduke, in March 1912, when three Hungarian newspapers revealed the existence of the top-secret Plan U—the archduke's 1905 plan to invade Hungary and shutter its parliament—and named Auffenberg as its author.

The revelation of Plan U was so scandalous that another deal had to be botched together in December 1912, just a year after the last one. Auffenberg was fired and Conrad warily recalled, Brosch noting from the Belvedere that anyone else would have been preferable but all of the other candidates were "old wives." Schemua had not worked out. He lacked stature, and with war looming, Archduke Franz Ferdinand, the inevitable army commandant, would need Conrad at his side.[15] The French embassy in Vienna found the crisis most interesting for the light it shed on the nonstop intrigues of the Hofburg and the Belvedere. The three newspapers that broke the Plan U story were all in the emperor's pay, which meant that Franz Joseph had deliberately outed Auffenberg to "strike a blow against Franz Ferdinand and his creatures." Such machinations, the French embassy observed, had the effect of reducing not just the effectiveness but also the caliber of Austria's top brass. Conrad turned up to replace Schemua as chief of the general staff, but no one could be found to replace Auffenberg. "No quality officer will take the job of war minister," the French noted. "These days the imperial war ministry is rightly viewed as a Hungarian subsidiary, and by now most senior officers are loyal to Franz Ferdinand anyway, and won't risk compromising themselves in *his* eyes by taking this position, for the emperor is just too old, and not worth the risk to a career."[16] Bolfras finally found someone close enough to retirement not to care: sixty-three-year-old General Alexander Krobatin, a rather harmless duffer who was discovered in the Skoda works in Pilsen supervising the manufacture of new artillery.[17]

The archduke and Conrad never resumed their old friendliness. The devoutly Catholic Franz Ferdinand resented the spectacle of Conrad's semipublic affair with a married woman, as well as the general staff chief's bellicosity, which simply could not be squared with Vienna's military weakness. Always intrigued by the idea of an Austro-Russian conservative entente (and seeing no solution to the riddle of how to fight a war with Serbia, Russia, and probably Italy and Rumania too), the archduke was swinging over to the peace policy of Berchtold and the emperor.[18] And yet there seemed little hope for peace policy either—the Serbs were spoiling for a fight, and Russia had no incentive to renew an Austrian alliance that had expired in 1878. Worse, Franz Ferdinand viewed Albania as analogous to Schleswig-Holstein in 1864, a territorial dispute that had caused the Austro-Prussian War. The Prussians had detached the Schleswig-Holstein duchies from Denmark, divided them with Austria, and then used the inevitable disagreements over the spoils as a pretext for war with the Habsburgs to settle the "German question" once and for all. Franz Ferdinand believed that the Russians were playing the same game in Albania, planning to "whittle down the borders of Albania" to beef up their "Serbian protégé" and provoke a war with Austria over the rump.[19] He could only hope that the Germans would support Austria and check the Russians.[20] If they didn't, Austria would go under. Even old Franz Joseph was aroused, asking nervously, "Is the army ready for war?"[21]

A tentative principals meeting at Schönbrunn on December 11, 1912, weighed Austria-Hungary's options. Foreign Minister Berchtold speculated that the Germans would probably not support an Austrian "military adventure" in the Balkans.[22] In fact, the Germans would; at a secret German council of war three days earlier in Potsdam, the kaiser and his generals had concluded that they *would* defend Austria-Hungary under all circumstances and that war should be invited, "the sooner the better," to defeat Russia and France before their military expansions were complete.[23] As usual, the Germans didn't think to share this resolution with the Austrians, and the Austrians didn't think to canvass their ally. As they would in July 1914, both powers operated in the dark as to the other's real intentions. With or without German support, Austria-Hungary's finance minister warned, the soaring costs of Austria's posturing would lead to a fiscal calamity. The army had called up 172,000 reservists to augment those already in the field. Half of them deployed to Galicia, the other half to Bosnia, and then fifty thousand more were called. Scenes of mutiny among Czech reservists in Pilsen, Prague, and Königgrätz—men who sang Serbian, not Austrian, anthems as they deployed—shocked the emperor. In Königgrätz (Hradec Králové), a crowd of two thousand blocked the road from the barracks to the train station and stoned the police who tried to disperse them. Several hundred more demonstrators waited at the train station and had to be driven away by troops with bayonets. The commander of the departing regiment was attacked in his train car by an angry mob. As the train got up steam, dozens more civilians lay across the rails to prevent the troops from leaving, and had to be dragged away to jail.[24]

Bismarck's old phrase "When the emperor of Austria says 'saddle up,' people saddle up" no longer applied. In Sarajevo, Potiorek estimated that at least a third of the reservists who arrived there for the Balkan War emergency were unusable—politically disaffected, physically unfit, or both.[25] Partial mobilizations such as this did not come cheap either: this little spurt of activity was costing 275 million crowns ($55 million), which amounted to half of the army and navy budgets for a normal peacetime year.

Costs like those threatened to bankrupt the monarchy if carried through to actual war. Conversely, could the monarchy afford to incur expenses like this and *not* strike? Conrad reminded all who would listen that the partial mobilization begun in November 1912—just three corps in Galicia and two in Bosnia—was costing

2 to 3 million crowns a day. Extra horses alone—to haul supplies, artillery, and reinforced cavalry squadrons—cost more than 30 million crowns ($6 million), yet everywhere the emperor turned, funds were denied. The Hungarian parliament refused even to consider War Minister Auffenberg's request for an emergency appropriation, and the Austrian Reichsrat stymied the request there with a filibuster. Eventually Franz Joseph—in a typical bit of Habsburg horse-trading—detached the Ukrainians from the filibuster with the promise of a Ukrainian university in Lemberg (Lviv), but it was too late: the desperate Finance Ministry had already sought a loan in New York on humiliating terms, as well as unpopular new taxes on income, capital gains, real estate, matches, tobacco, liquor, and, for the first time, the tips of waiters in coffeehouses.[26]

Only the former war minister seems to have profited from the crisis. Auffenberg's involvement in Plan U was one cause of his removal in December; the other was his insider trading on the shares of companies that received mobilization contracts. The tips were allegedly played at the stock exchange by a junior officer named Heinrich Schwarz, who would later commit suicide, leaving behind his correspondence with General Auffenberg.[27] Clearly Vienna was at the end of its rope. It could not go through this humiliating exercise—scandals, filibusters, subprime borrowing, demonstrations, and mutiny—ever again; it would rather risk war. "The Austrian army *needs* to wage war, not merely play at it. . . . All of this waiting around has cost Austria-Hungary 200 million crowns," a German newspaper fumed. "The peace-at-any-price crowd seems intent on buying the most expensive peace possible, while Serbia exhausts the Habsburg monarchy's financial resources, holding itself in perpetual readiness for war so that when war comes Russia will easily destroy a weakened Austria."[28]

But the Russians—who called up three hundred thousand reservists of their own in the crisis—blinked first, concluding that Albanian ports for Serbia were not worth a Russian war with the Germans and Austrians.[29] Russia, Austria, and the other powers convened an ambassadors' conference in London in December 1912 to contain the crisis and avert war. "In the negotiations here, the [Ottoman] Empire is laid on the block and hacked to pieces," the London correspondent of Vienna's *Presse* reported. "Macedonia is lost, Old Serbia, Epirus and the Islands, Albania neutralized under Great Power protection. All that's left to Turkey is a stump of Thrace around Adrianople."[30] Yet despite their losses, the Young Turks had survived another round. Entertaining foreign journalists in his office in Constantinople beneath portraits of Napoleon and Marshal Ney, Enver Pasha explained that by fighting for places like Scutari, Adrianople, and the four Greek islands at the entrance to the Dardanelles—and accepting every loss of ground as an opportunity to shovel Turkish foreign debt into Balkan hands—the Young Turks had paradoxically demonstrated their determination to maintain the fatherland.[31] It was hard to disagree with this logic; Turkey had shrunk but shored itself up for the long haul, a process that the Austro-Hungarians—obsessed with honor and historical rights—seemed incapable of. There was a new Sick Man abroad, and his seat was Vienna.

War did not come, but it almost had, and both sides drew the wrong conclusions from the scare. Franz Ferdinand's Österreichische Rundschau growled that Vienna had narrowly averted "a second Königgrätz" and had nearly been "hunted out of the Balkans."[32] Colonel Brosch marveled at the "unexpected outbreak of peace" when everyone had been tensed up for war.[33] Conrad assumed that the Russians had backed down because of his partial mobilization and that he could have gotten away with invading Serbia and Montenegro. Potiorek wrote that in the *next* crisis war would have to be undertaken, or else "the men and officers will assume that the political leadership has lost faith in the military." Austria could not call up the reservists a third time, "as in 1909 and 1912—and *not* use them." Any future provocation, in other words, would trigger a world war, yet the monarchy had become so unpopular with its own peoples that no less than a third of Austria-Hungary's soldiers would probably refuse to fight in such a conflict.[34]

Austria's foes also misinterpreted the crisis. The Russians concluded that the Austro-Hungarians had not invaded Serbia because of their fear of the Russian army, not because the Germans had restrained them.[35] The Serbs viewed their own provocative annexations as innocuous, and blamed the war scare on "sick old Franz Ferdinand's saber-rattling."

Germany, for its part, was glad that Austria had averted war—in the Balkans, at least. In Berlin, the kaiser wavered, like a man peering into a box of chocolates, between European and global mastery. He was transfixed by the bigger prizes in "Turkey, China and South America," where, as the Berlin papers reported, "the next decade will decide which of the economic great powers will win out over the others."[36] With such prizes within reach, the kaiser vowed that he would not be drawn into an *Existenzkampf* (war of national survival) against Russia, France, and Britain merely because "Austria did not want the Serbs in Albania." German general staff chief Helmuth von Moltke—who initially had judged war "unavoidable"—now trimmed his sails to the imperial wind, characterizing the war scare in the relatively peripheral Balkans as "Austrian foolishness."[37]

More foolishness was in store. With war clouds gathering over the Balkans again in May 1913, the Bulgarians threatening a second Balkan war to enlarge their share of Macedonia, the Austrian press reported a remarkable event. Forty-seven-year-old Colonel Alfred Redl, one of the most talented and reputable officers in the Habsburg army—a man who had made colonel at an age when most of his peers were languishing at captain—was found dead in a Vienna hotel room. He had thrust a Browning pistol in his mouth and pulled the trigger, exploding his palate and brain and dying almost instantly from the torrent of blood that exited his left nostril. Redl had checked in on Saturday and was discovered Sunday morning, slumped in an easy chair, caked with dried blood, the pistol on the floor under his right hand, operating instructions for the pistol—clearly not his own—spread on the table beside him. Two letters lay on the desk, one to his last commander, General Arthur Giesl in Prague, and the other to his brother, along with a curt suicide note: "I ask for understanding and forgiveness."[38]

The Austrian press swarmed hungrily over this latest mystery. It had been a busy year of scandals. First there had been the Dreadnought Affair, when Austria's first all-big-gun battleship, the *Viribus Unitis*, had been delivered overweight with a speed 50 percent slower than advertised. Admirals and shipyard directors had been fired, and Skoda, which had manufactured the offending guns and armor, had been publicly rebuked.[39] Then came the Jandric Affair. Cedomil Jandric, an Austrian lieutenant of Bosnian Serb extraction and a close friend of Chief of Staff Conrad's son Kurt, was convicted of selling technical data on Austrian artillery to the Russians. The army's investigation of Jandric led to another spy—Kurt Conrad's Italian girlfriend—and suggested that young Conrad himself may have been involved, removing top-secret documents from his father's study for sale to the Russians.[40] The impression of cynicism and avarice at the highest levels of the Habsburg state seemed confirmed by the Auffenberg Affair, which followed hot on the heels of the Jandric scandal. The Habsburg war minister was accused of insider trading on the shares of defense contractors and let go with a slap on the wrist. Now, when the hue and cry of that latest embarrassment had barely faded, one of General Conrad's best and brightest had been found dead by his own hand in a hotel room.

Colonel Redl, the press speculated, was the sort of over-worked flunky who had become common during the twenty-four years when Friedrich Beck, the emperor's rather lazy boon companion, had been chief of the general staff. Beck and his section heads had routinely dumped all of their tasks on ambitious subordinates like Potiorek, Conrad, and the recently deceased colonel. Redl had been requested by his final commander, General Giesl (the very portrait of the indolent Austrian general, three chins sagging down the collar of his tunic), precisely because Giesl remembered Redl from Vienna as a tireless worker bee. By all accounts, Redl never stopped working, arriving early at the office, working late, repairing to the coffeehouse to read the newspapers, and then returning to the office to work late into the night. He had been on the verge of being promoted to general but apparently had cracked under the pressure. Other reporters speculated that Redl's nerves might have been broken by dangerous "covert operations" abroad.

"We have no idea *why* he shot himself," the *Neue Freie Presse* conceded on Monday, May 26. "We hear that he came to Vienna in a car on Saturday night and was met by three officers, who

escorted him to his hotel room, conferred with him, then left."
After the officers departed, Redl left the hotel, dined at a nearby
restaurant, wrote notes and letters, took a short walk, returned
to his hotel at midnight, placed 3,000 crowns ($600) on the desk,
and shot himself.[41] He was discovered at five o'clock on Sunday
morning by his batman, who was sent by the three officers of the
previous day to awaken him. By midweek—after the batman also
killed himself—every paper was on to the story, the *Neuen Wiener Journal* reporting a "very odd funeral." Why had such a re-
vered officer been given a secret funeral, without military escort
and with civilian pallbearers and a covered coffin, and then rushed
without ceremony from the garrison morgue to an unmarked
grave in Vienna's vast Central Cemetery?[42]

By the end of the week, everything came out. The war
ministry—pushed by the tabloids, which had been speculating
since midweek on Redl's sex life—released a brief statement an-
nouncing that Redl had killed himself "because of homosexual
affairs that led him into financial difficulties that he mitigated
through the sale of classified military material to the agents of a
foreign power."[43] Put more simply, Redl had sold Austrian and
German military secrets to his Russian lovers for sex and money.
Each time he had tried to extricate himself, the Russians had
threatened to expose him. The *Presse,* which had held off on the
unsavory story while the tabloids tested it, now submitted as well:
"We had taken this dignified, beautiful officer for a dashing ladies' man, but in fact he seems to have 'fallen.'"[44]

The truth was that Alfred Redl had been a Russian spy since
at least 1905, when, as a forty-one-year-old captain, he had been
sent to study Russian in the Caucasus and had instead studied certain Russians a little too closely, a secret that his Russian hosts
kept as Redl climbed the ladder in Vienna.[45] As deputy chief of
military intelligence in Vienna, he had run counterespionage, en-
abling him to betray not only Austrian and German secrets but
also Vienna's best Russian informants. As general staff chief of
Prague's VIII Corps—one of the four Echelon B corps in Conrad's
floating reserve—Redl had betrayed the German-Austrian plans
for combined action in Poland and Galicia in the event of war with

Russia. The regularity with which classified Austro-Hungarian plans were discussed in the Russian press had finally triggered an internal investigation that led to Redl. His downfall was an envelope stuffed with 6,000 crowns that his Russian handlers had sent (from Germany) to his Viennese post office box but which he had not collected in time. It had been "returned to sender," where German officials opened it and put two and two together, something the Austrians had failed to do over the course of a decade.[46]

The Redl Affair, Auffenberg recalled, "delivered one shock after another," the last arguably the worst. Instead of interrogating Redl to discover the extent of his treason and contacts, the general staff officers who summoned Redl to Vienna had handed him a pistol instead and permitted him to shoot himself, presumably, as the British military attaché put it, "for the purpose of obviating unpleasant disclosures." Vienna's *Arbeiter Zeitung* spoke for most when it asked: "*How* was the enemy able to buy such a gifted and experienced staff officer of the Austrian army?"[47] The *Presse* found it "astonishing that such a highly talented officer, enjoying the boundless trust of his superiors"—he had even earned entrée to Franz Ferdinand's inner sanctum at the Belvedere as a *Vertrauensmann,* a trusted source—"could become a traitor to the fatherland." It would be impossible to overstate the humiliation the Redl Affair rained on Vienna.

Indeed, it was the implications of Redl's treason for the Austrian military that worried its leaders the most. Conrad—who had barely survived the espionage affair in April involving his son— did not want Redl now divulging his mentors (Conrad among them), accomplices, and methods.[48] It was Conrad, dining at the Grand Hotel on the Kärtner Ring when Redl was arrested, who had ordered the arresting officers to question Redl in his hotel room, then give the colonel a pistol and the option to kill himself. Conrad hoped in this blundering way to make the Redl problem disappear: the press would merely report that a distinguished officer had killed himself in the sort of despairing suicide that was only too common among Austria-Hungary's ill-paid officers.

In his hasty debriefing, Redl had cooperated minimally, taking most of his secrets to the grave, but what little his captors learned from questioning him and later cracking open the safe in his Prague apartment was horrifying: Redl had sold the Russians the latest version of Plan R—updated in 1912—including all mobilization and deployment plans, orders of battle and march tables, German mobilization plans for the eastern border (gleaned in Redl's personal meetings in Berlin with Moltke during the First Balkan War), the technical specifications of German and Austrian war matériel, and sketches of the Galician fortress complex of Przemysl as well as its provisioning arrangements. Redl sold the Russians secret general staff critiques of Austro-Hungarian maneuvers. He routinely warned the Russians of any organizational or technical reforms being pondered in the Austro-Hungarian war ministry, betrayed Austrian spies to the Russians, concealed Russian spies from the Austrians, falsely accused innocent Austrian officers of espionage (to maintain his reputation as a dogged spy hunter), and summarized the strengths and weaknesses of the Austro-Hungarian generals destined for army and corps commands. Redl's summary of Conrad as "an able tactician but no judge of men" seemed confirmed by the affair, which, the British embassy observed, "deeply embarrassed and discredited Conrad."[49]

For Franz Ferdinand, who had protected Conrad despite his bumptiousness, this flood of revelations was the last straw: it revealed gross incompetence on Conrad's part and handed critics of the Habsburg army on both sides of the Leitha all the ammunition they needed to further crimp military budgets and prerogatives. Among other items, Redl's safe in Prague had contained naked photographs of the cavalry lieutenant Redl had consorted with whenever in Vienna. "People are now saying that the army is a hotbed of abnormal sexual activity and perversions," one paper wrote. Another focused less on sex and more on money: "We are spending millions on the army on the assumption that at least there will be no treason, and now comes this incredible scandal: an officer at the highest level, spying undetected for fourteen years. What else can we conclude but this—that the army is a blind puppet, a preserve of feudal lords and bourgeois snobs, a disaster."[50]

No one could fathom just how the security culture in Conrad's general staff could have been so slack that Redl, the son of a Galician civil servant, could have escaped suspicion even while amassing the means to employ five servants, rent a luxury apartment in Prague, purchase a luxury apartment in Vienna, and stable four thoroughbred horses. Redl also drove a thirty-six-horsepower Austro-Daimler car worth 16,000 crowns at a time when hardly anyone owned a car, spent an estimated 100,000 crowns a year, and accumulated a fortune of 2 million crowns on a colonel's salary. Redl paid his servants alone 7,000 crowns a year, which was equal to the annual salary of two army majors. How could this ostentation have gone undetected?

The archduke, a religious man, was also outraged by Redl's homosexuality, which officers still referred to as *la Potsdamie*— the "Potsdam disease," a reference to its rumored prevalence in the Prussian court. It turned out that the hotel where Redl shot himself—the Klomser, just a short walk from the Hofburg—was the same place where Redl regularly drove from Prague to meet with his boyfriend, Lieutenant Stefan Horinka, whose apartment in Vienna's Josefstadt district had been, according to the landlady, the scene of "wild orgies." Redl would stop in for sex with Horinka and tell the landlady that he was "visiting his nephew"; she wasn't fooled, but did wonder how an army officer could dress and travel around so handsomely. The landlady's assumptions about Redl conformed to the general public skepticism about the army: "I assumed that he was engaged in some shady dealings at the ministry, probably selling draft deferments to rich fathers for their sons."[51]

This was the greatest gay scandal to hit Vienna since the emperor had exiled his brother Archduke Ludwig Viktor to the provinces in 1904, and it shined a light again on all of the things that the Habsburgs had hoped to cram into the shadows: steam baths, masseurs, and cruising for boys in the *Stadtpark,* the Prater, and along the Danube Canal, all haunts of the libidinous Redl. And all of this had happened on Conrad's watch. Redl's career had started under Beck but accelerated under Conrad, who even now refused to fire or discipline anyone for the Redl Affair other than Lieutenant Horinka, who received three months' hard labor and reduction in rank to private.[52] Franz Joseph was so sickened by the revelations that he turned most of his military authority over to Archduke Franz Ferdinand, whom he now made "General Inspector of the Combined Armed Forces," a step the emperor never would have taken otherwise. The last man to wield this authority—to command the army and navy and oversee the general staff—had been the old emperor's uncle, Archduke Albrecht, who had died in 1895.[53] Franz Ferdinand was at least as disgusted by the revelations as Franz Joseph was, but the pious archduke also considered Conrad's proffer of a suicide option sinful. He once again began pushing for Conrad's replacement, this time by someone who would clean house and restore discipline and morality. Generals Tersztyánszky and Potiorek were mentioned, despite Potiorek's own rumored homosexuality.

All of the Dual Monarchy—and not just the Austrian press and the military—fixated on the Redl Affair. Conservatives saw the episode as yet more evidence of the "social sickness" that was rotting Austria: "the striving for money and career, egoism, materialism, vanity, and the total neglect of moral behavior. All of this has penetrated even into the *k.u.k.* officer corps."[54] The Reichsrat exploded with indignation, demanded that the army turn the affair over to the Ministry of Justice, and rang with embarrassing questions: Why had Redl not been arrested and brought before a proper court-martial? How had he achieved such rapid promotion to the directorship of a vital war ministry department and the position of general staff chief of a corps? How had his extravagant lifestyle gone unnoticed? Why had he been permitted to take his own life? Why were the Germans not invited to take part in an inquiry, considering that Redl had betrayed their secrets too? Exactly which secrets had he sold? Was any future war with Russia now irreparably compromised? The army's feeble efforts to defend itself—"Redl wore the tunic of the emperor but was never really an Austro-Hungarian officer, because the officer corps is pure"—were ludicrous, elliptically anti-Semitic (Redl was Jewish and therefore impure), and dismissed as the hogwash they were.[55] The Hungarian parliament recoiled in horror at the revelations of ineptitude, corruption, and depravity in the already despised Common Army. Berchtold, who had been besieged by Conrad since late 1912 over the need to fight a war with Serbia "once and for all," now saw the siege lifted, as a deeply embarrassed Conrad fell silent.[56]

The guns of the Balkan League shortly broke the silence. All the league's member states had been nibbling at Macedonia since the 1890s—Bulgarians raiding Greek villages, Albanians raiding Serbs, everyone raiding the Turks—and they now opened their mouths and tried to swallow as much of it as they could.[57] Serbia had committed before the Balkan War to deliver most of northern and central Macedonia to the Bulgarians, but Belgrade, having been forced out of Albania by the great powers, now refused to cede the Macedonian territory. The Greeks, who had beaten the Bulgarian army to Salonika by just a day in November 1912, refused to cede any ground there or in Thrace. The Rumanians piled on, demanding Bulgaria's Danube port of Silistria as well as southern Dobrudja. The Austrians, reduced again to impotent spectators in their prime sphere of influence, watched abashedly, a Budapest daily opining in March that "the Austro-Hungarian monarchy has lost more prestige in the Balkan War than even the defeated Ottoman Empire."[58] The raw energy and élan of these young Balkan states, which were fighting the Turks (and each other) to unify their peoples, would not be overlooked by the bored, dispirited Slavs and Rumanians of the Habsburg monarchy.[59]

At the annual Austro-Hungarian army maneuvers in Bohemia in the summer of 1913, Archduke Franz Ferdinand took Conrad aside and told him that he wanted to lay on a second set of maneuvers for 1914. There would be the usual September maneuvers simulating war with Russia, but the archduke wanted to precede those maneuvers with a large-scale military exercise in Bosnia in June to intimidate the Serbs and serve as a long-overdue Balkan show of force. The archduke even had a date in mind, June 28—Serbia's national holiday, commemorating the Christian kingdom's defeat by the Turks in 1389 on the Field of the Blackbirds in Kosovo.[60]

While the Austrians plotted, the Bulgarians incited a second Balkan War, intending to redress the unequal results of the first. In July, they were thoroughly defeated by the other members of the now defunct Balkan League. Bulgaria's loss was Serbia's gain; Belgrade more than doubled its territory and increased its population by a third, claiming most of north-central Macedonia from Skopje south to Monastir (Bitola). Again, the Austrians were conspicuous by their absence at the peace terminating the war in August 1913, and the Germans further undercut their Austrian ally by affirming the terms of the peace over Austria's objections and agreeing to expanded borders for Rumania, Bulgaria, and Serbia.

The days when Vienna could disparage Serbia (as Aerenthal once had) as a "rascally boy" stealing apples from the Austrian orchard were clearly over, yet even in drastic times such as these, the two halves of the Dual Monarchy could not work together effectively. Meeting in 1913 to discuss an urgent increase to the military budget and annual draft contingent, the delegations that connected the Austrian and Hungarian governments became bogged down instead on the question of whether off-duty Habsburg officers could moonlight as security guards at the Hungarian parliament, or whether they must be disqualified as "troops of a foreign power."[61] The whole empire seemed to be crumbling. A piece in a British journal titled "The Break-Up of the Austrian Empire" had the subtitle "Perhaps Today, Possibly Tomorrow, Certainly the Day After." It predicted that the monarchy would shortly be partitioned by the Germans, Italians, Russians, Serbs, and, most mortifying of all, Hungarians.[62]

Habsburg army maneuvers in Bohemia in 1913 reflected this prevailing unease; they were the occasion for a public altercation between Conrad and Franz Ferdinand. Conrad actually stormed out of the maneuvers after accusing the archduke of ruining them. Franz Ferdinand responded in kind, calling the general staff chief "a Wallenstein," a reference to the victorious Austrian generalissimo of the Thirty Years' War who had conspired against the Habsburgs until his assassination.[63] The cause of the spat between Conrad and this latest Habsburg revealed much about the continued travails of the Austrian army. Maneuvers had degenerated under Beck, who had raced through them in a day or two to fit the emperor's shrinking energy and attention span and deployed ruses to magnify the size of the attacking force to appease the emperor's appetite for spectacle.[64] Conrad was more professional and up-to-date. He'd designed the 1913 maneuvers in two parts. A first period of four days would test the operational abilities of the commanders as two armies—fourteen thousand men to a side—approached each other over the rolling hills around Kolin and Budweis and deployed for battle. A second period of three days would test their tactical abilities.

Conrad's complaints about the archduke were, in this instance, entirely justified. Franz Ferdinand cut short the first phase of the maneuvers, depriving the commanders—Generals Brudermann and Auffenberg, who shortly would find themselves in real battles with the Russians—of the opportunity to reconnoiter an enemy army on the move and deploy to fight it. The archduke then abruptly terminated the battle phase at the moment when Brudermann's army was collapsing and ordered an exercise against a "flagged enemy" for the following day instead. This practice of taking troops from the defense, leaving flags in their place, and adding them to the attack had been widely used by Beck for dramatic effect but had been dropped by every other European army "because it led to situations not represented in war." More serious maneuvers by 1913 featured an unpicturesque but realistic "empty field," as cavalry dismounted and infantry and guns entrenched or took cover. Attachés referred to flagged exercises on a crowded field as "giving the girls a show," and indeed the archduke was overheard ordering a colonel to move his unit for the flagged exercise to a spot "where it could be seen more easily from the hill," where Franz Ferdinand sat with his wife and children.

Watching thousands of Austrian troops sweeping down the field in close order to assault a line of flags, the French attaché turned to his Serbian colleague and asked him, "Did you ever see any situation in your last two wars that offered better opportunities for a defender than this?" The Serb hadn't.[65] But the archduke was unfazed; he was overheard rebuffing Conrad's demands for greater realism thusly: "It's not necessary to teach our soldiers to die in time of peace."[66]

The Austrian press reported intrigues that went far beyond the maneuver field. General Rudolf Brudermann, "the darling of the Belvedere," had been on the verge of being annihilated by Auffenberg—the latter tainted by scandals involving Hungarians, money, and women, and present at the exercises for a measure of reclamation. Rather than watch his preferred commander lose, the archduke had abruptly stopped the maneuvers at the moment when Brudermann's army was dissolving, then ordered the flagged exercise to save face for Brudermann and deny Auffenberg the complete rehabilitation he so desperately craved.[67] Thoroughly disgusted, Conrad offered his resignation on the spot, but he was rebuffed by the archduke. Franz Ferdinand reminded Conrad that the army could not afford yet another scandal on the heels of the Redl Affair, for "Jewish and Masonic papers" would make a sensation of the two men's differences and Conrad's departure.[68] Reporting on the tension between Franz Ferdinand and Conrad, the Hungarian newspaper *Budapest* expressed indifference: "For the Hungarian public, it's irrelevant whether Conrad or some other general occupies the post, for there is no connection between their army and our nation. It's not our army and it doesn't fight for our national goals."[69]

Prevented from resigning, Conrad tried to make the best of his position. Meeting with the German kaiser in Leipzig on October 18, Conrad extracted a pledge of support from Wilhelm II in the event of a war with Serbia, which was already encroaching on the new country of Albania, created by the great powers just five months earlier. *"Ich gehe mit Euch,"* the kaiser rumbled—"I'm with you." That same day, the Austrians delivered an ultimatum to Belgrade demanding withdrawal from all disputed Albanian territory and threatening war if the demand was not met. The Serbs—who had lost ninety-one thousand men in the two Balkan Wars—evacuated the territory a week later.

Once again, as in the Scutari crisis of the spring, the Habsburg threat of war had walked the Serbs (and the Russians) back from the brink. It was good that it did, for Austro-Hungarian bluster masked severe shortages in the army, particularly in field artillery and machine guns. From Bozen, Colonel Alexander Brosch informed Auffenberg that in his regiment "everything [was] lacking: artillery, machine guns, shells, rifles, and rifle ammunition."[70]

Ignoring these omens, Berchtold congratulated himself that he had won another round with the Serbs, "even," as he grandly put it in a letter to Franz Ferdinand on October 21, "without [German] tutelage," although that seemed ensured, the kaiser having cabled his support to the emperor and his congratulations to Berchtold. "For once," Wilhelm II told the Austrian military attaché in Berlin, "Austria has shown her teeth; I hope she'll continue to do so."[71] Much of Berchtold's self-congratulation was owed to a too-rosy reading of the international situation; Berchtold still assumed that Britain regarded "a powerful Austria-Hungary as a European necessity"—to check Russia—and had helped deny the Serbs their seaports in Albania to prevent formation of "a great Slavic Empire" dominated by Russia.[72] These were big assumptions to take away from a messy skirmish with Serbia. ("Even an idiot gets lucky sometimes," was Brosch's acid judgment on Berchtold.)[73]

In fact, Vienna had lost most of its freedom of movement as a great power. There was no domestic consensus on foreign policy and the budget was a billion crowns in deficit. The old emperor was as dotty as ever—in a meeting with the British embassy staff in October, he rambled across the whole political field in the Balkans and, to the surprise of his hosts, concluded that "on the whole the Turks are the best element there."[74] Of course they were no longer there, a development that seems not to have altered the emperor's view.

Austrian leaders less senescent than the emperor were only too aware of their dire predicament. Britain's military attaché reported near panic in the War Ministry and general staff as the monarchy began to grasp just how weak it was. The war scare in the Balkans had forced the Austrians to consider how they would apportion strength in a real conflict, and they discovered that they would have too few troops to achieve *any* of their missions, whether against Russia, Serbia, Italy, Rumania, or even an uprising in Bosnia-Herzegovina. "I believe more and more that our purpose will merely be to go under honorably," Conrad scribbled despondently on Christmas Eve, "like a sinking ship."[75]

Externally, there was no escape from the German embrace. "They had been allied; they were now shackled," Churchill would later write. The German army—or the threat of it—had become Austria's only "means of life." Austria-Hungary desperately needed to confront Serbia before it grew even more powerful, but it could not fight Serbia without fighting Russia, and could not fight Russia without Germany. Berchtold was rushing a major review of Habsburg foreign policy to completion in the Foreign Ministry, and its implications only confirmed this assessment of Germany's importance. The review's central finding was twofold: that Serbia, increasingly under the influence of the army and the Black Hand (as well as its aggressive new Russian ambassador), was implacable and could only be curbed by battle, and that Russia would not hold back in such an event. The review noted that St. Petersburg was now pulling every lever it could find in the Balkans to weaken the Austro-Hungarian position. The Russians were inciting the Serbs and were trying to detach Rumania from its Austro-German alliance, and they might lure away the Bulgarians and the Turks as well, with French loans. There no longer seemed to be anything specific to negotiate about—just a cloud of pan-Slav agitation enveloping the Balkans and seeping into the largely Slavic Habsburg monarchy. This handed the initiative to Serbia, which now grasped that Tsar Nicholas II, who conflated Russian and Serbian nationalism, would never again abandon Belgrade. He'd risk alienating the army, which was the pillar of the regime, if he did. Thus emboldened, the Serbs would no longer shrink from Austrian bluster. If war came, they would embrace it, trusting that the Russians would kick in Austria-Hungary's eastern door and facilitate a Serbian conquest of Bosnia-Herzegovina, Croatia, and Slovenia.

Everything now hinged on Berlin, where the kaiser was having serious doubts of his own. Having promoted the *Ausgleich* since 1867, the Germans were deeply concerned about the looming succession in Austria-Hungary; they knew that Franz Ferdinand's ascension—which was considered imminent—would strike at the root of the already troubled partnership between Vienna and Budapest. Franz Joseph was eighty-four in 1914 and so feeble that whenever Archduke Franz Ferdinand repaired to his Bohemian country house or his Adriatic palace, a special train was kept waiting to rush him back to Vienna in case the emperor was stricken.

The archduke, not the emperor, opened the delegations in May 1914, because Franz Joseph was so ill. The emperor had not attended army maneuvers in years, the archduke going in his place.[76] But Franz Ferdinand was hated in Budapest for his anti-Hungarian views. Nor was he liked anywhere else. Even the Croats, whom the archduke had wanted to favor with their own capital at Zagreb and shared leadership of the monarchy, had deserted him by the early 1900s.[77] The Czechs too fell away; they spent the months before the outbreak of war in 1914 battling with the Germans of Bohemia for control of the Prague diet and the Austrian Reichsrat, a struggle that the Ukrainians of Galicia joined with attacks on the "Polish Club." Could Austria-Hungary survive if *every* nationality demanded entry to the privileged ruling club of Vienna and Budapest, or the right to break away altogether? Obviously not: in March 1914, Franz Joseph instructed his prime minister, Count Karl von Stürgkh, to adjourn the Reichsrat indefinitely and govern by emergency decree.

Conrad and Moltke had held intermittent staff talks since 1909 and had loosely agreed that in the event of a great war, the Germans would implement their Schlieffen Plan and knock out France while the Austro-Hungarians blunted any early Russian offensives in the east. Once France fell, the Germans would pivot east to rescue Austria from the Russian steamroller. That rough agreement was renewed at their last meeting at Karlsbad (Karlovy Vary) in Bohemia in May 1914. But there was a veil of obfuscation about the proceedings. Conrad's war plan called for the three-part division of the Habsburg army into a Russian group (twenty-eight divisions), a Balkan group (eight divisions), and a floating reserve (twelve divisions). A great European war would almost certainly flare in the Balkans but spread immediately to Russia, and so it was essential that the Germans receive Austria's assurance that Vienna would merely defend its borders in the south with the eight divisions of the Minimal Balkan Group and move everything else— forty divisions—briskly to the east to hold off the tsar's armies.

Like Germany, Austria was only too aware of its eastern vulnerabilities. A study prepared by Franz Ferdinand's military chancery in 1911 had concluded that the Austrians simply could not fight wars in Serbia and Russia simultaneously. To do so would isolate outnumbered Austro-Hungarian armies in the great space between Warsaw and Lemberg and virtually ensure their destruction.[78] The Russian army had become so vast in the twentieth century—six million troops—that even the entire two-million-man Austro-Hungarian army would have a hard time blunting its attacks. If reduced to a fraction of its strength by detachments to Serbia, the Austrians would almost certainly fail.

Still, given Conrad's nonstop fulminations against Belgrade, it was probable that he would attempt to fight the Serbs first. He would try to mass twenty divisions against Serbia's twelve—thus effectively implementing Plan B instead of Plan R—which would leave Austria's twenty-eight divisions in the east perilously exposed to the wrath of a Russian army three or four times bigger. Germany ignored this obvious danger. Moltke, who seemed chiefly concerned to deflect Conrad's requests for German troops in the east, decided to skip over the details. Vagueness suited both sides: it gave Vienna the flexibility to crush Serbia, and it gave Berlin the option to strip the Eastern Front bare and launch everything into France.[79]

Both generals, Moltke and Conrad, were whistling past the graveyard. The Russia of 1914 was not the clay-footed colossus imagined in the first drafts of the Schlieffen Plan ten years earlier. Crushed in the Russo-Japanese War, Russia had since reformed itself, adding quick-firing light and heavy artillery and overhauling its mobilization procedures. New double-tracked railways had been built from Moscow and St. Petersburg to Warsaw, and battle-ready units—endowed with more artillery than the Austrians—would now deploy quickly to the frontiers without pausing to incorporate slow-arriving reservists. The Russians felt confident enough to promise the French in 1911 that they would deploy eight hundred thousand troops to their borders with Germany and Austria-Hungary no later than fifteen days after the first mobilization order.[80] Though no one took such Russian promises all that seriously—it was an empire, after all, where the average reservist had to travel seven hundred miles from his home to his depot—the claims still suggested technological advance and a surprising optimism.

Meanwhile, the fraught situation in the Balkans made a war between Austria and Serbia all but inevitable, even though such a war would almost certainly provoke a Russian intervention for which German troops—diverted by the Schlieffen Plan and a likely Russian attack on East Prussia—would be unavailable. And Belgrade had the wind at its back. Despite Austria-Hungary's containment policy, the Serbs had doubled their territory and increased their population to nearly five million. Vienna was looking into the chasm. Fighting Russia and Serbia together, a British paper warned, "would be madness."[81] Yet Conrad was contemplating just that madness. He wanted it now, more than ever.

CHAPTER 4

Murder in Sarajevo

DURING THE HABSBURG ARMY'S ANNUAL MANEUVERS in Bohemia in 1913, Franz Ferdinand had instructed Conrad to plan two rounds of maneuvers for 1914. In addition to the normal September maneuvers simulating war with Russia, the archduke wanted a large-scale exercise with two corps in Bosnia for June 1914. This, it was hoped in Vienna, would frighten the Serbs (by simulating a war with them) and serve as a long-overdue Austrian show of force in the Balkans.

Franz Ferdinand, who would command the Austro-Hungarian army in any future war, would be on hand to direct the military exercises. This impending archducal visit to Bosnia—widely advertised in the Austrian and foreign press in March 1914—offered a tantalizing target to Serbian terrorists. Colonel Apis and the Black Hand wanted a terrorist spectacular to goad the Austrians, but they also wanted to drive Serbian prime minister Nikola Pasic to war by foreclosing all avenues of negotiation with Vienna.[1] Pasic was more prudent than ultranationalists such as Apis, and far less sanguine about the Serbian kingdom's ability to defeat an Austrian invasion while busy digesting so much recently annexed Macedonian and Albanian territory. To force Pasic's hand, the Black Hand began training three Bosnian students in Belgrade in the spring of 1914: Gavrilo Princip and two others. The plan was for Princip and his fellows to assassinate the archduke in league with four additional assassins, who would be recruited in Bosnia.

While the assassins struggled to equip themselves, Conrad struggled to keep his job. The archduke had publicly rebuked Conrad at the army maneuvers in 1913 and seemed intent on rubbing his new post-Redl powers as "General Inspector of the Combined Armed Forces" in Conrad's face. Though they reconciled—Conrad boasting to his mistress of the "honey-sweet words" the normally abrasive archduke had deployed to mollify him—Colonel Brosch's letters to Auffenberg in October and November 1913 took for granted that *der Wechsel,* the change, was coming, and that a new general staff chief who did not "diminish" and annoy the archduke as Conrad did would be selected. Conrad's replacement would probably be Potiorek ("who craves the job") or the archduke's new adjutant, Colonel Karl Bardolff ("who essentially ran the general staff during Schemua's tenure anyway").[2]

That those and other names were being leaked suggested the imminence of the change. Conrad heard the rumors and scuttled to the emperor to deflect the archduke. In October 1913, the beleaguered general staff chief had a long audience with Franz Joseph, who, learning that the archduke had soured on Conrad, was only too happy to take him on as a client. Conrad became the latest football in the constant scrimmaging between the Hofburg and Belvedere, with the emperor, who was repenting the broad new military powers he'd given the archduke during the Redl Affair, now guaranteeing Conrad his job and restoring his direct access to the Hofburg to undercut Franz Ferdinand. A protégé of the archduke, Conrad had previously been forced to correspond with the Hofburg via the Belvedere. Now his mail would travel in the opposite direction.[3] Most of Conrad's waking time must have been spent consumed like this—shifting between mentors and defending his shrinking turf. The rest of the time, he pondered Austria's shrinking freedom of action.

The Schlieffen Plan of 1905 required certain things of the Austro-Hungarians. They would have to hold the fort in Galicia and Poland until the Germans had beaten the French (in six weeks, according to the plan), but they would also have to beat back the

Serbs. During the Bosnian annexation crisis of 1908, when war had nearly come, Conrad had devised a superficially elegant plan to fulfill these obligations. For the unlikely event of a localized Austro-Serbian war, there was a Plan B (as in Balkan). For the likely event of an Austrian war with Serbia that dragged in Russia, there was a Plan R. To make it possible to fight either contingency, the Habsburg army was divided into three groups: Echelon A (*A-Staffel*, nine corps, twenty-eight divisions destined for the Russian front), Balkan Minimal Group (*Minimalgruppe Balkan*, three corps, eight divisions for use against Serbia), and Echelon B (*B-Staffel*, four corps, twelve divisions that would float between the two fronts as a general reserve). If an Austro-Serbian war could be localized, Echelon A would guard the Russian frontier while Echelon B joined forces with the Balkan Minimal Group to implement Plan B with twenty infantry and three cavalry divisions. If the Russians intervened—which everyone took for granted—Plan R + B would be implemented: Echelon B would entrain immediately for Galicia, reinforce Echelon A, and fight Russia with forty infantry divisions, while the eight divisions of the Balkan Minimal Group merely defended the borders of Bosnia-Herzegovina and Hungary.[4]

Such a plan had seemed feasible in 1908, when the Serbian army had been small and weak and the Russians had been recovering from their defeat against Japan, but by 1914 the odds had shifted: at least fifty Russian divisions and eleven Serbian ones would immediately face Vienna's forty-eight, with many more Russian reserve divisions to come and thousands of *komitadji* partisans girding to support the Serbian regulars. And whereas the Russian railways in 1908 had been primitive to the point where Schlieffen spoke of the "railwayless vastness" of Russia, by 1914 that vastness had been filled in with French-financed double-track railways that would punish any Austrian delay in the movement of troops to the east. Indeed, by 1914, Russian railways were *better* than Austrian ones. Russia had four single-tracked lines (which meant that traffic could flow in only one direction at a time) and five double-tracked lines (permitting two-way traffic). Austria had just seven single-track railways, and two of these had to stagger through the high Carpathians. By the grim arithmetic of the time, this meant that Russia could send 260 trains a day into the Polish-Ukrainian theater of war, versus Austria's 153.[5]

The simultaneous growth and modernization of the Serbian military under tough, battle-hardened generals meant that a punitive Austrian expedition across the Danube or Drina with a small army would no longer work.[6] As early as 1911, Conrad had discovered in war games that he would need at least fourteen divisions to beat the Serbs, an amount that simply could not be spared if there was also a war with Russia. And to thwart Austria completely, the Serbs had only to pull back from their frontiers and force the Austrians to undertake a time-consuming invasion of the mountainous Serbian interior. Indeed, Austrian maneuvers in 1907 and a war game in Vienna in 1913 had tested and confirmed the devastating stresses that would be placed on the ungainly Habsburg army by a Serbian fighting retreat. War minister Auffenberg had verified on the eve of the First Balkan War that *any* Austrian invasion of Serbia would have to use the broad avenue of the Morava Valley, not nibble at the strategically worthless northwest corner of the kingdom, where the Drina and Sava Rivers flowed together. But such a broad invasion on multiple lines of advance would require more troops and more time, neither of which the Austrians would have. On a visit to Dubrovnik in April 1914, Potiorek ran his own war game—a chess derivative using metal troop and supply indicators and two-minute moves constrained by logistical and terrain realities. To the amazement of all present, the Serbs won.

Potiorek's April war game would prefigure his August invasion of Serbia. Life would imitate art—a big gap opening between the Austro-Hungarian Fifth Army, operating at the confluence of the lower Drina and the Sava, and the Habsburg Sixth Army, crossing the Drina further south, permitting the Serbs to beat the two armies in detail. Yet the game's portents were all wasted on Conrad, whose reflections on the winter 1913 war game explain his bizarre decisions in August 1914. With all the difficulties Serbia presented, including bad roads, supply difficulties, and an entrenched enemy, Conrad's recommendations were foolhardy: "Lacking supplies, communications and a good overview, our only recourse will be a brisk, brave attack."[7] This underestimation of modern firepower had always been a characteristic of Conrad's general staff. His plans for war with Serbia in 1908 had taken a swipe at "timid" Japanese conduct in the Russo-Japanese War and suggested—on no evidence other than Conrad's feistiness—that "a more energetic command, a quicker start to operations, and a faster campaign would have minimized casualties."[8]

As the Serbian assassins began to assemble in Sarajevo, turbulence rocked Belgrade. Weary of mediating the struggle between Pasic and the generals for the right to direct foreign policy and administer the newly annexed lands in Macedonia and Albania, seventy-year-old King Peter resigned most of his functions and named twenty-five-year-old Crown Prince Alexander his regent in June 1914.[9] This did nothing to appease Serbian nationalists, who were enraged by the Austrian archduke's impending visit to Bosnia. As an exponent of "Great Croatia"—a Roman Catholic superstate embracing Croatia, Dalmatia, Bosnia-Herzegovina, Slovenia, and as much of Serbia as possible—Franz Ferdinand would be putting his stamp on the very provinces the Serbs claimed as their own. The date of the archduke's visit had also been spectacularly ill chosen, June 28, St. Vitus's Day: the anniversary of Serbia's fourteenth-century defeat in Kosovo and subjugation by the Ottoman Turks, and Serbia's bittersweet national holiday ever since. Franz Ferdinand could not have chosen a more provocative display of his contempt for Serbia or for the cautious methods of his uncle the emperor. "Don't let the archduke shine too much," Franz Joseph's adjutant had written Potiorek before the visit. "We don't want people forgetting about the emperor."[10] But the archduke was about to shine as never before.

The archduke—attended by Conrad and Potiorek—observed the exercise of the XV (Dubrovnik) and XVI (Sarajevo) Corps in the mountains southwest of Sarajevo on June 26–27, and then joined his wife, the Archduchess Sophie, for a tour of Sarajevo on the twenty-eighth. The full-scale Austro-Hungarian maneuvers would be held, as always, in September, and would simulate a Russian invasion of Galicia; this Balkan exercise was merely intended as a show of force and a warning to Serbia. The visit to

Sarajevo would be brief, with stops at an army barracks, the town hall, a new museum, a carpet factory, and lunch with Potiorek, all intended to flourish the Habsburg flag and assert Austrian rights to a province claimed by Serbia. The archducal party would be on a train out of Bosnia by nightfall.[11]

The archduke rose on June 28 in the Hotel Bosna in Ilidze, a spa located in a cool leafy glade outside Sarajevo. He dressed in the gala uniform of a cavalry general (blue tunic, black pants, and bicorn hat with green feathers), attended chapel in a hotel room that had been sanctified for his visit (at a cost of forty thousand crowns), and then clambered into the backseat of a waiting automobile. The open sports car was third in a line of six vehicles. Franz Ferdinand and Sophie nodded and smiled at the crowds lining the route into Sarajevo, while Potiorek, hunkered in the jump

Archduke Franz Ferdinand had ordered a special exercise with two corps in Bosnia in June 1914 to intimidate the Serbs. Here the archduke studies a map held for him by General Oskar Potiorek, a corps commander and military governor of Bosnia. It was the archduke's last full day on earth. He'd be shot in the streets of Sarajevo the next day.
CREDIT: Heeresgeschichtliches Museum, Wien

seat facing them, pointed out the principal sights. The seven Serbian assassins were strung out at intervals along the route. The first fired his Browning pistol at a range of thirty feet and missed. Franz Ferdinand turned and watched as Austrian police tackled the would-be assassin and shielded him from the blows and kicks of the crowd. With a keen sense of the emperor's hostility and unfailing instinct to do the wrong thing, the archduke cracked: "Hang him as quickly as possible, or Vienna will give him a medal!"[12] The second assassin threw a hand grenade, but the archduke's driver accelerated under it and it exploded beneath the next car, lightly wounding Potiorek's adjutant, Lieutenant-Colonel Erich von Merizzi.

The archduke was seething when he drew up at his first stop, the great pseudo-Moorish town hall finished in 1894. Finding the mayor of Sarajevo and his councilors arrayed in two rows, with Muslims in fezzes and baggy trousers on one side, Christians in tail coats and top hats on the other, the archduke brutally interrupted the mayor's obsequious greeting: "Mr. Mayor, what's the use of your speeches? I come to Sarajevo on a friendly visit and someone throws a bomb at me? This is outrageous!" Inside the town hall, the archduke calmed down. "Mark my words," he joked to his entourage, "the [assassin] will probably be decorated with the Order of Merit, in the good old Austrian style, instead of being 'rendered harmless.'"[13]

General Potiorek, who had insisted on organizing all security arrangements for the visit, was deeply embarrassed. Hoping for a better finish to the day than the start, he assured Franz Ferdinand that the archduke could safely complete his tour of the city as scheduled. Franz Ferdinand was willing but insisted on a change of route so that he could be taken to visit the lightly wounded Merizzi in the hospital. The archduke never having been in combat, this was the closest he had come to succoring a wounded comrade on the battlefield, and he now recklessly insisted on observing the formality. Potiorek agreed but neglected to communicate the change of plan to the mayor of Sarajevo and his driver, who were now leading the motorcade away from city hall on the original route. The archduke's driver dumbly followed the mayor into a turn onto Franz Joseph Street, only to be pulled up short by Potiorek, who barked at him to stop, back up, and continue straight along the quay toward the army hospital.

Cars were still enough of a rarity in 1914 that these were on loan from the Austrian Automobile Club, and the drivers were balky.[14] As the archduke's driver struggled to back out and turn with both sides of the road crowded with spectators, Franz Ferdinand drawled to Potiorek that "as far as assassins are concerned, one must really put one's life in God's hands." With the car stalled and trying to straighten out, the archduke and duchess sitting stiffly in the back, Gavrilo Princip—one of the three Bosnian students the Black Hand had recruited in Belgrade—stepped through the crowd and fired two shots at point-blank range: the first cut the archduke's carotid artery, the second bored into Sophie's gut. They both died in minutes.

When the bodies of Franz Ferdinand and his wife were laid out at the old Ottoman Konak—Potiorek's walled residence nearby—the archduke was found to be wearing seven amulets around his neck, each designed to ward off a different brand of evil. Sophie had a gold chain around her lifeless neck, with a scapular containing holy relics intended to guard her against illness or accident. These were the modern Habsburgs, who were supposed to save the Balkans from backwardness and superstition. Karl Kraus, the Viennese satirist, found more black humor in the woefully managed and tragically terminated visit: "The gunning down of the Heir Apparent to the Throne on the corner of Franz Joseph and Rudolf Streets symbolizes what it means to be an Austrian."[15]

Princip was immediately identified as a Bosnian Serb, and everyone in the archduke's entourage took for granted that the assassin was an agent of the Serbian government, which had been protesting Austria's occupation of Bosnia-Herzegovina for years. Potiorek, whose own inattention to detail had facilitated the assassination, now pushed for war "with everything he had," as a colleague put it, "to wash his slate clean."[16] Conrad, who learned of the assassination only when changing trains in Zagreb on his return from the Bosnian exercise, advocated the usual remedy: "*Krieg, Krieg, Krieg,*" as Berchtold summarized, "war, war, war."

In meetings with the emperor and cabinet, Conrad demanded "decisive action."[17] War Minister Alexander Krobatin leaned hard on Franz Joseph's adjutant to secure "an immediate declaration of war" from the emperor.[18] Most of the senior Austrian generals joined the vengeful chorus against the Serbian "assassin state" or *Meuchelmörderstaat*, and its "death dealers" or *Mordbuben*. "Give me just one corps and a division of reservists and I'll get the job done," General Michael Appel sputtered from his office in Sarajevo.[19]

In Zagreb, Croatian nationalists pondered genocide. "We are infested with Serb creatures; as of today let it be our goal to destroy them," the newspaper *Hrvatska* growled. "Srbe o vrbe," meaning "String Serbs up from the willow trees," became a popular catchphrase.[20] Austria-Hungary's legation in Belgrade—affronted by "the low level of mourning here, where people in the streets and cafés mock our misfortune"—hit the same note: "Serbia must learn to fear again. . . . We must use this opportunity to deliver an annihilating blow, without regard for any other considerations, in order to win a few more decades for the peaceful development of the monarchy and to punish this insult to the crown of the empire."[21]

Meeting with the Crown of the Empire himself at Schönbrunn on June 30, Berchtold was struck most by old Emperor Franz Joseph's sadness. Sad less for the archduke than the monarchy's predicament, the emperor teared up as he heard his options. Franz Joseph had shied from war since the debacle of 1866, but even he realized now that war, or at the very least the real threat of it, could not be averted. Princip's blow to the Habsburgs was too brutal and insulting. Still, the Hungarian veto on Austrian decisions was so well entrenched that Franz Joseph and Berchtold agreed that no decisions could be taken until Hungarian prime minister István Tisza arrived to state Budapest's views.

The meeting with Tisza later that day conformed to expectations. Tisza was against war with Serbia, and for nothing more than a scolding diplomatic campaign against Belgrade. He worried that any conflict with Serbia would trigger Russian intervention, and the Russians lay just across the border from Hungary. Having spent years in government shortchanging the Austro-Hungarian army, Tisza also had a better sense than most of the monarchy's military weakness.[22]

Hungary's craven position was a blow to Germany, which had long sought a pretext for a decisive showdown with Serbia. German chief of the general staff Moltke, who had pulled Conrad back from the brink of war in February 1913 with the argument that the German and Austrian peoples would not go to war over a minor issue like the borders of Albania, glimpsed opportunity in Austria's tragedy. The German and Austro-Hungarian peoples *would* fight to avenge the cold-blooded murder of the heir to the Habsburg throne. This was just the "slogan" that was needed to whip up the German and Austro-Hungarian masses.[23] But German hopes that the Austrians would seize the moral high ground, promptly crush Serbia, and then shift all forces to the east withered in the hot summer air—and not just because of Tisza's intransigence.

In Sarajevo, six of the seven assassins had been arrested and interrogated. One called himself "a Serbian hero," but the picture of Serbian government complicity in the assassination plot was muddy at best. Milan Ciganovic, a government employee who stored bomb-making materials in the closet of his Belgrade apartment, had connected the assassins with their military trainer, Major Vojin Tankosic, as well as Apis and the Narodna Odbrana. But these Serbian officials were rogues acting on their own, not agents of the government, an important distinction that the Austrians (and Germans) plowed over.[24] From Sarajevo, Potiorek warned that Bosnia-Herzegovina would become ungovernable if Vienna didn't strike back harshly against the Bosnian Serbs and their state sponsors. Conrad's informants in Bosnia told him much the same thing: the job of governance had to be taken away from the "Polish diplomats and court counselors" running the show in Vienna and given to the army. "It is time to sweep this place clean with an iron broom . . . at least 60 percent of the Serbs here are enemies of the state," he was told.[25] Even the peaceable Berchtold was coming around, on June 30 calling for "a final and fundamental reckoning with Belgrade."[26] The same day, the kaiser in Berlin exhorted the Austrians to war: "Now or never!"[27]

The emperor had hoped to huddle with Kaiser Wilhelm II when he came to Vienna on July 3 for the archduke's funeral, but the kaiser, fearing Austrian security arrangements as much as Serbian assassins, decided to remain safely in Berlin, where he read a letter from Franz Joseph asserting that the archduke's murder was the work of Serbian and Russian pan-Slavists. This conclusion allowed Germany to turn up the heat on its weak-kneed ally. Meeting with Berchtold's chief of staff, Count Alexander Hoyos, on July 1, the German journalist and envoy Viktor Naumann told Hoyos that *now* was the time to ask for unstinting German support "to annihilate Serbia." Naumann had been enlisted as an intermediary by the German government, and he brought this unambiguous message to Vienna in the first days of July: "The sooner Austria-Hungary goes to war the better; yesterday was better than today and today is better than tomorrow."[28] Berchtold, "allured by the glamour and force of the military men and fascinated by the rattle and glitter of their terrible machines" (as Churchill put it), avidly agreed, telling the German foreign secretary, Gottlieb von Jagow, that Berlin and Vienna needed "to rip apart the cords that our enemies are weaving into a net around us."[29] Berchtold would not be disappointed; the German kaiser was shocked by the assassination of a fellow royal (who was also a close friend) and was expected to write a blank check of support for Austrian action on that basis alone.

Four days after his meeting with Naumann, Hoyos arrived in Berlin as Berchtold's special envoy. He met first with Undersecretary Arthur Zimmermann at the German Foreign Office, where he outlined Vienna's goals: Serbia would be partitioned by Austria and its Balkan neighbors and essentially "wiped off the map." The assassination would be used "to fabricate a pretext for settling accounts with Serbia."[30]

It wasn't Serbia's extinction that Germany needed, however—merely its weakening as an Austrian gadfly and a Russian ally. At Potsdam, where the kaiser was preparing to depart the next day for his annual North Sea cruise, Austrian ambassador Count Ladislaus Szögyeni peddled a softer line than Hoyos and Berchtold, promising not to wipe the Karageorgevic realm off the map, but merely to "eliminate Serbia as a power-political factor in the Balkans."[31] This declaration was enough to secure the notorious blank check from the kaiser. Vienna was free to attack Serbia, and Germany would support Austria-Hungary even if Russia intervened "and let loose the great war."[32]

Meeting in Vienna's Westbahnhof on July 3, to see Franz Ferdinand's casket off to its final resting place in Artstetten, Conrad and Auffenberg held a whispered conference. Conrad averred that this time Serbia would *have* to be punished. Auffenberg agreed but pointed out that an invasion of Serbia would almost certainly expand into a wider war. Perhaps, Conrad said, but not necessarily. Auffenberg reminded him that the Austro-Hungarian artillery remained as deficient as ever, the army's glaring weak spot in any "struggle for life and death." The Habsburg army had just 96 guns per corps, while the Russians had 108, the French 120, and the Germans 144. The Austro-Hungarian guns were older too, of inferior range, accuracy, and caliber.[33] Conrad limply agreed: "I'm aware of that, but I'm in no position to fix that *now*."[34]

Conrad could not fix the artillery problem for all of the usual reasons, but also because he had planned a vacation in South Tyrol with his mistress, which, incredibly, he now took. The chief would be gone from Vienna for two entire weeks, from July 7 to 22, returning briefly on July 19 for a ministerial council meeting, but then hurrying back to Frau von Reininghaus at her chalet in Innichen (San Candido) for four more days. The German military attaché in Vienna—who did not take vacation—could get no precise information from Conrad's slumbering office as to what exactly the Austro-Hungarian army planned to do: what forces would entrain for Serbia, and what units to Galicia.[35] With Conrad gone, everyone else decided to take leave as well. Krobatin went off to a country house, and even the all-important chief of the general staff's Railway Bureau, Colonel Johann Straub, went on vacation, all the way south to the vineyards and beaches of Dalmatia. Seven of the army's sixteen corps furloughed their peasant troops to help take in the summer harvest; they would not return to their units until July 25. No wonder Conrad's general staff would find itself flummoxed by "technical difficulties" in August; no one had rectified them in July.

Although many in the German army hungered for a world war *now,* before the French and Russian army procurement and manpower programs were complete, Moltke remained prudent, noting the obvious: with the world united in horror at Princip's deed, which had at least a degree of Serbian government connivance, it would be better if Austria-Hungary seized the day, promptly invaded Serbia, and crushed the kingdom in single combat. Churchill, no friend of the Austrians, agreed that the murder was obscene, akin to Ireland launching a "pan-Celtic scheme to unite Ireland, Scotland and Wales" and assassinating the Prince of Wales "with weapons supplied from the Dublin Arsenal."[36] Even the Russians would find it hard to react, the kaiser predicting that Tsar Nicholas II would not enter a war "on the side of regicides." Decision makers in Berlin were united in believing, like Lady Macbeth, that "if it were done when 'tis done, then 'twere well it were done quickly."

In other words, Vienna had to exploit the momentum and sympathy of the crisis, cancel its vacations, and *move.* Mobilization was a three-week process: a week for reservists to report to their regiments, another week for the regiments to join their corps, and then a third week for the corps to join their armies on the frontier. Everyone was sufficiently confident that the Austrians would do the right thing that few summer leaves were canceled in the other great powers; on July 5, the kaiser told the Austro-Hungarian ambassador in Berlin that he "would be saddened if advantage were not taken of such a favorable juncture as the present one." That was a bare-faced incitement to war, reinforced the next day by German chancellor Theobald von Bethmann Hollweg, who urged the Austrians to strike, even if the "action against Serbia will lead to a world war."[37]

Having summoned the war clouds, the kaiser then departed on his three-week cruise to the Norwegian fjords, Moltke returned to the healing waters of Karlsbad, and Falkenhayn and the key war ministry and general staff department heads and section chiefs scattered to the lakes, spas, beaches, and mountains.[38] German chancellor Bethmann Hollweg even agreed that so long as Vienna's punitive expedition unfolded swiftly, there would be no need to notify Rome and Bucharest, as the Triple Alliance demanded. "Austria," Moltke wrote from his rest cure at Karlsbad, "must beat the Serbs and then make peace *quickly,* demanding an Austro-Serbian alliance as the sole condition," tactlessly adding, "just as Prussia did with Austria in 1866." The kaiser had given his blank check to Ambassador Szögyeni on the assumption that the Austrians would move fast—stepping across the Danube to corral the Serbian army and seize the Serbian capital—and present the world (and the Russians in particular) with a fait accompli.[39]

But "fast" was a word that had never been associated with the Austro-Hungarian military. The fact that Austria's duel with Serbia in 1914 mushroomed into a world war had much to do with the sluggish decision making of the Austro-Hungarian government and the torpid deployment of the Habsburg army. At a meeting of the Common Ministerial Council on July 7, ten days after the assassination, Hungarian prime minister Tisza still argued for purely diplomatic pressure on the Serbs and refused to support a deliberately humiliating ultimatum that the Serbs would have to reject. Hungarian public opinion weighed heavily on the prime minister, as most Magyars shrank from war for three reasons. First, the archduke had planned to reduce the size and power of Hungary; no one in Budapest wept for him. Second, Hungarians did not want to add yet more Slavs to the monarchy, so a war for Balkan or Polish annexation made no sense to them. Third, Hungarians recognized that a great-power war would likely result in one of two outcomes, Russian or German domination of central Europe and the Balkans; neither outcome would favor Budapest.[40]

Nor was Tisza encouraged by Conrad's review of the Austro-Hungarian plans for war. The staff chief was overconfident, suggesting that he had the means to strong-arm Serbia *and* fluidly shift forces to the Russian front as needed, so long as Russia's intentions became clear "by the fifth day of mobilization." He made no allowance for Tisza's chief concern, which was that the Rumanians might seize upon the opportunity of an Austro-Russian war to invade and annex Habsburg Transylvania.[41] No one in the room seemed to grasp the existential danger posed by Russia. The Romanovs could be beaten only if the Germans attacked them too, but the German Schlieffen Plan called for an attack on France first, which meant that the Austro-Hungarians would bear the brunt of the Russian steamroller. This too explained Tisza's caution.

Another full week was consumed arguing with Tisza, who insisted that a war, far from ameliorating Austria-Hungary's nationality problems, would "explode" them instead.[42] Conrad and Krobatin took the opportunity presented by this Hungarian dawdling not to finalize their war plans but to prolong their summer vacations. The Austrian legation in Belgrade fulminated at the delay, writing Berchtold that the Serbs were using the respite to "finish *their* war preparations and buy time for a Russian intervention that will wear us down."[43] General Auffenberg—on a vacation of his own—ran into the vacationing Austro-Hungarian finance minister on July 10 in the Salzkammergut. Bilinksi was taking his customary summer holiday in the Alps and, despite being the Austro-Hungarian money man and civilian chief of Bosnia-Herzegovina, had no idea that the monarchy was about to shift to a war footing.[44]

Tisza only came round to the consensus war view on July 14, when he was reminded by his fellow Magyar and foreign policy advisor Count István Burián that to do nothing about Serbia's mischief would merely embolden the Rumanians to practice the same destabilizing tactics in Transylvania, a largely Rumanian corner of Hungary coveted by Bucharest. Tisza did insist that no Serbian territory be annexed lest the monarchy's nationalities problem become even more vexing, to which everyone hastily agreed, Conrad confiding to Krobatin: "We'll see. Before the Balkan Wars, the powers also talked of the status quo; after the wars no one worried about it."[45]

Another week was lost as finishing touches were put to Vienna's ultimatum. On July 21, Berchtold finally carried it to the Kaiservilla in Bad Ischl, where the emperor spent his summers—even *this* one. The emperor, about to turn eighty-four and never the most acute commander in chief, read and approved it. The ultimatum demanded that Serbia "cease its attitude of opposition to the Austro-Hungarian annexation of Bosnia-Herzegovina," and then listed ten humiliating demands. Belgrade would be required to censor its own press to "remove anti-Austrian articles," eliminate anti-Austrian material from school instruction, fire bureaucrats and officers with anti-Austrian attitudes, arrest suspect army officers and government officials, stop shipments of illicit weapons into Bosnia-Herzegovina and Dalmatia, dissolve secret societies like Narodna Odbrana, and—most degrading of all—permit Austro-Hungarian officials to lead an inquiry (on Serbian soil) into the "subversive movement" and the "plot of June 28th."[46]

Had the ultimatum been delivered a month earlier, on the heels of the assassination, it would have been greeted with international sympathy, but by now—several weeks after the murder— the slow march of this démarche was such that Austria had lost its early edge in the crisis. Moral outrage had faded. The assassination was a month old, and in the meantime the archduke's corpse had been conveyed from Sarajevo to the coast, taken on a dreadnought to Trieste, transported by rail to a funeral in Vienna, and then transferred to the family crypt in Upper Austria, where it had been resting in peace for nearly three weeks. General Appel, commanding the Austro-Hungarian corps in Sarajevo, boiled with frustration: "We have lost two martyrs for Austria's honor; we are the insulted empire; our mailed fist is ready to smash them, yet still not even a mobilization order! We await it feverishly."[47] Worse, German indiscretions—leaking the contents of the Austrian ultimatum to Serbia to the Italians—had betrayed the whole operation. In St. Petersburg on a state visit, French president Raymond Poincaré made plain that he and the Russians knew what was going on and that Austria-Hungary would not succeed in localizing the war: Serbia, Poincaré declared, "has friends."[48]

Austria-Hungary's minister in Belgrade, Wladimir Giesl, delivered the ultimatum to the Serbian Foreign Ministry at 6:00 p.m. on July 23. The note was simultaneously published in the Austrian newspapers, with the clear implication that acceptance by the Serbs was neither desired nor expected. The Serbs had forty-eight hours to answer, and when they did, on July 25, they rather surprisingly granted all of the Austrian demands except those that required the intervention of Austrian investigators on Serbian territory, suggesting as an alternative that the matter be turned over to an international tribunal at the Hague.[49] In a bid for international support, the Serbs were trying to appear reasonable. But, prodded by the Germans and their own wounded pride, the Austrians were impervious to reason. Giesl read the Serbian caveats, deemed them unacceptable, broke diplomatic relations, and left the kingdom, crossing the Danube on a ferry to the Hungarian town of Semlin (Zemun). This was the signal for war.

But the lack of synchronization between Austrian policy (the ultimatum) and strategy (the mobilization) was astonishing. General Auffenberg, who shortly would be given an army, was still vacationing in Upper Austria, sitting down to lunch with his sister when his brother-in-law suddenly appeared on a bicycle waving a newspaper and crying, "The fuse has been lit; it's the ultimatum!" Auffenberg recalled his surprise: "Four weeks had passed since the shattering events in Sarajevo, so I had assumed that this crisis too would amount to nothing."[50] Woefully prepared though they were, the Habsburg generals exulted at the chance finally to fight. "Thank God, we've got a war!" General Viktor Dankl, commandant of the Austrian XIV Corps in Innsbruck, shouted to his headquarters staff on hearing the news. He summoned the post musicians to his office and ordered up a celebratory concert. Sir Maurice de Bunsen, Britain's ambassador in Vienna, observed "vast crowds parading till the early morning" in the Austrian capital, and hostile demonstrations in front of the Russian embassy. Bunsen expressed his dismay at the Viennese war fever: "The public clearly thought that this would be a war with the Serbs . . . summary vengeance for the crime in Sarajevo. . . . Few seemed to reflect that the forcible intervention of a Great Power in the Balkans must inevitably call other Great Powers into the field."[51]

That collision of great powers was precisely the contingency that Conrad was supposed to be hedging against. Conrad should have been using the month since the assassination to tee up a hasty attack to cripple Serbia before the other powers could engage, rather than vacationing with his mistress in the Alps. In all war planning since the 1880s, the Austrians had stressed the need to mobilize, move, and beat the Serbs quickly, for Russia would almost certainly intervene in a lengthy war, and the need to force rivers—the Danube, the Sava, the Drina, or all three—to get into Serbia would only protract the campaign.

On July 25, the Serbs evacuated Belgrade, shifting their government to Nis. With the government far from the frontier and the army grouped behind the Kolubara River around Valjevo and Arangjelovac, Serbia now presented an almost certain quagmire, not a lightning victory. While the Austrians had dithered, the Serbs had rushed their initial mobilization—300,000 troops and 542 guns—to completion.[52] This explained the consternation of contemporaries at the sluggishness of the Austrian reply to the assassination: Vienna had conceded the Serbs and the Russians four entire weeks to prepare for war.

Conrad had always insisted that the *Zeitfaktor,* or time factor, would be crucial in any showdown with Serbia, but for all of his bluster, he proved remarkably passive in the clinch.[53] He had authorized summer harvest leaves for active-duty troops, permitting tens of thousands of soldiers to return to their villages in June to assist with the harvest. Officers were also on summer leaves. So when the Serbs gave an unsatisfactory answer to the ultimatum and the emperor ordered a partial mobilization on July 25, Conrad had little real force to mobilize. When the emperor actually declared war on Serbia on July 28, *nothing happened.* Count Burián—who would replace Berchtold as foreign minister in 1915—would later use this passivity to defend Austria-Hungary against insinuations of war guilt: how could "the war have been contrived in a shadowy workshop," he hazarded, when "the Austro-Hungarian army proved so utterly unprepared for it?"[54]

Conrad's workshop, of course, was supposed to have been better prepared than this. The general staff chief had assured Berchtold on July 7 that so long as he knew Russia's intentions within five days of the start of mobilization, he would be able to manage a war on two fronts.[55] He now knew Russia's intentions: the tsar had ordered a partial mobilization in the Moscow, Warsaw, Kiev, and Odessa military districts the day the Serbs rejected the ultimatum. From the Russian capital, France's president had warned that Serbia "had friends." Clearly it was time for Plan R, not Plan B, but Conrad wouldn't see reason; he still wanted to fight the Serbs. That prospect, however, was looking less and less appealing. While the Austrian army struggled with its own partial mobilization—just two-fifths of the army—the Serbs were busily deploying their entire strength. By July 25, the Serbs had called up four hundred thousand men and had begun to assemble three field armies. The Russians were accelerating their mobilization, and the British were pressuring the Germans to force the Austrians to halt in Belgrade—that is, to punish but not partition Serbia—and negotiate an end to the July Crisis.[56]

Conrad downplayed the threat from Russia, still preferring to "sweep the iron broom" across Serbia.[57] His willful blindness was remarkable. Austro-Hungarian staff planning had always taken for granted that an Austrian war with Serbia would be but the *Vorstufe*—the first step—to a wider war with Russia.[58] Now Conrad buried his head in the sand and lashed out blindly. He wasn't the only one. Meeting late on July 28 with General Alexander von Uxküll, a close advisor to the emperor and former military attaché in St. Petersburg, General Auffenberg was stunned to hear Uxküll describe the Russian war preparations as a "bluff." Russia, Uxküll averred, "will not intervene."[59] Berchtold also was groping in the dark, blind to what Conrad was doing. Conrad ordered the twelve divisions of Echelon B not to Galicia but to the Serbian border, wildly assuming that the Russians would back down when faced with a real German threat.[60] "I was not pleased with the division of our army into two parts," Auffenberg recalled, with just twenty-three divisions against Russia (too few) and eighteen against the Serbs (too many), with seven divisions floating in between the two armies as a general reserve.

Conrad, in short, was setting the army up for defeat on all fronts. His superior, Archduke Friedrich, named *Armeeoberkommandant* (supreme commander) by the emperor after the death of Archduke Franz Ferdinand, lacked the acuity to amend Conrad's decisions. Meeting with the fifty-eight-year-old Friedrich—"Fritzl" to his intimates—Auffenberg was underwhelmed: "We had a short, trivial chat; as was always the case, the noble gentleman left an impression of abiding mediocrity; he will not inspire confidence at the head of an army of 2 million."[61] Fortunately, there was still a way out of the unfolding disaster. The British ambassador called on Berchtold on July 28, offered his good offices, and warned the foreign minister that he must not continue to "neglect the *European* aspect" of Vienna's grievance with Serbia. If he did, there would be a world war involving all of the powers. Berchtold told the British that the Russians would not intervene, "for we will assure [Russia] that we seek no added territory."[62] This was staggering naiveté for a man as prudent as Berchtold.

The Germans gave the final shove to war. Having appeared to support a "halt in Belgrade" option on July 30, when the kaiser enjoined Franz Joseph to accept the keys to "Belgrade or other fortresses" as collateral for Serbian cooperation in Vienna's investigation of the assassination plot, Wilhelm II abruptly reversed course, issuing a double ultimatum to St. Petersburg and Paris on July 31. "Decline the renewed advances of Great Britain in the interest of peace," Moltke instructed Conrad. "European war is the last chance of saving Austria-Hungary. Germany is ready to back Austria unreservedly."

Moltke ought to have added that a general European war was the only chance of saving Germany, Bethmann having declared that "the future belongs to Russia, it grows and grows and weighs on us like an ever-deepening nightmare."[63] Only war could nip that Russian growth in the bud, or so they thought in Berlin. These exchanges between Vienna and Berlin underpin the verdict of German and Austrian war guilt, all the more so because Moltke confessed that he knew what he was doing. There would be a "world war," Moltke wrote Bethmann Hollweg, and the great powers would "tear each other apart," with vicious results: "The culture of almost all of Europe will be destroyed for decades to come."[64] But no matter. Like the Austrians, the Germans felt that the military advantages they currently enjoyed would be drowned in two or three years by the big Russian and French military programs, which would add yet more troops, artillery, and infrastructure, leveling a playing field that was still tilted in favor of Germany because of its vast 1913 army spending program. "All postpone-ment," Moltke had told Conrad at Karlsbad in May 1914, "means a lessening of our chances."[65]

And like the Austrians, the Germans also suffered from a do-mestic political malaise. Bethmann Hollweg had been Reich chan-cellor for five years yet had never secured a reliable parliamentary majority; his role had been reduced to passing huge army and navy bills through the Reichstag and fending off increasingly bold at-tacks from the Socialists, the Alsace-Lorrainers (*"Vive la France!"*), and the Poles, who carped at every German-speaking school and official in their precincts. There may have been little Bethmann could have done anyway to arrest the drive to war. The chancellor complained that he was not "receiving good information on mili-tary events" and that the "decisions for war were being taken in the closed circle around the kaiser."[66] The Austrians would later recall the "fearful, nervous, hesitant, neurotic" quality of these harried decision makers in Berlin. They lacked "Bismarck's shrewdness" in recklessly declaring war on Russia on August 1 and then on France two days later. When Britain reluctantly added its weight to the co-alition against Germany on August 5—"to prevent the union of all of Western Europe under a single power"—the German reaction was furious (and idiotic): "One more enemy, just one more reason to close ranks and fight to the last breath."[67]

Austria-Hungary displayed none of this German brazenness in its own declarations, slouching reluctantly into a war with Rus-sia on August 6—"in view of the menacing attitude of Russia in the Austro-Serbian conflict," as Berchtold put it. Conrad was over-come with the pessimism that would mar his conduct of the entire war, declaring that "in 1912–13 it would have been a game with decent chances, but now we play *va banque*."[68] This was anything but reassuring, *va banque* being a gambler's term meaning "all or nothing." As usual, Conrad was acting as if he were the blame-less victim of events, not the chief driver of them. Tisza renewed his obstruction, insisting that the "halt in Belgrade" option first floated by the kaiser be pursued and that Berchtold "dispel the fairy tale" of Austrian aggression, but he was too late. In the quiet rooms of Schönbrunn, the elderly emperor had resigned himself to aggression. He sat quietly, secure, as his adjutant put it, "in our legitimate cause." The adjutant, General Arthur Bolfras, harbored few doubts, bluffly writing to Potiorek in Sarajevo: "One more time I raise my voice to cheer: *viel Feind', viele Ehr'*—many enemies, much honor."[69]

Bolfras would not be cheering for long.

CHAPTER 5

The Steamroller

THE NIGHT BEFORE GAVRILO PRINCIP SHOT Archduke Franz Ferdinand and Sophie in the streets of Sarajevo, sixty-two-year-old General Franz Conrad von Hötzendorf sat down to write one of his orotund letters to his mistress, Gina. War was coming, Conrad scribbled, and Austria-Hungary would not survive it; Russia and Serbia would be "the coffin nails of the monarchy." But Conrad would fight to his last breath anyway, "because such an ancient monarchy and such an ancient army cannot perish ingloriously."[1]

Conrad's bombast masked a darker truth: not only was the empire totally unprepared for the oncoming storm, but so was Conrad himself. Conrad's career as a writer and a bureaucrat had been brilliant, yet he had not actually heard a shot fired in anger in the modern age. Well known abroad for his tactical writings on the Boer War and other conflicts, his only combat experience had come as a staff captain attached to an infantry division in 1878 in Bosnia. He had rapidly ascended the ladder since his discovery by Franz Ferdinand in 1901, rocketing from a one-star general to a three-star in just five years, but the harsh challenges of modern war and the painful choices they imposed never seemed to darken his glittering career. "Conrad," Karl Kraus had prophesied before the war, "will remain the greatest commander only as long as the bugles are sounding and not the guns." Kraus was right, and this was about to become a problem.

Every inch the German hero to his mistress, Gina, Conrad was beginning to exasperate the Germans. With a population of 175 million, which was nearly twice the population of the United States and more than the populations of Austria-Hungary, Germany, and France combined, Russia would drown the Austrians in manpower unless Conrad brought every gun to bear on the Eastern Front immediately upon the outbreak of war.[2] Austria's forty-eight divisions—augmented by, at most, seventeen German ones—would have to hold the line against Serbia and defend Galicia and Poland against Russia's 114 divisions until the Germans had beaten France's eighty-eight divisions (in about forty-two days, according to the plan) and sent their army east to beat the Russians too. Russian manpower was so vast that there could be no thought in Vienna of offensive operations against Serbia once Russia entered the conflict.[3] From the first day of mobilization, the Austrians would have to roll everything east to beat back the Russian "steamroller," a term that had been coined by the awed British press to reflect Russia's seemingly infinite supply of men. The steamroller was the ghost in the machine, tormenting Conrad's every attempt to adapt the mind of his superficially elegant war plans to the matter of Russian might.

The Austrians would have to increase their own deficient troop numbers and strike an early blow to throw the steamroller—which would be busy augmenting the 1.4-million-man active-duty army with 6 million reservists—out of gear. The Austrians had already taken some measures to expand their available manpower: in 1912, the Austrians had increased the Habsburg army by reducing the term of service from three years to two, while stretching the reserve obligation from seven years to as many as twenty-seven. Troops could now be recalled for service in the reserves until age fifty. This was apparently the only way that a poor empire of 53 million could square off against a poor empire of 175 million.[4] The problem, which would shortly reveal itself, was that calling men soldiers on paper was not the same as making them soldiers in the field. Horrified by training costs, the monarchy still trained only a fraction of its eligible twenty-one-year-olds each year, so in the mobilization of 1914, most of the Austro-Hungarian soldiers appeared at their depots with little or no military experience.

Other sleights of hand fostered a reckless optimism in Vienna. By 1914, the Austro-Hungarians had gotten their mobilization time down to sixteen days.[5] They had also improved the combat readiness of the eight Landwehr and eight Honvéd divisions to a level where they could now be mobilized, classed as *Feldtruppen* (field troops), and merged in sixteen army corps alongside the thirty-three regular army divisions. That, of course, was a mixed blessing. Since the Landwehr and Honvéd—one-third of the army's total strength—had been originally conceived as a reserve army, counting them as first-line strength meant that the Austro-Hungarian army no longer had a trained reserve, whether to replace losses in the first wave or to defend an unexpectedly threatened point.

With no room in the budget for real reserve divisions, Conrad made do with notional ones: retired officers, one-year volunteer officers (educated men who had volunteered to serve just one year to escape conscription), and all of the untrained men that the army had been drafting but not actually inducting since 1900. These blessed holders of high draft numbers—the so-called *Nichtaktiven,* or non-actives—were the men who had escaped service in both the regular army (which had received the men with the lowest draft numbers) and the Landwehr/Honvéd (those with middle numbers) but would certainly be called to the colors in case of a major war. There was, in fact, nowhere to put these men if they were called up, as the Hungarians naturally had prevented the creation even of hypothetical reserve regiments to accommodate them, so in any general mobilization they would mill around uselessly. Eventually they'd be bundled into *Neuformationen* (new formations), equipped with uniform oddments and rifles from as far back as the 1870s, and ordered to march and fight after the most perfunctory instruction. The luckiest *Nichtaktiven,* of course, had long since emigrated to America, where they delightedly ignored the mobilization orders that wended their way across the Atlantic to factories in Connecticut, mines in Pennsylvania, or lumber camps in Michigan. The less fortunate, who had not made their escape before the war, were dignified with the name *Landsturm* or *Ersatsreserve* and lumped into undergunned, undersupplied *Marschbrigaden* (march brigades) that theoretically would furnish eleven reserve divisions but in practice were cannon fodder: "Men and officers alike were much surprised when arms and equipment were issued and *everything* had to be explained," one veteran dryly observed.[6]

With troop problems like these, Conrad might have been expected to adopt a more prudent strategy. If he were to have any hope of winning in the east, Conrad would have to concentrate his three-part army as quickly as possible. He would have to abandon all thought of sending Echelon B down to reinforce the Balkan Minimal Group in the fight against Serbia; instead, the forty divisions of the A and B echelons would have to be combined against Russia and the eight divisions of the Balkan Minimal Group left to deal with Serbia's dozen divisions.[7] By July 1914, only a fantasist could still imagine that an Austro-Serbian war could be localized and the twelve divisions of Echelon B—the four corps of General Eduard von Böhm-Ermolli's Second Army—safely dispatched to Serbia to join forces with *Minimalgruppe Balkan*. Austro-Russian relations had deteriorated so sharply after the annexation crisis of 1908 and the Balkan Wars that it was hard to imagine *any* scenario in which the Russians would permit an unfettered Austro-Hungarian invasion of Serbia. But Conrad proved an imaginative man.

Now that Russia and Austria were at war, swinging Echelon B into line against Serbia invited disaster. The Russians had improved their railways and converted dozens of reserve divisions into first-line divisions that could mobilize and strike swiftly, without having to wait for any reservists. Russia now had nine new railways, five of them double-tracked, running up to the frontiers with Germany and Austria. The tsar now would be able to put ninety-six infantry divisions and thirty-seven cavalry divisions—2.7 million troops in thirty corps—into the field quickly, with 2.3 million slower-moving troops from Siberia and Asia in reserve.[8] And everyone assumed that Italy's twenty-five divisions would eventually enter the fray against Austria. Everything hinged on Austria's

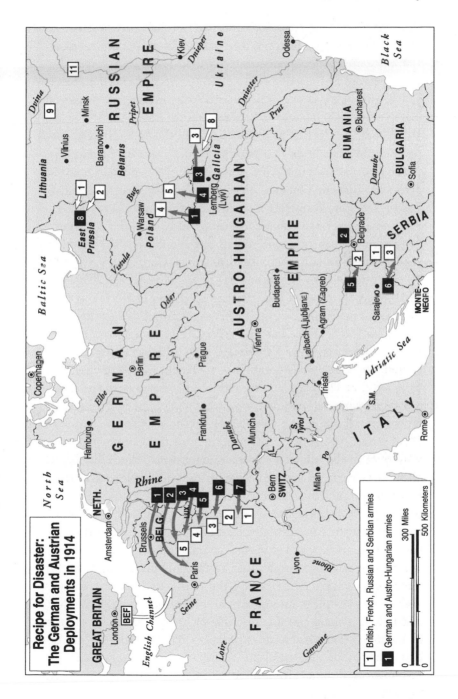

Recipe for Disaster:
The German and Austrian
Deployments in 1914

ability to hold long enough in the east for Berlin to win in the west and shift strong forces to the Russian front. But there was no assurance even of this prerequisite; in their last staff talks in May 1914, Moltke had merely said that he *hoped* to defeat the French and British in six weeks. If he didn't, Austria-Hungary would be like the little Dutch boy with his finger in the dam.[9]

Conrad had agreed to put his finger in the dam on the vague, never ratified condition that Moltke would contribute *something* to the Eastern Front in the first days of the war—perhaps a dozen divisions. Indeed, vagueness had been the keynote of Austro-German military cooperation since Schlieffen's accession in 1891. His predecessors had cooperated thoroughly with the Austrians; Schlieffen, in contrast, was noted for his wariness. He didn't trust Austria-Hungary's ability to guard German secrets and never trusted Austro-Hungarian promises to attack the Russians. Moltke, who succeeded Schlieffen in 1906, absorbed this skepticism about the Austrians and kept his communications with them vague. In May 1914 he had *seemed* to agree to a joint offensive, pledging offensive operations by a German Eighth Army in loose conjunction with a much larger Austro-Hungarian force operating from Galicia. The Eighth Army would be a down payment, to be followed by strong forces within a reasonable time in the east, after the French and British were beaten in the west.

Conrad, who was at least as wary of the Germans as they were of him—he regularly stamped documents "Not to be shared with the German general staff"—had been delighted with Germany's nebulous assurances, for entirely the wrong reasons.[10] He believed that he could eat his cake and have it too: do his thankless duty against the Russians, sloughing off most of the work to the Germans, and still win a glorious victory against the Serbs. Knowing that the next war would arise in the Balkans, Conrad had no intention of letting the Serbs slip the noose while he trucked the Habsburg army off to an inglorious holding operation in the dust and mud of Poland and Ukraine. He had tipped his hand slightly in January 1913, when he'd remarked to Moltke that the "unpredictable attitude of Russia" in a Balkan crisis might cause him to improvise on a day-to-day basis, *durch den Moment.*[11] When

Moltke hadn't demanded clarification of that alarming proposition, Conrad quietly—without advising the Germans—began improvising in the spring of 1914. Instead of pushing whatever troops he sent to Galicia right up to the Russian border, to relieve pressure on the Germans by threatening an Austro-Hungarian invasion of Russian Poland, Conrad decided to unload the troops far to the south, on the San and Dniester, where they could shelter behind the rivers and inside the fortresses, and buy time for the defeat of Serbia when the long-awaited war finally came.

This, of course, was the exact opposite of what the Germans thought that they had arranged with Conrad. Indeed, when Conrad had proposed something like this to Moltke in 1909, the German chief had reacted indignantly, pointing out that an Austro-German defeat of Russia "will itself solve the Serbian affair."[12] The Austrians, in other words, were supposed to arrange the fate of Serbia on the Bug, not the Drina.

But even as war with Russia crept closer in July 1914, Conrad still wanted to deploy safely and unthreateningly in Galicia to buy time for the destruction of the Serbs. In fact, he was quietly sending 40 percent of the Habsburg army to fight the Serbs.[13] On July 30, two days after the Russians began their "partial mobilization" of 1.1 million troops, Conrad told his chief railway planner, Colonel Johann Straub, that even though war with Russia was imminent, he *still* wanted Echelon B (Second Army) reserved for the Serbian front. Conrad even ordered a last-minute revision of the war plan that day. Whereas Echelon B was supposed to sit in its barracks until its final destination was clarified, freeing up the rails for the prompt movement of Echelon A to Galicia and Balkan Minimal Group to the Serbian frontier, Conrad now ordered a stunned Straub to move the Second Army to Serbia *immediately.* He even stripped a corps from Echelon A and ordered Straub somehow to move it to Serbia as well.[14]

Berlin was even more stunned by Conrad's freelancing. With Russia's general mobilization under way, the kaiser wired Franz Joseph on July 31 and warned him not to "fragment your main forces with any simultaneous offensive against Serbia." Moltke had become so wedded to the Schlieffen Plan—the notion of a fast

war in France followed by a leisurely destruction of the Russians—
that he had announced in April 1913 that German plans for a war
with Russia alone would no longer be entertained or even updated.
That this was stupid and irresponsible in no way diminished the
need now for all Austrian hands on deck in the east. Despite their
numbers, the Russians would be deploying with the biggest wet-
lands in Europe at their back: the Pripet marshes, swamps and
floodlands that extended from Belarus to Ukraine. "Assemble
your *whole* force against Russia," Moltke enjoined Conrad from
Berlin. "Drive the [Russians] into the Pripet marshes and drown
them there."[15]

Colonel Straub also protested the Serbian detour—"technically impossible" was his verdict—and requested "a few days'
grace" to reroute the torrent of trains and horse-drawn wagons.[16]
Having already squandered a month since the assassination of
Franz Ferdinand, Conrad now agreed to squander another week.
He announced the Austro-Hungarian mobilization against Russia
on July 31 but named August 4 as the first day of mobilization. He
would not begin meeting with his army commanders until August
2. The old saw "Austria, always a day late, with an army and an
idea" was on everyone's lips as time ticked by and Austria's momentum ebbed.

When the Russians and Germans proclaimed general mobilization at midday on July 31, Conrad found himself in the entirely predictable predicament of having routed half of his army
to Serbia for a war with a minor Balkan state. As usual, Emperor
Franz Joseph had no idea what was really going on. He assured
the kaiser that he was sending "the great majority" of his army
against Russia, but, as in most things, he was foggy on the details. The Germans weren't—the Second Army (Echelon B) was
supposed to anchor the right wing of the Austrian position in
Galicia, not invade Serbia—and the Germans were thunderstruck
by the slow-motion revelation of Conrad's *real* plan, as opposed
to the one he had seemed to agree upon with Moltke in May. It
was, of course, partly their fault. Germany's military attaché in
Vienna discovered to his amazement on August 1 that despite the
succession of international crises since 1908, Moltke and Conrad

had never agreed upon "measures to coordinate operations against Russia." Indeed, no "intimate arrangements" of any kind had been set down, merely sketchy oral agreements.[17]

Conrad, who had just blithely told his corps commanders that "all instructions remained in force despite the intervention of Russia," now phoned an astonished Colonel Straub and asked whether "the prevailing Balkan mobilization could be transformed into a Russian one." This was an abashed way of asking whether the five corps he'd ordered to Serbia on Thursday could be redirected to Galicia on Friday. Straub recoiled in horror; he had 140 trains a day rolling along seven lines to Galicia and four lines to the Balkans.[18] He had toiled through the night to implement Conrad's revisions and had already put 132 troop trains with the first echelons of the Second Army on the rails to Serbia. To undo the latest operation was nearly impossible; Straub (who had been vacationing in Dalmatia until now) promised that were it to be attempted, there would be "chaos on the railway lines for which I cannot take responsibility." Even if the trains could be stopped and reversed back to their depots, Conrad knew that an already demoralized army would become even more so if subjected to such a ludicrous about-face. Major Emil Ratzenhofer, head of the general staff's Russia Group, noted that the Second Army continued on its way to spare the telegraphs, which were overheating with conflicting orders, but also the fighting spirit of the troops: "we feared moral, political, and disciplinary damage; the men's confidence in the professional competence of their leaders would have suffered."[19]

Conrad, Straub, and Ratzenhofer—already bidding to rescue their postwar reputations—would have been wiser to fear what crushing defeats in Serbia and Russia, caused in part by their unruly mobilization, would do to the men's confidence. Redirected trains were nothing compared to lost battles. Conrad later professed to be surprised and let down by the rigidity of his railroads, but they were *his* railroads in times of war, and, in fact, he had known since July 1913—when Plan R + B had last been gamed—that he would have no flexibility. He had told the emperor in March 1913 that Echelon B could be fluidly shifted between the fronts; in July, a full year before the July Crisis, his railway experts had assured him that it really couldn't. In other words, Conrad would have to take the most prudent course early on, for once embarked, the men could not easily be turned around.[20]

But Conrad was never decisive. He hated making decisions because they committed him to a single course for which he might be held responsible. And he had never been prudent—not in his politics, not in his personal life, and not in war. Just as he would later attempt to recast every one of his defeats as the fault of incompetent diplomats or subordinates, he tried to recast the bungled mobilization of 1914 as the fault of Straub and Ratzenhofer. But as with the battles, it was *his* fault. He vacillated all through the July Crisis and then leaned hesitantly toward Serbia until he realized too late that he was making a terrible mistake, at which point he leaned back in the direction of Russia, but too late to undo the damage he'd already done on that front.

Ultimately, Conrad was more showman than strategist, and he now made a show of sticking with his Serbian plan even as he scrambled to undo it. Conrad had planned to lead the invasion of Serbia; with his presence required on the Russian front, he reluctantly conferred command of the Serbian operation on his old rival Potiorek. In August, he offered Potiorek an extra army to crush Serbia, but it came with strings attached; Conrad told Potiorek that the Second Army could be used only "for demonstrative purposes" during its transitional week on the Danube. The Second Army's staff merely raised a sardonic eyebrow at Conrad's bumbling: "One hoped to knock Serbia out quickly and then turn all forces against Russia—only this can explain the peculiar conduct of the high command." To Moltke, Conrad's general headquarters (*Armeeoberkommando* or AOK) pledged a prompt offensive against Russia with only temporarily diminished *deutsche Treue* (Germanic loyalty).[21] Meeting with the three generals he was placing in command of the armies in Galicia at the war ministry on Sunday August 2, Conrad ordered them to deploy their armies as fast as possible. Things that were lacking—reservists, guns, ammunition, supplies—would follow.

The astonished army commanders were handed notebooks from Conrad's Operations Bureau with their marching orders:

a deployment from the mouth of the San southeast to Lemberg and the Dniester, Dankl's First Army on the left, Auffenberg's Fourth in the center, Brudermann's Third on the right. The Second Army—which was supposed to nudge up on Brudermann's right, defending his southern flank at Lemberg and resting its own right flank on the Dniester, thus ensuring a measure of protection for the army against the Russian steamroller—was nowhere to be seen, for it was still chugging toward Serbia, against all expectations. That left Brudermann's Third Army in the air, without flank protection, ripe for envelopment by the numerically superior Russians.[22]

The Great War on the Eastern Front had not even begun, yet a glance at the map suggested that the Austro-Hungarians were going to lose it, thanks to Conrad's floundering. Auffenberg was troubled by the meeting with Conrad on August 2, remarking that the chief was importing into the field army the same staff culture of secrecy and opacity—officers called it Conrad's "Japanese style"—that had nourished the Redl Affair. Expecting a detailed exploration of the monarchy's military objectives, the relationship with the German army, and the balance between the Austrian armies aimed at Russia and Serbia, the Austrian generals bound for Russia (those destined for the Balkans were not present) got nothing of the sort. Conrad kept the meeting brief and spoke only of the "deployment areas" where each army would assemble. Beyond that, he offered *nothing*—not what they'd do once deployed, and nothing on the Russians or on Austrian plans in the event of success or failure.

What the generals immediately noticed were the revised deployment areas. Plan R + B had always pushed the Austrian army as far east as it could travel on the rails, to eastern Galicia, where it would be positioned to strike an early blow against the Russians. Conrad had quietly amended the plan in March 1914, pulling the whole army back in a *Rückverlegung* or "backward movement" to western Galicia. Why he thought this was a good idea is a mystery; the Austrians' only advantage in a war with the Russian colossus was a hasty attack. Moving the Austrian army all the way back to Cracow and the San River meant that it would either concede

Russia time to complete its mobilization or have to march needlessly over ground that it could have crossed in trains.[23]

Clearly Conrad had bungled everything; to fight the war he wanted against beatable Serbia, he had simply ignored the war he didn't want against unbeatable Russia, and prevaricated throughout to confuse everyone. Instead of having thirteen corps against Russia, he found himself with eight. Straub and Ratzenhofer had assured him that they could get the five missing corps— the four of the Second Army as well as Echelon A's III Corps—out to Galicia by August 23, but in fact, only two of the five corps had staggered into place on the Eastern Front by September 8, too late and too tired to intervene effectively in any of the pivotal battles.[24]

Unaware of Conrad's flip-flopping, Potiorek was stunned by the chief's admission on August 6 that the Second Army would not be lingering in the Balkans after all, but would instead make for the Russian front as soon as the railways were clear. Still, Potiorek was hopeful. Publicly, he promised "tactical success": he would envelop the Serbs with the two armies left to him.[25] Privately, Potiorek raged at Conrad's treachery: "How the supreme command could arrive at such a radical change in its decisions is a mystery to me," Potiorek grumbled. "It reveals much as to the functioning of the machine."[26]

The machine was already falling apart under the strain of a mobilization that assembled and equipped nearly two million men—the active-duty establishment, the trained reserve, and the untrained *Ersatzreservisten*—and then shipped them off to various, shifting points. And the Austro-Hungarian army took more work to assemble, outfit, and deploy than most. Because the army had been kept so lamentably small in peacetime, 75 percent of it was not even in uniform when Emperor Franz Joseph declared war. More than 1.5 million reservists had to be found, equipped, and formed into units that could be moved to the front.[27] No places could be found initially for the untrained reserves in the 106 standing regiments, which meant that in garrison towns all over the monarchy tens of thousands of men milled around for days and even weeks awaiting uniforms, arms and orders. A typical division—like the 9th, assembling in Prague and destined for

Serbia—reported chaos by the third mobilization day: "All saddles had to be replaced, and we're short 25,000 coffee rations, 40,000 salt-meat portions, and 1,700 kilos of zwieback." At every halt between Prague and the Drina River crossings, troops went missing "because they confused the departure time," or so they said.[28] Had they wanted to, the troops could have *walked* to overtake the trains that had left them behind. With exaggerated military caution forbidding any one train to travel at a speed greater than that of the slowest train traversing the worst track in the monarchy, the average speed of Austro-Hungarian mobilization trains was not much faster than a bicycle's. Overall, the Habsburg army took a month to deploy its strength to Galicia and Serbia, hardly the Germanic efficiency envisioned in Plan R + B.[29]

Conrad was still in Vienna, oblivious to the spreading shambles. On August 15, he had an audience with the old emperor at Schönbrunn. "God willing, all will go well, but even if it all goes wrong, I'll see it through," was the emperor's less than stirring farewell. The next morning, Conrad and Archduke Friedrich boarded an early train at Vienna's North Station and began rolling east toward the San River fortress of Przemysl, where the AOK would establish its headquarters. Conrad had lingered long on the platform with his mistress, Gina, before boarding; he had clasped her hands in his and demanded that she promise to secure a divorce and marry him "after the war."[30] As they traveled east, Joseph Redlich, Conrad's political advisor, noted the graffiti scribbled on the walls and railroad cars that they passed: a crude drawing of a gorilla with the caption "The Czar in civilian dress"; a gallows, with the tsar swinging from the noose above the words "The Russians and the Serbs, we'll beat 'em all."[31] Despite decades of decline, the Austrians still fancied themselves superior in every way to the Russian bear.

Trying to supervise the Eastern and Balkan fronts from Przemysl on the San, Conrad exhorted Potiorek to put aside his daily cavils about missing beef portions, bridging equipment, medicine, and telephones and focus instead on defeating the Serbs. He assumed that the Serbs would attack through Uzice toward Sarajevo and the Montenegrins toward Mostar, making some preemptive

Austrian attack desirable. On August 9, he wrote that "under no circumstances can we afford a defeat in the Balkans." It would be humiliating and would convince the "wavering states"—Italy, Greece, Bulgaria, and Rumania—to remain neutral, or even enter the war against Austria. ("I've just had the Bulgarian military attaché in my office," Conrad added, "and I told him that Bulgaria will be committing suicide if it doesn't attack Serbia at once.")

While the Serbs mobilized and twenty Austrian divisions marched up to the Drina and the Sava, Potiorek wrote long letters to the director of the war archive in Vienna, like this one on August 8: "I am going to be sending you daily evidence of my leadership methods, so that you can use them in the official history that you will be writing this winter." Potiorek's vanity was one of the only things not pricked by Conrad's flailing mobilization. Potiorek assumed that the war would be short and victorious and that he would play a hero's role. Each day he wrote the war archive director twenty pages of "daily events" for a future official history, including bluff Radetzkyan bromides such as this one: "The only difference between an Army Commander in war and peace is that in war the Commander spends even more time behind his desk and speaking on the phone!"[32] How would *this* commander know? Potiorek had never experienced war or combat.

When no Serbian attack came, Conrad, who was unaware of Potiorek's daily correspondence with posterity, wrote the Balkan commander on August 14 to urge an attack across the Drina with the Fifth and Sixth Armies, before the Second Army withdrew entirely: "Make *some* use of its presence and ability to demonstrate on the Sava-Danube." At first glance, the task that Conrad was setting Potiorek seemed simple enough. The Serbs—who drafted men in three classes, two "levies" of young men and a third of older ones—could mobilize three hundred thousand men in the first and second levies, and adding the third levy yielded a total of four hundred thousand men. But while their numbers were impressive, their armaments told a different story: there were just 381 rapid-fire field guns for the entire force, and crippling shortages of munitions, machine guns, and rifles in all three classes. In many Serbian units, one-third of the troops would have no rifle at all. Second-levy divisions had just half the field artillery of the first levy, the third levy even less.[33] Here was cause for some Austrian optimism, even if war with Russia was a certainty. Potiorek's force alone in August 1914 was equal to the entire Serbian army, had an empire of fifty-three million behind it, and had more guns and ammo.[34] Everyone in Vienna was confident of victory, at least on the Serbian front.

Reports of the first battles in France arrived as the Austrians struggled to deploy Conrad's North Army to Galicia and Potiorek's South Army to Serbia. General Viktor Dankl only arrived in Tarnow in southeastern Poland on August 10, where he halted briefly, and then continued on to Rzeszow, where he noted that his First Army lacked everything.[35] Joining his Fourth Army on the San River, General Auffenberg complained of the unexpected hostility of the Austrian population: "At Jaroslau, Dobromil, Rawa-Ruska, etc., not enough is being done to repress unreliable elements," chiefly Ukrainian priests and schoolteachers— *Moskalophilen,* Moscowphiles—who were betraying the location and strength of Austrian units to the Russians. Conrad ordered a brutal crackdown against all of these "hostile elements." Agitators and traitors were to be summarily shot or hanged. This must have been sobering, for the Ukrainians of this region had historically been the monarchy's most loyal people.[36]

Moving more briskly than Conrad, the Germans were stunned by the casualties sustained by their seven armies in France. The German forces there were divided into two groups, one operating between Metz and the Vosges, the other driving on Paris through the Meuse defile. The ferocity of the fighting in all sectors had left them reeling. Entire units had been wiped out by French artillery firing from covered positions, a result that the Germans reciprocated each time the French attacked. Both armies had assumed that this war would play out like the Franco-Prussian War, with large but manageable casualties and sharp flanking maneuvers, but this time the killing was on an industrial scale and the troops, who were too numerous on both sides to be flanked, were driven into trenches. German officers complained that there was no glory to be had in this artillery-driven *Maschinenkrieg,* or "war of machines."[37] A German cavalry officer mourned the new era: "In these fields, where Roman-Gothic legions once clashed with the riders of Attila, there is today only deadly battery fire, delivered invisibly and anonymously from miles away."[38]

At the as-yet-unblooded Russian headquarters in Belarus, optimism still reigned. Grand Duke Nikolai, the tsar's uncle, who had been cavalry inspector before the war and now found himself supreme commander at the Russian Stavka or general headquarters, spoke breezily of annexing Habsburg Galicia and grinding Bismarck's Reich down to its original harmless parts: "The German Empire must cease to exist and be divided up into a group of states, each of which will be happy with its own little court." A foreign ministry official at Stavka joked to the gathered generals, "You soldiers should be pleased that we've arranged such a nice war for you." One of the generals replied: "Let's wait and see whether it'll be such a nice war after all."[39]

CHAPTER 6

Misfits

IT WAS NOT LOOKING TO BE A NICE WAR in Austro-Hungarian headquarters, where Conrad was the proverbial one-eyed man in the kingdom of the blind. The emperor had appointed Archduke Friedrich (Fritzl) commander in chief of all Habsburg troops in the field. The post had been reserved for Franz Ferdinand, but he lay dead and the new crown prince, Franz Ferdinand's twenty-six-year-old nephew Archduke Karl, only a major when war broke out, was judged too callow. Although the ruddy, mustachioed fifty-eight-year-old Fritzl looked the part of army commander and had excellent genes—he was the grandson of an earlier Archduke Karl, who had defeated Napoleon at Aspern in 1809, and the nephew of Archduke Albrecht, who had defeated the Italians at Custoza in 1866—Friedrich himself was a run-of-the-mill Habsburg, bluff but diffident, and unlikely to curb any of Conrad's wild impulses. Friedrich had only soldiered in maneuvers, and there badly, managing to lose in all scenarios, a French report of summer maneuvers near Budapest remarking that "he allowed himself to be taken in the rear so maladroitly by his adversary that the referees had to intervene to rescue him; his corps was annihilated."[1] Auffenberg was stunned by Friedrich's appointment, remarking that "his big responsibilities as high commander far exceeded his small abilities."[2]

Conrad had seized the opportunity presented by the assassination to begin the process of strategic "dynamization" he had been advocating for years. No fewer than eight corps—a puzzling detachment in view of the now certain war with Russia—would strike into Serbia and destroy the royal army. On July 29, Austro-Hungarian monitors floating in the Sava and the Danube had opened preliminary fire on Belgrade, inflicting little damage on the Serbs, not least because the Serbian government had long since decamped to Nis and declared the capital an "open city."[3] Ground troops would be needed to complete the mission, which had been hopefully characterized in Vienna as a mere "punitive expedition," yet just as Austria's Second Army detrained and deployed on the frontiers of Serbia, Conrad announced that it would shortly be moved along to the Russian Front.

Archduke Friedrich preceded the sweaty men of General Eduard von Böhm-Ermolli's Second Army, who were crammed into stifling railway cars—forty-two men or eight horses per car—as they wended their way around the monarchy. Conrad had planned to locate general headquarters (AOK) on the Serbian front, but Russia's entirely predictable mobilization necessitated its immediate transfer to Galicia. Thus, Fritzl moved his headquarters to Przemysl just six days after scouting the Serbian frontier. The Good Soldier Svejk described the jumble of conflicting orders: "They never knew in which hole on what battlefield they wanted us in."[4]

"They," of course, were the Austrian brass, Fritzl and Conrad in Galicia and Potiorek in Sarajevo. With the Second Army, Potiorek would have 400,000 troops. Without it, he would have 290,000, not nearly enough to inflict a ruinous defeat on Serbia. The Serbs, after all, deployed 400,000 men when fully mobilized, plus 40,000 Montenegrins and whatever *komitadjis* turned out. Austria's Fifth and Sixth Armies, already in place, were "weak" armies, each counting just two corps, not the customary four. Until August 6, Potiorek had believed that he would have eight corps to work with. On that day, Conrad informed him that he would have the four corps of the Second Army only for "local cooperation" along the Sava, and only until August 18, when they would be moved to Galicia. Potiorek was furious, all the more so as he looked closely at the troops he *did* have for the long haul. The hot, tired men of the Fifth Army were malingering and taking liberties with the civilians they encountered near the Serbian border, provoking furious rebukes from headquarters: "The beating and imprisoning of innocent Austrian civilians must stop; the *k.u.k.* army must inspire fear and respect, but must be chivalrous and must not descend into evil and inhuman acts."[5]

Potiorek and Conrad seemed more interested in scoring victories against each other than against the Serbs. They had been rivals for years, both bidding for the post of general staff chief in 1906, and each acutely distrustful of the other ever since. Potiorek had toiled for years in Beck's back offices, doing the hard work of the general staff while Beck chased money, decorations, and women, and he had fully expected to be rewarded with the top job, only to see it given to Conrad.[6] His resentment of the injustice never faded, and in August 1914, Potiorek took Conrad's decision to shift the Second Army to Galicia as a personal attack, not a strategic one. He interpreted it as sabotage of his own Balkan war effort, and immediately began lobbying the Hofburg—where Potiorek had warm relations with General Bolfras—for independence from Conrad's AOK, which he secured on August 21. The seventy-six-year-old Bolfras, who had been decorated in Bosnia in 1878 and made a Hofburg adjutant ten years later, wielded considerable power in the army. He was the emperor's agent and well liked for his mild, conciliatory manner.[7] He also had a clear favorite in the Conrad-Potiorek feud: he viewed Conrad with suspicion and considered Potiorek a useful brake on the general staff chief. A Hofburg that had unfailingly chosen badly chose badly again. For all of his faults, Conrad was the overall army commander. The Hofburg had no business barging between him and his field generals, but it did. Rescued by the emperor, at least for now, Potiorek set to work figuring out how to accomplish the "punitive expedition" against Serbia along a four-hundred-mile border with poor communications and just a quarter of a million troops.

As in most things, Potiorek and Conrad had contrasting views on the question of how to deal with Serbia. Whereas Conrad envisioned a brisk operation in the second week of August, with Potiorek leading the Fifth Army across the lower Drina toward Valjevo, where it would encircle and destroy the Serbs fixed in place between Belgrade and the Macva by the Second Army, Potiorek had an entirely different conception of the unfolding campaign. Conrad saw the Fifth Army as the hammer crushing the Serbs on the anvil of the Second Army; Potiorek saw the Fifth Army, untrained in mountain warfare and unlikely to make much headway on the lower Drina, as the anvil against which the Serbs might be hammered by the Sixth Army, which would cross the upper Drina around Visegrad and then knife into the flank of the Serbian forces lured by the Fifth Army.

A more muddled plan of campaign couldn't be imagined. Conrad was demanding "a thrust into the Serbian heartland," while Potiorek was for lying on the ropes along the lower Drina until the Serbs descended and offered an unguarded flank to a Sixth Army that would require weeks to traverse friendly but undeveloped Bosnia and then get through the mountain wastes on the Lim and upper Drina.[8] Both plans were built on illusions and a deep ignorance of terrain and enemy movements. The Habsburg army hadn't prioritized aircraft before the war—procuring a fifth as many as the Germans, a third as many as the French, and half as many as the Russians—and so they lacked the surest way to track Serbian marches.[9] Conrad's plan assumed that the Second Army would draw off large numbers of Serbian troops, even though the Serbs *knew* (from Russian intelligence) that it was departing. Potiorek's plan assumed that the Fifth Army would survive despite the departure of the Second Army on its left and the slow arrival of the Sixth Army on its mountainous right. Most of the Second Army would be departing for Galicia on August 18, yet the Sixth Army would not complete its mobilization around Sarajevo until August 13 and would not arrive on the Drina before August 20. The Hofburg, which might have imposed a single direction on the army commanders, was lost in its own romantic reveries: "We are living through the lull before the storm," Bolfras wrote Potiorek. "I still cry: 'more enemies, more honor!'"[10]

The Fifth Army began crossing the Drina on August 12. Potiorek lamented the "difficult terrain" of the Macva region, made all the more difficult by a lack of bridging equipment, but told Conrad that he couldn't simply "sit and wait." He'd have less than a week to exploit the reciprocal action of the Second Army, and a week was not much time on ground like this: wooded, hilly, and buried in tall rows of corn, perfect ground not only for Serbian infantry but for Serbian guerrillas as well, the *komitadji* partisans, who had played a big role in the Balkan Wars and were thirsting for a part in this one as well.

Through it all, Potiorek remained weirdly sanguine. "The desk is his favored terrain," colleagues said of the sixty-one-year-old Potiorek, and it was true. The career *Schreibtischmensch* (desk jockey) remained in Sarajevo with his adjutant Merizzi, making no effort to familiarize himself with the Drina front. Potiorek had never been regarded as a leader of men. As the jovial Beck's deputy, he had been noted for his social awkwardness. Fellow officers noted his weakness at riding and with women. They called him a *Weiberfeind*, an enemy of women, either because he didn't like them or because he loved the office too much. Some whispered that he and Merizzi, twenty years younger and the son of an old friend, were a couple. Potiorek had made Merizzi his wing adjutant in 1903 and they had been together ever since. In Appel's judgment, both of them were misfits and afraid of their own troops, "*weltfremd und truppenscheu*," tending to hole up in their offices instead of acquainting themselves with their units. They created, as Appel said before the war, an "ivory tower" in the Sarajevo governor's palace that took no interest in the world outside. Everyone regarded Potiorek as a pompous ass, famous for his cold silence—broken only by mirthless laughter and vicious sarcasm—and his pretensions. He was easily caricatured in the popular press as having perfected the *Moltkeangesicht*, the mien of a Moltke. Grave and somber, Potiorek would be "a god of war only so long as ink, not blood, was flowing." In 1898, at the age of forty-five, Potiorek had commanded a brigade at Budapest, and a junior officer had said of him, "He bore the stigma of coming greatness on

Potiorek had perfected the image of a brilliant staff officer, and was taken as such by everyone except his rival Conrad, but he was vain and militarily inexperienced. As Karl Kraus accurately predicted, "Potiorek would be a god of war only so long as ink, not blood, was flowing."
CREDIT: National Archives

his forehead; everything he said was clear and true, and no criticism could penetrate his laconic, closed, unapproachable self." He lived in a "self-constructed world." This was most certainly not the man to command a messy war in the Balkans, and yet somehow, in its inimitable way, the Habsburg army had chosen him.[11]

Potiorek assumed that the guerrilla war against the *komitadjis* would be easy enough to stamp out with atrocities. Since 1878, Austria-Hungary had never shrunk from terror in policing the Balkans, and this war would be no exception. From the comfort of his former Ottoman palace, the Konak, Potiorek encouraged his corps and division commanders to proceed viciously: "The best method against the *komitadjis* is to kill them all, no quarter; kill the whole band down to the last man, then wipe out the village that harbored them and publicize the event widely."[12]

Potiorek was no less confident that he could crush the Serbian regulars too. Even if he missed his rendezvous with the Second Army—now a certainty—he continued to believe that the Serbs could be drawn down on the Fifth Army around Valjevo in large numbers and rolled up from the right flank by the late-arriving Sixth Army. He should have asked himself how the Fifth Army would even reach Valjevo. It would struggle just to cross the Drina, enjoyed no flank protection from the slow-moving Sixth Army, and would probably encounter entrenched Serbian guns and infantry in the hills between the Drina and the Serbian interior.

The Serbs, meanwhile, were not passively awaiting the Austro-Hungarian invasion. They had been actively planning for it since the Annexation Crisis of 1908. Serbia's commander in chief was the young regent, Crown Prince Alexander Karageorgevic, but the real decisions in army headquarters at Kragujevac were made by the army chief of staff, General Radomir Putnik, who had run the Serbian general staff and War Ministry since 1903. Although crippled by emphysema—Putnik would direct much of the war from a stretcher —the sixty-seven-year-old general was a shrewd strategist and a popular hero.

Taking the waters at the Austrian spa of Bad Gleichenberg in Styria when war broke out, Putnik was fortunate to have made it back to Serbia at all. Wheezing from his illness, he was detained while changing trains in Budapest on July 25, and released only after the quixotic intervention of Emperor Franz Joseph. Auffenberg was speechless: "Diplomatic relations had already been broken; we had captured the commander of the enemy army—a capable and iconic figure—and we let him go! Here was yet another proof of our political and military stupidity."[13] While Putnik's release was negotiated in Budapest, his aides dynamited his office safe in Belgrade to get hold of the only copy of Serbia's war plan with Austria-Hungary. Serbian officers, meanwhile, rushed to deploy their army for its third war in as many years.

Though the Austrians tended to sneer at Serbian "backwardness," the Serbs mobilized efficiently. Serbian recruits reported to the nearest of five "division districts," each of which could raise as many as four divisions: a first-levy division (men ages twenty-one to thirty-one), a second-levy division (ages thirty-two to thirty-eight), a third levy (those thirty-nine to forty-five), and a "final defense" division of boys eighteen to twenty and men over forty-five. Serbia was so poor that only the first-levy divisions received complete uniforms and modern rifles. The second, third, and fourth levies wore their own clothing and more often than not got single-shot black-powder rifles from the 1870s. After two wars in quick succession, everyone and everything was worn out or in short supply: officers, NCOs, technical troops, artillery, machine guns, shells, bullets, guns, horses, wagons, uniforms, tents, and kitchens. Plus, an ill-timed transition from the German 7 mm Mauser rifle to the Russian 7.62 mm Mosin-Nagant meant that even the first-levy divisions would not have a standard rifle or cartridge. Indeed, the Serbian army found itself with several different rifles and calibers in 1914, the Mauser and the Mosin-Nagant plus older Mausers captured from Turkey in the First Balkan War and 8 mm Männlichers captured from the Bulgarians in the Second Balkan War. Putnik, sent home by the Austrians the long way via Rumania, where he contracted pneumonia atop his emphysema, alighted finally at Serbian headquarters in Kragujevac on August 5.[14]

Putnik's deputy, General Zivojin Misic, had completed the deployment of the Serbian army in the chief's absence. This was no mean feat, as much of the army had to be brought north from the newly annexed Turkish areas of Macedonia and Kosovo, which had Europe's worst railways, having been constructed and maintained by the notoriously shoddy and corrupt Oriental Railway Society. Serbian locomotives and rolling stock, inadequate within the smaller borders of 1912, were thoroughly overstretched in the enlarged nation of 1914, all the more so because Serbia's coal had to be imported and was in short supply like everything else. Serbian combat divisions lacked everything: A third to half of the men in even the first levy's divisions had no rifle. Half of the army's battalions had no machine guns. The army's cavalry, artillery, and supply trains lacked horses. Only a fraction of the men received uniforms; the rest had to make do with an army cap and a tunic. Boots were unavailable. Instead, the troops were given *opanci,* the leather (in some cases) or cardboard (in most cases) curled-toe moccasin worn by the Balkan peasant.[15]

Prime Minister Pasic, having acceded reluctantly to war, was stunned by the appearance of this armed mob: "without clothes, shoes or tents." The Serbian officers were less worried. They would have agreed with the British military attaché in Belgrade, who noted that these poorly shod Serbs were "brave, enduring . . . and can live on next to nothing under conditions which would appall the average Britisher." The American minister was no less admiring: "Give the Serbian soldier bread and an onion, and he is satisfied."[16] Knowing this, Serbian officers had been rehearsing a war with the better-equipped Austrians since Vienna's occupation of Bosnia in 1878, with staff rides and exercises along the Drina, Sava, and Danube fronts every year. After the annexation crisis of 1908, the Serbs had settled on a firm plan: defend the kingdom until the broader European situation clarified, then take the offensive when Austria diverted troops to other fronts.[17]

Knowing that Russian intervention ensured just a narrow window, if any, for Austrian offensive operations in Serbia, General Misic deployed the three Serbian armies to counter all possible Austrian attack scenarios. His poverty of arms made the task especially difficult. Although every Serbian division was supposed to have forty-eight guns, the first-levy divisions rarely mustered more than thirty and second-levy divisions were lucky to scrounge a dozen, many of them obsolete French cannon from the 1880s with no crew shield or recoil mechanism.[18] Against this force, even Potiorek's South Army looked formidable.

Putnik and Misic placed the Serbian armies in northern Serbia along the lateral railway line from Valjevo to Palanka. The Second Army (four divisions), with the four divisions of the Third Army on its left, was assigned the heaviest task: to absorb and then counterattack the main Austrian blow. If the main blow descended from the north across the Sava, the Second Army would hit its right flank. If it came from the west across the Drina, the Second Army would knife into its left flank. The Third Army would join these counterattacks, or stand guard against Potiorek's Sixth Army if it arrived sooner than expected. The Serbian First Army—four infantry divisions and a cavalry division at Arangjelovac—would function as a general reserve for use against any of the encroaching Austrian armies.

Potiorek's First Invasion of Serbia
August 1914

Potiorek began the war on August 12, or tried to. Lacking most of its bridging equipment, General Liborius Frank's Fifth Army straggled up to the broad, fast-flowing Drina and . . . stopped. The summer heat was stupefying. Most of the men were reservists and were thirsty and overloaded with sixty pounds of gear, much of it (brushes, boot polish, and songbooks) superfluous. The area was a tactical nightmare: swampy, overlooked by high river banks on the Serbian side, and cluttered with woods, bushes, and cornfields. A brigade of the Austro-Hungarian 36th

Division sent half battalions across the Drina in boats to establish a bridgehead of sorts, but each boatload was greeted with withering fire from Serbian regulars and *komitadjis* on the riverbank. Still, a few Austrian companies clung to the east bank and even deployed a regimental band, which played the "Prinz Eugenmarsch" to keep spirits up as Serbian shells plunged in and machine guns chattered from nearby woods and cornfields that grew right down to the water's edge.[19]

The Austro-Hungarian Second Army was supposed to build its own bridgehead at Sabac on the Sava to draw off large numbers of Serbs, but it discovered that it had left behind its bridging equipment in the haste to mobilize. Frank's Fifth Army thus began crossing the Drina between Zvornik and Bijelina—where the river was broad and eighteen feet deep in some places—without any protection on either flank. General Arthur Giesl's VIII Corps required two entire days to clap together pontoon bridges and cross the river, against light Serbian resistance. Aviators overhead and officers on the ground described utter confusion on the Austrian side, as every stray Serbian shot from across the river ignited panic in the green Austrian ranks, with troops wildly returning fire (at nothing) and "horses breaking loose and galloping round and round the camp." When bridges were opened, the inexperienced Austro-Hungarian troops rushed onto them all at the same time, shutting down the bridges until order could be restored.[20] Smelling weakness, General Paul Jurisic-Sturm's Serbian Third Army stole closer to the Drina River crossings and deployed its guns.

The Austrian Second Army did push elements of the 29th Division across the Sava at Mitrovica on August 12, and more units crossed a hastily arranged pontoon bridge at Klenak on August 13. Vienna was briefly delirious with joy, newsboys bawling "Great victory at Sabac!" and Austrians eagerly snapping up the afternoon papers to read about it.[21] But with the VIII Corps still fussing with its Drina bridges, General Adolf von Rhemen's XIII Corps attacked on August 14 with only a smattering of Giesl's troops on its flank. Troops and officers immediately discovered that their camouflage "pike gray" (*hechtgrau*) uniforms were not very camouflage at all. Blue-gray instead of the more serviceable green-gray used by the Germans, they were too bright for any theater outside the boulder-strewn Italian Alps (for which they had been procured in 1908) and made fine targets in the lush green Macva.[22]

General Heinrich Haustein, commander of Austria's 72nd Brigade, noted that his men were "immediately demoralized by Serbian rifle fire as well as the lacerating impact of the enemy's 12-centimeter shells." In their mixed bag of old and new artillery, the Serbs had fifty-four 12 cm Schneider quick-firing howitzers, a battery of which appeared here to take Haustein under fire. Ordered to clear the road east from Ljesnica, Haustein's frightened brigade wilted. "Because of the poor physical conditioning of my men," Haustein wrote, "I had to rest them." While the units around them surged up and down their tracks, Haustein's brigade sat panting in the summer heat. When they finally began to move in the late afternoon, mounting toward the fortified village of Dobric, they discovered that they had no bullets. Their ammunition wagons had vanished.[23]

The 71st Brigade, moving into line beside the 72nd, had ammunition, but no hope against the thousand-foot heights around Plec; as the Austro-Hungarian troops struggled toward their objective, they were cut down by Serbian enfilading fire from entrenched machine guns as well as artillery from front, flank, and rear. The Serbs had even thought to hang hand grenades from the trees along the cart tracks, which they would explode with a rifle shot as the Austrians passed. "*Wenig gemütlich*, pretty uncomfortable," was one officer's recollection: "My men quickly lost all self-confidence."[24] Another Austrian officer noted that his men had been "worn down even before the fighting by tales of the *komitadji*, hunger, thirst, fatigue, lack of sleep and the unfamiliar noises of battle." The 16th Regiment pronounced itself "wiped out—only rabble made it off the hill."[25] The 72nd Brigade was terrified by the fall of heavy shell, the rattle of machine guns, and the rifle fire, which was so much more demoralizing because the Austrians felt its impact but saw nothing but bare slopes. "The enemy were so well entrenched that we couldn't even *see* them," Haustein reported.[26]

The 42nd Honvéd Division crossed the Drina at Zvornik with orders to push up onto the high ground at Krupanj to facilitate an eventual junction with the Sixth Army on its right and to cover the right flank of the VIII Corps troops engaged on the Cer Planina at Tekeris. With a well-armed division coming at them, the Serbs— first-levy troops from the Drina district—initially gave ground, falling back to Zavlaka. But as they interrogated their Honvéd prisoners, they began to understand that this was a rotten army. "We took five prisoners, three Hungarians and two Croats; they said they came from the 27th, 28th, and 32nd Regiments. Of the battle-worthiness of the 32nd, a Hungarian said they had poor morale, because the troops were city boys from Budapest, and that only peasants fight well. The officers," he added, "have to drive the troops into battle with their pistols. They spend their whole time menacing their own men, not fighting ours." The Hungarian unit had come from Osijek, and just the twelve-mile march to the trains that took them to Serbia had knocked out a third of the regiment with heat exhaustion.[27]

To the left of these men, VIII Corps' better-equipped 9th Division also crossed and went into action on August 14. General Giesl, who had hoped to expunge the shame of his long patronage of Colonel Redl, now saw that he wouldn't. He summarized the plight of his army: "non-stop battle, no water, searing heat, extreme exhaustion."[28] The brigades of Giesl's 9th Division were immediately set upon by Serbian partisans and regulars, who shot them up day and night. Inexperienced in modern warfare, the Austro-Hungarians moved at night with railroad lanterns in hand and on their wagons to light the way, and professed astonishment when the Serbs began shooting at the illuminated targets. The Austrians subsequently discovered that the Serbs heard their units coming from miles away because they were so noisy—the troops and teamsters bawling at one another, and unsecured gear rattling and banging around.

When the Fifth Army's 9th Division did engage the Serbs, the men fired wildly. Orders went out to collect all ammunition from the dead and wounded because the living were firing so promiscuously, usually without hitting anything. Even spent cartridges were to be swept off the ground and returned to Austria for recycling.[29] Reports from officers deplored the *planlose Herausschiesserei*, aimless firing in all directions, and the tendency to fire into the blue without first registering a target. Yet unless they could actually hear them blazing away, neither Potiorek—still in his office in Sarajevo—nor his corps and divisional commanders even knew where their units were much of the time. If the officers were off the telegraph grid, which they usually were, they tended not to report, provoking an outcry from General Giesl: "If you have no telegraph connection, use messengers instead, but get through! It must not happen that the high command spends the entire day searching for a single column of troops!" Even messengers, however, would lose their way in the wilderness beyond the Drina. "I'm here with the horses of the general staff," one galloper wrote from Kozjak on August 15, "but the telegraph here is not working and I have no orders. There is gunfire all around us. Please tell us what to do."[30]

Although Conrad met that day, August 15, with the Bulgarian military attaché in Vienna to assure him that "all Austro-Hungarian troops are inside Serbia and holding all of the key heights," the reality was less inspiring.[31] The fire- and logistics-intensive modern age had certainly slowed marches down, from a peak of fourteen miles a day under Napoleon to about eight or nine miles a day under the Elder Moltke in 1870, but the men under Potiorek were hardly moving at all. These ugly clashes along the riverbanks between Ljesnica and Loznica augured badly for the brusque attack strategy of Conrad and Potiorek. One officer noted that "tough resistance from small Serbian units—vastly inferior to us in numbers—made us realize that Valjevo was a lot farther away than just five marches."[32] The encircler, in short, was fast becoming the encircled.

But Potiorek still assumed that he had the upper hand. Far from the depressing realities of the front, he took for granted that Putnik would pull back and split his army into purely defensive cordons to guard the main Serbian towns. On the contrary, the Serbian commander was taking stock of Potiorek's blundering and beginning to take some calculated risks.[33] With little to worry about at Sabac, where the broad Sava was a natural brake on what little activity Conrad had authorized, Putnik could mass nine divisions in the space between Sabac and Valjevo and turn the bulk of that force against the Fifth Army on the Drina. The fact that most of the Second Army remained on the left bank of the Sava instead of crossing into action on the right confirmed to Putnik that it was headed to Galicia.[34] This was the signal for Putnik to launch the next phase of Serbia's long-standing war plan: the counterattack that would follow any reduction or redeployment of an attacking Austrian army. Putnik now linked the fighting at Sabac (to hold off the rump of Second Army) and at Krupanj (to fend off the Sixth Army) with the fighting on the Cer Planina to destroy as much of the isolated Fifth Army as he could.

Putnik's intuition gave him a vital advantage against the Austrian Fifth Army. Conceptually, Putnik viewed Sabac-Tekeris-Krupanj as a single space; he grouped the three fields of battle into a single "Battle for the Cer Mountains," and hustled his troops into those forbidding hills by forced marches.[35] Thus it was that the Austro-Hungarian 9th Division discovered large numbers of Serbian infantry and artillery in trenches around Tekeris on the Cer Planina when it pushed inland on August 16. With their numbers fleshed out with so many untrained reservists, who had never been taught to fight in open skirmish order with their rifles, the Austro-Hungarian officers packed the men into storm columns and sent them up the steep slopes raked by machine guns and shrapnel. Unfortunately, the Austro-Hungarians had not been trained to entrench either, that being interpreted by their officers as cowardice. So most of the Austro-Hungarian infantry had simply discarded their entrenching equipment on the march and were now forced to scrape out shallow rifle pits with their fingers.[36]

Still, Potiorek reported to Emperor Franz Joseph that he was making progress—probably because the South Army commander remained in Sarajevo, following operations with pins on a map. Before the war, the French had judged Potiorek an armchair general, "an erudite, office-bound theoretician," and he was proving them right. "We've thrown the Serbs back on the lower Drina at Ljesnica; they are retreating in disorder. Prisoners tell us that they will make a last stand at Valjevo," Potiorek scribbled confidently from his palace.[37] Putnik had confirmed in the meantime that the Habsburg Second Army was indeed bound for Galicia, and now grasped that the Austrian Fifth Army's unsupported push over the Drina toward Valjevo was the main effort. He wheeled his three armies forward in echelon.[38] The First Army, on the right, could strike toward the Sava or Drina as needed. The Second Army, in the center, could mass everything it had against Frank's Fifth Army around Ljesnica and Loznica. And the Third Army moved into line around Krupanj, to hit Frank in the flank while keeping an eye peeled for the Sixth Army.

Serbian colonels and generals were twelve to fifteen years younger than their Austrian peers, and they all had recent battlefield experience.[39] They thrust forward hungrily, scenting a well-armed (by Balkan standards) but clumsy adversary. The three Serbian armies could detach strength as needed to smash back any Austrian advance anywhere on the arc.[40] Putnik had been unable to do much in the Macva because the Sava and Drina protected the Austrian flanks once they were across and made it difficult for Putnik to slide in behind either the Fifth or the Second Army. The Serbian staff chief identified the Cer Planina, the chain of two-thousand-foot hills overlooking the Drina crossings at Ljesnica and Loznica, as the key point. The Austrians would have to take the heights to move east and protect their supply lines and flanks.

Marching day and night to reach the hilltop village of Tekeris before the Austrians could arrive in force, two divisions of General Stepan Stepanovic's Second Army destroyed the Austrian 21st Landwehr Division as it struggled to ascend Mount Cer and take Tekeris on August 16. This was no easy achievement considering that some Serbian regiments—awaiting continually postponed arms shipments from Russia—had fewer than two thousand rifles for twice that number of men.[41] No matter: for the men of the 21st Landwehr Division, mainly Czechs recruited in Bohemia, it was an infernal baptism of fire. They had crossed the Drina on August 14 after five days on the train from Prague and marched up to the Cer Planina that day and the next under a blazing sun with full packs and no drinking water. They had passed the night not resting but shooting at their own patrols and Serbian attacks, the latter delivered in the dark from the tall corn. They finally contacted the Serbs on a fifteen-hundred-foot height at eleven o'clock in the morning on the sixteenth. Pulled by their officers, they swarmed uphill, the Germans among them crying, "*Hoch das Sieg! Hoch Seine Majestät Kaiser Franz Joseph!*" The Czechs advanced far less enthusiastically, feigning wounds and going to ground in alarming numbers.[42]

With the 21st Landwehr pinned on the slopes, the Serbs counterattacked the division all day and night, severing their connection to the 9th Division and shooting down their officers, until the division's two headless, unconnected brigades dissolved and slid backward toward the Drina. Survivors recalled the Serbs pushing in under cover of darkness, screaming in German, "Don't shoot, we're Croatian infantry!" and then opening up with their Mausers. Each time General Frank approached the front to take stock of his army, he noticed ammunition wagons and field kitchens swarming with Austrian troops trying to hitch a ride to the rear; each time an Austrian was struck by enemy fire, a dozen unwounded comrades would volunteer to walk him to the rear. The rare Serbian prisoner would attract a crowd of escorts back to headquarters as well. "Iron discipline!" Frank roared. "There are far too many shirkers and malingerers!"[43]

"The army of His Majesty the Emperor Franz Joseph covers itself in ridicule," the French paper *Figaro* hooted from Paris.[44] One of the Austrian generals was not surprised in the least. The Serbs were hardened peasants, he wrote; the Austro-Hungarians were "factory workers, artisans and clerks, men used to an easy life of beer, mild weather and a roof over their heads." With all of these things lacking in Serbia, the fight simply went out of them.[45]

In Sarajevo, Potiorek seemed oblivious to the disaster on the Drina. He was spending his time winnowing out more conspirators in the assassination plot, proudly telegraphing Finance Minister Bilinksi on August 16 that a witness had "incriminated three more conspirators in the archduke's murder—a Belgrade theologian, a Bosnian lawyer, and a waiter from Banja Luka."[46] While Potiorek made his case in Sarajevo, the battle for the Cer plateau was itself dissolving into a sort of military tribunal, as some

Austrians fought, but large numbers tried every means to desert. When one of the 9th Division's brigades was ordered to launch an attack to win breathing room for the other, only a single battalion answered the call, and it was immediately destroyed by artillery and machine guns. The general in charge of this donnybrook put the tragedy down to yet more "misunderstandings," and noted that each defeat on this front involved an isolated, abandoned Austro-Hungarian unit surrounded and taken in cross fires by the better-organized Serbs.[47]

The Austro-Hungarian 9th Division never got going. The men had exhausted themselves crossing the Drina, first under blistering sun, then under a day or two of heavy rain; they had been stalled on the riverbank for three entire days, sleeping in the open on their sodden coats and cursing their officers and supply service. When they finally went into action on Mount Cer, they were decimated by Serbian fire. They retreated under "hailstones the size of hazelnuts" on August 18, the men crawling under supply wagons to shelter from the weather and Serbian shells. A measure of warmth was achieved only when the quartermasters were ordered to burn everything they had carried over to the Serbian side of the river.[48] Field reports brimmed with incidents of Austro-Hungarian malingering, particularly the wounded terrifying the unwounded with "alarming accounts of the enemy." General Frank—characterized by a colleague as "a senile old pedant"—was not the optimal commander anyway, with or without help on his flanks. He ordered men and officers to swap "heroic stories instead of these dreadful ones." If the dreadful stories continued, he growled, troops would be executed on the spot "for the Crime of Cowardice."[49]

The rare Serbian POW gave the Austrians glimmers of hope. Interviewing one, an Austro-Hungarian officer concluded: "The Serbs are exhausted and badly supplied; the officers add to their confusion; they have just one machine gun per battalion." But at least half of Putnik's troops on any sector of this front were veterans of the Balkan Wars, and despite deficient artillery and an already emerging shell shortage, they stood their ground, patiently mowing down the Austrian attacks.[50] One victim of this dauntless Serbian fire was the commander of Austria's 21st Landwehr

Division, General Arthur Przyborski, who was anything but a battle-hardened veteran. His colleagues called him a *"Ringstrasse general"*—a soldier-bureaucrat who had married War Minister Schönaich's daughter and cut his teeth on paperwork, not battles. Przyborski never caught up with the pace of this chaotic, fast-moving fight.[51]

Repulsed at Jadar and the Cer Planina, the Fifth Army wavered. Famished Austrian troops scrounged along the banks of the Drina for anything edible, eating green corn and unripe melons. There was little to drink either; wells appeared to be poisoned, the water green, sour, and causing cholera symptoms after two or three days. "We never even saw our distant [supply] trains," one officer scoffed.[52] Much of the Austrian supply business had been bid to civilian subcontractors, and Frank now ordered his officers to "shoot their horses, destroy their wagons, and kill the drivers on the spot" if they didn't work harder and exhibit more courage. The Austrians troops, meanwhile, would simply have to go hungry, their (well-fed) division commander lecturing them that "the non-delivery of supplies is no excuse to consume your field rations. . . . Supply in war cannot be first-class all of the time."[53]

With the air rushing out of his little war, Potiorek pleaded for more help from the Second Army on August 16, but Conrad amended the request: "Do only as much as can be done without slowing your departure" to Galicia, he ordered.[54] The Second Army's 29th Division accordingly crossed the Sava at Sabac on August 16, fought a tentative battle with a Serbian division, and then retreated in the afternoon. Potiorek fumed, scoring Conrad for wasting the units of the Second Army "like drops of water," instead of sending them in one great wave. Had Potiorek actually been at the front instead of in his office in Sarajevo (where he was now pressing an investigation of thirty Serbian teenagers), he would have noticed the hopelessness of the Austrian attacks, whether in droplets or waves.[55]

Throughout this initial invasion, the Austro-Hungarians had failed to adapt to modern firepower. Whereas German infantry companies were already employing open-order tactics—one platoon spearheading any attack in a widely spaced skirmish line followed by two platoons in open-order echelons—Austro-Hungarian companies were simply rushing forward in an easily targeted huddle of men. "Neither troops nor officers know how to attack with any cohesion," General Alfred Krauss wrote in his diary after assuming command of the 29th Division. "They just launch disorganized bayonet charges under any and all circumstances; the Serbs recognize this, lure us into these attacks, and then gun us down." Colonel Felix Schwarzenberg, who commanded a dragoon regiment in the gap between the Fifth and Second Armies, overheard infantry officers assuring their men "in the most scornful tones, 'Don't worry, the Serbs dig themselves in, but trenches won't save them when we go in with the bayonet.'" Schwarzenberg also noted the tendency of the Austrian field artillery to fight in the open, where it was easily shattered by entrenched Serbian guns, and to rain shrapnel uselessly over Serbian trenches because no high-explosive shells were available to uproot them. Shells were more expensive than shrapnel and so had simply not been procured, in the inimitable Austro-Hungarian way. This was an army fighting not the last war (1913) but *its* last war (1866). "Pray for Austria," an already demoralized Prince Schwarzenberg wrote his wife.[56]

With the Second Army slated to move to Galicia on August 18, Conrad agreed only to the temporary loan of General Karl Tersztyánszky's IV Corps, which, it was hoped, would do *something* to throw back the Serbs on the Sava and take pressure off the Fifth Army on the Drina. Tersztyánszky decided to attack elements of the Serbian Second Army on August 19 at Sabac. The plan was for the general's two divisions to seize the town of fourteen thousand with its important railway terminus and riverboat wharves and then work their way south on three parallel roads. The drive south was critical, for if it failed, Putnik would be free to turn his entire force against Frank's Fifth Army to envelop it from all sides. But the omens were not good: the Austrian generals had little precise information on Serbian movements and no definite plan beyond "pushing the Sabac bridgehead south."[57] Officers compared the terrain around Sabac to Italy, with high cornfields, fences, hedges, and dense little woods that blotted out overviews and made fire control difficult.

The Austrians took Sabac with little difficulty but made little progress on the roads south. An Austrian corporal in the 92nd Regiment recalled the march out of Sabac in the humid summer heat: "corn so high it swallowed up even men on horseback; everything got harder; we felt that we hadn't slept for days; we burned with thirst; sweat poured down our faces; we mopped it away with muddy hands and then licked our hands, to have something to drink." The men of the 92nd marched along their narrow road in broad columns that spilled into the fields on either side; they had to break trail, cutting through cornstalks, vines, clods of earth, waves of wheat, and patches of pumpkins and melons; row after row of men would stumble over the obstacles, and half the unit was diagnosed with blistered feet after a single march. Memoirs spoke mainly of the heat, thirst, and fatigue—and, on nearly every page, "the pitiless sun."[58]

Harassed by Serbian units nesting in the corn and trees, the Austrians blazed away in their usual fashion and quickly ran out of ammunition. The Serbs were brilliant at sowing confusion: "They place their caps and backpacks on the ground to draw our fire, and then slither away to new positions," an Austro-Hungarian officer dolefully reported. The Serbs used the corn like a fifth element, stringing themselves out in long, invisible skirmish lines and firing rapidly and accurately into the bunched Austrian units. Having emptied their pouches firing at knapsacks, caps, and other phantoms, the largely Hungarian 31st Division staggered toward Jevremovac with just their bayonets for protection; then they were hit in the flank by their own artillery. With men being shredded by friendly fire, they also came under attack from Serbian infantry, but didn't return fire because they were out of ammo and thought the Serbs were so close in on their flank that they must be fellow Austrians anyway. An entire Austrian regiment, Slovaks and Hungarians, broke into two shuddering groups and fled back up the road to Sabac. The rest of Archduke Joseph's division followed, enemy and friendly shells cracking and splintering among them and causing a panicky rush to the rear that effectively disarmed the division. The 3rd Bosnians were first decapitated and then wiped out, losing the colonel, his adjutant, and a battalion commander in a single spray of shrapnel, then two company commanders and fifteen lieutenants, along with 332 men, as they struggled to push the Serbs out of a wood commanding their road.[59]

One Austrian company found itself pinned down and out of ammunition; they were out of officers too, all of them having been killed, so the surviving NCOs bellowed for their reserves, a fresh company lying prone in a skirmish line behind them. But the reserves wouldn't come forward. "We screamed at them furiously—'cowards, c'mon!'" one of the survivors recalled. "But they wouldn't even lift their faces out of the dirt." As the advance company retreated over the frightened men behind them, they discovered that they were not so much frightened as dead, mowed down in a tidy row by a Serbian machine gun.[60]

Dispatched to Sabac by Archduke Joseph to obtain an explanation for the rout of the Austro-Hungarian 31st Division, a general staff major found "parts of the Hungarian 44th Regiment in the church square, dead tired. The unit had literally dissolved in panic." They had lost thirty officers, 487 wounded, and an untold number of dead; army surgeons estimated that three-quarters of these casualties were self-inflicted, the men in the rear accidentally shooting the men in the front in their panic. Shouted commands, horn signals, and the waving of flags had not stemmed the rout, with the Hungarians having fled into Sabac crying, "The Serbs are coming!" They weren't, just yet. That evening General Putnik learned from the French general staff that the Second Army was definitely headed for Galicia. "Attack now," the French advised, "a large part of their army is leaving." The French—being buffeted on the Marne, and desperate to relieve themselves of this pressure—guaranteed free deliveries of shells if the Serbs would only attack.[61]

General Andreas Griessler's 32nd Division crossed the Sava to the left of the 31st and fared even worse. Wheeling south, the division marched toward Vukosic through trees and cornfields that broke up their march order and hid them from their own artillery, bringing down so much friendly fire from the flank and rear that the division had to retreat from the fire of its own guns. "We must stop shooting at our own infantry and start shooting at *theirs*,"

Frank expostulated.[62] Serbian shells also fell with deadly precision because Serbian peasants ignited haystacks along both sides of the road to mark the Austrian advance.[63] Casualties lay everywhere, and the troops fired excitedly in all directions. If a cow or a child blundered into the high corn and rustled, the Austrians would unleash salvos of fire at it. Most of these troops were untrained reservists, and they had marched thirty-six miles over the past two days and nights and were on the edge of collapse.

Several hours passed as officers of the 32nd Division tried to douse the haystacks, calm the panicked units, and summon new troops and ammunition to replace the morning's losses. Eight guns were lost along with twenty ammunition wagons. Amazed Habsburg auditors later totaled the material discarded by a single regiment of this division: 886 backpacks, 1,200 tents, 400 cartridge pouches, 90 shovels, 280 haversacks, 400 coats, 1,250 pairs of shoes, and 40 wire cutters.[64] Whole field hospitals, with their patients still tucked in bed, were abandoned to the advancing Serbs.[65] After repeated orders from corps headquarters to resume the attack, General Griessler rode through hordes of stragglers and heaps of abandoned equipment to Jelenica, and reported that an attack was still impossible: the men continued to retreat, ignoring their officers, and so many units had broken up and mingled that they couldn't be reassembled anyway, nor had the men been fed since daybreak. It didn't help that this division combined men of four different nationalities—Hungarians, Germans, Serbs, and Rumanians—who often could not be made to comprehend even the simplest orders. But the corps headquarters kept demanding an offensive, and finally at seven-thirty in the evening Griessler reported that sufficient order had been restored to attempt one. Night was falling, however, so the men were ordered to camp instead. As they filed toward Cerovac, the Serbs mocked them from the darkness with animal cries: dogs barking, hens clucking, and owls hooting.[66]

Tersztyánszky later blamed his defeat not on the first-levy division from Sumadija that had decimated him but on Potiorek, who he asserted had prematurely called back his march beyond Sabac:

"We had advanced 10 kilometers inland from Sabac when we were ordered back to the north bank." But Tersztyánszky, who had been considered a coming man before the war, was snipping off his account at the moment when crushing defeat ensued. Whatever directions Potiorek had given him, they almost certainly would have proved useless in the face of this furious Serbian opposition.[67]

Nothing was achieved at Sabac other than atrocities. "We did have to institute sharp, repressive measures against the inhabitants of Sabac and its environs," Tersztyánszky sniffed. "They poisoned wells and shot at our backs, and I even heard that a twelve-year-old girl threw a grenade at us." Archduke Joseph, commanding the 31st Division, admitted that one of his Hungarian regiments rounded up and slaughtered an entire village after *komitadjis* fired into their flank.[68] When they weren't marauding, the Austro-Hungarians were sleeping: "The men were so exhausted by these exertions that they fell asleep at every opportunity, even on the briefest halts. They obeyed, but they had lost their verve."[69] Who could blame them? This draggletailed retreat of the Second Army across the Sava left the Fifth Army vulnerable to Potiorek's fantasies. With most of the Second Army rolling east to Russia, Potiorek now imagined that Frank's exhausted, riddled army— initially conceived of as the anvil—could now perform the role of hammer, striking southeast to crush the Serbs against the anvil of the Sixth Army.

Potiorek's Sixth Army was finally completing its halting deployment along the upper Drina on August 18, the emperor's birthday. Potiorek had hoped to lay conquered Serbia at Franz Joseph's feet as an eighty-fourth-birthday present, but he was instead looking at almost certain defeat. Even as Potiorek planned the next phase of the campaign—a majestic advance by the Fifth and Sixth Armies toward the Kolubara River, which flowed between Belgrade and Valjevo—shattering news arrived from the front. Putnik had massed five divisions on August 19 and punched a six-mile gap between the two corps of the Fifth Army. Ordered to counterattack, the Austro-Hungarian troops refused. Frank's men were streaming across the Drina, ignoring Potiorek's telegraphed commands "to hold the line at all costs."[70]

Meanwhile, IV Corps yielded Sabac in the military sense. In the literary sense, General Tersztyánszky held the line, insisting (from the comfort of his saloon car to Galicia) that his divisions had actually triumphed on the Sava: "I never had the feeling that we'd been defeated . . . but since my troops may not understand this, I'm having a sketch of the battle prepared so that the officers can show it to the men."[71] There was no fooling Potiorek, however; he knew that the Serbs had delivered the first clear-cut Entente victory in the war. "This day of joy has turned to a day of mourning," he scribbled in his diary. To Frank he wrote, "Keep fighting at all costs; help is on the way!"[72] But it wasn't: the troops in the north were bound for Russia, and the troops in the south were blundering through high mountains and had no idea what was happening, because Potiorek had never told them. "Of the overall situation we knew next to nothing," a colonel in the Sixth Army wrote, "and what we did know we learned quite by accident, when someone else's orders were mistakenly delivered to us."[73]

Potiorek was overwhelmed by his responsibilities. He had advanced his armies so ponderously that the Serbs were able to achieve local superiority in every clash with the Austrians. The Serbs also equipped themselves with cast-off Austro-Hungarian equipment, one Habsburg officer observing an entire Serbian division wearing pike-gray Austrian coats. With each Austrian reverse, the Serbs appeared to gather strength.[74]

Potiorek now imagined that he might still save the day by bringing his as yet unblooded Sixth Army into action. After some embarrassing incidents inside Bosnia, when Sixth Army columns shot large numbers of Bosnian gendarmes, mistaking them for Serbian *komitadjis,* the entire force marched slowly up to the Drina at Visegrad.[75] It was clear to everyone on this mountainous front that the Sixth Army would never catch up with the Fifth Army, or make much progress into Serbia at all. The mountain brigades, jogging alongside mules carrying wicker hampers filled with ammunition, wrested fortified outposts from the Serbs slowly and with difficulty. "Nothing much known of the enemy here," the 4th Mountain Brigade reported from Cigla on the Lim River. "We took a trench on August 22, but there's another behind it." Each step forward—even against no resistance—took forever, officers noting that the unconditioned men would stop at "even insignificant obstacles" and pause for long rests. At night the men hardly slept because of "ceaseless shooting; the men imagine enemies behind every rock, and fire nervously all night long, ruining everyone's rest and wasting ammo."[76]

The left-hand units of the Sixth Army crossed the Drina at Visegrad and began a hopefully dubbed "general advance to the east" that immediately bogged down in the time-consuming mountain warfare that Putnik had counted on to slow the advance of Potiorek and permit the destruction of Frank. The 7th Mountain Brigade passed through Visegrad and then spent the entire day on August 20 trying to break through Serbian positions on a nearby mountain. Austrian casualties multiplied so quickly that stretcher-bearers couldn't keep up with the torrent and simply administered first aid among the rocks and trees. As the Austrians pushed toward the summit—the officers congratulating themselves that they were loosing *Sturm um Sturm* (charge after charge) despite withering defensive fire—growing numbers of Austrian infantry were shot in the back by their own comrades, who were so panicked by Serbian artillery, machine guns, and grenades that they fired wildly uphill, killing friendly troops.

Dismaying numbers of Austro-Hungarian officers were also shot trying to herd their men forward. Taught to lead from the front and keep their heads up to direct and observe fire, officers were easy marks for Serbian sharpshooters (or their own frightened troops). A battle that had begun at dawn did not end until dusk, when the Serbs retreated to their next defensive line, leaving the Austrians to count their casualties: 23 dead, 128 wounded, and 26 missing. Casualties were particularly heavy among the officers.[77] Clearly the Sixth Army—theoretically supposed to curve northward to meet the Fifth Army in a great envelopment of the Serbs at Valjevo—was not going to make the rendezvous. The Sixth Army vented its frustration in the same manner as the Fifth Army, burning Serbian huts, plundering, stealing livestock, picking the fields bare, and shooting hostages to cow the local population. "This is conduct unbecoming of a civilized army," one

Austrian general sputtered to his troops, but no one listened. Potiorek's classical plan of campaign was proving totally unsuited to Balkan realities.

On the main front, the Fifth Army's VIII Corps had already retreated across the Drina, abandoning General Adolf von Rhemen's XIII Corps on the east bank. Rhemen's corps never succeeded in lashing together its constituent parts, the 36th Division complaining from start to finish that it had been doomed by the non-arrival of its sister formation, the 42nd Honvéd Division. The Honvéds—Croats recruited around Zagreb—felt doomed in their every brush with the Serbs: "They laid their coats on the ground and then climbed trees to fire at us." The Honvéds fired at the coats while the Serbs fired at the Croats.[78] The already beaten Austrian 21st Landwehr Division, meanwhile, completely dissolved, littering the field with its equipment. "Unfortunately our armed forces are not all stamped from the same press," was the Hofburg's icy comment on the largely Czech division's "odious conduct."[79]

Even more odious conduct was going on behind the lines. Terrified by *komitadji* attacks and furious at their own humiliation, the Austro-Hungarian army savaged the civilian population of the Macva in a wave of atrocities. The irregularities of this Balkan war made them feel justified. Troops reported booby traps buried in the roads and Serbian civilians poisoning their drinking water. They reported that Serbian infantry were putting on Austrian uniforms and shouting commands in German to confuse Austro-Hungarian troops, or raising white flags and then shooting any Austrians who came across to accept their surrender. They reported Serbian wounded shooting Austrians in the back. They reported Serbian front-line troops yelling, "Mi smo vasi" (we are your friends) to demoralize Slavic units, or fooling everyone by yelling, "Nazdar, Domobranzen" (hey there, we're Croatian Honvéds) and pretending to be Croats (or Serbs from Austria-Hungary) until the Austrians closed in and were greeted with lead. For their part, the Austrians—trying to replace their heavy casualties with march battalions from the monarchy—confused themselves. The new-model army introduced after 1866 contained so many German, Hungarian, or Croatian-speaking Landwehr units that orders regularly went out in the wrong language, causing end-less "friction and hostility," as one officer put it.[80]

Ultimately, it was easier just to blame the Serbs. "What else can we do?" General Rhemen thundered. "They are a culturally backward people. How can we cling to our European culture and remain within the laws of war against *them*?"[81] Although Rhe-men cautioned troops to distinguish between Serbian perpetrators and innocents, the troops generally didn't bother. One reason the invasion force contained so many Croats—from the Dubrovnik, Sarajevo, and Zagreb corps districts—was that Vienna recognized that this was its last chance to wield Catholic Croats against Or-thodox Serbs in an excoriating war of religion and culture.[82] In Krupanj, men of the 42nd Honvéd Division bashed a group of old men and boys to the ground with their rifle butts and then hanged any who were still breathing. Near Loznica, Austrian troops took civilian hostages and then executed them in reprisal for an attack on their supply lines. When an Austrian infantryman was found with his throat cut, sixty hostages were killed and nearby villages burned to the ground. In Ljesnica, the Austrian VIII Corps con-ducted mass executions with firing squads. The largely German 73rd Regiment plundered the town for two hours, killing and rap-ing, and then hung Serbian civilians alive. Orders from division to "cease all of this unwarranted plundering and destruction"—"for wc are soldiers of a *Kulturarmee*, after all"—were largely ignored, not least because Potiorek had explicitly ordered the taking of hos-tages, reprisal hangings, and arson by all units on August 13.[83] Sixty-eight Serbs were subsequently discovered with their eyes gouged out and thirty-four with their noses cut off. A soldier of Austria-Hungary's largely Slovenian 97th Regiment reported that his unit had been authorized to "burn and kill everywhere" to quell Serbian resistance.[84]

None of these atrocities, however, stemmed the Austrian rout. With its flank exposed by the collapse of the 21st Landwehr Di-vision, the 9th Division also was savaged. They had the misfor-tune to be attacking toward Tekeris on ground that the Serbs had graphed in peacetime for artillery practice; the shells thus landed with astonishing accuracy. The division fell back, yielding a dozen

Austrian troops shoot Serbian villagers. "This is conduct unbecoming of a civilized army," an Austro-Hungarian general wrote disgustedly after witnessing repeated atrocities against Serbian civilians in 1914.
CREDIT: Heeresgeschichtliches Museum, Wien

guns to the pursuing Serbs.[85] Standing on Mount Cer, the Serbs watched the rout of the hated *Schwabas:* "You could see their columns retreating in all directions; we sent small pursuit detachments of infantry and guns to keep contact."[86] Some of those pursuit detachments, two battalions and a battery, overtook the Austrians and attacked them. The Serbs cornered elements of the 42nd Honvéds and the 36th Division in a gully east of Mramor and poured in rifle and artillery fire. Within minutes the Czech 28th Regiment had lost "hundreds of dead and wounded." Those strong enough to flee clawed their way up the sides of the gully like spiders, looking for a way out. Thousands of them would huddle alone or in small groups in the hills for two entire days before finding their way back to their units.[87]

Austrian officers were reminded of their duty: "During mass panics or demoralizing speeches, you are required to shoot the criminals on the spot."[88] But there were too many criminals and not enough officers, so many of the officers having already succumbed to wounds or illness, and no amount of capital punishment would fortify this army anyway. The Fifth Army had crossed the Drina with eighty thousand troops; it retreated back across the river having lost a stunning six hundred officers and twenty-three thousand men. Virtually every unit had lost its best officers and 20 percent of its ration strength. "A normal military campaign is not possible with *our* troops and *our* equipment in *this* country," an Austrian officer harrumphed as Frank's division fled across the Drina.[89] Obviously the Austrians should have thought of that beforehand.

The abandonment would be nearly complete on August 20, when the third of the Second Army's four corps began rolling east from Sabac to Galicia. Böhm-Ermolli's army would be caught between two stools—leaving Serbia too early to affect the fighting there, and arriving in Galicia too late to be of any help there. Count István Burián, the Hungarian minister to the Court of Vienna, expressed the growing frustration of Austria and Hungary: "What horrible effect in the Balkan states, in Italy and Rumania. When will we have some the victories?"[90] The IV Corps had a last stab at victory on August 23, when the men were ordered to cross the Sava with "only their backpacks" (implying a rapid, pitiless attack unencumbered by supply trains), but became so disorganized crossing the river in the dark—some on steamers, some on bridges—that the attack had to be called off, and the men dispatched first to bed and then to the east. "The men are shattered," Archduke Joseph concluded. "At every opportunity they throw themselves on the ground and fall asleep."[91]

Potiorek had hoped to find victory on the thinly defended upper Drina, but here too he was beaten. The Sixth Army, which was supposed to have worked in concert with the Fifth and Second Armies, arrived too late and too distant to cooperate. Potiorek finally left Sarajevo and arrived on the upper Drina in time to lead the isolated Sixth Army to its river crossings and win minor engagements at Visegrad and Priboj on August 20 and 21. But sixty-five miles still separated him from the battered Fifth Army, which had lost more than a quarter of its strength and an eye-popping forty-two guns in the battles on Mount Cer.[92] On August 24, Potiorek sounded the retreat all along the line—"further offensives would be pointless"—and pulled the Sixth Army back across the Drina.

As IV Corps abandoned Sabac, it visited the same atrocities on the population there that Sixth and Fifth Armies had inflicted on the towns and villages along the Drina: scores of Serbian men, women, and children were locked in a church for several days and then shot by firing squad as the Austrians retreated, bringing the rough total of Serbian civilians killed in this Austrian attempt to "West Europeanize" Serbia to thirty-five hundred.[93] Just ten days earlier, Potiorek had exhorted the Sixth Army to "teach the Serbs to submit respectfully to Austria-Hungary, as in the days of Prince Eugen and Radetzky."[94] There was nothing Radetzkyan about this retreat. The Austrians, sickened by their defeats and random acts of wickedness, pulled back into filthy camps littered with their own excrement. "The men must be taught to use latrines and to stop fulfilling the demands of nature in the open," an VIII Corps general fumed. "They must also be required to salute superiors at all times."[95]

Potiorek blamed everything on Conrad, saying, "I never knew with any certainty whether the units of Second Army would remain for me . . . I must be given untrammeled command of *my* theater . . . AOK must stop communicating with *my* subordinates." But the defeat was unquestionably his. He had remained too long in Sarajevo and then drifted from one remote rear-area headquarters to another, never grasping the hard facts of this war.[96]

Alerted by Hungarian officers to Potiorek's fecklessness, Tisza wrote the emperor a letter on August 23 that summarized the Balkan commander's folly: "Frontal attacks are being launched against fortified positions without any proper reconnaissance or even artillery preparation, which has led to monstrous casualties . . . among the widely separated columns that the Serbs overpowered separately at Sabac-Loznica, while the entire Sixth Army, too far to the south, could never even be employed."[97] Tisza heaped scorn on the idea that Austria-Hungary could defeat Serbia with the bulk of its troops deployed against Russia, and urged the emperor and Berchtold to face facts, forget about Serbia, and mass everything against Russia.

But the Hofburg was not ready to give up on Potiorek and his Balkan dreams just yet. The South Army commander at least had the virtue of writing the emperor letters, and Conrad didn't. "Oh well," Bolfras consoled Potiorek on August 24, "things will start to go better for you; after all, the world is round and has to keep spinning!"[98] It was not spinning any longer for the seven thousand Austro-Hungarians lying dead in the hills, woods, and villages along the Drina. Thirty thousand more Austro-Hungarians had been wounded, and four thousand captured along with forty-six guns and thirty machine guns. Serbian losses were low by comparison—three thousand dead and fifteen thousand wounded—and their morale remained solid. The Serbs jeered the Austro-Hungarian defeat, calling the Habsburg army "rabble," Tisza "a snake," and the monarchy "a criminal against humanity."[99] As thousands of wounded Austro-Hungarian troops dispersed to hospitals and homes in both halves of the monarchy, they spoke freely about the disaster in Serbia, drawing rebukes from the high command: "Men and officers alike must be told in their mother languages to stop alarming the civilian population with all of this bad news. Having stood in the heat of battle, none of them have the necessary overview or calm to describe the situation accurately." With his usual obtuseness, General Frank recommended "sharp punishment" for all.[100]

Externally, Vienna tried to hush up the defeat, assuring the neutral states in late August that Austria was winning. Italy was not buying it; there newsboys chanted, "Great Austrian defeat," crowds demonstrated for war with Austria-Hungary, and troops marched past the Austrian embassy and consulates whistling the Garibaldi hymn and the *Marseillaise*. The Italians looked increasingly warlike.[101] Internally, Austro-Hungarian towns were placarded with official bulletins attempting to explain the defeat: with Russian intervention in the war, the invasion of Serbia had been nothing more than a "sideshow" *(Nebenaktion)* and "jab" *(kurzer Vorstoss)* to "weaken and repulse" the "immensely more numerous Serbian army," and those Austrian measures had succeeded, permitting an "orderly withdrawal from Serbian soil."[102] Inside the Hofburg, Bolfras labored under no such illusions. He reminded Potiorek that victories in Serbia were needed "to create the political constellation that will make our mission in the Balkans easier." "*Was nun*—what's next?" Bolfras queried anxiously.[103]

CHAPTER 7

Krásnik

CONRAD WAS ASKING THE SAME QUESTION: "What's next?" He'd always prided himself on his military acumen, but he'd begun the war on Austria-Hungary's Eastern Front in the most confused way imaginable. He had little contact with the Germans, who liked him even less than he liked them, and he had left behind a foundering campaign in Serbia that remained a drain on scarce resources. Potiorek retained his hold on two weak armies—more troops than were needed to defend Austro-Hungarian territory, but not enough for a second invasion of Serbia. Here on the Eastern Front, the Germans and Austrians had talked before the war about thrusting from north and south, respectively—the Germans from East Prussia, the Austrians from Galicia—to pinch off Russian Poland, which bulged westward from the body of the Russian Empire. They'd even talked about crowning such a campaign by detaching Poland and Ukraine from Russia and forming them into an Austrian-run buffer state between Russia and the West.[1] But to contemplate an invasion of Russia, Conrad needed his *entire* army and needed to be on the Russian frontier. Instead, he'd deployed his diminished forces a hundred miles west of his easternmost railheads, hoping to buy a little more time for the defeat of the Serbs.

All of Conrad's conflicting strategic notions and occult faith in his own "war luck" *(Kriegsglück)* came to naught. Fearing even

169

a symbolic defeat in the east while they were so heavily concentrated in the west, the Germans held their small number of eastern troops back for the defense of East Prussia, not a converging attack with the Austrians into Russian Poland.[2] Conrad's own dithering in Serbia meant that Austria-Hungary built to a strength of just thirty-one divisions on August 28, and thirty-seven divisions by September 4, when a third corps from the Second Army—the fourth lagged behind as a sop to Potiorek—finally rolled in from Sabac. One of these late-arriving Austrian officers would complain to a journalist that the war in Serbia had sickened him: "Our orders were to kill and destroy everything. That is not humanity." He would call the senior Austrian generals "brigands."[3] They were also dawdlers, and the Germans did not bother to hide their contempt, the Austro-Hungarian ambassador reporting from Berlin the resentment felt in German military and government circles at "the lack of pressure and speed on our part, the failure to divert Russian troops from Germany" while the Germans battled in France.[4]

Berlin's complaints were loud enough that Franz Joseph's new ambassador there, Prince Gottfried von Hohenlohe, urgently advised "a prompt offensive against Russia to prove that the two empires are sharing the burdens of this war equally."[5] By M+30, the Russians had already mobilized forty-five infantry divisions and eighteen cavalry divisions in Galicia, as well as the eleven infantry divisions of the Russian Ninth Army, which were gathering at Warsaw to join an invasion of Germany or Austria-Hungary. The speed of the Russian deployment mocked prewar Austrian calculations, which had predicted just twenty-four Russian divisions by M+30, not the fifty-plus that were now hunkering on the Austrian and German borders.[6]

Austria-Hungary's only chance in a Russian war had been to strike quickly, before the Russians could mobilize in depth; Conrad had squandered that chance. Though the first shot in the campaign had not even been fired, defeat seemed inevitable, not least because the Austrians were already running out of shots. They had conscripted most of their munitions workers, which meant that the big arsenals at Vienna, Steyr, Pilsen, Budapest, and Pressburg were not producing at anywhere near full capacity. By mid-September, they were making just 3.5 million rifle bullets and 9,500 shells daily, and were having trouble shipping even these small quantities to troops at the front.[7] A pathetic cable from the Austro-Hungarian minister in Munich to Berchtold on September 8 conveyed the news that the Germans would send Austria 2.5 million rifle and machine gun cartridges previously dismissed as "past their sale date" *(veraltet)* and "suitable only for the Chinese army."[8]

Deployed on the San and the Dniester, behind adequate fortifications, Conrad at this late date should not even have contemplated an offensive. Using the bridgehead at Przemysl—an ancient crossroads ringed by modern forts, earning it the nickname "Verdun of the East"—Conrad could have defended Austria-Hungary against the looming Russian steamroller: three million Russians against fewer than half that number of Austrians. Six Russian armies (the Third, Fourth, Fifth, Eighth, Ninth, and Eleventh) were descending on a three-hundred-mile front to envelop just three Austro-Hungarian armies (the First, Third, and Fourth), as well as General Hermann Kövess' fluctuating group around Lemberg, which comprised whatever troops straggled in from Böhm-Ermolli's Second Army in Serbia. The Russians had spent a $500 million French loan in 1913 improving their roads and railways into this theater and had completely reversed Austria's logistical advantage. Now they could move more trains and troops into the Galician border region than the Austrians.[9]

True to his breakneck nature, Conrad elected to attack anyway, even against these hopeless odds and without German cooperation. "We cannot find any suitable sphere for a chief of staff with such soaring plans," Franz Joseph would later say of Conrad, but, characteristically, the emperor did nothing to arrest Conrad's soaring plans in August 1914.[10] With his right flank resting on unfortified Lemberg, Conrad gambled that he could thrust northeast with his left—the eighteen divisions of his First and Fourth Armies—and envelop and destroy the two Russian armies assembling around Lublin and Chelm. If Conrad smashed them both, he would find himself victorious on the Bug, without even having to await the (German) decision on the Seine promised by Moltke.

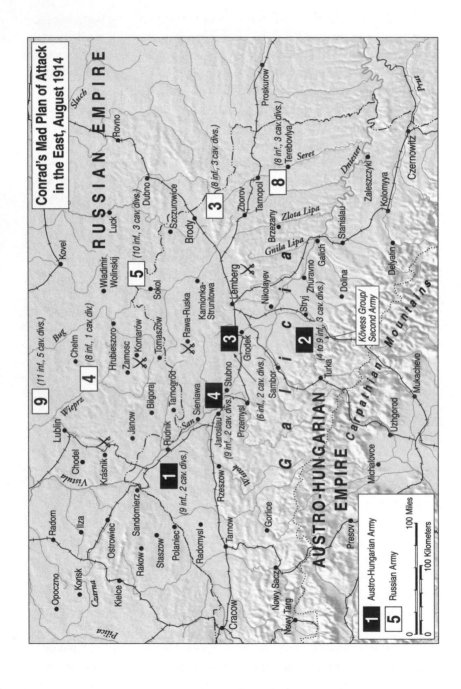

Conrad's Mad Plan of Attack in the East, August 1914

For a peevish man like Conrad, it was hard to resist such a prospect, but he should have. Even if he defeated the two Russian armies around Lublin, there were two more armies behind them in reserve, the Eleventh and Ninth, and it was inconceivable that he would defeat them as well, for he lacked reserves, transport, and ammunition. In his prewar planning, Conrad had projected this Habsburg offensive with a strength of more than thirty divisions on his left wing, which would curl around and envelop the Russian units mobilizing in Poland and Galicia. Now he found himself with just eighteen divisions on his left, not nearly enough to overawe the Russians, whose fifty-two divisions (thus far) were deploying at a faster clip than anticipated and in greater strength: Russian divisions had more battalions and machine guns than Austrian ones and so were, on average, 60 to 70 percent stronger. They also enjoyed crushing artillery superiority, having twice as many field guns and three times as much heavy artillery. Decisively outgunned by the Germans, the Russians were far superior to the Austrians.[11]

Conrad's gamble was all the more reckless because his divisions would now have to *walk* a hundred miles just to reach their points of attack. Conrad must have known that the marches alone would destroy his largely civilian army. Conrad's memoir of his youth recalled his only experience of war, in Bosnia in 1878, and how the summer heat then had inflicted "unspeakable agonies" on the men, causing mass straggling and even suicides.[12] Had Conrad stuck to the original deployment plan, his troops would have crossed those hundred hot miles in rail cars. Instead, they stumbled along on foot, eating the dust of their supply trains, cavalry, and artillery under a scorching sun. Livestock—the seventy oxen, two hundred pigs, and three hundred sheep that would be butchered in stages to feed each Austrian corps—added to the misery, lowing, bleating, and egesting all over the march routes.

Otto Laserz, a *Kaiserjäger* from Tyrol, never forgot the marches in "steaming heat"; the men were let off their trains from Vienna at a tiny village called Lubien Welki and then ordered to march ninety miles to Lemberg, a three-day struggle that would have been accomplished in a couple of hours on the rails. By the second march day, every man was stricken with lice and thirst. They'd guzzle the contents of their canteens in the first hour and go miles between wells, where the men would line up by rank and wait for a drink of warm, brackish water that inevitably brought diarrhea. These *Kaiserschützen*—Landwehr troops from the recruiting districts of Vienna, Styria, and Tyrol—also wondered why they were campaigning in flat Galicia with ropes, crampons, and ice axes, as well as hobnailed mountain boots that sank deeper into the Galician sand than the normal army shoe. Bureaucracy was a religion in Austria, and so no one—not even Laserz' commandant—had dared leave the unsuitable items behind without exculpatory paperwork, which, of course, no bureaucrat had thought to do. And so the men were already wilting, "feet burning, back and shoulders aching." One of Laserz' men fell far behind the march column on the first day and reappeared in the afternoon; Laserz noted that "he'd thrown everything away—the mountain gear and even his backpack and haversack, and now he was finally smiling. This is what it's like to march fifty kilometers in a day in Galicia in the summer."[13]

Nor did Conrad bother to secure his right flank as he moved his thirsty, staggering army north through the still Galician landscape—dusty villages of steep-roofed thatched houses and three-domed churches alternating with a limitless, empty plain. ("We knew nothing about this Austrian province, only that it produced oil, salt, filth, lice and lots of Jews," one curious Austrian trooper noted in his diary.)[14] Neither Austria-Hungary's cavalry, which crossed into Russia on August 15 to reconnoiter, nor the monarchy's aviation noticed two entire Russian armies, the Third and the Eighth, gathering around Proskurov and Tarnopol and advancing from the east. Austria-Hungary's fledgling air corps had been all but grounded in August by friendly fire, the excited peasant troops firing on their own airplanes whenever they passed overhead.[15] Initially briefed on the different markings and silhouettes of Austrian, German, and Russian planes and instructed to fire only at the Russian ones, undiscerning Austrian troops were shortly told not to fire at *any* of them.[16]

Austrian troops enter a Galician village in August 1914. "We knew nothing about this province," one Austrian infantryman wrote. "Only that it produced oil, salt, filth, lice, and lots of Jews."
CREDIT: Heeresgeschichtliches Museum, Wien

In theory, the new weapon of aircraft, with its ability to re-connoiter at long range (two hundred miles, out and back), was supposed to shorten the period of deployment and accelerate the onset of battle by providing precise, real-time knowledge of the enemy, but it was having as little impact here as in Serbia. The miserly Austrians had just five planes at Lemberg; three of them didn't work, and one of the two that did crashed inside the Russian border on August 12.[17] In his usual way, converting hindsight to foresight, Conrad blamed others: "They called me a fool when I recommended 1,200 airplanes for the army; now they see that I was right."[18] Of course as chief of the general staff, he could have insisted on airplanes, but he hadn't. Thus, his North and South Armies were still blundering around the old-fashioned way.

The resolutely old-fashioned Austro-Hungarian cavalry proved hapless in their border skirmishes with the Cossacks, driven back on all points with heavy casualties and complaining of their loads and armament. "Everything was lacking," Auffenberg scribbled after learning of the rout of his 6th Cavalry Division in fighting around Tomasow.[19] Many of the Austrian cavalry had been all but unhorsed by the choice of a heavy parade-ground saddle that rubbed their unseasoned mounts raw and sent thousands of troopers limping back to their bases on foot, leading their wincing horses behind them. Those that went forward, scouring a 250-mile-wide front and penetrating as far as 100 miles, were greeted with unexpectedly ferocious fusillades, a Russian lieutenant recalling that in these early days of the war his overwrought bumpkins would fire "twenty rounds each at a single Austrian cavalryman," effectively disarming entire units until the next ammunition supply arrived.[20]

Somehow the vast Austrian cavalry screen missed the great bulk of the Russian army altogether, persuading Conrad that "there was no sign of any significant movement from the east against his right flank."[21] In his memoirs, the Russian Eighth Army's Aleksei Brusilov expressed surprise at the "small number" of Austrian troops he encountered on the border around Tarnopol, and the alacrity with which those he did encounter surrendered, and divulged information. The Austrians, it turned out, believed that the Russians were taking time to complete their mobilization, not advancing.[22] Austrian general Hermann Kövess' Group—two corps screening eastern Galicia until the arrival of the rest of Second Army from Serbia—warned as early as August 23 that the entire Russian Eighth Army was massed around Proskurov and

The Austrians had overinvested in cavalry before the war and these *uhlans*—like the rest of the Austrian horse—failed to locate the Russian armies in August 1914, despite scouring a 250-mile front and penetrating 100 miles into Russia. Airplanes were a better choice for reconnaissance.
CREDIT: Heeresgeschichtliches Museum, Wien

crossing the frontier. A plane was cautiously dispatched. "This afternoon an airplane will be sent to reconnoiter; officers must make sure that our troops don't shoot it down," an anxious staff officer wrote that day.[23] The situation was worse than that: *two* Russian armies—the Eighth and the Third—were closing from the east. They had been marching in the cool nights and sheltering through the hot days in woods, thus avoiding aerial detection.[24]

Conrad was feeling better now; Gina had sent him a locket containing a miniature portrait of the Elder Moltke, the Prussian general who had crushed the Austrian army in 1866, and the Austrian chief looped it hopefully around his neck.[25] But he was no Moltke, as was made plain by his mad decision to attack with such paltry forces into a vast space from which he would easily be engulfed from both flanks. The decision was even more baffling in view of the earlier *Rückverlegung* (backward movement) and the foot marches now required to reach forward positions that could have been reached earlier and more easily on the railroad. Conrad belatedly argued that this offensive north was the only means to secure the Galician capital of Lemberg as well as its oil wells, roads, and railways, catch the Russians off guard, and preempt their inevitable, overwhelming assault on the rest of Galicia, the Carpathians, and Hungary. On August 20, General Auffenberg traveled to Przemysl to meet with Conrad, Archduke Friedrich, and the new crown prince, Archduke Karl. Auffenberg expected to discuss operations; instead he found Conrad and Fritzl sitting in sulky silence. Potiorek had announced big victories in Serbia for the emperor's birthday on August 18 but was now saying that he was beaten.

Both Conrad and Fritzl complained of German faithlessness and Moltke's dogged focus on the Western Front, although the latter remonstrance struck Auffenberg as silly: "even the best commander cannot chase two rabbits at the same time." The Germans would have to deal with the French and British and only then turn to the Eastern Front. Conrad had "nothing to say about his ideas for operations, and nothing to say about the enemy." Fritzl's face was "clouded with worry." Only the crown prince was cheery, but that was because no one had bothered to brief him. Auffenberg also met with AOK's German military mission—General Hugo Freytag-Loringhoven and Colonel Karl von Kageneck—and found them in a foul mood. The Germans had run out of patience with Conrad's sluggish arrangements. Returning to his own army headquarters near Jaroslau, Auffenberg pronounced himself depressed. In his diary he wrote: "We're not in a good situation. The war has been badly prepared and badly begun. The terrain is against us, as is the whole world. Even Japan has now declared war on Germany!"[26]

With the Germans still trying to win the war on the Bug by winning on the Seine, Conrad's only real option was to wait. He had let Austria-Hungary's advantage in the war's early days dribble away. Instead of rushing forty divisions to the Russian border,

General Moritz von Auffenberg was a close confidant of Franz Ferdinand and had been war minister in 1911–1912. Given command of the Habsburg Fourth Army in 1914, Auffenborg did not conceal his nervousness. "We're not in a good situation," Auffenberg wrote as he prepared to invade Russia. "The war has been badly prepared and badly begun."
CREDIT: National Archives

Conrad had detoured to Serbia, let the thirty divisions that did reach Galicia off their trains far from the frontier, and then spent the last week of August and first days of September hauling in the last divisions of the Second Army at Stanislau on the Dniester. By then, the Russians had mobilized 2.7 million troops: ninety-six infantry and thirty-seven cavalry divisions. With numbers like this (and the Germans still focused on the Western Front), the Russian general headquarters (Stavka) could threaten a total encirclement of the little Austrian North Army. With two Russian armies (the Fourth and Fifth) in the north around Lublin and Chelm and two more armies (the Third and the Eighth) around Dubno in the south, the Russians threatened both of Conrad's flanks. By attacking on the Vistula and south of Lemberg, they could surround the Austrians in the bowl between the San and the Carpathians.[27]

Conrad wasted more precious days pondering what to do, the reality of the Russian advance conflicting with his own increasingly deranged notions. Gina had pronounced him a Moltke, so a Moltke he would have to be. Late on August 22, Conrad finally spoke to his generals. He ordered General Moritz von Auffenberg's Fourth Army at Jaroslau and Viktor Dankl's First Army on its left to march northeast, Dankl toward Lublin and Auffenberg toward Chelm. General Rudolf Brudermann's Third Army and the units of Second Army that had arrived from Serbia would strike east from Lemberg toward Brody. Reading Conrad's orders at 8:00 p.m., Auffenberg was most struck by the fact that "they contained very detailed march tables, but no description of the overall plan, of what we were expected to *do*." There was no *Leitidee*, no "guiding idea."[28] This was Conrad's style—making things up as he went along, molding events retrospectively into firm plans if they succeeded and disowning them if they failed.

Conrad's entire plan was flawed from the outset. Driving on Lublin and Chelm to cut the Russian railways to Warsaw and Brest-Litovsk and menace the Vistula forts from the south and east only made sense if the Germans were menacing them from the north and west. The Germans weren't. They had been defeated on August 20 at Gumbinnen and were reorganizing their army in East Prussia. This meant that Conrad's pincer, at best, would grab air; at worst, it would itself be mauled by Russian pincers and prevented from retiring in good order to the San, which shielded Cracow as well as the roads north and south into Germany and Austria-Hungary.

Conrad's March 1914 plan had envisioned an attack by the nine divisions of Dankl's First Army on the flank of any Russian forces that engaged the nine divisions of Auffenberg's Fourth Army, with Böhm-Ermolli's Second Army as a reserve. But as the Second Army dribbled in from Serbia, Conrad redirected it not toward Dankl and Auffenberg but toward Brudermann's Third Army, which now faced the Russian Third and Eighth Armies. In fact, given the gathering Russian storm, the Second Army had to reinforce the Austrian right, but, thanks to Conrad's Serbian excursion, it arrived too slowly to be of any use there either. As in Serbia, this meant that the Austrians would be too weak everywhere for a decisive battle anywhere. Dankl's diary confirmed this: "Behind us," he wrote, was "nothing"—just the possibility of a German corps that might push down to Tarnow or Cracow to connect the Austrian and German armies. There were otherwise no reserves to exploit a successful attack or rescue a failed one. The three and a half Habsburg armies in Galicia were all that Austria-Hungary had to cope with the Russian steamroller. And they were not even formidable, Auffenberg feeling compelled to write his generals during the march to the frontier that "even though the Russian artillery has many more guns than we do, I'm convinced that the traditional excellence of our artillery will nullify that advantage." He had to be joking. Russian heavy artillery and high explosives would make short work of Austrian "traditional excellence." Auffenberg recalled learning more about the armies of Dankl and Brudermann from the heavily censored Austrian newspapers than from Conrad, who told his generals nothing about his plans as they matured. Auffenberg called this Conrad's "system of secrets," and the general staff chief would later use it to rewrite the history of 1914 and cast himself as a victim of incompetent subordinates.[29] Conrad retrospectively claimed that his three armies were part of a great interlocking system whose best defense was the offense—the First and Fourth Armies would wheel south to hit any Russian armies that attacked the bait of the Third Army in Galicia—but that was a brazen fabrication, and assumed far too much anyway: that the Habsburg field armies would be able to move fluidly along a three-hundred-mile front increasingly crowded with Russian forces.

Conrad's maneuvering was even more astonishing in view of the fact that he had gamed this maneuver in early 1914 at a *Generalbesprechung*—generals' conference—in Vienna involving all of the commanders now committed to the operation. Back then, one army had secured the flank and rear at Przemysl, while three armies had struck east to envelop the Russians. That was one army more than they had now, and even with four armies in the game, Conrad had noted the awesome difficulties: boggy roads, a rainy Baltic climate, and Russian fortifications at Warsaw and Ivangorod (Deblin) that would stop Austrian operations cold and require big (and presumably unavailable) German reinforcements.[30]

For all of his faults, Conrad at least directed the Austro-Hungarian war effort. Russian efforts were still disputed by multiple power centers, none of which had made up its mind how to fight this war. The scene of the Russian deployment posed tremendous challenges. Poland, a province of the Russian Empire since 1815, was a salient, with German East Prussia to the north, German Silesia to the west, and Austrian Galicia to the south— the "tongue of Poland" jutting from the Russian mouth. How to defend this salient and in which direction to launch offensives to aid Russia's allies in the West became a political football lustily kicked around by the tsar's generals.

Tsar Nicholas II had appointed his uncle, the fifty-eight-year-old Grand Duke Nikolai, commander of his vast army in 1914, but the grand duke's Stavka did not wield real power. General Vladimir Sukhomlinov did. War minister since 1909, Sukhomlinov had emerged as the army's Rasputin, a self-promoter who deftly played on the prejudices of the tsarina and insinuated himself into the tsar's inner circle. He had structured the army more to augment his personal power than to project its own, shuffling the post of Russian general staff chief as many times in the seven years before 1914 as Germany had done in the previous hundred years.[31] In these distracting office politics Sukhomlinov had a free hand, the tsar and tsarina protecting him despite revelations of corruption because of Sukhomlinov's loyalty to the Romanovs (and Rasputin) and the general's fashionable disdain for the Russian parliament or Duma.

What this meant in 1914 was that even as the Russian army deployed to the frontiers, it lacked the ability to settle on a coherent plan and shift reserves between the northern and southern groups. The army commands—a Northwest Front under General Yakov Zhilinsky and a Southwest Front under General Nikolai Ivanov—treated themselves as permanent fixtures, inelastic and irreducible, the prestige of their commanders (and Sukhomlinov, who mentored both) tied to the size of the force and the priority assigned it. Whereas the German and Austro-Hungarian headquarters could shuttle corps between their various fronts to reflect changing operational realities, the Stavka couldn't. Even had Grand Duke Nikolai tried to shift resources from one army to another, he would have had to request the shift from Sukhomlinov, who would veto or amend it if it upset any of his protégés in the

Grand Duke Nikolai (l.), General Sukhomlinov (c.), and Tsar Nicholas II (r.) at Russian maneuvers just before the war. Though Nikolai would serve as commander in chief, Sukhomlinov had the tsar's ear and wielded real power in the army. As wily and corrupt as Rasputin, Sukhomlinov confused more than aided the grand duke's high command. CREDIT: National Archives

field armies. Given that the grand duke's principal aides, Generals Nikolai Yanushkevich and Yuri Danilov, had been handpicked by Sukhomlinov (over the grand duke's objections), there was no way for this to happen anyway. The grand duke would ask for changes and Yanushkevich would pronounce them logistically impossible.

As Conrad struggled to finish the war in Serbia and strike into Russia, the Russians struggled to agree on what they were doing. The grand duke's new headquarters—halfway between the Northwest and Southwest Fronts, in a train on a siding in the town of Baranovichi in Belarus—was overshadowed by long-established, fixed Russian headquarters in Warsaw and Kiev, the first focused on the German threat (Russia's prewar Plan G), the second on the Austro-Hungarians (Plan A). The Warsaw and Kiev headquarters were nurtured by Sukhomlinov, which meant that they had little need for the Stavka and no interest in cooperation with each other. The Warsaw generals knew they would need every available gun and bayonet against the Germans; the Kiev generals wanted to knock out Austria-Hungary first, not least because everyone feared for Poland if it was successfully invaded. The tsars had been repressing the Polish language, church, and nobility for more than fifty years, and if the Austrians or Germans gained a foothold in Russian Poland, they might actually be welcomed as liberators. The Stavka, under pressure from Paris and London to overweight the German option and take pressure off the Western Front, was supposed to resolve these debates but didn't, the grand duke bursting into tears of frustration at his own impotence when appointed generalissimo by a tsar who neither liked nor trusted him, preferring Sukhomlinov for his military advice.[32]

Even though Russian prewar planning had called for a focus on Austria-Hungary and a strict defensive against the Germans, French pleas for a diversion in the east demanded a last-minute revision of the old Plan G and the preparation of an offensive. General Zhilinsky, who commanded the Northwest Front from headquarters at Bialystok, would be the man to lead the diversion. Another *Sukhomlinovets*, he had been Warsaw military governor before the war and the very man who had promised (in his own turn as Russian general staff chief in 1911) to deploy eight hundred thousand troops by M+15 to relieve pressure on the French.[33] With twenty-five German corps swarming into France in August 1914, the tsar agreed to send Rennenkampf's First Army and Samsonov's Second marching into the lake and forest country of Masuria to distract the Germans. Entrusted with this distraction, Zhilinsky was unlikely now to see the wisdom of cooperation against the Austrians or a sharing of reserves, which were accumulating in the rear of the two fronts as Russia's mobilization progressed. The Stavka ordered Zhilinsky's two armies into East Prussia so abruptly that when they marched on August 17, they had fewer than four hundred thousand men, not the eight hundred thousand promised. Still, they outnumbered the Germans in the east two to one, which gave cause for hope.

The Russians now found themselves with thirty-four infantry divisions headed for East Prussia and forty-seven bound for Galicia.[34] In the Southwest Front headquarters at Rovno, described by the British military attaché as "a typical Russian frontier town, dirty and dusty, the streets swarming with Jews who stare and gape at strangers," General Nikolai Ivanov held sway; his staff chief was General Mikhail Alekseev.[35] Ivanov disposed of four armies, General Anton Salza's Fourth Army and General Pavel Plehve's Fifth facing southwest from Lublin and Chelm, Nikolai Ruzski's Third and Aleksei Brusilov's Eighth facing west from Tarnopol—Ruzski north of the town around Dubno and Brody, Brusilov south of the town. Only two thin tributaries of the Dniester, the Zlota and Gnila Lipa streams, stood between him and Lemberg, the grand Galician capital.[36] When not quarreling with Ivanov (the front commander), Alekseev (the front chief of staff) argued for a downward chop from the right against the Austrian lines of retreat to Cracow. Others argued for a flanking attack from the left that would roll around the Austrians from the south and trap them in a pocket between Lemberg and the Carpathians.

General Danilov at the Stavka pushed both plans, arguing that Russia's superior strength would permit a double envelopment from *both* flanks of Conrad's North Army. The Fourth and Fifth Armies would flank Conrad on the left, while the Third and Eighth Armies rolled up his right. Ivanov—a gruff, competent veteran of the Russo-Japanese War—saw that he might annihilate the entire Austro-Hungarian army in a single battle. With just thirty-six divisions in the East, Conrad was already outnumbered two to one, a ratio that would worsen as the Russians brought more divisions up from the interior.[37] Alekseev would have liked to advance his two armies on the left (the Third and Eighth) to gain the line of the San and trap the Austrians in Galicia, permitting an encirclement by the two armies on the right (the Fourth and Fifth). But with the French absorbing a quarter of a million casualties in the first month of the war, the Stavka decided to lead with the armies on the right, which were closer to German Silesia and more likely to get Berlin's attention.[38]

A great encounter loomed, as both sides believed they were readying for a decisive blow—Conrad on the Bug, Ivanov on the San. Ivanov, who by now had learned a great deal about the thinness of the Austrian forces before him from talkative villagers along the Austrian march routes, saw that the way really *was* open to encircle Conrad's North Army. The fifteen divisions of Salza's Fourth Army and the eighteen divisions of Plehve's Fifth Army would drive westward to cut Conrad's communications with Cracow, Salza advancing on Rzeszow, Plehve on Rawa-Ruska. The eighteen divisions of Ruzski's Third Army would drive into Lemberg, while the fifteen divisions of Brusilov's Eighth Army crossed the Dniester south of the city to flank any Austro-Hungarian forces attempting to defend it. Centered behind this great movement, Plehve's army was positioned to aid either push—the envelopment of Lemberg, or the thrust toward Cracow.[39] The British military attaché recalled the excitement in Ivanov's headquarters as battle approached, but also the pessimism expressed by a Russian gunner, who was a husband and a father of five. When someone slapped him on the back and assured him that he'd soon be home with his family, the gunner demurred: "They say it's a wide road that leads to the war and only a narrow path that leads home again."

Russia's Fourth and Fifth Armies moved south on their wide roads, directly toward the Austro-Hungarian First and Fourth Armies moving north. With the Russian Third and Eighth Armies slowed by the poor roads in eastern Galicia, a series of rivers coursing north and south into the Dniester, and quarrels between Ruzski and his staff, the Austrians enjoyed a respite from the Russian steamroller. Supply and communications remained the Achilles' heel of the Russians. They were even less motorized than the Austrians, with just ten cars and four motorcycles for an army of 150,000, and fewer than seven hundred vehicles for the entire army of several million men.[40] Russia's supply service was a scandal, defeated at every turn by sloth and corruption. Touring the Warsaw headquarters of the Russian Line of Communications Command in mid-September, the British military attaché reported what he saw: "The whole place was in an indescribable state of filth; everyone was waiting . . . and all seemed content to wait." There appeared to be no actual system of supply; available horses were "dreadful scarecrows"; prisoners, deserters, and convalescents wandered around unsupervised.[41]

In no apparent hurry to develop their awesome power, which lay scattered on the fringes, the Russians were conceding the Austrians even odds in the Polish salient, for the moment. Three hundred and fifty thousand Austrians ranged themselves there against the same number of Russians. Anticipating victory, Conrad even appointed a military governor for soon-to-be-conquered Warsaw.[42]

A week of skirmishing preceded the first great battles, revealing crucial differences in Austrian and Russian tactics. The Russians had a healthy respect for firepower; the Austrians didn't. Skirmishing for control of Belzec in Russian Poland on August 15, an Austrian cavalry division leading the Fourth Army into battle summoned a nearby battalion of Vienna's 4th Deutschmeister Regiment, and the battalion appeared, led not by a major or a captain but by the regimental commander—Colonel Ludwig Holzhausen—and his entire staff. "A man's first taste of battle is like a boy's first kiss," soldiers liked to say, a mystery that held them all in thrall as they surged toward their baptism of fire.

The Russians—Cossacks and some infantry—had prudently dismounted and taken cover in buildings, behind walls, and in trees; they watched in disbelief as Holzhausen strolled to the front of the Austrian skirmish line, drew his saber, and walked the battalion forward. The official Austrian report of the colonel's inevitable demise spoke of his "crazy-brave, death-defying attitude," which "fired the men and drove them forward." Whether it was Holzhausen's attitude or the Cossack bullets nipping at their flanks that drove the men forward is hard to determine, but in a firefight that lasted ninety minutes, Holzhausen perished immediately. "A bullet cut his carotid artery; he died in seconds," one of the colonel's battalion commanders noted. Thirty-eight *Deutschmeister* died with him, and fifty-one were wounded—12 percent casualties in a minor skirmish.[43] This foolhardy machismo—incomprehensible in view of all the ink that had been spilled on the dangers of modern firepower—would decapitate one Austrian unit after another in the days ahead.

On the left wing of the spread-eagled Austrian armies, the 6th Cavalry Division entered Zamosc on August 22 and was surprised to discover strong Russian forces there. Austria's 3rd Cavalry

Division was driven back on Krásnik, but not before spotting big Russian columns advancing from Radom and Ivangorod (Deblin), in other words toward the rear of the Austrian First and Fourth Armies.[44] A lone Austrian airplane, puttering up from the mouth of the San on the twenty-second, spotted at least five Russian corps hurrying southeast from Chelm and Lublin. Southeast! This suggested that the Russians were turning everything against Brudermann at Lemberg, exposing their flank to an Austrian *Nordstoss* or "northern blow" by the armies of Dankl and Auffenberg.

With a careless disregard for the Russian reserve armies *behind* the armies he had before him, Conrad ordered the *Nordstoss*. Dankl agreed that the "northern blow" presented the opportunity—on paper at least—to "smash in the enemy left and drive the Russians off to the East."[45] But the whole enterprise seemed far-fetched. There were assuredly huge reserves behind this already large Russian force, and Conrad really had only the vaguest idea where the Russians were in the vast space between the Dniester and the Bug. On August 23 he told his armies only this: "We estimate eight to ten Russian divisions deploying between the Bug and the Vistula, none of them operational before September 1."[46] In fact, there were at least thirty-four divisions in that space, and they were all operational. But there was no restraining Conrad; as the Austrian staff history put it, "the wish was the father of the thought," and Conrad wished for a great war-winning stroke. Such was his reckless enthusiasm that he even ordered the Third Army—all that remained to defend Lemberg and North Army's right flank—to prepare to march north and join the "general offensive." With Brudermann now committed to the *Nordstoss*, Kövess was to cross the Dniester and deploy defensively in the space between Lemberg and the village of Przemyslsany, and there await the rest of Bohm-Ermolli's Second Army, which was trickling into Stanislau.[47]

Already things were falling apart. Even as the Third Army began to move north, alarming reports of big Russian forces to the east arrived in Conrad's headquarters in Przemysl: infantry masses closing from Zbaraz, Brody, and Tarnopol, and cavalry and infantry at Husiatyn. Kasper Blond, an Austrian officer attached to the army hospital in Czernowitz, described what it felt like to have masses of Russian forces closing around him: "Our army had already left; now there was a river of fleeing civilians—men and women, children and seniors, some on foot, some in wagons, all headed south, or trying to head south. People were paying exorbitant prices for a cart. People were milling about holding a few possessions in their hands. You saw girls and women walking in their nightgowns; now and then a droshky crammed with people and furniture would break through the mass of pedestrians." Jews crowded into the hospital seeking protection from mobs that had already sacked their shops.[48]

Desperate to strike the Russian flank, Conrad had exposed his own. But he persisted, repeating the order for the "general offensive" on August 22. He doubled down everywhere he could, ordering the Second Army's III Corps—one of the few units east of Lemberg—to defend the city against any Russian forces coming from the east, but to stand ready at all times to march off to join the Nordstoss. All that remained to defend Lemberg was XII Corps, the 11th Division and three cavalry divisions that had been so worn down by their exertions since mid-August that they could hardly be counted as combat units. "I must remind you that the 1st Cavalry Division has been in nonstop combat since the first days of the war and has been reduced from 3,800 sabers to barely 2,000," General Arthur Peteani reported. "We urgently need rest."[49] The troops arriving from the Balkans were to cross the Dniester at Stanislau and face north.

With the Nordstoss cocked and ready to launch, Conrad anticlimactically ordered the armies to rest on August 22. With so many reservists in the ranks, the men were tired and lame. Dankl remained sanguine, jotting in his diary on the twenty-third that "the Russians posed a danger, but a small one." Ignorance of Russia's real strength fostered the delusion that "they will have no choice but to yield to our superior forces." Although Dankl felt some nervousness, he didn't worry too much. He was feeling in a victorious mood as his army headed for a collision with Salza's: "It's just a shame that things aren't going this well in Serbia."[50]

The war in Serbia, of course, was two weeks old, and AOK worriedly transmitted some early lessons learned to the generals of the North Army. One was, "We must take care not to depress the good spirits and energy of the troops with unnecessary exertions." Of course, the whole deployment of the North Army, which had begun a hundred miles west of Lemberg, was an unnecessary exertion, but there was worse to come. "Officers must take care not to launch frontal attacks, know the terrain, know what the enemy is doing, go around the enemy flank, and never attack into unsuppressed enemy rifle and artillery fire."[51] Yet Auffenberg's army, which had just staggered through the woods, sand, and marshes of the Upper Tanew River and come to rest on the line Narew-Tereszpol, was even then girding to charge into unsuppressed enemy rifle and artillery fire. One officer recalled the approach to battle as a battle itself—waist-deep bogs, soft sandy tracks that swallowed the men up to their knees, then dusty roads, blistering heat, muddy water, and no food or drink because supply wagons were even less able to negotiate this terrain than the men.[52]

Dankl too blundered into battle on August 23, when his First Army collided with General Anton Salza's Russian Fourth Army east of the San River at Krásnik. Ivanov had directed Salza to advance to the line of the San and hold it from its mouth to Jaroslau. Dankl had arrayed his army to envelop this Russian thrust, with X Corps pushing forward on the right, V Corps in the center, and I Corps trailing on the left. Dankl had just written in his diary that he hoped to meet the Russians on the line of heights west of Krásnik, and now he did.[53] Salza had sent his XIV, XVI, and Grenadier Corps forward on a broad front, threading through the villages of Zaklikow, Janow, and Frampol. Sweating under the August sun and floundering in the deep sand and marshes, Dankl's left wing units, the 5th Division and 46th Landwehr Division, struck the Russian 18th Division north of Zaklikow.

In the center, the 37th Honvéd Division struggled with linguistic problems as much as with the Russians on the wooded heights above Janow. Orders arrived in German, yet because of Hungarian punctiliousness they had to be distributed in Magyar, often to units that couldn't speak or even read Magyar.[54] On the

"Thank God, it's war," General Viktor Dankl exulted when Austria declared war on Serbia in July 1914. "The Russians pose a danger," he hazarded, "but a small one." Little more than a month later, Dankl's Austro-Hungarian First Army lay in ruins, crushed by the Russian steamroller.
CREDIT: National Archives

right, Dankl was able to concentrate five divisions against the two of Voyshin's XIV Corps, which found themselves sprawled across twenty miles of swampy, rolling, wooded ground south of Lublin. It was a rare instance of Austro-Hungarian superiority in men and guns, and Dankl surged ahead to exploit it.

Dankl believed that he was linked to a vast Europe-spanning victory. "The Germans in France are also making great gains!" he scribbled excitedly in his diary.[55] Here on the western edge of Russian Poland, however, the fighting was cruder than anything seen in France. With V Corps in the lead, the Austrian 76th Regiment lost six hundred killed, wounded, or missing in three frontal assaults to seize the hilltop village of Polichna. Moving in masses up a long bare slope, the troops were scythed down by artillery and machine guns, and then stumbled into the village in clumsy columns, where they fought hand to hand and house to house in what would most charitably be described as a Pyrrhic victory.

Common sense suggested that Austria-Hungary could not afford a war of attrition with the Russian Empire, yet that was

"A man's first taste of battle is like a boy's first kiss," Austrian officers liked to say. It was anything but. Brutally sacrificed in bayonet charges, the Austro-Hungarian infantry died in droves.
CREDIT: Heeresgeschichtliches Museum, Wien

exactly what the Austrians had embarked on with ruinous tactics like these. No one seemed to notice; Austrian officers on the scene wrote daft after-action reports to put a gloss on the lamentable slaughter. *"Jeder Mann ein Held"* (every man a hero), the commander of the 76th proudly asserted. The poor wretches would have to be heroes with tactical direction like this.[56]

The 33rd Division, joining the attack on Polichna from the right, climbed toward the village as if this were a war of the eighteenth century: two battalions arrayed wing to wing, a third in a second rank behind them, and the fourth in reserve. The 14th Division attacked in the same fashion, with its four battalions in thousand-man clumps, sweating up the hill to Polichna. Most of its battle had to do with recovering survivors of the 76th Regiment, a job made more difficult, an Austrian colonel wrote, "by our own artillery, whose shrapnel missed the enemy and struck us."[57] Battling for the villages of Frampol and Goraj to place a Russian pincer on the San, Salza sent his XVI and Grenadier Corps against the Austrian V and X Corps on the right. Firing from elevated positions, the Austrians drove them off, then counterattacked, capturing hundreds of prisoners and nineteen Russian guns. Salza ordered a retreat to the northeast, a few kilometers back to the next line of heights on the road to Lublin.[58]

Austria's pike-gray uniform, which did not camouflage troops in Serbia, was not concealing them here either. "We were always visible in our pike gray, the Russians, in their dirt-colored uniforms, far less so," an officer wrote.[59] Explaining the ghastly casualties to a German officer at AOK, Conrad blamed more than just the uniform. He faulted the legacy of the Austro-Prussian War, noting that the Habsburg army's "ill-timed bravado stems from 1866," a war in which the Austrian infantry had attacked just like this. Perhaps Conrad was right; low budgets, peace, and slow promotion since 1866 meant that Austria-Hungary's regular officers in 1914 were old (most captains were over forty, and many of them were approaching sixty), fat, and incapable of new tricks. Senior officers who couldn't mount a horse were placed in cars, but they quickly broke down, the monarchy lacking the rubber imports to manufacture spare tires. "Drive more slowly and carefully on these bad roads," Conrad's supply director hissed. "There's nothing wrong with our tires, it's the way you drive."[60]

Despite gruesome casualties, the Austrians carried the day. They chased the Russians out of key villages like Polichna, occupied Krásnik, dug trenches, and settled in for a night that shook men and officers alike. For most, it was their first taste of battle, and it was horrid. "Sleeping in the open on a battlefield strewn with corpses and wounded men, who cried and pleaded through the night, was an experience that most of us will never forget," the commander of the Austrian 83rd Regiment wrote.[61] As a delighted Kaiser Wilhelm II awarded Conrad the Iron Cross, Conrad ordered Dankl to close up with Auffenberg's army, which was now reinforced with three divisions from Brudermann's. This assembly—Dankl, Auffenberg, and Archduke Joseph Ferdinand's

XIV Corps—was now ordered to press the attack toward Lublin. Dankl's left wing was still "in the air," without flank support, but the Germans promised a corps of Landwehr troops to reinforce it. Though speed was everything at this point, Dankl wasted considerable time on the twenty-fifth exchanging formalities with one of Fritzl's adjutants, who had been dispatched from Przemysl to offer the archduke's congratulations for the victory at Krásnik, for which Dankl had to prepare his own elaborate reply.

Although Dankl was at the end of his logistical rope—his nine divisions had outrun their supplies and were pressing into the gut of at least eighteen Russian divisions—he didn't seem to know it. Dankl wrote on August 25 that he and Auffenberg could now proceed to "hurl the Russians back to Lublin and beyond." Taking stock of his own victories, he boasted that "the Russians are giving up everything—prisoners, guns, flags—and fleeing the area." But a flyer report confirmed that large Russian forces continued to stream along the Vistula toward Dankl's left flank and rear. "He who flanks is himself flanked" was an old Napoleonic bromide, and it was true here: the further Dankl advanced, the more Russians appeared behind him. Conrad had redirected Dankl's X Corps to guard the right flank of Auffenberg's II Corps, leaving Dankl more exposed than ever. With no troops to spare anywhere, Conrad was playing a shell game, switching corps here and there to plug holes, but opening new ones with every move.[62] Both Dankl and Salza now looked south for relief: the Austrian to the four corps of Auffenberg's Fourth Army, the Russian to the four corps of Plehve's Fifth Army. Like wrestlers circling each other on a mat, the Austrians and Russians drew closer, both preparing to lunge at the other with as much strength as they could muster.[63]

CHAPTER 8

Komarów

STILL THINKING THAT HE COULD WIN the Great War in the east with a bold maneuver, Conrad now added a southern stroke to the fading *Nordstoss*. He detached Archduke Joseph Ferdinand's XIV Corps from the Third Army and ordered it to attack Plehve's left flank in a potato field near the soon-to-be-notorious town of Rawa-Ruska. The Austrian corps was led in by Colonel Alexander Brosch's 2nd *Kaiserjäger* Regiment on August 26; they were getting their first whiff of battle, one soldier remarking to another when their (bronze) cannon opened fire for the first time: "Brother, those guns are going to fire all the way to Kiev! Now the Russians are really done for." Of course they weren't. In this action, as in most others, the old Austrian cannon were largely ineffective, failing to hit or even locate Russian howitzers that were firing indirectly from behind a distant chain of hills.

The *Jäger* Alpine infantry—still encumbered with their ropes, picks, ice axes, and crampons—stumbled through the potato field in two long skirmish lines. Undergoing their baptism of fire, the men were immediately disabused of the glories of war. Dozens of white and red clouds cracked overhead, and the troops felt shrapnel for the first time. One *Jäger* named Johann Komaromi described the reaction of the Austrians: "We fell out of our lines and cringed into little groups, trying to get as far from the

195

raining darts as we could." But the nature of shrapnel was to land everywhere, "behind us, in front of us, to the left, to the right." Six shells cracked immediately over them, causing panic, the men "running confusedly in every direction" to escape the barrage. Komaromi crawled on his belly to the top of a hill and saw . . . nothing. "Not an enemy to be seen," he wrote. A curiosity of war on the Eastern Front was that the Russians, unschooled in Western trench art, simply dug deep slit trenches without breastworks or parapets and vanished inside them. The Austrians wouldn't notice Russians in their path until the *muzhiks* stood up and fired.[1]

With Russian shrapnel spraying overhead and head-fused shells landing and hurling the sod forty feet in the air, the *Jäger* platoons descended the height in rushes, sprinting a hundred yards, then kneeling to cover the approach of the following group. They found the Russians in the next wood and returned the Russian salvos with individual fire. As the other regiment of their brigade advanced into line, they turned the Russians out of the wood with a flank attack. The Russians retired to another wood and kept up their fire.

After several hours the Austrians took that wood too, but still the Russian artillery thundered from invisible positions far away, landing shells with astonishing accuracy in their midst. In this little episode from the emerging Battle of Komarów, all of the defects of Austrian tactics and strategy were revealed. The Austrians had entered the war with the essentially nineteenth-century view that grit and determination would overcome firepower and manpower on the battlefield. "Entrenched and hiding in woods, the Russians offered very small targets for our rifles, forcing us to storm ahead with the bayonet," Brosch's regiment reported.[2] This, of course, was the Russian plan: to goad the Austrians into the open and kill them. The Russian infantry, no match individually for the *Jäger,* had inflicted heavy casualties with their salvo fire, and the Russian artillery, well situated a couple of miles behind the infantry, had never ceased killing Austrians. After taking the second wood, the Austrians should have entrenched or withdrawn out of range of the Russian guns; instead, they were bluffly rallied by their officers—*"Kaiserjäger Ihr weicht?"* (you're not scared, are you?)—and told to attack again toward the faraway gun line, a last charge that killed yet more crack troops for no apparent gain. The Austrians were also gratuitously exposing their officers to certain death; Komaromi's battalion and company commander were both killed on this first day of the war. His platoon leader, who grimly laughed off the casualties with *"Heute rot, Morgen tot"* (here today, gone tomorrow), would be killed a week later.[3]

The war was not going particularly well for the Russians either. In every clash with the Russians the Austrians noted poor fire discipline. Russian infantry were not allowed to fire singly, only in volleys commanded by their officers. Even then, they invariably fired high, killing and wounding more unsuspecting Austrian troops in the rear echelons than in the front. Everywhere the Russians had been, the ground was littered with little black cartridge clips, evidence of their profligacy. These trigger-happy *muzhiks* were threatening to disarm the Russian infantry; a single Russian division could easily fire off 4 million rounds in a single day of fighting at a time when monthly Russian production for the entire army of 115 divisions was 59 million rounds. Put another way, the three cartridge factories in Russia were producing 700 million rifle rounds a year for an army that was firing that quantity every month.[4]

The Russian artillery was already experiencing the shell shortage that would afflict it for the entire war. Russian planners had focused on mobilizing their vast army but given little thought to maintaining it in the field. "The immensity of the requirements," General Danilov recalled, "surpassed the wildest expectations." The Russian general staff had assumed that shell production of three hundred thousand units a month—which amounted to one or two shells per day per gun—would suffice, and it clearly wasn't. Gunners were firing hundreds of shells a day, and at a rate of two million a month they were rapidly exhausting stocks that simply could not be replenished because Sukhomlinov's War Ministry had actually closed the Russian shell factories and packed their workers off to the front when war began. Imports were hard to come by too, for Russia's ports were inaccessible—the Black Sea closed by the Turks, the Baltic by the Germans.[5]

To exploit the recent victory at Krásnik and pursue the beaten enemy, Dankl ordered the two corps still under his control to advance on August 26. They hadn't gone far when they found the Russians not in retreat but in strong positions on the next row of heights around Rudnik, trenches dug and artillery deployed. This, in a nutshell, showed why the Austrians would never win this war. The Russians had more men and even more artillery. Auffenberg had jauntily asserted that the "traditional excellence" of Austria's artillery would overcome Russia's advantage in batteries and caliber, but it wasn't overcoming anything. The Russian artillery was hitting the Austrians effectively at a range of five miles, whereas the Austrians with their old bronze guns needed to close to two miles or less to make their guns accurate. The Russians also had more artillery everywhere, which meant, as a despairing Austrian report put it, that "the enemy was always able to dedicate a fraction of his artillery to destroying our attacking infantry," while the rest destroyed the Austrian artillery, causing "enormous casualties."[6]

Artillery, however, was only one of the many reasons the war was going badly for Austria-Hungary. What few Austrian machine guns there were broke down because the crews had decided to smear them with lard to prevent rusting, which caused the guns to jam. ("Clean every trace of lard from every machine gun immediately," Conrad's AOK bellowed from the sidelines.)[7] The Austrians lacked the means to move quickly, leverage their infantry with artillery and machine gun fire, or deal any kind of decisive blow. At best, they were like a small Russian army without the benefit of Russian artillery. Russian rifle fire was notoriously inaccurate, but, as one Austrian officer put it, its sheer volume—"they opened up with huge, uninterrupted, rolling salvos from long range"—terrified the Austrian line, not least because the Austrians were generally forbidden to return fire, being "under strictest orders to conserve what little ammunition they had." This poverty of arms and ideas had been apparent before the war, yet Conrad had glossed over it for years.

Standing around in the August heat, contemplating the Russian trenches at Rudnik, Dankl's generals discussed how to proceed. They put off the attack for a day, then struck into the wooded heights on August 27. Every unit took heavy casualties, the Austrian artillery doing nothing to disturb Russians in defilade. The colonel of the Austrian 83rd Regiment overran a Russian trench and took the surrender of a Russian colonel and several hundred men of his regiment. As the Russian emerged from the trench, waving a white handkerchief, he congratulated the Austrian on the "bravura" of his men. "Mine," he declared, "would never attack like *that*," which, in view of all of the dead, irreplaceable Austrians lying around, was not really a compliment. The Russian was sent to the rear with the other prisoners, his parting words to the Austrian colonel: "Take off those yellow officer leggings you wear; we see them from far away and we fire at them."[8]

Both armies were still groping in the dark, merely guessing at the other's location, but Ivanov, characterized by the Austrian general staff as a "smart, methodical, outstanding leader," now began to connect the dots.[9] He guessed that the left wing of Dankl's army was the left wing of the *entire* Austrian North Army; he located it on the road from Tomaszow to Zamosc, then ordered Plehve's Fifth Army to hurry southwest and hit it in flank and rear. Salza was to halt on the heights of Goraj, hold the Austrians, and let Plehve bite into their flank. Ruzski was to plow straight ahead with the Russian Third Army. Using the roads to Lemberg and Rawa-Ruska, he'd be positioned to attack the Austrian Third Army at Lemberg or roll up the Austrian Fourth and First Armies from the south.

Unaware that he was in danger of being engulfed from both flanks, Dankl pressed his attack, herding his weary troops toward the Wiznica stream and then across it. Dankl's I Corps—the 5th and 46th Divisions—struggled toward Wilkolaz. The seventy-one-year-old Salza, ordered to hold at Goraj, instead retreated toward Lublin. Ivanov fired him on the spot, promoting General Aleksei Evert to take his place.

Dankl's X Corps advanced into Goraj and found the field littered with Russian rifles and other equipment.[10] In the crude three-day battle of Krásnik, 144 Austro-Hungarian infantry battalions, 71 cavalry squadrons, and 354 guns had ranged themselves against a roughly equal Russian force, and the Russians had had the worst of it, losing twenty thousand men and twenty-eight guns. Though he had lost fifteen thousand troops of his own, Dankl was awarded the Maria Theresa Cross for valor, so great was the emperor's relief at having finally scored a victory in the war. In Vienna, *Das Lied vom General Dankl* (The Song of General Dankl) was hastily composed, eight stanzas depicting the "Russian hordes, flooding across the steppes from the north," as "countless as grains of sand on the beach," and bent on "murder, pillage, and arson." Dankl, the hymn sang, drove the "Russian dogs" all the way back to Lublin, his troops "eagerly pursuing with lusty war cries," Dankl in their midst, hacking the dogs back with his sword until "there were no more Russians to be killed."[11]

For a moment, Conrad's aggressiveness seemed to have paid off. His heady prewar predictions that he would split the Russians like a chisel and drive them into the Black Sea and the Pripet marshes seemed within reach.[12] Dankl had dealt a heavy blow to Salza's army, and Auffenberg was coiled to hit Plehve's. The Russian situation was all the more disturbing when viewed alongside the news from East Prussia, where the German Eighth Army—reinforced with two corps and a cavalry division from France—was embroiled in the Battle of Tannenberg in the last days of August, crushing two Russian armies of the Northwest Front, inflicting 300,000 casualties, capturing 650 guns, and threatening to push into Poland and join hands with the advancing Austrians. "Thousands of Russian prisoners, and Hindenburg is still counting them!" the newswomen in Berlin called to passersby (the newsboys all being at the front).[13]

But German victories did not ensure Austrian ones. *Das Lied vom General Dankl* notwithstanding, there actually was no end to the *Russenhunde,* or "Russian dogs." They had just briefly receded, and certainly not as far as Lublin. Every night, the few Austrian units able to rest were invariably awakened by Cossacks (or rumors of them), and the "wild firing in all directions" that ensued killed and wounded far more Austrians than the Cossacks ever did.[14] Still, the German Kaiser awarded old Franz Joseph the Pour le Mérite—Prussia's highest decoration, the coveted "Blue

Max"—on the twenty-eighth, as thanks for these early victories, if you could call them that.

Dankl attacked again on the twenty-ninth into the next line of hills and absorbed devastating casualties. Evert's Fourth Army was concentrating more troops and pushing them west to find Dankl's flank. In the center, Dankl's 33rd Division wrested the village of Piotrkow from the Russians, but not before losing thousands more men to artillery and infantry fire. The 83rd Regiment alone lost four hundred men and six officers on the twenty-ninth. Austrian officers were still dumbly advancing in battalion columns to *Sturmdistanz*, storm distance, and then ordering their frightened men to fix bayonets and lope that last *Distanz* into Russian rifle, machine gun, and shrapnel fire.

The Russians had a survival instinct lacking in the Austrians. They would lie up against the lip of their trenches pouring fire into the Austrian bayonet charges until the first wild-eyed Austrians arrived at the edge of the trench. At that precise moment, every Russian in the trench would throw his hands in the air and surrender as one. "I mention this fact," an Austrian colonel later wrote, "only to confirm that our enormous casualties were not the result of Russian attacks, but rather Russian defensive fire." Whereas Austrian officers led from the front and died in droves, Russian officers preferred the rear; "only in the rarest cases did we ever see Russian officers near the front line; most were well back and well covered." With peasant cunning, the Russians were fighting more intelligently than the Austrians. The next day the depleted Austrian 83rd took delivery of its first "march battalion"—raw recruits and reservists—who had been sent from the regiment's Transylvanian depot to replace the dead and wounded active-duty troops. The war of attrition had begun.[15]

Thanks to Russian floundering, Conrad had—against all odds—advanced into the space between the Bug and the Vistula, frustrating Russian attempts to cross the San, encircle him, and separate the German and Austro-Hungarian armies. For the moment, he held the initiative. But the moment was passing. The Stavka was redirecting Plehve's Fifth Army as well as General Platon Lichitski's Ninth Army to surround and pinch off Conrad's left. Lemberg, on Conrad's right, was about to be crushed under the Russian steamroller. Although Conrad later claimed to have estimated the Russian armies threatening Lemberg at just ten divisions, that was merely another of his whitewashes. In fact, he had ample warning of the approach of two entire armies, the Russian Third and Eighth, with sixteen divisions.[16] But Conrad yearned for a great victory and hoped that if he only pressed the *Nordstoss* harder, the Russians would crumple. But pressing the *Nordstoss* harder—and taking more troops from his right to bolster his left—merely ensured that his right wing at Lemberg was even more vulnerable to attack. If the Russians smashed it in or crabbed around behind it, Conrad would lose every inch of conquered ground in the north, and probably the armies there as well.[17]

Blind to these considerations, Conrad ordered Auffenberg to press the attack with Dankl toward Lublin. Auffenberg, spread over a sixty-mile-wide front, stumbled on August 26 into the flank of the sixty-four-year-old Plehve's Fifth Army, which was itself stumbling toward Dankl's right flank.[18] Throughout, Conrad was engrossed in his romantic envelopments, spending valuable time on the twenty-sixth chatting with his political advisor, Joseph Redlich, about Gina. With the guns of August booming around them, Redlich pronounced himself disgusted; he liked Conrad but deplored the general's "pessimistic-sentimental outlook" and his obsession with his married mistress. Redlich was most struck by Conrad's melancholy and "boundless naivete." The chief was "like a child in his judgment of life and the world . . . in no way distinguishing himself from the average general staff officer" in his thinking. Bound by office routines and his "senile" doting on Gina, Conrad was incapable of the deep thought and decisive action needed to put the Austro-Hungarian army on solid ground.[19]

With little direction from Conrad, Auffenberg took the opportunity to hit Plehve hard, hoping that he could envelop him with Dankl from the left and Archduke Joseph Ferdinand from the right. Here was another rare instance of the Austro-Hungarians enjoying even odds with the Russian steamroller, Auffenberg's 156 battalions and 470 guns against Plehve's 144 battalions and 526 guns. Auffenberg marched his II Corps toward the lovely

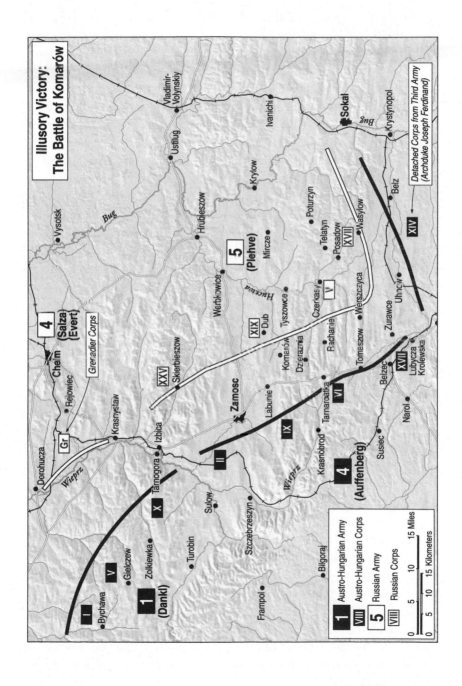

Illusory Victory:
The Battle of Komarów

Renaissance town of Zamosc and wheeled his IX and VI Corps forward in the direction of Komarów, an elevated market town surmounted by a brick church that commanded the surrounding fields. Archduke Joseph Ferdinand's XIV Corps, beating its way up from Lemberg, would sweep in to the right of VI Corps, brushing the Bug with its sleeve to complete the encirclement of Plehve.

On August 26, four Austrian divisions of the II and IX Corps battled along the old imperial road of Zamosc against the Russian XXV Corps. Archduke Joseph Ferdinand, who was wearying of his ever-changing orders, rested his men at Wielkie. It was well he did, for Conrad now changed his mind again and ordered the archduke not to cooperate with Auffenberg after all but to turn around and march back to Lemberg to support Brudermann. Auffenberg would have to make do with his own forces. He extended his VI Corps far to the right to take the place of Archduke Joseph Ferdinand's departing corps. The VI Corps' 15th Division now found itself in the unenviable position of having to do with one division what had been planned for five.

Dankl's army rested on the twenty-sixth, rising only to reply to Russian artillery fire from north of Krásnik. For August 27, Dankl planned a renewed advance; despite exhaustion and casualties, Conrad still regarded the First Army as the left pincer of the *Nordstoss*. Evert's army seemed to be retiring on Lublin. On the twenty-seventh, Dankl attacked with two corps and wrested some villages from the Russians, absorbing more heavy casualties. The omens were nevertheless good, as three Russian corps were observed retreating before the onslaught. Dankl—who moved his headquarters into Krásnik on the twenty-seventh, to a building that had served until the previous day as the headquarters of a Don Cossack regiment—now planned to move to Duza and Belyce. But his army was nearly broken by several days of fighting and marching. His I and VI Corps were devastated and urgently needed march brigades to replace their casualties. Dankl ordered rest for the twenty-eighth.

Despite the slowing of Dankl's pincer, Auffenberg glimpsed victory. Evert—brought in to stiffen Salza's wilting army—was still retreating to the north, leaving Plehve's Fifth Army exposed.

On August 27, the second day of battle, Auffenberg ordered General Svetozar Boroevic's VI Corps to attack the flank of Plehve's XIX Corps at Rachanie; Boroevic made early gains but then foundered, his 39th Honvéd Division losing half its strength to Russian fire. Pacing back and forth in the garden of the palace in Oleszyce hearing the distant thunder of the guns, Auffenberg was handed an early casualty list and goggled in disbelief: "It said that the 39th Honvéds had taken 50 percent casualties. I refused to believe it, but more precise information arrived later confirming that some units had lost even more than that."[20]

On the right, General Friedrich Wodniansky's 15th Division attacked Pukarczow, but already his men were "wilting from heat, thirst and sleeplessness." Like Dankl's men at Krásnik, these largely Hungarian troops humped up the high ridges chosen by the Russians for their trenches and into withering fire. Wodniansky's 5th Regiment alone lost eight officers and three hundred men in these attacks, in part because no one could be found to operate the unit's machine guns.[21] One of Wodniansky's brigades, fighting for a wooded crest around the village of Maloniz, arrived at the top to find "our entire skirmish line—230 men—lying dead." The Russians had killed them all, and then withdrawn a hundred yards to slaughter the next wave, a battalion of Bosnians: "The Russians were too well concealed; each time we sent a skirmish line forward it was immediately mowed down." One officer after another—the major, the captains, the lieutenants—were all cut down trying to lead the men forward in desperate scrambles. The major died in the front rank, roaring: "Men, now show your loved ones at home what heroes you are!" Eleven officers were killed and seven wounded, including the author of the report, a captain who had run past a Russian machine gun and been raked with bullets: left cheek (grazed), belly (grazed), saber (disintegrated), and left shoulder (shot through).[22] The other company commander was literally blown into a swamp by a shellburst, where he lay dazed, concussed, and unable to move.[23]

The Austrian army was just not big enough to fight the Russians; the Habsburg divisions were becoming lost in the vast spaces and losing their connection to units around them. This allowed the Russians to infiltrate those spaces and fire into the Austrian flanks and rear. Ordered to press on, Wodniansky couldn't, for he had Russians in front of him and all along his right flank. To reach them and their spitting guns, he would have to cross the swamps of the Huczwa.[24] Back in Belzec—the market town that would become a notorious Nazi death camp in 1942—General Boroevic tried to maneuver his VI Corps forward by telephone, telegraph, and couriers. Reports of Russian troops arriving from the southeast and hurrying toward Komarów suggested that Auffenberg's success would be fleeting.[25]

Later claims of a great Austrian victory at Komarów hardly seem justified by records of the action. Only a day into the battle, Auffenberg's overstretched units were, as one general put it, "falling apart, on the brink of chaos." The men had not slept or been properly fed in days. They were literally falling asleep while marching and even while fighting. The 15th Division had marched twenty miles on the twenty-fifth, twelve miles on the twenty-sixth, and fifteen miles on the twenty-seventh—all without a hot meal. They had slept no more than six hours over the course of those three days. Boroevic kept promising to "compensate" them for these exertions with extra rest days, but the rest day was always *übermorgen*, "the day after tomorrow." When these weary, furious men took Tomaszow, which before the war had been a Russian garrison town, they plundered the Russian barracks and officers' apartments, stealing what they could carry away and destroying everything else.[26] They were going mad with fatigue.

While Archduke Friedrich scolded Auffenberg from Przemysl—"You must stop these outrages, which ruin the army's image abroad and make the men believe that plundering is acceptable"— Conrad was launching another of his operational outrages. With Plehve apparently pinned in a pocket at Komarów but Boroevic unable to close the pocket on the right, Conrad—who had just cabled Auffenberg that the situation of the Third Army at Lemberg was "unfavorable"—nevertheless now ordered Archduke Joseph Ferdinand to turn around (again) with his long-suffering XIV Corps and rejoin Auffenberg.[27] The men, having already marched south on the twenty-sixth through sand and swamp, now turned around and crossed the same ground in the opposite direction, losing an entire day. These forced marches—thirty miles a day, for no apparent purpose—were killing the corps, which was losing nearly 10 percent of its strength every day to "straggling."[28]

General Josef Paic, the archduke's staff chief, kept a diary that recorded the backing and filling ordered by Conrad from his office far behind the lines. On the twenty-sixth: "hard marches by the men to intervene in the battle of Fourth Army; just as we were distributing orders for an attack, the phone rang and we received *new* orders to march back in the direction of Lemberg to support Third Army in *its* battles east of the city." Paic's staff worked for four hours to redirect the corps, knowing that "the change of direction and the new marches would have an extremely demoralizing impact on the troops." Four hours after that, at 1:15 a.m. on the twenty-seventh—as his supply trains and field artillery were already rolling south, trailed by the sleepless infantry—Paic received yet another set of orders from Conrad: "Suspend the march to Lemberg and carry out the *original* plans."[29]

With XIV Corps turning in ineffectual circles, Auffenberg grasped General Karl Huyn's XVII Corps, a new unit formed just days earlier, and commanded its 19th Division to advance from Belzec toward Plehve's forces, which seemed torn between regarding themselves as prey or predator. For now, Auffenberg still felt like a predator; Archduke Peter Ferdinand's 25th Division had taken Zamosc on the twenty-seventh and had been greeted by the city fathers with bread and salt on a silver salver, the traditional tokens of submission to a conquering army. Peter Ferdinand's staff chief recalled that "morale was high and our casualties were slight." Still, he noted that here too, on the left-center, the Austro-Hungarian troops were on the edge of collapse. They had been marching and fighting without a rest since the twenty-first. "We should have pursued the Russians, but we couldn't. We needed a rest day." They rested on the twenty-eighth, Archduke Peter Ferdinand settling into the luxury rooms of the Hotel Zentral.[30]

Auffenberg reverted to the original plan, which was to swing Boroevic's corps forward to pin the Russian XVII and V Corps on the bend of the Huczwa, then bite into their flank with Archduke

Joseph Ferdinand's corps, returning from the south. But Boroevic's corps was dead tired, scarcely able to march, let alone fight. When Conrad grandly ordered Auffenberg late on the twenty-seventh to press the attack all the way to Chelm, Auffenberg was stunned. "To Chelm?" Auffenberg sputtered. "And for this they took away a third of my army and gave it to Brudermann?" The eventual return of those units—for the second time—could no longer affect the outcome of the Battle of Komarów; the reinforcements would arrive too late and too weary. "What must these troops think of us?" Auffenberg scribbled in his diary. "We've sent them zigzagging around under steaming heat on roads of sand."[31] To solidify his right wing for Archduke Joseph Ferdinand's arrival, Auffenberg woke his 15th Division just after midnight on the twenty-eighth and sent them forward to wrest Tyszowce from the Russians and shore up the Fourth Army's right. After slopping through the swamps of the Huczwa, they were set upon in the darkness by the Russian V Corps. Already roughed up, the Austrian division now shattered completely, losing four thousand men and twenty guns in a pell-mell retreat.[32]

Desperate to seal a victory, Auffenberg was trying to find the flank of the swelling Russian army. He planned to keep moving northeast, toward Chelm, but was alerted by aerial reconnaissance that "strong enemy forces on the line Chelm-Tyszowce are closing on the army's right wing." This was Ruzski's Third Army, sliding northwest to rescue Plehve and flank Auffenberg before the Austrian could flank him. Alarmed, Auffenberg ordered Archduke Joseph Ferdinand to close up beside Huyn's XVII Corps, reconnoiter aggressively with a cavalry division, and fend off every attempt by Ruzski or Plehve to strike Auffenberg's right wing in the flank.

Colonel Brosch's 2nd Tyrolean *Kaiserjäger*, one of Archduke Joseph Ferdinand's regiments, marched day and night to make their rendezvous with Auffenberg, one veteran recalling the long slog from the Komarów force down to the Lemberg one and then back again: "There was Auffenberg; here was Brudermann, and we marched here and there under a hot shimmering sun—over rolling green hills and ancient forests—toward an infinite blue horizon." The troops who had skirmished near Rawa-Ruska three days earlier marched away and were now marching back, marveling at the space and the stillness of Russia, which swallowed them up like flyspecks. On the twenty eighth Brosch's light infantry slouched wearily into Belzec, "this poor, plundered, extremely filthy Jewish village," and were poised at long last to swing their southern pincer into Plehve's left flank.[33]

Conrad in Przemysl continued to believe that he was dealing a war-winning blow, wiring Auffenberg on August 27 that "the outcome of this campaign now hinges on the successful completion of these promising attacks on the left wing." Auffenberg was surprised. "Nothing could be expected from XIV Corps, it had been left too far behind by AOK's ever-changing orders," exposing his army and Dankl's—the "left wing" mentioned by Conrad—to Plehve and Ruzski.[34] Conrad was deaf to all of these caveats. "He was," Churchill later wrote, "one of those apostles of the Offensive for whom machine guns and barbed wire had prepared so many disillusions."[35] The apostle now ordered Auffenberg to press on dauntlessly with all available forces; local reverses anywhere on the field must not turn into retreats.[36] On the actual battlefield, Austrian officers already sensed that the battle and probably the war were lost, joking darkly, "*Zum Schluss hat doch jeder noch ein Kugel*" (Well, at least we've all saved a bullet for the end). General Wodniansky wasn't joking: he pressed his pistol to his head and shot himself that night.[37]

Resting on August 28—the lull before the storm—Auffenberg's divisions awaited instructions for the twenty-ninth. Conrad wasn't much help, for his mood careened wildly from punchy optimism to brooding melancholy; having earlier boasted of a war-winning blow, he was now disputing history with the Hofburg, already pronouncing the war unwinnable and insisting that if only the emperor had heeded his calls for preventive war in 1909 or 1912, all would be well. "It's a malicious freak of fate that it's I who must now bear the burden of that neglect," he griped in a spectacularly ill-timed letter to Bolfras.[38]

Conrad's officers were also contemplating fate; they knew that the Russians before them had to be bludgeoned to death before they could regroup and reinforce. Marching and fighting faster than was prudent, in order to mollify the French, who were fending off the Germans on the Marne, the Russians had been badly disorganized in these first battles, a fact confirmed by their slow reaction to the blows of Dankl and Auffenberg. It seemed to justify Conrad's fitful optimism, as the Austrian XIV Corps—now the right wing of Auffenberg's Fourth Army—advanced to within two days' march of the army's left at Zamosc. But the Stavka eventually reacted, diverting the Russian Ninth Army to the Southwest Front to prevent Dankl from joining his army with Auffenberg's, and to stem the Austrian advance. The Russian Fourth Army's command had imploded under the strain, the army commander, Salza, firing Voyshin for the debacle on the twenty-third, only to be fired himself by Ivanov, who then reinstated the demonstrably inept Voyshin. Incompetence seemed to reign as freely here as across the way in Przemysl. But two Russian armies—the Fourth and the threat of the Ninth—sufficed to stop Dankl, and the diversion of Ruzski to rescue Plehve would stop Auffenberg as well.[39]

To polish off Plehve before Ruzski could rescue him from the south, Auffenberg had spent a long night in Oleszyce drafting plans, which he distributed at six-thirty in the morning on August 29: "General offensive of the Fourth Army with every rifle available, for the imminent decisive blow."[40] Huyn's XVII Corps— now under General Karl Kritek, Huyn having been cashiered for "nervousness"—was the clasp joining the Fourth Army to Archduke Joseph Ferdinand's XIV Corps. It too was supposed to sweep Plehve up from the right, crushing him in a pocket at Komarów.[41] Having supposed that the mutiny against Huyn—"we'll shoot him ourselves if you don't do something about him," Huyn's staff chief had phoned the AOK—had stiffened his right, Auffenberg now found that it hadn't. Kritek's divisions made no more progress than Huyn's, their brigades shot down by Russian artillery and machine gun fire as they tried to get across the Huczwa and press into the heart of Plehve's position. Each time the Austrians took a ridge, they would find the Russians had merely decamped to the one behind it and dug in there with their machine guns. The little woods that dotted the field filled with Russian infantry, who fired into the flanks of every Austrian attack. If an Austrian machine gun opened fire, three or four Russian guns would answer. All the while, Russian shells were falling, gradually killing most of the officers in the 34th Regiment and the division's two *Jäger* battalions. The 19th threw in its last reserves, but they too retreated under Russian fire.[42]

Things were no better on the left, where General Blasius Schemua—given command of II Corps after his removal from Conrad's position in 1912—groped ahead. Archduke Peter Ferdinand commanded Schemua's 25th Division, and, having rested on the twenty-eighth, the archduke left the comforts of the Hotel Zentral in Zamosc on the twenty-ninth and resumed his march east. But Peter Ferdinand's 50th Brigade came immediately under Russian heavy artillery fire from Komarów. For troops supposedly trapped in a pocket, the Russians were behaving with admirable aggressiveness.

Archduke Peter Ferdinand ordered his division to attack toward the village of Dub and seal the pocket, an objective that was starting to seem outlandish in view of the accelerating Russian counterattacks. Expecting to find a Landwehr division on his left, the archduke spotted Cossacks instead. His artillery was its usual ineffective self, spraying shrapnel harmlessly over the Russian trenches while the Russian heavy artillery lobbed in shells that triggered panic in the archduke's 25th Division as well as in the divisions on either side of it. With two Russian armies, Plehve's Fifth and Ruzski's Third, closing around them, every Austrian unit along this quaking front assumed that the Russians had broken their line and were grasping at their flank. When night fell on the twenty-ninth the exhausted men slept where they stood, reserves a hundred paces behind the skirmish line, with no cook fires and no noise. Whispered orders were conveyed from Schemua to the archduke to the 10th Division to renew the attack at first light, but the archduke was told that the 10th Division would have to rest on August 30, as "the men are broken."[43]

Conrad's failed strokes around Komarów and the reserves he shifted there to support them had consequences at Lemberg. With Brudermann's army weakened by the detachment of XIV Corps to Auffenberg, the Russian Third and Eighth Armies struck toward Lemberg on August 26. They threatened not only to smash in Brudermann's center but to double-envelop him from the flanks as well. Whatever fleeting success the Austrians had achieved at Komarów was now being undone at Lemberg. With Russians everywhere, a sense of imminent doom affected everyone. The war minister, General Alexander Krobatin, sent a cable from Vienna to Przemysl urging Conrad to silence the "terrifying and depressing gossip" bubbling out of his headquarters and armies.[44]

But by now everyone was terrified and depressed. Having lost his XIV Corps to Auffenberg, Brudermann now had to hold Lemberg with just two and a half corps: his own XI Corps as well as Second Army's III Corps and a division of the XII Corps. The Serbian detour was proving disastrous, as three additional divisions desperately needed at Lemberg were still chugging slowly through Hungary on their way from Sabac. At best, Brudermann might eke out nine divisions against at least sixteen Russian ones; he'd survived this long only because of bad roads and Ruzski's inveterate caution.[45] With four corps in hand, Ruzski continued to swallow the Redl-era assumption that the main Austro-Hungarian effort would be a *Südstoss* from Lemberg, not the *Nordstoss* to Komarów, which he still took for a feint. Certain that thirty Austrian divisions, not nine, lay in his path, Ruzski was crawling toward Austria's eastern capital, averaging just five miles a day on his own territory, even less on Austrian ground.

Ruzski's tardiness gave Conrad the false hope that he could still seal the victory at Komarów, even though doing so would mortally weaken Brudermann. By now even the Austro-Hungarian line troops were becoming aware of just how vastly outnumbered they were; rumors of Russian strength and Austrian inferiority were so entrenched that Brudermann ordered the death penalty for anyone caught spreading them. "Reinforce discipline," he growled, "before it's too late."[46]

It was too late. Flogging Ruzski forward, Ivanov finally began attacking toward Lemberg in the last days of August. He was aided by appalling Austro-Hungarian indiscretion: generals around Lemberg were discussing their plans on unsecured telephone lines, which the Russians listened to raptly. Belatedly learning of this

Russian espionage, Conrad reacted furiously, demanding that his officers adopt a Joycean code when speaking on the phone. Lemberg would henceforth be referred to as "Uzldampf," a corps "Ulmklotz," a division "Ulmtexas," and so on.[47] "Uzldampf," of course, was the fourth city of Austria-Hungary and the junction of four vital railways. Conrad could not afford to lose it, on grounds of both prestige and military necessity, yet by August 30, Ivanov had massed three times as many troops for the assault on Lemberg as Brudermann had defending it. Ruzski would hit Lemberg from the east, Brusilov from the south.

All of this flailing around Lemberg alerted Auffenberg and Dankl to the fact that Krásnik and Komarów were not so much victories as preludes to their own envelopment and defeat by a much larger and apparently more competent Russian army. Both Austrian generals now slammed on the brakes, realizing that every step forward would pull them deeper into a Russian pocket, not the other way around. A twenty-mile gap promptly opened between the Austrian First and Fourth Armies near Zamosc, and Plehve galloped through it to safety. Having tasted victory in the north, Conrad watched in frustration as Plehve—dismissed before the war as a "*kranker Greis*," a sickly geezer—got away.[48] Auffenberg blamed Archduke Peter Ferdinand for drawing back with his 25th Division on August 31 and "giving back much of what had been taken." Peter Ferdinand was supposed to have closed the ring at Komarów "with every available rifle and gun," but he had pulled back upon hearing reports that there were Russians behind him. "Awful disappointment, he threw away the fruits of victory," Auffenberg wrote, virtually guaranteeing—Archduke Peter Ferdinand was a Habsburg, after all—that Auffenberg's insider-trading scandal, which had been quashed in 1912, would be rediscovered, dusted off, and pushed to an embarrassing and career-ending censure in 1915.[49]

Archduke Peter Ferdinand's general staff chief wrote his own account of Komarów and blamed much of it on poor communication from Auffenberg. The army commanders had agreed early in the campaign that the efficient delivery of orders was more important in this theater than any other due to the sketchy infrastructure and vast spaces of Russia, which could take days to cross with dispatches, but Auffenberg's orders and objectives invariably arrived late or not at all. This dawdling gave the Russians time to fill in gaps and march reserve troops and guns to the rescue. The Austrian divisions by now were running out of shells and bullets, and confronting reinforced Russian units that were better supplied. Efforts to join Habsburg units wing to wing invariably failed— the phrase "contact with neighboring units impossible because of swamps" recurring in almost every report.

At 2:00 p.m. on August 30, Archduke Peter Ferdinand learned that the divisions on his wings had been hit by overwhelming enemy force and driven back. The archduke and every commander along the front of the Fourth Army now understood that the envelopment of the Russians at Komarów that Auffenberg, Conrad, and the army's press bureau were clamoring for was impossible. In fact, the Russians were bidding to encircle Auffenberg. At 4:00 p.m. that day, Archduke Peter Ferdinand wrote Schemua: "We're faced with a choice—either retreat toward Zamosc, yielding the great gains we've made thus far, or, by throwing in the last man this afternoon in one last attack, strike toward Dub for victory." Auffenberg, desperate to pluck victory from the jaws of defeat, sent Major Prince Auersperg galloping from headquarters to Peter Ferdinand's command post with orders to "continue the advance and finish the encirclement of the enemy at Dub."[50]

By now, however, even an Auersperg prince couldn't move the Austro-Hungarian 25th Division; it had shot its bolt. Auffenberg's own memoir of the battle confirmed that the Austro-Hungarian troops no longer believed in the Dub gambit: "Complaints by troops in the front lines were getting louder and louder." They could feel Russians all around them, and they wouldn't hold. To the archduke's left, the 4th Division hadn't appeared, and the 13th Landwehr Division—Germans, Czechs, and Ukrainians—had dissolved into panicked clumps of men who refused to stand their ground. Looking to his right, Archduke Peter Ferdinand appealed to the 10th Division to add its weight to a last push. Citing exhaustion of everything—men, beasts, guns, and munitions—the

10th demurred. Everyone was worn out from the marches up from the frontier, the battles, the lack of sleep, and the frequent panics. Still, the archduke took a last stab at it. Using his Habsburg aura—and his status as the most senior divisional commander on the spot—he ordered the 10th Division to give its "Bestes und Letztes," its best and last effort, and join a concentric attack with his division toward Dub. Hours later, as darkness fell, the division commander's answer to that dynastic order came back, carried through the woods and swamps by a courier: "1,500 paces east of me are Russian positions—trenches with eight machine guns and artillery. Attacks on this position all day by my 36th Regiment and 12th *Jäger* Battalion have been repulsed with heavy casualties. Until these positions are destroyed by our own artillery, any renewal of the attack would be futile."

The Austrians retreated, clinging to the boast that they'd won great victories at Krásnik and Komarów. But they were victories only in the sense that a boxer who wins the first round on points but gets knocked out in the second can claim to have won the bout. With soaring immodesty, Auffenberg called Komarów "the greatest maneuver battle of the war and indeed of all the wars of the monarchy," which was to say the greatest victory in five hundred years. He judged his performance at Komarów at least as impressive as the Elder Moltke's at Königgrätz, commenting that "the war booty of the victor was about the same in both battles: 1866—18,000 prisoners, 182 guns; 1914—20,000 prisoners, 200 guns."[51] Of course, relatively speaking, this was nothing like Königgrätz, for the twentieth-century Russians would easily replace twenty thousand men in a way that the nineteenth- (or even twentieth-) century Austrians could not. Still, Auffenberg was hastily given the noble predicate "von Komarów" and a cash gift of eight thousand crowns by a grateful emperor. Partial victories were better than none at all.

CHAPTER 9

Lemberg and Rawa-Ruska

DEPLETING BRUDERMANN to strengthen Auffenberg produced nothing at Komarów and catastrophe at Lemberg. Yet Conrad, characteristically, now attempted to fall back on the very commander he had so recently undercut. With Auffenberg and Dankl all but beaten, Conrad ordered Brudermann and the rump of Böhm-Ermolli's Second Army to salvage the disaster on the Eastern Front. March east, Conrad ordered Brudermann on August 25, and "drive back the enemy forces, thus securing the flank and rear of the whole army."[1] The *Nordstoss*, in other words, was dead and buried. Ever the apostle of the offensive, Conrad was attempting to replace it with an improvised *Südstoss* from Lemberg. Needless to say (Krásnik and Komarów had said all that needed to be said about the prospects for Austro-Hungarian offensives), this offensive, by a small army with small artillery, would probably not go well. Otto Laserz, a reservist with III Corps' 4th Regiment, was roused with his fellows from a deep sleep at midnight on the twenty-sixth and ordered to march to the train station at Lemberg. Groggy with sleep, the *Deutschmeister* filed through the dark streets of the city and into the vast Art Nouveau station, which had been finished only ten years earlier at great cost to carry Austrian trade east and symbolize the permanence of Habsburg rule in Galicia.

217

Packed into boxcars, the troops rolled east toward Przemys-lany. Two streams blocked the approach to Lemberg from the east: the Gnila Lipa (rotten lime) and the Zlota Lipa (golden lime). Bru-dermann hoped to entrench behind the streams and drive the Russians off. Arriving on the Gnila Lipa, the sleepy men were ordered out: "Everyone out, grab your gear, line up, move!" Laserz recalled the confusion and the excitement, for none of the Austrian troops had ever been in battle: "Where was the enemy? Where were the Cossacks?" Nowhere, actually. The troops filed back to the station and saw their first wounded men, rolling back from the Zlota Lipa in carts. "How's it going at the front?" the troops called excitedly. The wounded just stared blankly at them or waved feebly. Laserz' unit got back in their boxcars and rolled toward the Zlota Lipa with the doors open, hearing the thunder of the guns. They piled out at Dunajov and formed into a skirmish line.

On the hill before them, the men of the 4th Regiment watched a battery of Austrian guns deploy; within minutes it was bracketed by Russian shells and shrapnel. One burst followed another, red flame and black smoke, geysers of earth, or the white overhead puffs of shrapnel, all aimed at the artillery. The Austrian gun crews began to dodge desperately between their guns, and one gunner broke free and ran screaming down the hill toward Laserz' platoon until he too was obliterated by a shell. While Laserz distributed ammunition to his men, he saw General Hermann Kövess, who was commanding fragments of the Second Army until Böhm-Ermolli's arrival from Serbia, standing on the Dunajov railway embankment, looking this way and that, trying to make sense of the noisy battle.

Laserz' group tramped through a lumberyard and saw a group of hussars—"exhausted, sleepy, their faces worn by fatigue and fear"—sprawled on the ground. The infantry, Germans from Vienna, saluted them eagerly as they marched past, calling, "*Österreichs Heer, Austria's army!*" but the hussars, Hungarians all, regarded them sullenly. Laserz' platoon came to a meadow and had begun crossing it when a Hungarian marching band broke from a wood on the far side and ran right past them, dragging their horns behind them: "*Granat! Granat!* Shells, Shells!" Finally

Austro-Hungarian dressing station near Lemberg in August 1914. "How's it going at the front?" passing troops called excitedly. The wounded just stared blankly at them, or waved feebly.
CREDIT: Heeresgeschichtliches Museum, Wien

the infantry arrived at the Zlota Lipa, "a deep narrow muddy stream." They tore up a fence, threw it over the stream as a make-shift bridge, and crossed. The fence broke, and they fell in, the men flailing to the far bank and crawling up it through the slime. "Our beautiful new pike gray uniforms, ruined, sopping wet and black with mud," Laserz grumbled.

Trails of black mud through the flattened grass showed the men the way forward, and they slithered ahead on their bellies in a skirmish line, most of the men muttering that their cigarettes and chocolate had been ruined by the water and the muck. They crawled into a wheat field, Russian rifle fire hissing overhead, and came upon "our first dead soldier: a Hungarian in uniform with all of his equipment, lying on his right side, arm outstretched, deathly pale, staring at us with dead open eyes, blood trickling from his nose and mouth." Soon the Austrians were crawling past more casualties; they rose to a crouch and ran forward in rushes, finally locating the Russians in a wood six hundred yards away. The battalion let off a salvo, "1,000 rifles firing at a stroke," and then charged. Here was all the madness of Austro-Hungarian tactics in 1914: the Russians were six hundred yards away, concealed in a wood, and the Austrians rose—the whistles screaming in their ears—and began running in *Laufschritt,* a sprint. Now the Russian machine guns opened up. Laserz saw men fall away shattered and bleeding as well as a cyclone of dirt and dust exploding from the ground as bullets struck all around him. They came abreast of a Hungarian unit and crowded in beside them, running and firing toward the Russians, who remained invisible except for the flashes of their rifles.

Resting on their bellies, the Austrians resolved on another rush forward to shorten the range, but the Hungarians were firing "like madmen" and wouldn't stop, preventing the Austrian unit from going forward. While one lieutenant ran across to silence the Hungarian rifles, another rose to lead his platoon forward. Laserz never forgot the face: "frightened, white as chalk, gripping the pistol in his right hand with white-knuckled fingers, looking first at us and then at the wood" occupied by the Russians. The lieutenant was killed instantly; in fact, he had already been shot when Laserz noticed him and began yelling, *"Niederlegen!* Lie down!"

The buglers blew the storm signal and the whole company rose to its feet, into a withering fire. Another lieutenant led the charge, "waving his saber, screaming and yelling." He was overtaken by the company commander, "Captain Beyrer, who sped forward like a white cloud, in his white linen pants." The Honvéds also stormed forward; Laserz remembered one stumbling up beside him, utterly blind because he was holding his trenching tool in front of his face as a shield. As they neared the wood—men falling left and right, the air filled with roars, screams, and shouted prayers—a group of Hungarians entered the wood, then burst back out of it in panicky retreat. Laserz reached the wood and found it abandoned. As was their custom, the Russians had held it long enough to inflict maximal casualties on the Austrian bayonet charges, then retired. Laserz saw his first badly wounded soldiers—"half naked, covered in blood, screaming in agony."

Coming face-to-face with some Russians who had lost their way in the trees, Laserz jerked his rifle to his shoulder, and the

Russians, "big blond-bearded chickens," threw their hands in the air and surrendered. The Austrians studied these prisoners and were most impressed by the simple peasant smocks the Russians wore for battle dress: *"Du, die haben keine Knöpfe!* Hey, they have no buttons! Can you believe it? These guys have no buttons!" Then they took their first souvenirs, mainly Russian caps and bandoliers. Strolling back to the edge of the wood, Laserz saw the casualties—dead Austrians and Hungarians strewn across the meadow, and wounded ones "moaning and wailing" as the sun set and the wood darkened.[2]

Laserz' unit was a small piece of Brudermann's much-reduced Third Army. Several divisions had been sent to Auffenberg, and three more were still on the rails from Serbia. But, ordered by Conrad to attack, Brudermann—like Laserz—collided with the Russians at the Zlota Lipa. Weaving through the green, lush land, III Corps' 6th Division slammed into the same obstacles as Laserz' 4th Regiment on their right. "We'd walk right into Russian positions that we hadn't even seen," a staff officer noted, "and be hit at point-blank range with shrapnel and rifles." Instead of retreating, the Austrians attacked, their officers dully intoning (to mollify Conrad), "despite heroic efforts, very heavy losses, and repeated storm attacks, the men made no progress." When units did push into the Russian line and call for flanking attacks, they were told that the flanking attack could not be delivered because every Austro-Hungarian unit was already fully engaged by "vastly superior Russian forces."[3] In this sloppy action—what historians would name the First Battle of Lemberg—Brudermann had sallied against what he took for an isolated Russian corps. Fooled by Ruzski's lethargic advance, he only now grasped that he was attacking not a corps but an entire *army,* the four corps of Brusilov's Eighth Army, and was outnumbered three to one.

On Brudermann's left, General Desiderius Kolossváry led the Austro-Hungarian XI Corps to an uncertain fate, his instructions reflecting Conrad's continuing incuriosity about Russian strength: "Advance on the left of our III and XII Corps to cover their attack on the enemy, who has crossed our border at Brody and Tarnopol."[4] That was it: "the enemy." Conrad said nothing about the Russians' strength or location. Kolossváry accordingly marched east from Lemberg, planning to occupy the Bug crossing at Busk and assail the flank of whatever Russian forces were engaged by the two corps on his right. The march alone, with tenderfoots on dusty roads in steaming heat, left Kolossváry's corps prostrate for a day. They rested on August 26, while Brudermann disposed his other units as if he were Napoleon at Austerlitz, planning to fix the Russians in place and then smash in their flanks with the corps (like Kolossváry's) on his wings. Easy meat during Habsburg maneuvers in 1913, where Brudermann had been decisively beaten by Auffenberg, Brudermann was faring no better in real war. Oddly, he anticipated no threat to his flanks, believing that a division detached to either side would secure him against envelopment and that "the battle will be *decided* in the center by the *unified* attack of the two divisions of our XII Corps against whatever enemy units are facing our III Corps." The imprecision of his plans—"whatever enemy units," in an age of telephones, airplanes, and automobiles—was as striking as the onslaught of the Russians, who at that very moment were closing on Brudermann.[5]

One hundred and ninety-two Russian battalions tramped toward the ninety-one Austro-Hungarian battalions of XI, III, and XII Corps. Resuming his weary march from Lemberg, a still unsuspecting Kolossváry found Busk already in Russian hands; he faced south to aid the two corps to his right, requesting that the 44th Landwehr Division and 11th Honvéd Cavalry Division of Archduke Joseph Ferdinand's XIV Corps "attack the flank and rear" of the Russian forces in his path. The result was not the one he expected: "The 44th Landwehr Division refused, and the Honvéd Cavalry Division never replied." Having been sent up to Komarów and then recalled to Lemberg (a third time), the archduke's corps had been marched into the ground and was effectively hors de combat. "In view of these unforeseen circumstances," Kolossváry reported, "my corps was unable to intervene effectively in the battle." He had a go at ineffectively sending his brigades without the flank protection that XIV Corps would have provided toward the Russian positions at Krasne and suffering—as he delicately put it—"rather large" casualties, "quite large" among the

Once considered Austria's "boy wonder" and "hope of the future" and a court favorite of the emperor and the archduke, General Rudolf Brudermann was crushed at Lemberg and Rawa-Ruska. The boy wonder was relieved of command and sent back to Vienna. CREDIT: National Archives

officers. Half of his guns were destroyed by Russian artillery fire.[6] The Austrian 80th Regiment fired at the Russians at Krasne with even less effect than usual. They discovered after the battle that they'd been mistakenly supplied with the blank cartridges used in peacetime maneuvers instead of live bullets.[7]

The Russians, meanwhile, flooded the Austrian center and flanks. Austro-Hungarian staff officers—who were getting information on Russian movements not from their cavalry but from Galician refugees who were streaming back through their lines—scribbled worried messages in blue pencil and sent them galloping back to Lemberg: "Division forced to retreat by *very* numerous enemy forces; our casualties *very* heavy."[8] Having loaned XIV Corps to Auffenberg, Brudermann had only nine divisions of his own and two of the Second Army's to hold the entire right flank of the Austrian position in Galicia. His losses were appalling, many units losing two-thirds of their effectives. In the center, east of Przemyslany, which was a big, prosperous market town, General Emil Colerus' III Corps tried repeatedly to drive the Russians back . . . with bayonet charges. This was entirely the wrong approach, and every brigade reported "very heavy casualties." Invisible and immune to shrapnel in their deep, narrow trenches, the Russians awaited every Austrian attack, then rose as one and flattened it with salvo fire. As the Austrians fled from these Russian fusillades, the Russians counterattacked into the openings and hit the Austrian flanks.[9]

As Brudermann and Kövess retired ten miles to the next river line, the Gnila Lipa—just twenty-five miles from Lemberg—the arrival of more units of the Second Army from Serbia on the right increased the Austrian strength in this critical sector to fifteen weak infantry divisions (for a total of 145,000 men) and 828 guns. But it was like a finger in the dike against Brusilov and now Ruzski, who was dividing his strength between this fight and the one against Auffenberg, yielding a total of sixteen strong Russian infantry divisions, comprising nearly three hundred thousand men, with 1,304 guns.

Brudermann stubbornly ordered more attacks on August 27. Still sounding like Napoleon, he assured his generals that the "Fourth Army is driving victoriously into Russia" and that all that remained was for his Lemberg army to "deliver the blow that will decide the entire war." He ordered his three corps to attack again from Rohatyn and the other villages along the Gnila Lipa, with cavalry to guard the flanks. The Second Army, with General Eduard von Böhm-Ermolli finally on the scene, would wheel forward on the right to engulf the Russians. Indeed, every night during the last week of August the disbelieving generals of the Third and Second Armies would receive orders from Archduke Friedrich and Conrad to "resume the attack" at first light.[10] But every Austrian attack ended the same way, shot to a standstill by Russian defensive fire and then enveloped from the flanks by Russian counterattacks.[11] Panic shot down the roads behind every Austro-Hungarian unit, the supply trains running off—as they always did—but even well-disciplined units firing at each other. "A battery of our 44th Field Artillery Regiment mistook our Bosnians for Cossacks and shelled them for five minutes—32 were killed and many wounded," the 6th Division dolefully reported. The division commander and his staff were in a farmhouse studying their maps, the Bosnians resting outside, when the guns opened fire, nearly exterminating the headquarters as well.[12]

The Austrians were pummeled backward, losing ground and touch with neighboring units. "No contact with the 22nd Landwehr Division since early this morning," General Colerus reported late on the twenty-eighth.[13] In Przemysl, Conrad phoned Brudermann's staff chief, General Rudolf Pfeffer, and refused to credit Pfeffer's explanation of what was happening at the front. "But where is the XI Corps *fighting*?" Conrad sputtered. "What's III Corps *doing*?" Pfeffer told him that their attacks had been shredded and that they needed to retreat behind the Gnila Lipa. "But if you'd only followed *my* instructions," Conrad retorted, "then you wouldn't be talking about a *retreat*." He slammed down the phone and turned to his adjutant, Major Rudolf Kundmann, snarling, "Es ist geschlagen! They're beaten." He began to compose a new narrative for posterity: "He's retreating! Because of this insubordination, things are going wrong."[14]

Conrad, the "château general" par excellence, ordered more attacks on the Gnila Lipa for August 29–30, while the Austrian divisions there looked for any cover they could find from plunging Russian fire and the sun. General Alfred Krauss, who liked Conrad, was reminded now that the chief was "at heart always a tactician, with no interest in strategic and operational questions, such as how to deploy a mass army in fighting condition, and how to move, feed and supply it, and furnish it with real plans."[15] Conrad was now confirming that verdict, with his heedless yammering about attacks when all was so obviously lost in the strategic sense. Kolossváry reported that most of XI Corps could march and fight no longer; the marches and battles of August 25–27 had exhausted them. "Our fighting fitness has plummeted; we cannot be regarded as full-strength for some time," he noted, adding that "employing lightly trained march brigades as 'operative units' equivalent to trained field troops is plainly not working. We'll do our best."[16]

Most of Brudermann's Third Army was crammed in a space barely five miles long, and it made an excellent target and was easily flanked. The Second Army's VII Corps jabbed daily at the Russians on their front, but when they discovered Russians crossing the Dniester from the south behind them, they stopped jabbing and retreated instead.[17] Conrad howled in frustration. Why weren't the men of the Second and Third Armies *attacking?* General Pfeffer asked Conrad to come to the front to see for himself what was happening, but Conrad replied that he was too busy in Przemysl. "Too bad," Pfeffer later wrote. "One glimpse of the Russian ring of fire would have cured his delusions."[18] To appease Conrad's offensive spirit, Pfeffer proposed thrusts that could not even be attempted.[19] With two heavy howitzer batteries per division—the Austrians had none—the Russians simply pulverized the Austrians from long range.

In this First Battle of Lemberg, twenty thousand Austro-Hungarian troops were captured, along with seventy guns. Brusilov, sweeping around Brudermann's right flank, was surprised at the number of cannon, machine guns, wagons, and prisoners abandoned by the retreating Austrians. The thousands of wounded on both sides were surprised at the lack of attention paid to them. Brusilov had been assured by his medical director that he had beds for three thousand wounded at Berezany; thirty-five hundred wounded men and officers were sent there, only to find that there were beds for just four hundred and the rest had to be laid on the ground in the open.[20]

Brudermann was sounding less Napoleonic on August 30, when he finally grasped the facts of the matter: "After a multiday battle against an overwhelming enemy, the army must retreat and regroup at a new line." He indicated the Wereszyca River, which lay *west* of Lemberg.[21] The war was barely a week old, and Conrad was on the verge of losing the fourth-largest city of Austria-Hungary and the capital of Galicia. His armies were being hammered apart in distant, unconnected actions—Dankl and Auffenberg around Krásnik and Komarów, Brudermann and Böhm-Ermolli at Lemberg. Had the Russians been better organized, they might have destroyed the entire Austrian North Army, but they were still moving slowly, and Ivanov, who had shifted his headquarters back to Kiev, still refused to believe that the armies of Dankl and Auffenberg represented Conrad's main striking force. Like Ruzski, he took them for a mere flank guard and kept peering toward Lemberg, looking for the armed hordes he assumed were coming up to reinforce Brudermann and carry the war into Russia.

If the Russians couldn't comprehend the extent of Conrad's bungling, his own soldiers could. By now, the Austro-Hungarian troops recognized the stupidity of their commanders, who persisted in sending them into the teeth of Russian trenches and battery positions with fatuous explanations like this: "The Russians rarely fire shells, because theirs don't explode."[22] That was news to these scarified men. In fact, it was the Austrian artillery that was proving harmless, the AOK learning from Russian POWs that the Austrian gunners were setting their shrapnel fuses to burst too high, permitting the Russians to run safely under the falling debris.[23] Austrian runs at the Russians, meanwhile, were anything but safe. An Austrian colonel explained how this happened: although in peacetime studies and maneuvers, officers had been trained "always to seek the flank and go around the enemy," in the heat of battle the macho watchword was *gradaus,* "straight up the gut"—no feints, no flanks, just "a hearty, crisp attack that fitted better with the Austrian tradition 'always to attack.'" This instinct killed monstrous numbers of Habsburg officers, "who felt compelled to sacrifice themselves pointlessly, to inspire the men."

Within a few days, even such obviously heroic inspiration had worn thin: the platoon leader would race toward the Russians and be killed, while the platoon itself would hang back. This prompted a subtle change in Austrian tactics. Now the lieutenant would delegate the hero's role to an NCO and follow in the second line, "spade and rifle in hand, employing lethal force against any of the men who hung back and refused to attack."[24] Many Austrians surrendered to the nearest Russian to escape certain death, but this did not always end well either. One Austrian prisoner described his capture: "We were disarmed, robbed of our valuables—watches, money, knives etc.—and we were shut in a pigsty for three nights with nothing to eat but raw potatoes. On the fourth day, we were released only to be forced to go forward in the Russian skirmish line and point out our positions to the enemy."[25]

While Ruzski picked his way over the Gnila Lipa, Brusilov—who had taken Tarnopol on the twenty-seventh and then Halicz, the old Galician capital on the Dniester, on the twenty-ninth—turned north toward Lemberg and into Brudermann's unguarded flank. In its prewar study of Russian generals, Conrad's staff had been especially leery of Brusilov, noting, "He's tough, smart, and dynamic." Now Brusilov proved them right, shrewdly taking Brudermann between two fires, his own and Conrad's. From the calm of his chancery in Przemysl, Conrad ordered on August 31 that Lemberg be held at all costs "for political and military reasons." Brudermann despondently complied, ordering his units and Böhm-Ermolli's to group themselves in an arc around Lemberg, using every little brook and hill for cover, but to "retreat to the west if pressed hard." Austro-Hungarian cavalry divisions were ordered to close up with the infantry on the flanks, dismount, and entrench. It was like Custer's Last Stand.[26] The Russians pressed hard, rolling up the flank, and the Austrians were soon retreating, Brusilov's aircraft spying masses of Austro-Hungarian troops boarding westbound trains at Lemberg station and other masses retreating on the roads toward the San River.[27]

Reeling backward, Brudermann yielded Lemberg on September 2 and retreated to the Grodek position, a line of heights behind the Wereszyca River. He placed III Corps in the center at Grodek, XI Corps on the left, and XII Corps and the 34th Division on the right. Brudermann tried to buck up his demoralized army: "The Third and Second Army have slowed a numerically superior enemy in his march west. . . . Now Fourth Army is turning to support us in a combined attack on the enemy—the hour for our revenge on this overconfident foe has come!" But his words fell on ears deafened by Russian artillery and by the lies and hyperbole emanating from the Austrian high command.[28]

With Austria's eastern capital—which had been regarded as the springboard for operations into Russia—now in Russian hands, all levels of the Austro-Hungarian army had to question the competency of their leadership and even the ultimate purpose of their efforts. Brudermann's staff chief later blamed the disaster on Conrad's *Schlamperei* (sloppiness): "The reason for the defeat was simply AOK's error-prone mobilization and total misreading of the Russians. . . . It was only now—during the battles for Lemberg—that AOK discovered that the main body of the Russian army was *here*."[29] Trailing the retreating Austrians, Stanley

Hungarians of the late-arriving Austrian Second Army hurrying to the front near Lemberg in August 1914.
CREDIT: Heeresgeschichtliches Museum, Wien

Washburn, an American war correspondent for the *Times* of London, visited wounded Austrians in the hospitals of Lemberg and was surprised to discover that "the ordinary enlisted man in the Austrian army had no idea whatsoever what the war was about." The Austro-Hungarian casualties knew nothing about Russia, even less about Serbia, and none even knew that Britain and France were in the war.[30]

Ever mindful of his image, Conrad knew that scapegoats would be needed for the loss of Lemberg. He fired Brudermann's general staff chief, General Rudolf Pfeffer, along with several corps, division, and brigade commanders. In his memoirs, Conrad would blame the defeat on the "passivity" of Brudermann, who had failed to implement the chief's otherwise winning plan of campaign.[31] But there was no winning plan, and Brudermann would have had a hard time executing such a plan even if it did exist, for the Austrians found themselves all but immobilized by Russian fire and their own creaky logistics. As in Serbia, the whole Habsburg army was limping along at a snail's pace thanks to its overlarge corps (forty-five battalions each) and its superfluous supply trains.

These Austro-Hungarian armies contained one horse-drawn wagon for every three combatants. Efforts before the war to create lighter, more mobile corps had stalled in the irreducible face of Habsburg bureaucracy, and so the army marched with gargantuan impediments. One disgruntled general noted that whereas Japanese officers had fought the Russians for a year and a half without baggage—two Japanese officers sharing a single suitcase for the entire campaign in Manchuria—Austro-Hungarian generals in 1914 were each allotted two entire "personal wagons" for clothing and other effects as well as three additional wagons for their divisional or brigade headquarters. Each of those headquarters was, in turn, allotted sufficient wagons to carry fifty-three hundred pounds of additional baggage—twice the luggage carried by an entire five-hundred-man battalion—for just three men, the general and his two aides. Overall, an Austro-Hungarian division trailed about 105 of these wagons as well as 45 for the troops, 45 more for their ammunition, 7 for food, and then field kitchens, bakeries, and ambulances. It was a wonder the generals could even locate their guns among the trunks of clothing, books, crates of wine, and canned delicacies.[32]

With impediments like these, it was hardly surprising that Archduke Friedrich now cabled the German kaiser urgently demanding a German relief offensive and "loyal fulfillment" of Berlin's alliance obligations, whatever that meant in this vast, fluctuating war. Conrad wired Moltke four times in the last week of August demanding that a dozen German divisions—four corps—be detached from the Western Front and committed to operations here in the east.[33] The Germans, fully engaged on the Marne against a million French troops and having already shattered two Russian armies at Tannenberg and the Masurian Lakes (northwest of Conrad's Russian front), were thunderstruck.

At German great headquarters in Koblenz, the Austro-Hungarian military liaison, General Joseph von Stürgkh, noted a sharp deterioration in relations with his ally. The operation Conrad proposed was impossible; with the unsubdued armies of the Russian Northwest Front on his flank, Moltke could not very well order Hindenburg's Eighth Army to plunge southeast to aid the Austrians. This was the view even of Austrians in German headquarters, who now spoke of conflicting "party lines": Conrad's, and everyone else's. Looking over the maps, Stürgkh and General Alexander von Üxküll—the graying captain of Emperor Franz Joseph's horse guards—judged Conrad's plan *"ein Ding der Unmöglichkeit,"* an impossible thing. The kaiser took Stürgkh aside and heatedly said: "Our little army in East Prussia has diverted twelve enemy corps, and destroyed or defeated them; hasn't *that* made your Austrian offensive any easier?"[34]

Apparently not. While Austro-Hungarian engineers poured gasoline over mountains of food around Lemberg (as starving troops shuffled past), Conrad sat down to a hearty breakfast in Przemysl, jauntily remarking to his companions that were Archduke Franz Ferdinand still alive, "he would have me shot" for the loss of Austria's eastern capital and its massive railway facilities. No fewer than one thousand locomotives and fifteen thousand railcars were left to the Russians. Arriving in the magnificent city, the *Times'* war correspondent surveyed its parks, boulevards, and grand hotels and judged it "the greatest prize taken by any of the belligerents in this conflict so far."[35]

The archduke had warned Conrad before the war about the danger of loading peripheral fronts with too many troops and the main one with too few, yet Conrad, in his determination to crush the Serbs, had ignored the warning.[36] Galicia's Ukrainians were now paying the price for the gulf between Conrad's aspirations and reality. Although Ukrainians formed the majority of Galicia's population, the Austrian leadership began to view them—as they had judged the Serbs of Bosnia—as unreliable, ordering Ukrainian officials, teachers, and priests to leave the province and relocate to Moravia, along with their Greek Catholic bishop. In western Galicia, a thousand Ukrainian notables were interned for possible Russian sympathies. Austrian staffs were given a map, the *Nationalitäten Galiziens,* that depicted the expansive "Russophile" sections of the vast province: the entire southern fringe from Neu Sandez to Lemberg, and the eastern border from Rawa-Ruska around to Tarnopol, with large pockets in the interior as well.[37]

To restore Austrophilia, Archduke Friedrich ordered atrocities: "individuals and even whole communities guilty of treasonous behavior should be struck down with maximum ruthlessness."[38]

With a bloodthirsty archduke on one flank, knout-swinging Russians on the other, and cholera blooming everywhere Austrian troops appeared, the Jews of Galicia—the monarchy's densest Jewish area—gathered up what portable property they had and fled to Vienna, where they settled in the Leopoldstadt quarter and began to perfect the mechanisms of the black market in state-rationed goods such as bread, flour, meat, fat, milk, and coal. Even as they purchased from Galician Jews, the Viennese deplored their *Schleichhandel*, black market, and began to speak darkly of a "Jewish question."[39]

To strike blows against the enemy, as opposed to his own population, Conrad changed course again. Reports from Austrian pilots revealed that Ruzski's Third Army was turning northwest, away from Brudermann, presumably to hit Auffenberg in the flank. Confident that Brudermann could hold Brusilov on a river line west of Lemberg, Conrad had agreed that the Third and Second Armies should evacuate Lemberg and retreat to the Wereszyca River, pulling the Russians after them. Why Conrad thought that an army smaller than the one that had deployed on the Gnila Lipa would do better behind this river than behind that one—against an even larger Russian army—was just one of the many mysteries of this campaign.

Conrad directed Brudermann and Böhm-Ermolli to hold the Russians on the Wereszyca while Auffenberg wheeled southeast with the Fourth Army through Rawa-Ruska to strike the Russian flank. The Third and Second Armies would hold the Russians long enough for the pincer to bite. Conrad's remote manipulation of his battered army like pins on a staff map would have been comical had so many men not been worn out, maimed, or killed by his cascade of errors. Like Potiorek, Conrad gave no indication that he understood real war at all.[40] After the exertions of the past week, Auffenberg could hardly move, let alone fight, so many of his horses having perished from wounds, hunger, and fatigue. "Take horses from the supply service for the ammunition columns; take horses from the ammunition columns for the field batteries," Boroevic counseled his generals. When not fighting, the men were ordered to capture as many stray animals as they could and put

Ukrainian civilians hung by the Austrian army in Galicia. "Individuals and whole communities guilty of treasonous behavior should be struck down with maximum ruthlessness," Archduke Friedrich ordered in August 1914. These are Ukrainians executed for suspected Russian sympathies.
CREDIT: Heeresgeschichtliches Museum, Wien

them back in harness. Soldiers whose rifles had been lost or damaged were told to scour the ground for a replacement.[41]

Auffenberg's Fourth Army, which had marched north since the Russian retreat from Komarów on August 30, was now ordered to turn around and march south. "Armies are not chess pieces," Auffenberg grumbled. The revised plan made no sense, not least because Conrad knew that Ruzski was wheeling north and offering his front—bristling with artillery and machine guns— not his flank.[42] Twice the Fourth Army traversed the battlefield of

Komarów, the second time gagging from the reek of death. Fourth Army units swerving around to the south in a pouring rain "that turned the roads to slime" stared in horror at the ground around Komarów: "countless corpses, ours and theirs mashed together, dead horses, and all the litter of war." The troopers naturally began to doubt the probity of a high command that had been urging them on to Lublin and now was driving them with no less urgency in the opposite direction.[43]

Turning in such a tight space, the Austro-Hungarians blundered into each other and the Russians, who were closing in all around them. Confused skirmishes tore through the night, everyone firing nervously at everyone else.[44] On the Wereszyca, generals received the usual furious telegrams from Conrad criticizing their "passive defense" behind one slender river barrier after the next and the "continual retreating." Conrad ordered his generals to attack instead, "to improve the overall situation." But officers actually present at the front found that further attacks, as one senior staff officer put it, were "humanly impossible. The men could not be driven to even one more bayonet attack; they were crushed by the non-stop marching and fighting and lack of sleep." Ordered to attack at Horyniec, the 8th Regiment went forward a few steps, but "dissolved and began running back when the first shrapnel burst overhead."[45]

General Auffenberg inspected a group of Russian prisoners on August 30. He was tremendously impressed by their drab, dirt-colored uniforms, observing that even at two hundred paces they blended into their surroundings so well that he couldn't make them out. He chatted with the Russian officers, most of whom spoke German. One of them indicated the corpse-strewn battlefield and said: "And all of this, for *what?*"[46] Auffenberg may have asked himself the same question; he could see that the victory he had claimed at Komarów was about to be dashed. He began concocting an alibi for posterity: "Hardly had the thunder of the guns died out at Komarów than we were directed south to aid our threatened comrades of [Third] Army." The Russians would "hurl ever larger numbers against our feared Fourth Army in the blood-soaked fields of Rawa-Ruska." In his diary he added: "I had done all that I could do."[47]

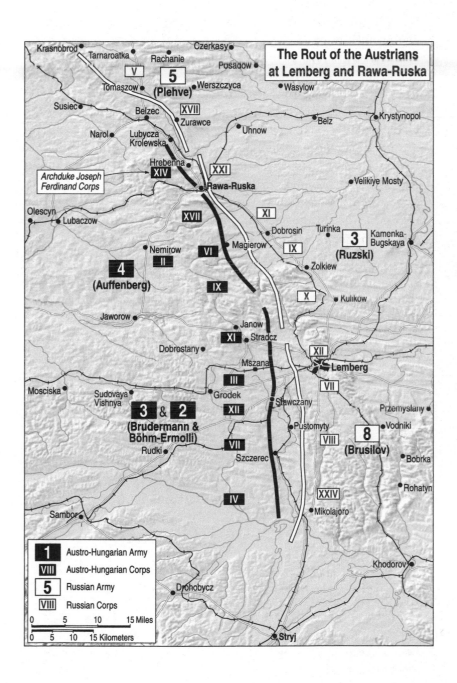

The Rout of the Austrians at Lemberg and Rawa-Ruska

The Russians were deploying ever larger numbers along the line from Krásnik down to Lemberg, and the Austrians were in no condition to hold them back. They were outnumbered, and—thanks to Dankl's retreat from Krásnik—about to be enveloped from both flanks. Colonel Joseph Paic, the staff chief of the Austrian XIV Corps, recalled finding six Russian divisions on his front, and three more plus an entire Russian cavalry corps on his flank.[48] Exhausted and running out of everything, Austrian troops were ordered to collect rifles from their fallen comrades and to grab the contents of their cartridge pouches as well. Gunners were ordered not to destroy their guns if threatened with capture, but merely to "remove and bury the gunsight for later use, if the gun is ever recaptured."[49]

Auffenberg was astonished by his new orders; the only logical course, he believed, was a retreat to the forts of Przemysl and the San River. The broad river and modern forts might halt the Russian pursuit and allow the Austrians to regroup and join themselves wing to wing with the German forces that were beginning to arrive from the west (not because the French were beaten, but because the Austrians kept losing).[50] But Conrad was not prepared to retreat just yet. He kept the Hofburg in the dark with vague telegrams that were reproduced for the myopic emperor in large-print editions with coarse-scale maps. General Bolfras, the emperor's adjutant, abetted the deception with soothing margin notes like this one on August 30: "Your Majesty, the situation is not as bad as it might seem."[51]

But it was. The Third Army was already broken; it would not hold up a corps, let alone Brusilov's entire Eighth Army. Everyone was summoned to the front and given a rifle, including engineers, teamsters, and the local Polish and Ukrainian militias, who arrived in iridescent peasant blouses, compounding the chaos. On September 4, Brudermann tried to galvanize his weary army, assuring the troops that Auffenberg had won "a complete victory, seizing 20,000 prisoners and 200 guns."[52] He ordered his generals to prepare a march east to retake Lemberg in conjunction with the Fourth Army descending from the north. In the same orders, he mentioned a "gap between our Third and Fourth Armies," and

fretted that the Russians might plunge into it. They did. Brudermann sent three cavalry divisions to seal the gap, but they were
brushed aside. Far from blaming himself for the debacle, Conrad
blamed Brudermann, pronounced him "ill," and packed him off
to retirement. It was a dismal end for a general described twenty
years earlier as Austria's "boy wonder" and "hope of the future."[53]

There was something ineffably shabby about the way Conrad
and Archduke Friedrich created scapegoats for their failures. Fritzl,
a mediocre commander at best, had acceded to all of Conrad's ca-
prices, and now wrote the emperor (who liked Brudermann) a long
letter explaining why the general had to go: "In the multi-day battle east of Lemberg and then in the fighting retreat to the Grodek
position, General Brudermann exercised too little control over his
subordinate generals, who ended up doing whatever they wanted
without any unified command." This was a lie to hide the fact that
Brudermann had done everything that Conrad had ordered, and
had merely been overwhelmed by the weight of Russian numbers,
which Conrad had always underestimated. Brudermann took the
fall anyway, the emperor's only consolation the usual one: a cash
gift of six thousand crowns and continued active duty (and full salary) as a "supernumerary officer" instead of retirement.[54]

On September 5, an indiscreet—and badly informed—princess yelled out of the window of her coach in Vienna that Auffenberg had retaken Lemberg, a rumor that swirled through the
streets of the city and was picked up by the afternoon newspapers.
Within a day, the story had to be retracted, further depressing morale in the capital.[55] Conrad replaced Brudermann with General
Svetozar Boroevic, who immediately noted his new army's lack
of "discipline and obedience. Apathy and lack of confidence," he
reported, "have entered its ranks."[56] Boroevic was struck by the
inexorable collapse that followed every heavy Russian barrage:
"In every battle so far, large numbers of our troops—even entire
units—retreat without authorization when the enemy guns open
up." Sending reserves to relieve those fugitives didn't help, "because *they* won't attack either."[57] Undeterred, Conrad ordered
more attacks for September 7–9. The Second Army was finally at
full strength, and he was determined to use it.

But as Conrad drained his left wing to bolster his right, the situation to the north became catastrophic. As Auffenberg marched south, he opened a seventy-mile gap between himself and Dankl, which the Russian Fifth Army poured into. A new Russian army, General Platon Lichitski's Ninth, began groping for Dankl's other flank around Krásnik. Ivanov now glimpsed an opportunity to envelop all three corps of Dankl's army before they could gain the safety of the San. Russian civilians delightedly joined the fight, ringing church bells and igniting smoke and fire signals to alert their army to the presence of Austro-Hungarian troops, who could be pinpointed for Russian artillery with a burning thatch roof.[58]

Nearly encircled, Dankl, who had driven almost to Lublin in the last days of August, fled for his life. His divisions were harassed the entire way by emboldened Russians, who left their trenches and tried to cut Dankl off. One of his regiments lost an entire thousand-man battalion on the retreat: dug in for the night on September 5, they were overrun in the morning by a Russian column and captured unscathed.[59] Dankl retreated behind the San on September 9, and Viennese musicians shelved their copies of *Das Lied vom General Dankl*. The "Russian dogs" had not been beaten after all.

Now in command of the Third Army, Boroevic assured his disbelieving men on September 9 that "all of our armies are now beginning to wring significant successes from the enemy."[60] That would have been news to Auffenberg, who was fighting at Rawa-Ruska, thirty miles northwest of Lemberg, without protection on her flank and hounded by Ruzski's Third Army on his front and and two of Plehve's corps behind him and on his right. While enerals struggled against the Russian horde, Conrad in Prze-vrestled with the problem of Gina. "If I lose [this war]," he ed to his political advisor, Redlich, on September 9, "I'll woman too, a horrifying thought, for then I'll be alone it of my life."[61] The chief press officer in AOK, Colo-ilian von Hoen, spoke of Conrad's encroaching "se-commander was hardly sleeping, and while his army at up half the night writing long letters to Gina and ar-old mother. Redlich was stunned by Conrad's oesn't believe in his own historical calling to be simo against Russia."[62]

With four armies, fifty-two divisions, and half a million men in the field, this Battle of Rawa-Ruska (also known as the Second Battle of Lemberg) was Austria-Hungary's biggest battle of the war. Conrad's third and youngest son, Lieutenant Herbert Conrad, died in it. Herbert's 15th Dragoons were part of Archduke Joseph Ferdinand's wandering XIV Corps, and on September 8—their mission and direction having been changed by Lieutenant Conrad's father for the fourth time—they trotted into a mass of Russian artillery and infantry near Rawa-Ruska. Torn by falling shells, they attacked the Russians, who fired shrapnel as the dragoons galloped toward them and then opened up on them from both flanks. Attempting to attack machine guns, artillery, and entrenched infantry on horseback, the dragoons got no closer than three hundred yards before being thrown back with the loss of twenty-four dead and sixty wounded, Conrad's son among the dead.[63]

Crushed by the loss of his favorite child, Conrad later tried to clean this battle up for history as well, suggesting that he had intended Auffenberg to slide like a stiletto into Ruzski's ribs as the Russian pursued Boroevic west; however, Conrad's orders at the time revealed that he knew that Ruzski had stopped his pursuit of Boroevic and wheeled north to disengage Plehve instead. This led to an artless head-on collision, which the Austrians had no hope of winning. Auffenberg, with 175 weary, depreciated battalions, stumbled into battle with two entire Russian armies—the 180 battalions of Ruzski's Third Army and the 180 battalions of Plehve's Fifth Army.

Colonel Alexander Brosch von Aarenau, Franz Ferdinand's military secretary before the war, found himself on the leading edge of this clash on September 6. His 2nd *Kaiserjäger* Regiment had been pushed and pulled around all week by Conrad, first given to Auffenberg, then sent in pursuit of the Russians after Komarów, then called back toward Lemberg to assist in the defense there. Now they reeled south from Komarów through bogs, woods, hot sun, cold rain, horseflies the size of a man's thumb by day, mosquitoes and bewildering blackness at night. Ordered to close up with XVII Corps, Brosch repeatedly signaled his whereabouts to them, but no one acknowledged the message.

Brosch began to grasp that he was being surrounded, which, like the rest of XIV Corps, he was, by the Russian Fifth Army from the north and the Russian Third Army from the south. Archduke Joseph Ferdinand had just wired Auffenberg: "Something is coming at us from the north; still not sure exactly what." It took this Russian pressure finally to stymie Conrad's daily mischief. He had just wired Auffenberg from Przemysl, ordering him to summon XIV Corps *back* to the northwest, this time to support Dankl's First Army, which had turned about and was retreating from Krásnik toward Tarnow with the Vistula on its right and the Russian Fourth Army feeling for its left. Now, according to Conrad's latest orders, XIV Corps was supposed to march back to the north to protect that exposed flank.

It was like a cruel joke, but this time only a regiment of XIV Corps could be dispatched on the fool's errand: the rest were locked in by the Russian Fifth Army, which now spilled into the yawning gap between Dankl and Auffenberg. Preparing to eat and spend the night in one grubby Galician village, Karow, Brosch's troops were forced in the evening to leave it and retreat through a dense wood to another grubby Galician village, Hujcze, on the other side to escape encroaching Russian forces, that unknown "something from the north" mentioned by Archduke Joseph Ferdinand. The regiment wearily slouched down to the southern edge of the wood by Hujcze, just a few miles northeast of Rawa-Ruska, in the evening of September 6. "What happened there," General Joseph Paic wrote in his summary of the battle, "gives us a lesson in the interaction of night, woods, swamps, and indescribable fatigue. Even elite troops and their leaders, in this case the *Kaiserjäger*, can be undone by these things."[64]

Emerging from the woods, Brosch's men found not a silent village but a Russian camp. Brosch, in the middle of the Austrian march column—with a company on point, then a battalion, then the regimental command post, with two battalions behind—struggled to deploy his men as the Russians, just as startled as the Austrians, poured ragged volleys into the wood. General Schneider, who was commanding the nearby Austro-Hungarian 5th Brigade, rode over to confer with Brosch, and an officer overheard their exchange: "Bravo! You've done well! There's light at the end of this tunnel!" the general shouted, to which Brosch replied: "We can't do anything else, we've got to keep moving." Conrad's hunters were only too aware that they had become the hunted.

As Brosch and Schneider worked to tie their brigades together and escape the Russian noose, Brosch emerged into a clearing amid Russian tents, wagons, horses, and a motor pool. With the Russians furiously counterattacking to secure their camp and the road to Rawa-Ruska, which was already filling with Russian supply trains and artillery, Brosch swerved off to the right and led his exhausted regiment cross-country on a fighting retreat to the west, with Russians emerging from the woods the Austrians had just exited and from the villages around them. Brosch was killed, along with dozens of his men.[65]

Brosch's fate was the Battle of Rawa-Ruska in a nutshell. General Karl Kritek's XVII Corps, just south of Brosch, had been in continuous action against the Russians since September 5. Slopping through the rain and bogs, snatching an hour or two of sleep in the open or in lousy peasant huts, they had repeatedly dug in beside their roads and tracks to repel Russian attacks, which arrived without warning from the north, south, or east, and sometimes from all three directions. The 6th *Jäger* Battalion spent the entire day on September 6 in such a hastily dug position, sprayed with Russian artillery and machine gun fire and unable to eat because food couldn't be carried to the beleaguered troops. As night fell, the Russians attacked with infantry. The Austrians beat off the last attack, then slept an hour or two; soon September 7 dawned with more Russian attacks. By the end of that day, most of the officers who had not been killed at Komarów were lying dead or wounded, along with 150 more troops. There were also scores of "missing," which was the official term for men whose bodies had not been recovered, usually because they had surrendered.

Austro-Hungarian counterattacks all along the Fourth Army front were driven back by Russian fusillades and artillery.[66] Archduke Joseph's XIV Corps, having been ordered up and down Poland by Conrad for seven frustrating days, was now told to strike south at Ruzski's Third Army. The archduke was disgusted, Paic noting in his diary on September 7: "That which we'd been trying to do, yet had been repeatedly prevented from doing, was now ordered done when it was too late to do."[67] Indeed, Conrad's planned flank attack on Ruzski was itself being mauled in the flank—by Ruzski. Plehve, meanwhile, was surging down from the north, killing off units like Brosch's, and encircling Auffenberg from the flank and rear.

On Auffenberg's right wing, Archduke Peter Ferdinand, who had failed to grasp the nettle at Dub, struggled now to grasp the sleeve of the retiring Third Army, so that the Russians couldn't split Auffenberg from Boroevic as they'd already split him from Dankl. The fighting here was as savage as it was further north in Brosch's sector, and equally pointless, from the Austrian perspective. A Russian patrol of just six men blundered into two entire battalions of Austrian infantry sheltering in a wood and threw up their hands in surrender. "No," one of the Austrian officers said in Czech, "let us surrender to *you*," and the disbelieving six-man patrol led their two thousand Austrian captives back to the Russian lines.[68] That any of this surprised Conrad was remarkable; in his prewar musings on modern firepower, he had agreed that ever since the Franco-Prussian War, troops could not be exposed to stiff defensive fire without risk of demoralization. On a visit to Austria before the war, Japanese officers had revealed that in their conflict with the Russians they'd had to substitute green troops for veterans in many assaults, for veterans wouldn't attack machine guns more than once. Conrad's own study of the Franco-Prussian War had concluded that even the best Prussian units had cracked under sustained pressure.[69]

Boroevic's musings on military history were more immediate; he'd enjoyed a brief respite in the Grodek position behind the Wereszyca. This line of heights, swelling from the confluence of the Dniester and the Wereszyca, would have been a strong position had the Russians not had sufficient forces to outflank it from all sides. Among the disgraced Brudermann's last communications to his army was this one on September 6: "Russian newspapers are reporting jubilantly that they have routed our Third Army." The troops' mission now, Brudermann declared, must be "to make the Russians eat their words." He continued to chide his officers for their less-than-discerning tactics: "I must remind you of the fundamental difference between casualties *acquired* in battle and casualties *suffered*. Casualties acquired in hard fighting do not disturb troop morale and indeed lead to victory; casualties suffered because of poor leadership discourage the troops and lead to ruin."[70] Evincing a total disregard for the distinction, the Russians piled on, Brusilov recalling that "those were troops we had *already* beaten . . . they were demoralized."[71]

Conrad ordered more attacks for September 8. He seemed finally to be grasping the tactical reasons for his defeat. "The Russian way of fighting seems to be this," he wrote his by-now frantic generals: "Defensive in trenches with strong artillery behind and on the flanks, usually well hidden, so as to achieve surprise once our infantry attacks have already been launched. They usually keep these positions for a day, inflict maximal casualties on us, and then retire to a new position to repeat the game."[72] This "game" was not exactly a Russian innovation; it was precisely the technique that had been used by the Prussians to destroy the Austrian army in 1866: the operational offensive married to a tactical defensive. That is to say, the enemy army would march offensively into Austro-Hungarian territory, then stake out formidable defensive positions to shatter the inevitable Austrian counterattacks—"inevitable" because Austrian army traditions, forged in the days of muskets, foolishly continued to vaunt the tactical offensive *(gradaus)* despite the supervening invention of machine guns and quick-firing artillery. Conrad's belated discovery that he and his pike-gray columns were being duped again, though dispatched in all directions on September 7, would not discover most of the scattered and beaten Austro-Hungarian generals until September 10, when they wearily glanced at it, scribbled the obligatory *gelesen* (read) in the margin, and filed it.

By now, everyone in the Austrian camp had tired of the game. Conrad ordered the Fourth Army to attack alongside the Third Army, but no one moved.[73] Wheelhorses were too tired to pull, troops too tired to march. The Austrians dug in behind the Wereszyca, but officers worried that even in trenches behind the river, the men would not hold. The entire Austro-Hungarian II Corps began retreating when rumors of Cossacks in their rear alarmed the men. The 3rd and 8th Divisions also began retiring, their wagon trains crowding together and causing panic. From Przemysl on September 9, Conrad fantastically complained that these "spontaneous retreats" were "ruining the otherwise successful attack of my army." As usual, he was more concerned to protect his dissolving reputation than to fight the war he had before him.[74]

On September 10, Conrad and Archduke Friedrich made their first of just three wartime visits to the front. Conrad, Fritzl, and Archduke Karl motored up from Przemysl to the Grodek position behind the Wereszyca, visited with Boroevic, ordered a last effort, and then hustled back to the safety of the San.[75] In his usual passive-aggressive manner, Conrad scolded Auffenberg that "since he'd rested in his positions yesterday while the other armies advanced victoriously," now he'd have to "redeem himself by attacking and subduing the Russians" at Rawa-Ruska and joining the "concentric attack on Lemberg." In fact, "the concentric attack on Lemberg" was another of Conrad's fictions; it was more like a desperate fight for survival by four bedraggled armies, all of which were marching west to the safety of Przemysl, not east to the relief of Lemberg. Dankl's First Army had been chased back to the San, pursued by the Russian Ninth and Fourth Armies. Auffenberg was being savaged by the Russian Fifth and Third Armies, Boroevic and Böhm-Ermolli by Brusilov's Eighth.

Having ripped Dankl and Auffenberg apart, Plehve was poised to thrust into the gap between them to reach the San. If Plehve reached the river crossings first, he'd be positioned to envelop the entire Austrian North Army, including the Third Army at Grodek and the Second Army on its right, which were themselves on the verge of being enveloped by Brusilov's Eighth Army. On September 11—the sixth day of the Battle of Rawa-Ruska, with flyer reports describing a vast Russian encirclement—Conrad ceased bloviating and ordered the Austrians to retreat toward the San River and the ring of forts around Przemysl, which they were already doing anyway.

"Tactically," Conrad later wrote, "the situation wasn't bad, but the operational situation was untenable." With the Russians hanging around the necks of the four Austrian armies, only a man

On September 10, Conrad (l.) and Archduke Friedrich (r.) made the first of only three visits to the front in the entire war. Here they stand uncertainly in the Grodek position, hearing the sounds of battle. Their German attachés stand at a discreet distance behind them. CREDIT: Heeresgeschichtliches Museum, Wien

in a quiet office in the fortress of Przemysl could distinguish operations from tactics at this hour. Moreover, as Auffenberg protested, *"who* placed the army in this operationally unfavorable predicament, so that all tactical exertions and successes were *bound* to fail?"[76] The fourteen-day Austrian retreat intensified, under the worst conditions—a thirty-mile-long convex bow from Grodek to Rawa-Ruska, with all of the armies and their roiling supply trains crowded onto a single hardened road and sandy tracks on either side. The Russians did not miss the opportunity to undertake a classic parallel pursuit, jogging along the flanks of this disordered Austrian retreat and charging in to sow yet more chaos and make off with Austrian prisoners, guns, and supplies.

Auffenberg later described the difficulty of evacuating the Austrian armies through this space, their paths blocked everywhere by artillery, field hospitals, ammunition and supply columns, telegraph and aviation units, and bridging equipment, much of which had to be abandoned to the Russians to make room for the fleeing troops.[77] The Fourth Army was ordered to burn all of the food and ammunition that had been dumped in Rawa-Ruska, and then destroy the town as well. Austro-Hungarian troops retreating in the vicinity of Galicia's railway were ordered to pull up the rails as they went.[78] Archduke Joseph Ferdinand's XIV Corps, which had already spent itself in the attack on Plehve, was all that Auffenberg had to secure his rear. These men had been marching and fighting for two weeks without rest. Ordered by Conrad to fight and open the line of retreat west to Jaroslau, which was already in Russian hands, the archduke simply ignored him and went south, conduct that only a Habsburg prince could get away with.

On September 11, threatened with total encirclement, Auffenberg retreated to the southwest. In the line for three weeks without a rest, Auffenberg's combat strength had plummeted to just ten thousand rifles.[79] The American correspondent Stanley Washburn goggled at the casualties at Rawa-Ruska, which seemed inconceivable to a man freshly arrived from Minneapolis: "The casualties on both sides were nearly 150,000—almost as many as the combined armies of Lee and Meade at the Battle of Gettysburg."[80]

In the bloodbath, Auffenberg's Fourth Army had lost half of its officers and most of its men. The Galicians—Ukrainians, Poles, and Jews—were killed in large numbers too; those who had survived thus far huddled in the cellars of their huts while the war thundered overhead. Touring the field in the wake of the Austrian retreat, Washburn expressed shock that roughly a million men had been engaged on little more than "a ten-acre lot." The fighting had been desperate; he saw evidence that "the Austrians had even tried to dig shallow trenches with their hands." He walked across the little salient, "stepping from shell hole to shell hole, each surrounded by strips of blue uniform, bones and bits of humanity blown to pieces by high explosive shell." About 120,000 of the 150,000 casualties mentioned by Washburn had been Austro-Hungarians, herded onto the ten-acre lot and butchered by Russian artillery fire. "War," Washburn sourly concluded, "is the survival of the unfit. It is always the best of the officers and the men who stay and are killed."[81] Conrad now set about sacking the unfit survivors. He had already fired Brudermann, Pfeffer, and Huyn; he now fired Schemua too. Boroevic vacated Grodek, leaving a rearguard of excuses: "Overwhelming attack on [Fourth]

Army prevents us from exploiting the victories we have won here at Lemberg; AOK has ordered the entire army back to the San."[82]

By the middle of September, the Austro-Hungarian North Army was safely behind the San River, where the forts of Przemysl offered a measure of protection. Conrad's four armies, the First, Fourth, Third, and Second, were so jumbled that several days passed while the thousands of *Versprengten* (stragglers) were sorted out and dispatched down various roads to their units. Auffenberg recalled long columns of Jewish refugees trying to extricate themselves from the war zone and the barbarous Russians.[83] Having tasted victory—or a semblance of it—at Komarów, Conrad now looked disaster in the face. The Russians had taken ninety square miles of Habsburg territory and threatened his lines of communication to the monarchy and Germany. Russian losses of 230,000 men in the campaign could be borne far more easily than the Austrian loss of 440,000.[84]

Having earlier taken credit for Auffenberg's exertions at Komarów, Conrad now unkindly blamed them for the defeat: "Auffenberg struck in a direction at Komarów that made it impossible for him to assist quickly in the Battle of Lemberg."[85] As was increasingly his habit, Conrad blamed the Germans too: "The Germans have won their greatest victories at our expense, and left us in the lurch; they have sent troops not to join us in the great struggle around Lublin, but to defend the stud farms and hunting lodges of [East Prussia]."[86] Austria-Hungary's ambassador in Berlin joined the fracas: "The Germans are blinded by their delusions of victory and always underrate our achievements. . . . We have held off the entire Russian army, permitting the Germans to accomplish great and relatively easy victories on the fine roads and railways of France." These complaints, of course, utterly disregarded the fact that the Germans had been pulling their weight on two fronts and—despite the stalemate in the west—were continuing to send troops eastward from France's "fine roads and railways" to the rutted paths of Ukraine and Poland.[87]

While the Central Powers quarreled, the left wing of Brusilov's army was overrunning the heaths and hunting lodges of Bukovina and its pretty capital, Czernowitz, which would change hands fifteen times during the war. Brusilov's vanguard rode all the way to the easternmost passes of the Carpathians, which opened into Hungary. With his left collapsing and his right outflanked, Conrad reassembled his forces around the fortress of Przemysl under pouring rain. The Austrian generals feebly exhorted their men and officers to pull themselves together. Auffenberg sounded like a management consultant: "A precondition of success and good spirits," he wrote his officers on September 15, "is the willingness of everyone to commit themselves wholeheartedly to the task at hand (marches, battles) so that everyone understands that there is *purpose* to what we are doing. . . . Nothing is more dangerous than apathy and despair."[88] But apathy and despair were all that was left. The Habsburg army had come unglued; if it had ever descried a "purpose" in the AOK's gawky arrangements, it certainly didn't anymore. Austro-Hungarian POWs in Russian captivity were observed to be "sickly and delicate, weak and undersized," appearing not "to know anything about the war."[89] Those still in the Austro-Hungarian ranks were shirking in record numbers. "Why is it that after every clash with the enemy *thousands* of stragglers circulate in the rear of our army, far from the fighting?" the AOK furiously queried. "You must discover the cause of this phenomenon and correct it."[90]

Everyone knew the cause: unending defeat. Large numbers of NCOs—a rare species to begin with—were being demoted (*degradieren*) for refusing to implement orders. Troop morale had hit rock bottom, and with the technology and leadership Austria-Hungary had, everyone knew that no corrections were coming. The Austrians had lost scores of guns in the retreat, and many of those they had extricated lacked gunsights, the crews having removed and buried them in obedience to earlier instructions. Too late, Conrad ordered the gunners to bring the laying devices with them, not leave them in the black earth of Galicia. There would not be much fire anyway, as he also ordered his generals to "stop wasting shells; shell use must in every case be proportioned to the relative importance of each moment in a battle," a truly bewildering directive.[91]

Boroevic didn't bother "proportioning" anything other than retreat and the minimum rest required to facilitate it. He ordered his generals to avoid even rearguard actions with the pursuing Russians—"to speed the marches west"—and to search the ground around them for rifles of any make or caliber, the Austrians who preceded them having thrown away so many of theirs in the retreat. Panic had cratered Boroevic's Third Army; late on September 16, he warned the armies retreating on either side of him to beware of his force, telling them, "Whole regiments are streaming into Przemysl; they are famished; they are looting shops and committing excesses."[92] He also distributed a memo that expressed astonishment at the tactics employed thus far, including frontal attacks with the bayonet, inadequate trenching, and no suppressing fire with machine guns and artillery. It was as if the Habsburg army wanted to kill itself.[93]

With Brusilov's Eighth Army tickling one flank and Lichitski's Ninth Army the other, the Austro-Hungarian North Army resumed its weary retreat on September 17. The Russians had already thrown seven bridges across the Lower San, which rendered it useless as a defensive moat and opened up the possibility that Przemysl and its outlying forts might be encircled and besieged with the entire North Army trapped inside. Leaving a big garrison at Przemysl, Conrad and Fritzl retreated with the rest of the North Army in the direction of Cracow and the barrier of the Wisloka River.[94] By the third week of September, Conrad estimated that there were sixty-four or more strong Russian divisions pressing hard against his forty-one weak ones.[95] The Austrians expressed astonishment at Russian troop numbers; they were outnumbered everywhere, Brusilov's single army having as many men as the Austrian Second and Third Armies combined. Just a year earlier, Franz Ferdinand's military cabinet had mocked the Russian army in an op-ed titled "A Bankruptcy." The acid description of the Russian retreat from Mukden in 1905 would have served this beaten Habsburg army just as well: "Something invisible and intangible now afflicted this army; the power of suggestion was broken; a dirty little secret exposed itself."[96]

On September 21, Conrad ordered a further retreat—to the Dunajec River, a tributary of the Vistula. The Second, Third, and Fourth Armies would dig in there. After a meeting in Neu

General Svetozar Boroevic took over the Austro-Hungarian Third Army after Bruder-mann's defeat at Lemberg and immediately noted its demoralization: "My troops are streaming back, famished; they are looting shops and committing excesses." The war was only a month old.
CREDIT: National Archives

Sandez with Hindenburg and Ludendorff, who commanded German troops in the east, Conrad agreed to detach the First Army for service with the German Ninth Army north of the Vistula. A worsening shell shortage was on everyone's mind; so much ammo had been fired off or surrendered, and there were no stockpiles in the rear.[97] Even with German assistance, Austrian defeat seemed inevitable. Auffenberg had abandoned so many guns and supply wagons in his retreat that the derelict vehicles would be visible from the air for months. He now excused himself with recondite analogies: "Didn't Blücher abandon *his* entire train before Leipzig in order to change his line of operations? And yet Blücher he remained."[98]

Auffenberg would not be so lucky. On September 29, Conrad and Archdukes Friedrich and Karl arrived in Auffenberg's camp at Zaklycin and presented him with the Grand Cross of the Leopold Order and the thanks of the old emperor. The next morning, preparing to resume his retreat with the red enameled Grand

Cross pinned to his breast, Auffenberg was met by a general staff courier sent up from the AOK with this letter from Archduke Friedrich: "Your Excellency, during my visit yesterday I came to the conclusion that your nerves have suffered badly from the recent events, and that you no longer trust in the power and potential of your army." Auffenberg was ordered to report himself "ill," transfer command of his army to Archduke Joseph Ferdinand, and return to Vienna. Auffenberg was aghast: "Here I was, the Victor of Komarów, being relieved of command by the Loser of Lemberg." Conrad wrote Auffenberg to soften the blow but—in his usual way—ended up dwelling on his own travails: "The entire blame for this infelicitous war is going to be laid at my doorstep, and I'll have no choice but to seek a quiet corner to escape the scorn of my fellows."[99]

On October 2, Auffenberg took leave of his army, pronouncing himself ill (with arthritis) as agreed, and handing command over to Archduke Joseph Ferdinand.[100] The whole army was suffering aches and pains much more serious than Auffenberg's. North Army had suffered 50 percent casualties, for a total of 100,000 dead and 220,000 wounded; many divisions had lost two-thirds of their effectives. Even the French—in their red trousers, dark blue tunics, and dense assault columns—had lost only one in three in the first month of the war.[101] Mass surrenders by disloyal Austro-Hungarian units augmented the casualties, delivering about 120,000 unwounded Austrian troops into Russian hands, along with three hundred guns.

The war in the east was barely three weeks old and Conrad had already lost over a third of the Austro-Hungarian army, as well as the best part of its officers and NCOs. "Our normal tactical units have been so ripped apart in the fighting thus far that command is extremely difficult," Boroevic reported in October. "I have far more strangers under my command than familiar old comrades."[102] The old comrades were dead or in Russian captivity; in Vienna's 4th Regiment, only seven officers came out of Galicia alive.[103] "If war was once a chivalrous duel," General Arthur Bolfras commented from the Hofburg, "it is now a dastardly slaughter." More cannon fodder was urgently needed, Bolfras jotted. "Mars has become voracious."[104] The Habsburg War Ministry nervously placarded the monarchy with appeals for donations to a new fund for the unexpectedly large and unbudgeted numbers of widows and orphans left behind by the troops who had already been sacrificed.[105]

Boroevic urged Conrad to abandon Przemysl entirely so that its 150,000-man garrison would not also be lost, but Conrad—who had tried to cut off funding for the fortress before the war—now poured in funds to prepare it for a siege. He rushed 27,000 workers to the San to build out Przemysl's fortifications. They strung 650 miles of barbed wire, dug 31 miles of trenches, and constructed 7 belts of strong points, with 200 battery positions and 24 forts. Twenty-one villages and 2,500 acres of forest were razed to clear fields of fire, time-consuming work that was completed thanks to the slow Russian advance. Six Russian divisions finally settled in for a siege in late September.[106]

Having moved the AOK to Neu Sandez in the Dunajec-Biala position, Conrad found himself trapped in the tight space between the Vistula and the Carpathians, with Russian armies closing in from every side. Conrad found it hard to move or even supply what remained of the North Army because so many of its horses had died. Generals were told to stop asking for ammunition, because it couldn't be sent.[107] Poking around the edges of this broken army, the American correspondent Washburn was struck by the massive casualties and the casual way in which they were discarded. "On the outskirts of a village huge trenches had been dug, beside which the dead were ranged in crowds; peasants drove up with wagonloads of stiffened corpses, split faces leering gruesomely. Like bits of pig iron, they were dumped out of the carts. Where was the romance of war?"[108] It was gone, and cholera and dysentery were now racing through the Austro-Hungarian ranks.[109] Only the Germans could save them now.

CHAPTER 10

Death on the Drina

IF AUSTRIA-HUNGARY'S ENTIRE NORTHERN ARMY was in need of rescue, so too were its forces in the Balkans—and no one more than the man at their head. General Oskar Potiorek had been the butt of jokes since the August fiasco. People called him "incompetent," an "imbecile," and worse.[1] Determined to silence his critics, Potiorek planned to invade Serbia again in September. This was risky; with Conrad in full retreat in Galicia, Potiorek would have to make do with even fewer troops than he'd had in August: just the depleted Austro-Hungarian Fifth and Sixth Armies, with no help from the old Echelon B troops, which had finally wended their way to the Eastern Front.

To close the yawning gap between the Fifth and Sixth Armies, Potiorek moved the Sixth Army northward to the middle Drina. This made matters even worse: instead of threatening the Serbs from two angles, the Austrians were now attacking on a single axis, which made General Putnik's job that much easier. And this time Austria's troop numbers—174 battalions—barely equaled Serbia's.[2] This made defeat even more probable than in August, but the Hofburg and Conrad's AOK seemed not to notice. Bolfras insisted that Potiorek "salvage our military honor at any price." Conrad, preoccupied with the rout in Galicia, struck a gloomier note, telling Potiorek that he could attack, but he must not expect

253

reinforcements and must "avoid all further defeats at the hands of Serbia." It certainly sounded like a lose-lose proposition, but Potiorek—desperate to prove himself and as certain as Conrad that "only the offensive will succeed"—vowed to bring the Serbs to their knees before the onset of winter.[3]

Never enthusiastic about Potiorek's bid for redemption, Conrad and Archduke Friedrich authorized it only when the four divisions of the Serbian First Army—responding to Russian demands for a Serbian attack into Austria-Hungary—crossed the Sava near

Potiorek's Second Invasion of Serbia
September 1914

Belgrade on September 6 and began marching into southern Hungary. It was a weak demonstration, more political than military, but Berchtold and Tisza demanded that something be done, and Potiorek still enjoyed considerable indulgence at court, where Bolfras and the old emperor wrote Potiorek warm letters praising him for his detailed reports and contrasting him favorably with the "secretive, laconic" Conrad.

Emperor Franz Joseph's headquarters in Vienna increasingly resembled an old folks' home, with the seventy-five-year-old Bolfras and the eighty-four-year-old emperor gnashing their teeth over Conrad's willfulness ("It's intolerable that a *k.u.k.* army commander and his staff should regard themselves as completely independent of the All Highest Court") and waywardness ("At least his departure to the North means that he *must* telegraph us every evening at 9:00 p.m.") and praising Potiorek for his accessibility ("We appreciate your detailed daily reports, which are so much better than AOK's, which invariably arrive late in the night"). Berchtold too sided with Potiorek, seeing a determined assault on Serbia as the only way to rope in neutrals like Bulgaria and prevent the formation of an opportunistic new Balkan League against a weakened Austria-Hungary. Conrad, who was trying to reorganize plans for the month of September, discovered that his defeats in August had given hostages to fortune: "Who is directing the overall conduct of Austria-Hungary's war?" he sputtered to Bolfras. "His Majesty? Or the Military Cabinet? Or the Ministry of Foreign Affairs?"[4]

Ever the bureaucratic adept, Potiorek was easing himself into the vacuum opened by Conrad's blundering. "Potiorek is vain," Conrad had raged while still in Przemysl. "He can't stand to see the Serbian campaign put on the back burner."[5] But Potiorek had found that propagating hopeful fiction to the Hofburg was the best way to get the Serbian campaign put back on the front burner. The Balkan commander's daily reports contained a great deal of rosy nonsense, which partly explained the Hofburg's willingness to authorize the renewed, quite hopeless invasion. "The Serbs have retreated to Nis. . . . Their regiments have been decimated, and their morale is bad," Potiorek reported in late August. They were running out of ammunition, guns, and shoes, and half their wounded lay untended in the open for lack of hospital beds, doctors, and medicine. Serbia's French 75 mm cannon could fire twenty shells a minute, yet Serbian industry produced just 260 shells a day. Surely the Serbian army couldn't fight yet *another* campaign. Potiorek reported two days later that King Peter had fled with his treasury and archive to Skopje, and that the Macedonian and Albanian areas that Serbia had annexed in the Balkan Wars were "in a state of insurrection." The Serbs, to hear Potiorek tell it, were on the brink; just one final shove would send them over the edge.[6]

The real insurrection, however, was in the Austro-Hungarian ranks, where, impressed by the incompetence displayed by their generals in August, troops on all fronts stopped saluting and obeying. Officers spoke in the first days of September of a total disappearance of formalities and control. On the Serbian front, General Adolf von Rhemen ordered "draconian measures" to restore discipline, reminding officers to "share the privations of the men" and compel everyone, even the sick and wounded, to rise and salute "higher-ranking personages."[7] Other officers chewed over the tactics of August and recommended changes. Remarkably, the Austro-Hungarians were giving themselves here, as in Galicia, a crash course in tactics that had been standard since 1866. General Rhemen reminded the officers of the 36th Division that they should never attack with massed walls of infantry and reserves, but should instead "wait for the artillery to soften up the enemy" and then "use the terrain to advance in rushes in small groups" after patrolling and scouting the enemy positions.[8]

General Giesl admonished his corps to mask their campsites, douse their cook fires, dig trenches and battery positions, and clear the corn and trees around them to have fields of fire.[9] General Krauss reminded his units that barbed wire had to be strung in such a way that it would slow attackers, but also permit the defenders to sally on a counterattack. Left to their own devices, Austro-Hungarian infantry were deliberately wiring themselves in so that they couldn't be expected to attack the Serbs. Krauss also deplored the tendency of Habsburg officers to drive their men into suicidal frontal attacks without artillery support or any coordination with the flanks: "Why are all of our attacks being launched frontally without any effort to envelop the enemy from the flank?"[10] Artillery and shells remained in such short supply that the Habsburg infantry were rather ambitiously ordered to take over critical functions of the guns: "All counterbattery fire should henceforth be undertaken by machine guns and infantry alone."[11] Behind the lines, the Austrians directed their fire at Bosnia's Serbian population. Hundreds of prominent Serbs—priests, teachers, lawyers, and local politicians—were rounded up. Thirteen hundred were sent into internal exile and 844 were taken hostage to deter sabotage in the rear of Potiorek's invasion.[12]

Too late, Bolfras began to have misgivings about Potiorek. The general, who had spoken so dismissively in late August of a severely weakened Serbian army, was now warning of an invincible one: 160,000 troops at Valjevo, 50,000 at Uzice, and 15,000 more at Belgrade. The Serbian Third Army had pushed three divisions up to the river crossings at Loznica and Ljesnica, just as they had in August. And with no forces on the Sava or the Danube, the Austrians were not exactly putting the Serbs on the horns of a dilemma. Putnik knew exactly how and where the Austrian invasion would proceed, and Potiorek was already lowering expectations in Vienna, describing the "deep depression" *(Deprimiertheit)* of his Fifth Army and characterizing only his Sixth Army as truly effective. In his usual woolly way, Bolfras wasted time puzzling over the last defeat instead of preventing the next one. "It's just not clear to me," Bolfras wrote Conrad on August 31, "why General Potiorek sought a decision on such difficult terrain, crossing rivers and fighting in hills without mountain-equipped troops." Potiorek, meanwhile, was poised to repeat the August folly under even more adverse circumstances.[13]

With two Serbian divisions still north of the Sava, Potiorek improvised a defense of the realm. General Alfred Krauss was given a scratch corps of four new brigades and ordered to throw back the invaders, while Frank's Fifth Army was ordered to cross the Drina immediately to cut the line of retreat of those Serbian marauders. Krauss drove the Serbs back on September 7–8 and pushed up to the Sava around Sabac in the space previously occupied by the Second Army. The Serbian inhabitants of Syrmia, who had rejoiced at the Serbian invasion and plundered the homes of local Germans and Hungarians, were now plundered themselves, and then burned out by Austrian gendarmes, a vengeful process with a legal name: *devastieren.* "No, war is definitely *not* pretty," Prince Felix Schwarzenberg observed as he trotted through the smoking streets of Surcin and paused at the Orthodox monastery at Fenek. It had been looted and burned by Austrian troops: "a thoroughly depressing and shameful sight."[14]

As in August, Frank's Fifth Army struggled to get across the Drina on September 8. The Fifth Army covered the front from Sabac south to Loznica, where its right wing met the Sixth Army's left. Every effort by the Fifth Army's 9th Division to throw bridges across the river was thwarted by the Serbs, who raked the bridges and engineers with artillery and machine gun fire. The division pushed just two thousand troops across on September 8, and the same number the next day. Three entire regiments ended up huddled on a narrow beachhead under withering Serbian shell and shrapnel fire. Terrified by the barrage and the apparent helplessness of their own officers, men began to wade into the river as if to swim back to the other side. *"Ausharren!"* their officers angrily shouted. "Hold on! Dig in! There will be no retreat from this spot!" But as the Serbian shells continued to fall and every Austrian effort to get off the muddy bank was driven back, they did retreat, back to the left bank.[15] There they found comrades who had not made it across amusing themselves with the local Bosnian women, who complained of sexual assaults and troops forcing their way into their homes.[16]

The Austrian response to all of these challenges was, as ever, wrongheaded. While Frank ordered some of his officers to tutor the men "in the religious tenets of Islam," others led his 36th Division into the by-now typical slaughter, involving ill-equipped, unprepared Austro-Hungarian troops storming Serbian rifle and battery positions that were cleverly integrated into the riverfront villages themselves, wending under hedges and fences and even through buildings, the straw roofs of peasant huts providing shade and cover from aerial detection.

Many of Frank's units failed to get across the Drina at all; their boats beached on sandbars, leaving the troops exposed to Serbian fire. Men and officers drowned or were struck down by the fire of their own troops on the left bank. Those who used the bridges had to pummel their way through retreating Austrian troops, one officer noting that as soon as a pontoon bridge was completed on September 8, the largely Croatian 79th Regiment, which had been laboriously ferried across to the right bank in the night on boats, bolted toward it to try to escape back to the left bank. General Johann Salis, on the left bank, had to charge onto the bridge with companies of the 37th Regiment to halt the retreat of the 79th from the right. He found the men of the 79th in a familiar state of panic, with each one swearing that he had been *ordered* to retreat; it dawned on their officers that enterprising Serbs had crept in close and yelled "retreat" in German, providing all the pretext that was needed. The Fifth Army had lost 143 officers and 4,400 men in a single day, September 8, without even gaining a foothold on the Serbian side of the river.[17]

On the Sava, the 21st Landwehr Division tried now to take pressure off of the divisions on the Drina. Elements of the 21st Landwehr crossed the Sava at Poloj on September 8 and immediately ran into the same high corn that had flustered the Second Army. Blundering through it, they came under fire from *komitadjis* hidden in the fields and trees. Turning in circles, their formations destroyed by ropes of trampled corn, they returned fire and succeeded only in shooting each other in the back. Out of ammo and nearly disbanded by fear, the Czech and German infantry began running back in the direction of the river. Halted by their officers—"There will be no thought of a retreat! This position must be held!"—they briefly dug in, but then came under fire from their own artillery, which uncorked a panicky resumption of the retreat all the way back to the Sava. Pursued most of the way by their own guns, which mistook the Austrians for Serbs and lobbed shells into their midst, they arrived at the river to find no engineering troops to row them across. The 7th Landwehr Regiment lost five officers and 174 men, without even glimpsing a Serb.

The wild-eyed survivors were deaf to reason and commandeered any boat they could find to paddle themselves over to the north bank. The VIII Corps commandant, General Arthur Giesl, who would be sacked for this episode, fulminated at his officers the next morning: "Every one of my troop commanders must work harder to repress cowardice, steel the hearts of the troops, and summon our full strength for offensive operations."[18]

Giesl, like every other Austro-Hungarian general in this sad war, was whistling past the graveyard. No offensive operations were working, owing to the now familiar combination of Serbian resolve and Austro-Hungarian blundering. Whereas the Serbs were already implementing changes that every army would introduce in the course of the war—deploying only a skirmish line in the forward trench and leaving the bulk of the infantry in reserve trenches farther back—the Austrians were still massing their troops well forward on narrow fronts, which made them easy targets for the Serbian artillery and infantry, as well as their own artillery, which would regularly hit their own men instead of the enemy's.[19]

Potiorek began to weave excuses for the inevitable defeat. He reported the "scandal at Loznica," where two entire Austrian corps failed to get across the Drina against light Serbian resistance. He asserted that the unfolding disaster was their fault, not his, and he forbade officers to retreat under *any* circumstances: "No retreat: any officer who orders one will be court-martialed, any man who does it will be shot."[20] Other generals merely noted the uselessness of Austrian tactics. With their scripted prewar maneuvers against flagged enemies, the Austro-Hungarian artillery had never trained for this fluid kind of warfare. They wasted their fire, scattering random barrages wherever they suspected Serbian troops, instead of focusing on agreed-upon targets and saving ammunition, either for counterbattery fire or to hit Serbian reserves when they moved up to reinforce the front lines.[21]

The corps of the Sixth Army were supposed to facilitate the crossing of the Fifth, but they too struggled to get across the Drina. As in August, the hilly terrain slowed progress to a crawl. Well entrenched with their artillery on the mounts overlooking the upper and middle Drina, the Serbs fired down on the ill-equipped Austrians.[22] Like the other armies in the war, the Austrians were feeling the effects of an acute shell shortage. Frugal war ministries had not stockpiled shells because their chemical ingredients deteriorated if not used, and none of the armies had expected a great war in 1914. (France would shoot half of its entire inventory of shells in the first *month* of the war.) Conrad and Potiorek now argued bitterly over the shells remaining to them, each man thinking the other was hoarding or wasting ammunition. "Be very frugal with your fire," one corps commander jotted. "Soon the factories of the monarchy will be unable to send us any more shells."[23]

Kriegsmetalle (war metals) were in such short supply that Emperor Franz Joseph had just appealed to his people for all the metal that they could spare: fire irons, trash cans, doorknobs, candlesticks, belt buckles, church bells, and cutlery. "Our army *needs* metal," he pleaded. Indeed it did; now Austrian guns were permitted to fire only when an "obvious target presented itself" and every battery commander agreed that the target was "real and appropriate." The massed fire of all guns was strictly prohibited.[24] With fire support like this, the Austrian infantry was picked apart everywhere. Reports from the 4th Mountain Brigade south of Jagodna confirmed the shocking parsimony of the Austrian artillery: "Under fire all day on September 14, we repeatedly asked for artillery fire on the wooded heights and were told that no 'suitable target' existed. We then asked the 5th Mountain Brigade to rake the height with its guns and it too replied: 'No suitable target presents itself.'"[25] Even as the men were ordered to conserve, they were warned that "everything around here that is not promptly used up will be sent to our troops in the Russian theater," a truly Svejkian paradox.[26]

A Landwehr unit of the Sixth Army's First Division was overrun in the night of September 8 when the Serbs approached in the dark, called, *"Landwehr! Feuer einstellen. Hier 84er!"*— "Landwehr, stop shooting, we're the 84th!"—and then charged in, firing and killing. The next day the Serbs battered the division, annihilating their skirmish line and then shooting down every reserve formation that came up. One regimental commander was a

Croat, and he briefly rallied the men in Croatian, urging, *"Dalmatinei dojte se!"* but the effect was ruined by the German brigadier, who appeared behind him bawling (in German), "Men of the Landwehr, hold the line! Reinforcements are coming!" Men who had responded to their Croatian colonel ran from their German general and began flowing in waves to the rear; each time an officer stepped into their path to turn them around, they would flow around him and keep going.[27]

Potiorek was trying to re-create the conditions of August, with Krauss' "Combined Corps" on the Sava filling the role of the Second Army, while the Fifth and Sixth Armies hammered across the Drina to unite with Krauss. But only the Serbs were hammering. They permitted elements of the Fifth Army to cross at Ljesnica on September 13 and then destroyed them in a whirlwind of shells and bullets. The rest of the Fifth Army watched the slaughter from the left bank.[28] With nowhere to go on the Drina, Colonel Felix Schwarzenberg took his dragoon regiment over to Mitrovica, dismounted, and crossed the Sava. The dragoons waited on the opposite bank for their horses, which never arrived. There were not enough boats to ferry both men and horses, so the prince and the dragoons stood down. "None of us had trained in peacetime to fight dismounted, nor were we properly outfitted for the task; we had only about 50 rounds for our carbines, no spades to entrench with, and we were clad in red trousers and red caps that glowed like wildflowers, and tall riding boots and spurs that made marching impossible."[29] A cavalry that had been procured for the parade ground was proving useless in war.

Even in the first days of this renewed push, the Austrian troops displayed remarkable apathy. A general staff captain touring the trenches of the 53rd and 96th Regiments found them filthy, unimproved, and littered with discarded equipment—backpacks, coats, belts of ammunition, rifles, and even unexploded artillery shells. Men sat sullenly in the dirt, ignoring their tongue-tied officers, who did well in German or Hungarian but not the ten other languages of the monarchy. The captain observed that the trenches and traverses were all collapsed from shelling, yet no one bothered to repair them. When he summoned military police to make the men work, "the gendarme evinced neither understanding nor interest in what I was ordering."[30]

Supplies were as scarce in September as they had been in August, and the Serbs made them even scarcer by infiltrating parties of two or three men into the Austrian supply lines at night and heaving grenades into their midst to cause a stampede. Without a regular food supply, the men plundered, provoking more rebukes from the generals: "Henceforth every plunderer shall be shot by a firing squad on the spot." Austrian generals puzzled over a paradox of the campaign; their troops would plunder Serbian civilians out of house and home and then promptly round up the dispossessed families and escort them far to the rear on "humanitarian" grounds. "No more escorts of old folks out of the battle area!" General Krauss admonished on September 19. "Too many troops are doing this, and weakening the battle front."

Krauss also noted an alarming increase in self-wounding, Austro-Hungarian troops shooting themselves in the left hand to remove themselves from battle. Eighteen men had presented themselves in a single day at a field hospital in his sector with bullet wounds in their left hand. "Each one told the same story: 'I was accidentally shot by comrades in the night while working in the trench.'" Krauss judged the explanations "not credible" and ordered that every hand injury be immediately examined by a doctor. Self-wounders would be hung, to encourage their fellows.[31]

Whereas thousands of Austrians surrendered more or less willingly to the Serbs, providing the Serbian general staff with much useful information, few Serbs gave themselves up for capture. "The Serbs don't hold up their hands, as the big childlike Russians [do]. They fight as long as they can stand," a war correspondent noted.[32] Those Serbs who did yield were found to be in deplorable condition, poorly armed and equipped, some with as few as four days of military instruction.[33] Still, they held on, and the intelligence-starved Austrian generals began offering bounties for the capture of Serbian personnel: two hundred crowns for an enlisted man, a thousand crowns for an officer.[34] The rewards were necessary, for Serbs had a disincentive to surrender: Austrians executed many of the Serbian prisoners they took because they weren't wearing uniforms. The Serbs weren't trying to deceive anyone, as Putnik's despairing cable to the War Ministry in Nis in mid-September made plain: "A high percentage of my men are fighting barefoot, in just underwear and shirts, without any military insignia; the enemy are shooting them as insurgents. We urgently need uniforms and 200,000 pairs of shoes."[35]

The foreign press caught wind of the renewed Austrian difficulties here and in Galicia and predicted the monarchy's early collapse. Many in the Dual Empire attributed the dire prognostications to the tsar's propaganda mill, rather than to actual events on the ground, which, of course, were the direst propaganda of all. Tisza in Budapest phoned Berchtold in Vienna on September 15 and demanded that he set the record straight: "You must correct the Russian lies in the foreign press and point out that we've been standing alone against the Russian main force and have even inflicted some major defeats on them, and that on the Drina our troops are conducting a victorious offensive deep into the heart of Serbia."[36]

Serbs rarely surrendered; those who did—like these men—were found to be in deplorable condition, poorly armed and equipped, some with as few as four days of military instruction.
CREDIT: Heeresgeschichtliches Museum, Wien

That would have been news to the troops still stuck on the Drina. On the front, Austro-Hungarian generals struggled to communicate or even equip themselves. Staff cars flying black-and-yellow pennants were driven across the Drina and Sava to speed the flow of orders between units. No one reckoned with the likely reaction of Austro-Hungarian sentries, few of whom had ever seen or even heard of an automobile. When the cars approached, the terrified bumpkins opened fire. Even Austrian troops who knew a car when they saw one opened fire, greedily crediting rumors that French bankers were sending cars stuffed with cash to support the Serbian war effort. "No more firing on military automobiles," Krauss' supply chief fulminated. "The drivers can't hear you over the sound of their engine when you tell them to stop." He also ordered an end to the "rumors about money-bearing automobiles from France." Sentries were abusing the drivers and pawing through their classified dispatch cases in search of the rumored cash. [37]

Supply problems only exacerbated the failure to communicate. Austro-Hungarian march battalions that arrived to replace casualties had to scrounge for everything, including backpacks and rifles. Sick and wounded troops were stripped of their gear to clothe and arm the newcomers. Even lightly wounded men were immediately relieved of their arms and uniforms, the War Ministry in Vienna ordering commanders on all fronts to "disarm and disrobe—down to their underwear—all casualties." [38] Although ordered to improve their infantry assaults by "cutting 'storm lanes' through the Serbian wire and securing the breaches with sandbags on the flanks," the entire force ran out of shovels, sandbags, picks, and wire cutters, "not," as General Othmar Panesch put it, "because they've worn out, but because the men throw them away so as not to have to carry them!" [39]

This second invasion of Serbia bogged down in the twelve-hundred-foot hills around Jagodna at the end of September. The 1st and 6th Mountain Brigades repeatedly attacked the Jagodna heights on September 20, 21, and 22. Blinded by rain and fog and engulfed by mud, they stumbled up steep, wooded slopes into Serbian fire in massed columns and were cut to pieces, the 1st Mountain Brigade alone losing 372 dead, 1,445 wounded, and 712 missing. The Croatian battalions of the 6th Regiment struggled day and night, their officers recalling the difficulty of directing the battle when the opposing officers were shouting similar orders in the same language to contending groups of lethally armed men. The first battalion lost two-thirds of its strength in the fighting, about 800 men, and buried 1,300 Serbs. Like the Russians in Galicia, the Serbs practiced defense in depth, with parallel lines of trenches, one behind the other, that made Austrian breakthroughs nearly impossible.[40]

Potiorek had finally shifted his headquarters from the comforts of Sarajevo on September 24, but only as far as Tuzla, which was still inside Bosnia and a hundred miles from the nearest fighting. Perhaps Potiorek needed the respite, for he was battling Conrad at least as hard as he was fighting the Serbs. He still enjoyed direct access to the emperor via Bolfras, but Conrad was laboring to block that access and divert Balkan munitions (and influence) to the east. When Bolfras released a shipment of shells and bullets to Potiorek on September 20, Conrad began a weeklong battle that ended with Bolfras sheepishly dumping Potiorek—"here there's no court camarilla"—and agreeing that Potiorek would make no more direct communications with Vienna, but would submit his reports and requests through Conrad instead.[41] Conrad had finally severed the Balkan commander's direct access to the emperor, ensuring (at last) that the fight with Russia, not the one with Serbia, would receive priority in Austro-Hungarian military planning.

Beyond Tuzla, things were looking up. The Germans reported good news in the west: they were flanking the French and British on the Oise, had the French on their heels at Verdun, and had begun to reduce the French forts on the eastern frontier.[42] Stalled at the Marne, the Germans were trying to restart their failed August offensive and carry operations through to the elusive victory on the Seine that would theoretically unlock victory in the east as well. Potiorek's Sixth Army had less thrilling news to report: they finally wrested control of the Jagodna heights, but at a cost of twenty-five thousand new casualties. Fatigued, demoralized and all but disarmed by shortages of ammunition, the Sixth Army could do no better than the Fifth. Taking stock of the Pyrrhic victory at Jagodna, Bolfras and the emperor expressed their usual belated dismay: "*Wer hat diesen Unsinn befohlen?* Who ordered this insanity?"[43] Potiorek had, and his flaccid September campaign left behind a poison legacy. After this second defeat, the emperor couldn't simply walk away from the southern front without walking away from his Balkan dreams as well. The loss of prestige would be too great. This was an empire, after all, that had bid for Balkan supremacy and still had visions of Salonika. And yet every gun in Austria-Hungary was needed for the wobbling Eastern Front. That left the Habsburg army in a dangerous predicament: too weak to reinvade Serbia, and too weak to counterattack Russia with any hope of success.

Austro-Hungarian ministers in the neutral capitals clamored for information. From the Austrian minister in Bucharest: "Serbian communiqués here speak of the annihilation of our regiments, a 'panicky' Austrian flight across the Drina and the Serbian reconquest of Loznica and Ljesnica. Shall I deny this?" From the Austrian minister in Athens: "I need details on the battles on the Drina; the Serbs are portraying them as great Serbian victories." From Sofia, the Austrian minister warned that the pro-Austrian government there would probably fall if new defeats in Serbia were confirmed: "Bulgaria was shattered by news of the Austrian retreat in the northern theater, but events in Serbia weigh even more heavily on the local situation."[44]

In all, forty thousand more Austro-Hungarians were lost in the September fighting in Serbia, without any gains.[45] Archduke Friedrich released a jaunty statement on October 1 from his headquarters near Cracow, pronouncing the "overall situation favorable." Russian power was "breaking," German troops were "deep in France," and "Serbian resistance [was] faltering." *This*, Fritzl concluded, "is the truth of the matter—explain it all to the men in their mother tongues."[46]

Potiorek had a great deal of explaining to do, and he officially terminated the offensive on October 4, blaming the halt not on his own fumbling but on the shell shortage: "We can't attack without first destroying the enemy trenches, but for that we need prolonged heavy bombardments." General Krauss agreed, assuring Potiorek that he did not lack "offensive spirit," but considered it "a crime to continue running headfirst into a wall and sacrificing thousands of our brave troops so uselessly."[47]

These may have been the wisest words uttered on the Austro-Hungarian side thus far, but they were not yet the view of the army commanders, who still worshiped at the altar of the offensive. Behind the scenes, Potiorek began agitating at the Hofburg for a *third* invasion, improbably asserting that Serbia—which kept beating Potiorek—was finally on the ropes: "What's left of Serbia's army is concentrated at Valjevo, scarcely 180,000 effectives." Serbian casualties—estimated at 600 officers and 60,000 men since the start of the war—could no longer be replaced. Belgrade's court and government would shortly move even further south, this time from Nis to Skopje. Morale, Potiorek reported, was "bad," even worse among the Serbian population, which was racked by cholera and typhus and which had begun to resist conscription and the military authorities. "Just one more attack," Potiorek pleaded on October 1. "Just one more attack will prove decisive."[48]

CHAPTER 11

Warsaw

Austro-Hungarian floundering in Galicia and the tumultuous retreat nearly to the Carpathians struck the Germans dumb with amazement. At German great headquarters on the Western Front, Austria's military liaison noted that Conrad's swift, artless defeat had finally gotten Germany's attention: "They'd always considered the war against Russia 'our thing,' but our defeat at Lemberg and retreat from Galicia suddenly made the war in the east as vital for them as for us." Now the Germans no less than the Austrians could feel the shuddering approach of the Russian steamroller. After the repulse on the Marne, Moltke had been fired and replaced with General Erich von Falkenhayn, who noted the obvious: a Russian advance through the Carpathians would be "catastrophic for the overall war situation," wrapping Russian armies around Silesia, a prime German industrial region, and thrusting them into the heart of Hungary.[1]

The war was barely a month old, yet Vienna seemed to have reached the breaking point. Potiorek had twice been beaten in Serbia, and all three of Conrad's offensive thrusts—at Krásnik, Komarów, and Lemberg—had been crushed, his troops driven all the way back to Cracow. Conrad's four armies had suffered so many casualties that burial parties could not keep up, and the corpses were simply stacked like firewood, where they swelled, rotted, and burst.[2] In Galicia alone, the Habsburg army had lost 100,000 dead, 220,000 wounded, and 120,000 POWs, as well as 216 guns and thousands of rail cars and locomotives.[3] When Potiorek's 81,000 casualties were added in, it was clear that the whole army—reduced by half a million troops—was hanging by a thread. Men in their forties were already being called up and sent to replace the monstrous casualties.[4] Survivors of the August battles were crowding the eastern rail stations trying to hitch rides home on trains for the sick and wounded, while newcomers, many of whom had never even fired a rifle, stepped off their trains, many dressed in gaudy surplus uniforms from the Victorian era and without rifles, shovels, blankets, or medical supplies. In the Austrian army's palmiest days before the war, the French had judged it "two or three generations behind the west." Now it looked even more backward.[5]

The Schlieffen Plan had pledged big German reinforcements for the Eastern Front after six weeks, but there was no sign of them. Embarrassed by their defeat on the Marne in September, German great headquarters told Conrad as little about it as possible. They did not even bother to tell him that Moltke had been fired and replaced as general staff chief by Falkenhayn. A week after Falkenhayn's appointment, Conrad was still addressing his letters and cables to Moltke.[6]

Moltke, Falkenhayn . . . it hardly mattered anymore to Conrad. He blamed them both for the Austrian rout. He attributed the failure of the Germans to cooperate with his thrust into Poland not to their massive battles in France and Belgium but to Kaiser Wilhelm II's desire to protect his "stud farms and stag hunts" in East Prussia. Conrad had known in early August that the Germans, with seven armies engaged in France, would not be taking the offensive in the east as well, but he still acted as if he had been betrayed. It seemed the best way to exonerate himself for his terrible opening act. He increasingly viewed himself as a blameless scapegoat, "an outlaw." In love with another man's wife, he mooned and blubbered over his loneliness: "I have no home, no woman. Who will be at my side in my later years?" The German attachés in AOK headquarters at Neu Sandez reported that Conrad had "lost all confidence in his army."[7] He was even mooting the idea of a separate peace. "Why," Conrad wrote Foreign Minister Berchtold, "should Austria-Hungary bleed needlessly?"[8]

Fifty-three-year-old General Erich von Falkenhayn, who had replaced Moltke on September 14, heard Conrad's complaints with no small degree of wonderment. Germany was well on its way to losing two million dead or wounded in the first six months of the war. The proud Prusso-German army was increasingly taking on the appearance of a motley *Volksheer* or people's army, as reserve and *Landsturm* forces were called in to replace the soaring casualties. Whole cohorts of professional officers and NCOs had been wiped out. German infantry companies were commanded by corporals. Pensioned generals (including Paul von Hindenburg and Remus von Woyrsch) had been recalled from their retirements to take up new challenges.[9] France's successful stand on the Marne meant that the war in the west would not be over by October. The Germans would not be able to deliver the "overwhelming force" to the Eastern Front that Moltke had promised Conrad at Karlsbad in May 1914; victory on the Seine would not unlock victory on the Bug. Instead, as an Austrian diplomat jotted, "Russia's massive superiority in troop numbers has become the dominating factor in this war."[10]

In view of the Habsburg army's collapse, German troops would somehow have to be found for the Eastern Front. The Austro-German alliance was already unraveling under the strain of the conflicting priorities of Berlin and Vienna, which were succinctly put by the new Austro-Hungarian ambassador in Berlin, Prince Gottfried von Hohenlohe: "Bethmann Hollweg now speaks of Germany's primary aim as 'securing Germany's future'; for us, the same principle of a 'secure future' applies, but can be only achieved through a defeat of Russia, whereas the German future depends first and foremost on the defeat of France and England."[11] The Austrians worried that the Germans, blinded by "hysterical Anglophobia," might themselves rush to conclude a separate peace with Russia before the fatal "imbalance of power" in the east had been corrected.

Vienna assumed that Berlin might even barter *Austrian* territory to get the territorial gains the Germans wanted in Belgium and France. Thus, Hohenlohe defined his diplomatic task as "creating a mood" in Berlin that would see "Germany's future secured through total victory in the east—through the *total annihilation of Russia.*"[12] That was not exactly Berlin's mood, but the Germans did recognize that they had little choice but to thrust into Poland, restore Austrian confidence, and force back the Russian steamroller. If the Austrians, clinging to a narrow strip between Cracow and the Carpathians, were pushed over the mountains and the Russians pursued them into Hungary, then German Silesia would be outflanked and probably lost. Germany's only European ally would also be lost, leaving Berlin without the Austrian army or even the fig leaf of a "coalition" to disguise its vast ambitions. In mid-September, the kaiser and his generals agreed that "direct assistance to the Austrians is now politically essential."[13]

While the Germans planned to rescue the Austrians by invading Russia, the Russians were planning to rescue the French by invading Germany. French ambassador Maurice Paléologue shuttled between the tsar, Sukhomlinov, and the grand duke deploring Russia's focus on Austria-Hungary and reminding the Russians that "the surest way to beat Austria is to beat Germany." When Sukhomlinov protested that his army had lost 110,000 men at Tannenberg *trying* to beat Germany, Paléologue countered that fresh efforts were needed, and soon. France had lost half a million men in its first battles with the Germans and was on the ropes.[14]

After peevish negotiations in the last days of September, Grand Duke Nikolai did agree to launch a drive on Berlin as soon as he had finished off the Austrians, but Tsar Nicholas II overruled his uncle, insisting that the attack on Germany begin at once. This was good news for the Austrians, and bad for the Russians. The grand duke pulled twelve corps out of Galicia and added them to eight fully mobilized armies—three in the center, two each on the flanks, and another in East Prussia. He would drive back any German attacks and then deliver the relief that the French and British had been demanding since August: a Russian thrust with two million men through Silesia to Berlin. General Nikolai Yanushkevich, the grand duke's staff chief, ordered "preparation of an offensive, of the greatest possible weight, with a view to deep invasion of

Germany, proceeding from the middle Vistula to the upper Oder." This, of course, was easier said than done; it had been Russian policy before the war *not* to build hardened roads and railways west of Warsaw, in order to slow down any German invasion of Russia. No thought had been given to how this would affect a Russian invasion of Germany.[15]

But with just seven German corps against this gathering Russian horde, the Germans were not idly awaiting the grand duke's drive on Berlin. *Their* roads were good, at least as far as Poland. Hindenburg and his staff chief, Ludendorff, planned a late autumn campaign across the Narew and toward Warsaw, to unhinge and throw back the Russians. With East Prussia secured by Tannenberg, Hindenburg sought a similar decisive result in Poland that would justify a reorientation of German strategy—an *Ostaufmarsch* or "eastern deployment" instead of the apparently fruitless western one still being pursued by Falkenhayn. Whereas Falkenhayn was continuing Moltke's (and Schlieffen's) France-first strategy, Hindenburg wanted a Russia-first approach, to exploit the incorrigible inefficiencies of the tsarist empire. But with the Russian mobilization finally complete and Conrad retreating instead of advancing, Hindenburg's Warsaw operation would be risky. Without an Austrian pincer from the south, the Germans would have to bludgeon their way alone through Russia's fully mobilized strength.

As they would throughout the war, the German commanders in the east, Hindenburg and Ludendorff, exceeded their orders and did what they wanted to do. Falkenhayn was preparing to hit the British with what he hoped would be a knockout blow in Flanders; he expected Hindenburg merely to shift German forces toward Cracow to bolster Conrad and hold the eastern line defensively, but Hindenburg opted for an offensive instead. He and Ludendorff argued that such an operation would threaten the Russian flank and rear and take far more pressure off Conrad than a flat-footed deployment in Silesia or Galicia.

In the east, in other words, Hindenburg was aiming as doggedly at Warsaw as Falkenhayn was aiming at Calais in the west. Warsaw—a city of eight hundred thousand, with barracks,

The Battles of Warsaw and Lodz Oct. – Nov. 1914

German Army

Austro-Hungarian Army

Russian Army

0   100   200 Miles

0   250 Kilometers

hospitals, magazines, and a belt of modern forts—was the third-largest city in Russia, the chief railway hub of Poland, and the natural headquarters of the Russian army. Its loss would force the Russians to pull back their entire front and relocate general headquarters to some peripheral place like Vilna or Bialystok. Calais would be the springboard to conquer England, Warsaw the springboard into Russia.[16]

Wedged in between the Vistula and the Carpathians, Conrad had painted himself into his own peripheral place. He was fortunate that his pell-mell retreat had taken him so far so fast that the Russians had outrun their own radius of supply and could not finish him off. As Churchill would put it, "In the West the armies were too big for the country; in the East the country was too big for the armies."[17] A Russian officer noted that the Austrians and Russians had marched so fast—the Austrians in retreat and the Russians in pursuit—that it took a long time for the Russian supply trains to catch up; some days his unit would go from daybreak until ten at night without a crumb to eat. Even when food arrived—some army bread, a slaughtered ox—he found it hard to eat: "I've become a vegetarian; they slaughter these cows to feed us; there are guts, organs, stomachs and eyes lying everywhere, dark pools of animal blood, sometimes the bawling beast will run right past you, its throat already slit, and then fall down beside you, bleeding and kicking the air."[18]

Ludendorff's idea was to exploit these Russian difficulties. Engaged in stripping the German Eighth Army to create the Ninth Army at Breslau (Wroclaw), Ludendorff asked Conrad to chip in Dankl's First Army for a renewed offensive. When Conrad hesitated—viewing every request from the Germans as a personal affront—Hindenburg reminded him that only the offensive could overcome worsening odds on every front: "a greater success will be achieved through envelopment," not passive defense, he coached Conrad on September 22. Privately, German headquarters scorned this Austrian passivity, Colonel Max Hoffmann writing in his diary: "Everything is fine here except for the Austrians. If only the brutes would move!"[19]

This time the brutes were willing. Conrad judged this his last opportunity to envelop the Russians in the Polish "tongue." With this infusion of German troops, Berlin and Vienna would muster nearly eighty infantry divisions in the east, against eighty-five Russian divisions. Beset by organizational problems and the need to detach armies to the Baltic and Black Sea coasts as well as to the Caucasus to fight the Turks, the Russians would not achieve an overwhelming superiority in manpower on the Eastern Front until the middle of 1916. It had been precisely this Russian sluggishness that had given hope to proponents of the Schlieffen Plan. The Russians were also feeling the loss of thousands of regimental officers and NCOs in the battles of August and September; their places now had to be filled by new recruits, who lacked experience and conditioning.[20] Austria-Hungary, in other words, still had a chance to win in the east, if it acted quickly and decisively in concert with the Germans.

Conrad scraped together his last intact forces—"the last man, the last artillery piece, the last machine gun." For once he was not exaggerating; with a paltry annual production run of just 150,000 rifles, the monarchy was running out of them, so many troops having surrendered theirs to the Russians or Serbs. Field artillery regiments found themselves with more crews than guns because so many cannon had been abandoned to the Russians.[21]

Conrad naturally believed that he, not Hindenburg, should command all allied German and Austrian formations in the east. "Why," Conrad raged to Bolfras, "is the German Ninth Army reporting to its own great headquarters in Mézières instead of to [me]?" Having once favored cooperation with the Germans, Conrad now resented being pulled north: "Why are we being asked to give up operations on the San to help the Germans at Warsaw?" But by now Bolfras was only too willing to subordinate Conrad to Hindenburg, or even to replace Conrad with an entirely new AOK: Archduke Friedrich perhaps, with Ludendorff as his all-powerful staff chief.[22]

Ludendorff, like Hindenburg, was a force to be reckoned with. By reducing the Eighth Army to just two corps, Ludendorff was able to mass the new Ninth Army with four corps, a reserve division, and a cavalry division around Kattowitz (Katowice) in Silesia. Before the war, Ludendorff had emerged as a ruthless department head inside the German general staff, taking over much of Moltke's work and acquiring little fear of Falkenhayn, who, as war minister, had represented a more moderate and reasonable faction than Ludendorff's.[23] By now Ludendorff was working at cross-purposes with the kaiser and Falkenhayn's *Oberste Heeresleitung* (OHL) in France. OHL, the German supreme command, wanted merely to hold in the east while striking decisively in the west, forcing Hindenburg to telegraph the kaiser regular threats of resignation to wring more independence (and troops) from Falkenhayn, who felt that every premature detachment of troops to the east would doom his efforts in the west.

Now a *Generaloberst*—a virtual field marshal—Hindenburg could not really be ordered around by anyone anyway. Conrad chafed at the politics involved in every decision by this "marvelous triangle" of the Eastern Front: himself, Ludendorff, and Falkenhayn. Colonel Max Hoffmann noted the tension: "When one gets a close view of influential people—their bad relations with each other, their conflicting ambitions—one must always bear in mind that it is certainly worse on the other side among the French, English and Russians, or one might well be nervous."[24]

It was certainly worse on the Russian side. After his halting conquest of Lemberg, Ruzski had been rewarded with command of the Northwest Front, where he replaced Zhilinsky, who had been disgraced by defeats at Tannenberg and the Masurian Lakes. But instead of taking the fight to Hindenburg, Ruzski took it to Ivanov, his former boss on the Southwest Front. Ivanov wanted to exploit the collapse of the Austrians and press on to Cracow and Budapest. Ruzski slammed on the brakes, insisting that no offensives be undertaken and that reserves instead be collected to defeat the gathering German thrust through Warsaw to the Russian interior. Taking stock of his poor communications, Ruzski even mooted a "strategic retreat" to the Niemen. He pondered abandoning Warsaw, that great road hub and strategic prize, and pulling back to Kovno.

Were Ruzski to withdraw as threatened, Ivanov would have to go back too, yielding even Lemberg to guard his flank. With all of its reserves already apportioned by Sukhomlinov, the Stavka found itself with little ability to impose a single direction, or even move units around in the true spirit of a "general headquarters." East Prussia absorbed twenty-five Russian divisions and Galicia another thirty, leaving just thirty divisions for the central offensive demanded by the tsar and the western allies. Grand Duke Nikolai expressed "fright" at the pessimism and querulousness of his generals, but he had few levers to move them. The commanders on each operational front controlled a vast hinterland as well as rails and rolling stock, and they had become adept at rebuffing the Stavka's calls for cooperation with unanswerable logistical counterarguments.[25]

It took the Germans finally to move the Russians. On September 28, General August von Mackensen's Ninth Army began marching to the Vistula along roads so muddy that the carts and troops were forced to stumble through the plowland on either side. The officers marveled at the "lack of middle-class culture" in Polish towns, a shabbiness of architecture, display, and street life that was, as one German put it, "as frightful as the American West."[26] Ludendorff, who had pressed hard for this autumn offensive, had not expected conditions to be so bad so soon. He described the mud in Poland as "knee-deep," even on the great Cracow-to-Warsaw post road. Guns and carts sank up to their axles and had to be heaved forward by wet, tired troops. Officers recalled Napoleon's observation a century earlier, when he had come this way: "God has created a fifth element in addition to water, air, earth and fire: mud."[27]

Like Napoleon, the Germans had soaring plans. In an uneasy compromise between the France-first and Russia-first strategies, Hindenburg and Ludendorff were preparing for an intensive "second war" with the Russians once—as Hoffmann put it—"France was crossed off the list of great powers." On this campaign, Hindenburg brought along the king of Saxony—a prince of the German Empire—to be installed in Warsaw as "king of Poland" once the Russians had been driven out.[28] Lieutenant Harry Kessler, marching with the German Ninth Army, mused about victory: Russia would be beaten and Poland detached as a self-governing German dominion "along the model of Canada or Australia."[29]

A British officer marching with the Russians noted that they suffered even more than the oncoming Germans; "so defective was the state of the roads" that his unit required nine days to traverse 120 miles. Another foreign attaché, serving with the Russians at Lublin, described roads there "broken up by heavy artillery and pontoons, and covered with several inches of liquid mud."[30] Sukhomlinov's war ministry had made even less provision for the foul weather than Ludendorff or Conrad, and so these Russian troops shivered in their sodden summer uniforms and squelched through the mud barefoot or in sodden hemp clogs. On October 5, the only marginally better-shod Austrian Fourth, Third, and Second Armies crossed the Viskola and the thirteen divisions (one hundred thousand men) of the First Army closed up wing to wing with the German Ninth Army at Opatów. One of those Germans was unimpressed: "The Austrians make a clueless and disorganized impression. Many do not understand German. . . . In general, even the Russian prisoners make more of a military impression than these Austrian tramp soldiers, who arrive everywhere too late."[31]

The Austrians relieved the town and fortress of Przemysl on October 9. Like MacArthur in the Philippines, Conrad had vowed to return, and he had. Some of Boroevic's troops cleared fifteen thousand Russian and Austrian corpses from the fortress' perimeter, while the rest joined the Second Army's pursuit of the retreating Russians toward Lemberg. But their pursuit shortly slowed and then stopped altogether. Like the September battles in reverse, the Russians withdrew from river line to river line, shooting up every Austrian attempt to pursue them. Unlike the Russians in September, the Austrians lacked the manpower to go around the Russians, so they attacked frontally, with the usual result. "The battle today," General Otto Meixner wrote on October 12, "was indecisive; none of my groups could push through." On the thirteenth: "It appears that we're no longer dealing with rear-guards, but with strong enemy forces." On the seventeenth: "This morning we began our attack as ordered. It quickly broke down under heavy fire from the flank. We slept in the same position we woke in."

The Russian retreat had stopped and they had settled into the very Grodek position the Austrians had yielded in September. Getting shot by Russians sheltering in the same position in which they had so recently sheltered to shoot Russians must have been deflating, even more so because the Austrians were attacking without artillery support. On October 21, Meixner expressed his consternation: "General Colerus has ordered that due to the shortage of shells, attacks must only be attempted where success can be anticipated without artillery support."[32] That was nowhere on this front.

Dankl's First Army followed the Vistula northeast in the same half-hearted fashion, crossing to the left bank and making for Sandomir. The Austrians marched until they met resistance, then halted. Although the Austrians had broken the Russian codes and the Germans had discovered the complete Russian order of battle on the corpse of an officer on October 9 (revealing three Russian armies, the center of the Russian phalanx, concentrating behind the Vistula), Conrad lacked the strength to exploit the intelligence. For their part, the Russians sought ways to get at the Germans and exploit Austria's infirmity. They needed to do *something* lest they yield more of Poland to the German advance and expose the flank and rear of Ivanov's Southwest Front in Galicia. If that happened, the whole Russian army would have to retreat, permitting the Austrians to retake Lemberg and the Germans to take Warsaw while finishing off the French and British in the west.

The guiding concept now in Russian headquarters was that the Austro-Hungarians were weak and could be held in check by a small force while the bulk of the Russian army turned to attack the Germans. Brusilov was entrusted with the smaller force: the Third and Eighth Armies as well as a newly formed Eleventh Army. Ivanov took the Second Army from Ruzski's front and added it to his command of the Fourth, Ninth, and Fifth Armies. Crossing back over the Vistula, Ivanov marched north; by mid-October, the First, Second, and Fifth Armies were massing around Warsaw, the Fourth around Ivangorod (Deblin), and the Ninth at Sandomir.

Sixty Russian divisions faced eighteen German ones. Hindenburg later applauded it as the "grand duke's greatest plan": count on Austrian passivity, lure the Germans toward Warsaw, and then envelop Mackensen's overeager Ninth Army from the flanks.[33]

The grand duke's plan was fine on paper, but all of the Russian armies were dogged by crippling shortages. With their ports on the Baltic and Black Sea closed by German and Turkish blockades, the Russians had to rely on imports from Archangel (two thousand miles from the front and iced over for half the year) and Vladivostock (eight thousand miles away). It took Russian ports a full year to accumulate as many ship arrivals (1,250) as British ports handled every four days, which certainly gave a glimpse of the tsar's supply problem. The grand duke and Ivanov pleaded for a suspension of operations until shell stocks could be replenished, but the tsar and Sukhomlinov, pressured by the French, drove the generals forward, the desperate Russian gunners improvising shells out of ration cans, gas pipes, and scrap metal.[34]

On October 10, the Russians began to cross the Vistula to attack. While the German Ninth Army came under attack at Warsaw, the Austrians were pummeled on the San and south of Przemysl by the Russian Third and Eighth Armies. From October 13 until early November, this Battle of the San raged along the Polish-Ukrainian borderland. Archduke Joseph Ferdinand, who had replaced Auffenberg in command of the Fourth Army, alternated excuses ("for more than three months we have been fighting a Russian force twice our size") with exhortations ("find those sectors where we can fight the enemy on equal terms") and strategic nonsense ("only the strong can waste time; the weak must save it").[35] Nothing worked, and the three hundred thousand men of the Austrian Second, Third, and Fourth Armies were roundly beaten again.

Boroevic had to deploy machine guns to stem the rout of his Third Army on the San; one of his regiments, the largely Hungarian 34th, was depleted by mass suicides, as the exhausted men killed themselves rather than soldier on.[36] The Third Army had been Boroevic's for two months, yet he was still lamenting the things he had observed in September: "too many men are walking

away from the battle line, and no one stops them." His 44th
Landwehr Division retreated, leaving hundreds of precious rifles
neatly stacked for the pursuing Russians. "Those rifles were taken
from our wounded per regulations," Boroevic raged, "and no one
thought to transport them to safety?"[37]

The Germans had misread Russian intentions and were forced
to retreat from Warsaw, a decision announced on October 18.
Having agreed earlier to the loan of Dankl to cover Mackensen's
right, Conrad was now compelled to use Dankl's First Army to
cover the retreat, advancing the First Army to attack the flank of
the Russian Fourth and Ninth Armies as they crossed the Vistula.
In the last week of October, the Austro-Hungarian First Army
was badly beaten opposite Ivangorod, the great moated citadel
fifty miles south of Warsaw. Supply was abysmal—the Austrians
had not seen their field kitchens for days, and the scrawny wheelhorses were dying in their traces. An Austrian staff officer, asked
to report on the condition of the 37th Honvéd Division during the
battle, reported thus: "Severely exhausted by days of round-the-
clock marching and fighting, the troops can only be driven forward with acts of violence; even the officers are broken men."[38] A
battle opened to cover the German retreat was then converted by
Hindenburg into an opportunistic offensive to lure the Russians
after Mackensen, then cross the Vistula with the main German
body and hit them in the flanks. But Dankl, seeking validation
after his dispiriting retreat from Krásnik, opened up his own de-
fenses to tempt the Russians over the Vistula and enclose them.
He let them across but failed to enclose them, which had the effect
of surrounding the surrounders, now from both flanks—Ruzski
from the north, Evert from the south. Hindenburg resumed his
retreat, damning the Austrians as he went. They couldn't seem to
do anything right.

Pursued by the Russian Fourth and Ninth Armies, Dankl retreated all the way back to Cracow, then on to the Nida River,
where he rested in the crook behind Hindenburg's right flank. His
army, like Archduke Joseph Ferdinand's Fourth, had dissolved.
Accosting a leaderless band of Austro-Hungarian troops, a German officer was stunned by their fearless indifference. "Why are

you straggling?" he demanded. "Are you footsore, exhausted?" No, they growled, glancing in the direction of the front, "but why should we let ourselves be shot to pieces up there?"[39] The Austrian officer chronicling the decline of the 37th Honvéd Division described their behavior on the retreat: "Extreme demoralization— in Opatów, I found drunken men of this unit weaving through the streets; they had guzzled a cask of rum; the whole place was jammed with retreating wagons; a more depressing spectacle couldn't be imagined."

Neighboring Austro-Hungarian divisions seethed with ethnic hatred for one another, further poisoning the already sickened Habsburg army. "The mistrust that has arisen between the adjoining troops of the 5th Division and the 33rd Division is based on the extremely heavy casualties suffered by a regiment of the 5th when a regiment of the 33rd surrendered en masse instead of covering the retreat of their comrades from an exposed position," one of Dankl's corps commanders explained to him on November 15. What he was really saying—still a taboo subject in the Habsburg army—was that Czechs and Germans had been slaughtered because Hungarians had surrendered to save themselves rather than fight to extricate their comrades. The event in question had occurred on October 26. On December 13, the pedantic Dankl was still entangled in it, even though it was the sort of depressingly ordinary donnybrook that happened every day everywhere on this front: "I remain confused as to what specific circumstances caused the unauthorized retreat of the [Hungarian] 26th Regiment," he wrote the 5th Division commander, who was advocating on behalf of the Czechs and Germans of the 93rd. "Your attachments do not clarify the matter. Go back over this event and document it thoroughly in writing, so that we can determine whether actions were indeed taken that did not correspond to the 'no retreat' order in force at the time."[40]

Hindenburg was also litigating, against Conrad's impetuosity; by now relations between the two headquarters were so sour that the German referred to the Austrian as "that man," as in "that man hit the Russians too soon, when they were only partially across the Vistula instead of waiting for the main body to cross."[41]

They hated the sound of each other's voices—Conrad's warbling Viennese accent contrasted with Hindenburg's "Berlin Guardsman's tone" *(Berliner Gardeton)* that delivered pronouncements with the clipped officiousness *(Schnoddrigkeit)* that made every Austrian—Conrad most of all—feel small.

The Austrians by now were so weak that they could not even parry a fragment of the Russian army. Conrad begged Falkenhayn for more and more German troops. One day Falkenhayn took his Austro-Hungarian military liaison aside and said, "General Conrad has written me a letter in which he says that thirty new divisions are necessary for the Eastern Front. . . . I'm sure he's right and I concur, but, tell me, *where* shall I find those divisions?"[42] Once more, however, the quarreling Austrians and Germans were spared by Russian hesitation. After Warsaw, the Stavka could not decide whether to emphasize the southern, central, or northern fronts, so they promoted all three. "Frankly speaking," Ivanov grumbled, "it's impossible to detect in the Stavka's instructions either an exact task or a fixed objective."[43]

On the Austrian front, the Russians crossed the San in the night of October 18. This meant that Przemysl, which had been briefly relieved on October 9, would have to be either abandoned or shut up for another siege. His reputation already in tatters, Conrad did not dare abandon the fortress, and so for a week trains rumbled into Przemysl every fourteen minutes unloading supplies for a six-month siege and carrying out the fifteen thousand men who had been wounded in the struggle for the town. A Russian on Przemysl's war-torn perimeter was struck by the squalor of his first siege: "The images are very depressing; corpses to left and right, ours and theirs, some fresh, some many days old. . . . Most memorable are the skulls, the hair, the fingernails and the hands of the dead. Here and there feet poke out of the ground, from corpses that were not buried deep enough. The heavy wheels of our battery make cracking noises as we roll over them. We saw an Austrian who had been buried alive; he'd come to, freed himself, and then died. He lay there lifeless, his head and hands above the ground, the rest below. My God, how long can you see such things before you lose your mind?"[44]

Spared these horrors, Conrad still seemed to have lost his mind. His management of the defense was appallingly slipshod. With everything collapsing, Przemysl was either a bridge too far—beyond the means of Austria to defend—or an indispensable symbol of Austro-Hungarian resistance to the Russian steamroller. If he held it as the latter, Conrad needed to evacuate the civilian population of thirty thousand and reduce the garrison to the bare minimum of about fifty thousand troops needed to hold the town and its detached forts so that the Russians would be unable to starve them out. He took none of these precautions. The civilian population remained, along with 135,000 troops, leaving a bloated, largely useless, and voracious population that the Russians could simply surround and leave to starve. No one believed that a Habsburg relief army would arrive in time, or at all. "The Austrians are thought to have sixteen regular and five reserve corps left in the field," the British military attaché jotted from Warsaw, "but they are mere skeletons. The Russians have taken 1,000 guns and 200,000 prisoners. Are the Austrians beaten?"[45]

Since the late summer defeats at Lemberg and Rawa-Ruska, Conrad's war had swirled sluggishly around the basin between the San and the Carpathians. Forced behind the San in September, Conrad spent most of October—to Germany's amazement—trying to cross back over it in order to make his army in some way effective. But the Russians, having failed to envelop Conrad before he reached the safety of the San, now turned the tables and used the river barrier to prevent the Austrians from cooperating with German operations around Warsaw. In a depressing sequence of skirmishes along the river—the San battles or *Sankämpfe*—the Austrians struggled to get back into Poland and the Russians struggled to keep them out.[46]

In the three-day Battle of Opatowka in early November, Dankl's First Army lost another forty thousand troops and pulled back behind the Nida. Conrad now gave back everything that had been (briefly) retaken. As most of the Austrians regrouped behind the next river barrier—the Dunajec-Nida position just east of the Cracow forts—Conrad's North Army increasingly resembled a rabble. General Karl Lukas, who had experienced problems with the Czechs of his 19th Division in July, was overwhelmed by them in October. In a line that might have been penned by the sniggering Svejk, he implored: *"Viribus Unitis!* With United Forces! Let's just do our best and give everything we've got, life and blood, for our beloved emperor."[47]

Conrad gaped at his casualties and the spiraling cost of the war, noting that just a few months of combat operations had cost the empire four billion crowns, the equivalent of seven years of prewar military spending. Yet despite these expenditures, Austro-Hungarian shell production remained embarrassingly feeble, even by 1914 standards. The monarchy produced just 116,000 shells in December 1914 for an artillery establishment that was firing off 240,000 rounds every *week.* Only regular deliveries of German shells kept them going.[48] Conrad instructed his army commanders to compile "feats of arms" that could be mashed into propaganda and used "to inspire the war-lusty youth of the monarchy," but there were no feats of arms to describe. The *Kampfschilderungen* (battle stories) requested would only serve to demoralize Austria's youth.[49]

The Austrians took some bittersweet consolation from the German retreat. Their ambassador in Berlin groused that Hindenburg's "wreath of glories" remained weirdly intact despite the retreat from Warsaw back to German territory, and despite German contingency plans to blow up the Silesian coal mines if the Russian pursuit continued.[50] It wouldn't, and the Germans knew it. Unlike the Austrians, the Germans had a realistic sense of their own capabilities and those of the enemy. Ludendorff had calculated that a German retreat of seventy-five or a hundred miles—demolishing all (Russian) railways, roads and bridges along the way—would suffice to save his army and stop the Russians. And indeed, without rails beyond the Vistula, the Russian advance did peter out after just three days, an observer noting that "the Germans were retreating in that leisurely way which indicated that their retirement was anything but a rout."[51] Hoffmann, who had served as an observer in the Russo-Japanese War and still relished the anecdote about Generals Samsonov and Rennenkampf quarreling and punching each other on the railway platform at Mukden, had predicted a similar Russian breakdown in his war diary: "Nothing can go wrong; if we have to retreat, the Russians can only follow us for three days."[52]

By November 1, the Russian pursuit had stopped. The Germans, using the military railway that ran the entire length of their border with Russia, were able quickly to reinforce every threatened point. Unlike the Austrians, the Germans had perfected this kind of speedy deployment. "At every station as you approach the frontier," the British travel writer Henry Norman had observed before the war, "the lines expand into a dozen, each alongside a platform, obviously that trains may be filled and emptied quickly to hurl the military might of Germany northward." Cash to fill those trains with soldiers and shell and prolong the war flowed in from occupied territories such as Belgium, where the Germans levied a monthly "war contribution" of 40 million marks to defray a war bill that was mounting to 1.25 billion marks a month.[53]

But there was no disguising the fact that even with heavier German participation, the Russians had parried the swipe at Warsaw (the "Calais of the east") and survived another round. The Central Powers found themselves back where they had begun the operation a month earlier. By now, the two governments were hardly speaking, Austria's minister in Dresden noting that he was being told nothing by German military authorities and was reduced to "loitering in the train stations to observe the passage of troop trains from east to west," which, from the Austro-Hungarian perspective, was entirely the wrong direction.[54]

On November 1, the kaiser formally appointed Hindenburg commander of all German forces in the east. Ludendorff was chief of staff to this new *Ober-Ost* command at Posen (Poznan) and Hoffmann chief of operations. "All German forces in the east" comprised two armies: Mackensen's Ninth Army and Prince Leopold of Bavaria's Eighth. They were embroiled in a strategic debate with Falkenhayn and the kaiser, a debate that would not be resolved until Falkenhayn's dismissal and replacement by Hindenburg in August 1916. Falkenhayn had no appetite for Russian operations. He was committed to the battle at Ypres, which offered a great strategic prize—the Channel ports—if carried through to

In November 1914, Kaiser Wilhelm II (c.) appointed Hindenburg (l.) and Ludendorff (r.) to command all German forces in the east from a new headquarters (*Ober-Ost*) in Posen. The two generals battled with Falkenhayn for resources and influence, seeking to decide the Great War in the east, not the west.
CREDIT: National Archives

victory. If the Germans gained control of these ports, they could directly pressure Great Britain with U-boats and surface ships. That might compel the British to negotiate and withdraw their wealth, industry, and navy from the war, permitting the Germans to fight the French and Russians on more equal terms.

Falkenhayn considered it foolhardy to focus on the Russians. The tsar had only to enlist "General Winter" and retreat away from the Germans to buy time for yet another attritional campaign while the British busily expanded their army and navy and Italy—in all probability—entered the war on the side of the Entente. Thus, Falkenhayn refused all reinforcements to Hindenburg and counseled him instead to hold a winter line in the east while Falkenhayn carried through to victory his operations in Belgium. Falkenhayn even pondered a separate peace with the Russians to facilitate concentration against France and Britain.[55]

Ludendorff continued to assert that he could win the war in the east, even as Falkenhayn doubled down for the Ypres offensive, which he launched on November 4.[56] The six corps that Hindenburg had been expecting were instead committed to Falkenhayn's "race to the sea," which left *Ober-Ost* and the Austrians with a total of just 75 divisions against 135 Russian divisions. Undeterred, Ludendorff reconcentrated the Ninth Army at Thorn (Torun). He and Hindenburg gave Falkenhayn's apparently sacrosanct France-first strategy a novel twist. They (grudgingly) agreed that France and Britain would remain the focus of German efforts, but added that the defeat of the British Expeditionary Force and Kitchener's call for "new armies" in Britain after the devastating casualties of the summer and fall offered a one-time opportunity: to finish the war in the east in the winter of 1914 and then transfer all German (and Austrian) fighting strength to the west in the spring of 1915 before the new British divisions were available. In just a matter of weeks, with relatively light forces, Ludendorff and Hindenburg had managed to stop the Russian steamroller in its tracks. They now intended to finish it off.

CHAPTER 12

The Thin Gray Line

LUDENDORFF HAD NO INTENTION OF LOSING. With the Russian Second and Fifth Armies resuming their weary march on Germany, *Ober-Ost* planned to reprise the Tannenberg feat with a similar stroke: move rapidly onto the flank of the Second Army—already Ludendorff's victim once at Tannenberg—smash it in again, and then drive southeast to the city of Lodz with Mackensen's Ninth Army. Lodz was the only place with good roads, railways, and quarters in a region otherwise bereft of billets and communications. It was a strategic keypoint for both sides, and Hindenburg planned to bring forty-two Austro-German divisions against forty-nine Russian divisions to seize the city and use it as an eventual springboard for a new eastern offensive.

Ludendorff imagined that victory at Lodz would decisively open the door to Warsaw. Based there, the Germans and Austrians might finish off Russia and—as an Austrian diplomat put it—"redraw the borders of northeastern Europe." Everyone was confident enough to begin speculating on what to do with the Russian carcass. Bethmann spoke of a "liberated Ukraine"—presumably liberated just long enough to be subjected to Germany or Austria. Vienna and Berlin angled for Poland, and the Germans assumed that they'd receive Russia's Baltic provinces and Finland as well. Poland was the knottiest issue; neither the Germans nor the Austrians really wanted it, for it contained too many Poles, who would merely weaken future governments in Berlin or Vienna with their nationalist demands. Yet Poland could not be left to the Russians, who needed to be maximally weakened and pushed away from the German and Austrian borders; nor could it be given its independence, lest it become a great power in its own right or a French satellite. With the war far from decided, this "Polish question" still lay some distance down the road.[1] But that distance was closing, and the Polish roads rising to meet the Germans now would not be blocked by snow until December, and they'd freeze in mid-November, facilitating fast German marches and preventing the Russians from entrenching. If the Germans could strike quickly into the heart of Poland, they might be able to catch the Russians in the field and deal them a crushing military defeat before the year was out.

Using eight hundred trains, Mackensen shuttled the Ninth Army north to Thorn. Then on November 11 he wheeled southeast and, covering his left with the Vistula, struck toward the Russian flank between Lodz and Warsaw. In just five days, he had moved a quarter of a million troops onto the Russian flank in complete secrecy. This, as the British attaché with the Russians put it, was "a masterpiece of organization," launched just fifteen days after the German retreat from Warsaw.[2] Back in the Dresden train station, where he had earlier complained of the east-west flow of German troops, Austria's minister confirmed that "troop trains are now moving west to east."[3]

This eastward movement of German troops, meanwhile, was reshaping events in the western theater. Having failed to win the "race to the sea" to outflank the British in Flanders, Falkenhayn grimly settled down to a war of attrition on the Western Front. He fortified his trench line in Belgium and France and released three infantry corps to Hindenburg. A British observer with the Russians judged the German troop movements "amazing—some of the men [the Russians] took prisoner, their entire corps and divisions, had been rushed up from Belgium, back again, sent into Austria, and then brought back to East Prussia."[4]

This ability to shift nimbly on interior lines between the two fronts gave the Germans the chance to execute Hindenburg's favored strategy: defend in the west and win in the east. To land that winning blow, Berlin dug deep for new sources of men (forty-five- to fifty-year-olds were conscripted for the first time) and money. The Reichstag voted a second round of war credits in November. Thus bolstered, Hindenburg built his Eastern Army or *Ostheer* to a strength of twelve corps (with six more promised) and seven cavalry divisions. Conrad, his fortunes and importance sinking by the day, watched jealously from the sidelines, his only comment "*Vederemo*—we'll see."[5]

Most striking about the German forces arriving from the west was their state of mind; having been exposed to more fire than the easterners, they exhibited more psychoses. One German officer in the Carpathians noted that of ten men sent to his unit from France, three suffered nervous breakdowns. One would sit for hours staring at the ground and reciting long passages from *The Odyssey* in Greek.[6] But it was still early days in the war, and these shell-shocked men accounted for only a fraction of the overall troop strength in the east.

With the ground hardened by frost, those Germans of sounder mind marched quickly, covering fifty miles in four days, and smashed the lone corps of the Russian First Army on the south bank of the Vistula. The Germans then thrust into the gap between the First and Second Armies and pushed the four corps of General Sergei Scheidemann's Second Army back on Lodz, a city of 500,000, on November 18. As the Russian First Army reeled back toward Warsaw, Ludendorff gathered in 136,000 prisoners and prepared to envelop the Second Army. His analysts estimated that the Germans and Austrians together had killed, wounded, or captured 1.25 million Russians since the start of the war, and that even the Russian steamroller could not absorb losses like these forever.

Evidence from the battlefront seemed to justify German optimism. Captured Russians confirmed that they had neither food nor ammunition; their orders were to attack unarmed and pick up rifles from the dead and wounded. Wounded Russians were instructed not just to await first aid but to look around for an

By November 1914, the Germans calculated that they and the Austrians had killed, wounded, or captured 1.25 million Russians in just three months of combat. Russian prisoners, like these, lacked everything: rifles, ammunition, food, and any notion as to what the war was about.
CREDIT: Heeresgeschichtliches Museum, Wien

unarmed comrade and offer him their rifle. This predicament partially explained the German drive for war in 1914: the Russian Great Army Program of 1913 was not projected to fill the rifle gap in the Russian army until 1918, and this gap and many others had clearly not even been narrowed in the first year of the program.[7] For the duration of the war, 35 percent of the men in an average Russian infantry division would have no rifle at all; German officers chuckled that the Russians were so short of artillery that they were begging the Japanese to return the guns lost in the Manchurian War. The Russians were also trying to buy rifles and ammunition in Japan, and were offering five rubles to peasants who would bring any rifle—German, Austrian, or Russian—to a Russian unit.[8]

The Russian artillery had fired an average of forty-five thousand shells a day for the first hundred days of the war, and the ammunition shortage was so severe that Russian officers were now being told to "push the troops forward and pull the munitions back," which was not good news for the troops. The Russians were estimated to be down to a million shells or less, and they had only a single munitions factory (Britain had 150) and could not easily import new factories because the French and British had already claimed all American exports; even if the machines were shipped to the faraway Russian ports, they could not be installed anywhere near the fighting fronts.[9] Sensing victory—so welcome after the stalemate in the west—Kaiser Wilhelm II departed for a ten-day visit to the Russian front. The German generals now spoke excitedly of a war-winning *Zug nach Osten*, or drive to the east.[10]

Ruzski, who was in command of the Northwest Front, finally understood on November 15 what was happening. Mackensen's move was not a feint; it was the main effort, and it was aimed at Lodz, the heart of the empire's textile industry and a key winter-billeting area on the road to Warsaw. Ruzski had left only a corps of Rennenkampf's First Army around Lodz, directing the rest of it to advance into East Prussia. He now ordered Rennenkampf back, to join the battle at Lodz. Ruzski ordered Evert to continue advancing west with the Fourth Army to engage any Austrians who came forward and divert any German reinforcements, then swung his Second and Fifth Armies around to face north. He boldly directed his First Army to drop down and encircle Mackensen.

Plehve, commanding the Russian Fifth Army, had already extricated himself from Auffenberg's trap at Komarów, and now wriggled clear of Mackensen's. Sixty-five years old—the same age as Mackensen—Plehve was a born commander, a witness in his headquarters recalling that he "grasped the situation with extraordinary quickness and gave his decision rapidly and firmly."[11] Countermarching seventy miles in three days over frozen roads, Plehve's Fifth Army beat Mackensen to Lodz, and then attacked the right wing of the attempted German envelopment.[12] Rennenkampf's emboldened First Army approached the German left at Lowitsch (Lowicz). Mackensen arrived outside Lodz to find seven Russian

General August von Mackensen had fought in the Franco-Prussian War and served as Wilhelm II's military history tutor. Reputed to be the best horseman in the German army—hence the hussar tunic—Mackensen had vied with the Younger Moltke for the job of general staff chief in 1906 and was a natural choice to command the German Ninth Army in the east in 1914.
CREDIT: National Archives

corps already there. Suddenly the German was in danger of being encircled by a Russian force twice the size of his own. Sensing a decisive battle, Grand Duke Nikolai moved the Stavka from Baranovichi to Skierniewice, a village east of Lodz.

As at Warsaw, Ludendorff had gambled and lost. Russian plans had been so muddled, first forward, then back, that he had assumed that their latest movement back on Lodz heralded a panicky retreat across the Vistula, not a grim determination to hold the line. Like Mackensen, Ludendorff gobbled the bait and rushed headlong into the trap being laid by Ruzski. Where the fighting was heaviest, north and west of Lodz, the Russians outnumbered the Germans; being so close to the city's supplies, they also had sufficient ammunition for once, while the Germans, at the end of long supply lines, were running short. Valued less than ammunition, Russian wounded were left to die and rot. Mikhail Rodzyanko, the president of the Duma, debarked near the front and saw seventeen thousand wounded Russians sprawled in the cold mud. Most of them had been there for five days, and no one had even dressed their festering wounds.[13]

While they grappled with Plehve, the Germans were also eavesdropping on Russian radio transmissions, as they had been doing every day since Tannenberg. They charted Rennenkampf's slow progress toward Lodz and knew that whatever advantage they still enjoyed was slipping away. Mackensen gambled that he still had time to send General Reinhard von Scheffer's reserve corps—fifty-five thousand Germans in six divisions—east of the city to close the ring around the two Russian armies that were there. The Austrians were supposed to have done this; Conrad had ordered the Fourth Army to sally from behind the Wisloka (where it had crept from the Dunajec), attack from the south, and "complete the catastrophe of the Russian armed forces in Poland," but it hadn't. Fighting to cross the Vistula, the Austrians were stopped cold by the Russians, who had one army on their right (Third) and another on their left (Ninth), a by-now familiar predicament for Archduke Joseph Ferdinand's Fourth Army. Attacking across pontoon bridges into Russian shrapnel and machine guns, the troops experienced casualties so high that some Fourth Army divisions had to be renamed brigades. Drummers and musicians were converted to riflemen. The conversion was explained thus: "Because we just don't need music anymore."[14]

Shadowing the Austrian retreat on November 20, a Russian lieutenant named Fedor Stepun noted the squalor and dashed hopes the Austrians left in their wake. Stepun was reminded of old Marshal Kutuzov, who had fought Napoleon to a draw at Borodino and explained looting and atrocities in war this way: "Whenever you cut down a tree, sawdust flies." Now Stepun arrived amid all the sawdust of war. "We entered a town the beaten enemy troops had just left. What a picture of misery. . . . The streets and train station were filled with civilians who had tried and failed to get away with their property. Five trains were stuck in the station; personal belongings were piled on the platforms and crammed into every railroad car: beds, couches, mattresses, toys, paintings, albums, women's clothing, hats, Jewish prayer books, lamps, coffee, a meat grinder."

Cossacks on horseback—each of them trailing an extra horse or two liberated from the locals—picked through the heaped-up

Cossacks dancing in camp. "Here's the difference between soldiers and Cossacks," a Russian officer observed. "The soldier will take what he needs; he has pangs of conscience. The Cossack has none; he takes everything, the necessary and the unnecessary alike."
CREDIT: Heeresgeschichtliches Museum, Wien

chattels; some dismounted to replace their worn saddles and blankets with sofa cushions and tablecloths. "Here's the difference between soldiers and Cossacks," the Russian officer observed. "The soldier will take what he needs; he has pangs of conscience. The Cossack has none; he takes everything, the necessary and the unnecessary alike." Across the street, the Roman Catholic church had been looted: urine, vomit, and excrement streaked the walls, the Latin Bible lay on the floor, and two dead Austrian soldiers sprawled in the entrance, one young and handsome, the other old and ugly. "Their pockets, as is the case with every dead soldier, had been turned inside out; everybody here is greedy for gold."[15]

Little of this misery penetrated the sheltered leadership of the Habsburg state. Far to the west, General Stürgkh was spending a raw November day touring the 1870 battlefields of Gravelotte and St. Privat with Tisza. As they poked around the tidy French villages, assembling their knowledge of the Franco-Prussian War, Tisza said: "To this day, I am still wondering *who* ordered the offensive in August against Serbia. Once war with Russia became unavoidable, all offensives against Serbia were to have been shelved. How it is that we went ahead and invaded Serbia remains a big hole in my knowledge. I am convinced," Tisza concluded, "that we would not have lost the Battle of Lemberg had Conrad only sent Second Army promptly to the east."[16]

Lemberg, of course, was ancient history to the Austro-Hungarian troops in the east, who were reeling back toward Cracow, "retreating west again on roads we had come to know so well," one *Jäger* officer jeered. Desertion spiked, and the Fourth Army ordered an investigation into the disappearance into Russian captivity of two entire regiments totaling eight thousand men along with their colonels and officers on November 25. Inside Cracow, the Fourth Army went on a thieving rampage, the fortress commandant forming a civil guard "to protect private property from the assaults, vandalism, and burglary" practiced by Austria's own troops. In the Austrian countryside, peasants quickly learned to fear the approach of the emperor's army. Unit reports echoed with incidents of robbery, extortion, and beatings. On December 1, General Dankl vowed to punish the "escalating cases of plunder by our own troops against our own people," a vow that would be difficult to enforce in this atmosphere of chronic defeat and retreat.[17]

The Austrian *Nordstoss* of August had given way to the Great Retreat of September, then to the San Battles of October, and now settled into an even drearier Battle of Cracow. Several Russian armies closed around Conrad's shrunken Austro-Hungarian force, which was supposed to be bravely thrusting forward to join forces with Mackensen's Ninth Army at Lodz, but was instead huddling in its trenches 150 miles to the south. With the Austrians inert, Ruzski drifted over to threaten the Germans with catastrophe. Ludendorff had spoken grandly of a "second Sedan" at Lodz, with the Austrians and Germans encircling the Russian armies there, but Mackensen now grasped that he'd have to perform the feat alone. Although outnumbered in the long run, Mackensen still thought he could win in the short run if he could knock out the Russians before Rennenkampf arrived in force.

The Russian Second Army certainly *felt* defeated. As General Reinhard von Scheffer's fifty-five-thousand-man corps moved onto his flank, the Second Army's new commander telegraphed Ruzski that he was surrounded, to which Ruzski, who was studying his maps, marvelously replied: "No, you've surrounded *them*, now demand their surrender." Indeed he had. Marooned at Lowicz— midway between Lodz and Warsaw—Scheffer's corps found itself with no connection to Mackensen and frantically began to back-pedal. The ground was too hard for trenching, so soldiers on both sides fought in the open, slid into streambeds, or raked together tree limbs and sandbags for protection. These were easily blasted away by artillery and machine guns. Where old trenches coincided with the new lines of battle, they were occupied, but the frozen ground prevented wet from soaking away, so blood, feces, and urine accumulated in a sludge that never froze, making this winter war even more squalid than the campaigns of summer and fall.[18] Walking along one of these foul trenches, an observer paused to record a grisly sight: "I came upon a raven perched upon the face of what had once been a man. It had picked his eyes from their sockets, and torn away his lips, and portions of the flesh of his face. It flapped off slowly, with a sullen croak."[19]

Ludendorff damned Conrad's inaction. Had the Austro-Hun-garian North Army advanced powerfully on the German right, Ludendorff believes, the Central Powers would have enveloped the Russians. Instead, the Russians were poised to envelop the Ger-mans.[20] An Austro-Hungarian officer attached to a German corps in France reported that "all people talk about here is Austria, and Hindenburg's regular complaints about our lack of toughness. . . . They say German troops can march sixty kilometers when neces-sary; ours can't make more than thirty; they say German troops can campaign without baggage; our troops can't."[21] In German great headquarters, Stürgkh puzzled over the organic differences between Germans and Austrians: "The Austrian is forever confus-ing the personal and the professional; the German has eyes only for the professional and leaves the personal aside. To the Austrian, the form and manner in which a task is assigned is more important than the task itself, whereas the German looks only at the task. To the German, the Austrian lacks energy and substance."[22]

With the Austrians sitting on their hands and the Germans on the verge of a great defeat, Ruzski watched in frustration as the Germans escaped. Rennenkampf—disparaged since Tannenberg as "*Rennen ohne Kampf*," or "Run without Fighting"—had run away again, this time closing too slowly from the north and permitting Scheffer to extricate his entire force (as well as ten thousand prisoners and sixty guns) from the Lowicz pocket. A Russian captain provided an explanation for the unwarlike torpor: summoned urgently from Tilsit to trap the Germans, he force-marched his regiment sixty-five miles in three days to the nearest train station, where no train awaited. The men spent twenty-four hours on the platform without food, drink, or shelter from cold winds. When the War Ministry finally discovered them at Mittau (Jeglava) and sent a train, it took two entire days—still without the troops having a crumb to eat—to crawl along to Warsaw. There they entrained for Lodz, still without food, and arrived on the outskirts, detrained, and were sent into the trenches, without sleep or a meal. Troops raved with hunger and literally fell asleep while shooting. Officers stumbled up and down the trenches, "muttering like sleepwalkers, beating the soldiers with the flat of their swords."[23]

Scheffer didn't sleep either. He was awake for seventy-two hours straight while his great escape unfolded in the last days of November, the Germans retreating through heavy snow that compounded the confusion in the Russian command. Lodz was a draw, with the Germans losing thirty-five thousand men—but the exhaustion of Russia's troops and shell stocks meant that the Stavka could contemplate no more offensive operations. Bullets were running out too, some Russian infantry divisions firing two million rounds in just three days of combat.[24]

The Russians had also lost an eye-popping 70 percent of the combat strength of their First and Second Armies to death, wounds, sickness, and captivity. Rennenkampf, who had barely clung to command after his failures at Tannenberg and the

Masurian Lakes, did not survive this humiliating episode. Widely suspected of treason because of his German origins, he was relieved of command, and driven out of the army. Grand Duke Nikolai had fifteen Russian officers shot for their hand in the fiasco. Touring the notoriously corrupt army supply office in Warsaw, the grand duke had only four words to say to the officers gathered there: "You steal, I hang."[25]

Passing by a field hospital near Lodz, a British correspondent noted thousands of wounded men laid out in the snow, transport to the rear being (as usual) unavailable; "outside one tent a great heap of amputated arms and legs lay on the ground." He was struck by the number of men who had lost one or both eyes to shrapnel darts.[26] In all, the winter battles had cost the Russians another half million troops, as well as 70 percent of their frontline officers. Now Russian conscripts were being sent to the front without any rifles at all, which partly explained the relatively light German losses of a hundred thousand.[27] Even though the vast spaces in the east enabled a war of movement—only one and a half German divisions occupied a frontage that would have been held by five German divisions in the west—the Russians lacked the mobility, boots (Ruzski spoke of a five-hundred-thousand-pair deficit), and artillery to polish off the overstretched Germans. Indeed, the Russians would never threaten German territory again in the war.

Austro-Hungarian territory was another matter. The Germans having proven too redoubtable, Ivanov proposed at a war council with Ruzski and the grand duke on November 29 that "the way to Berlin lies through Austria-Hungary." Ruzski had absorbed 75 percent casualties battling the Germans and was all but hors de combat.[28] The Russians would have to reboot yet again, this time focusing on their more vulnerable Austrian opponent. The grand duke agreed and authorized a reorientation from the Northwest back to the Southwest Front. Ivanov would now take the reins, leading a drive on Cracow and then over the Carpathians.

Conrad too wanted a fresh start. With the Russians pressed back to a line just west of Warsaw and four new German corps arriving from the stalemated Western Front for the *Ostheer*, he was fighting to remain relevant. He took out his frustration on Hindenburg, pronouncing accounts of the heroic German escape from Lodz "naive" and speculation that Hindenburg was preparing a counterstroke with his beefed-up force of nine corps and three cavalry divisions "childish." Remember, Conrad hissed, "the 'people's hero' has been *defeated*," but the Austrian general's credibility was at the vanishing point.[29] On December 6, the reinforced Germans did take Lodz and advanced to within thirty miles of Warsaw. It seemed only a matter of time before Emperor Franz Joseph agreed to subordinate the feckless Conrad to Hindenburg and Ludendorff in a new joint Austro-German *Ober-Ost*. "How on earth can we pursue even a tolerable foreign policy," the emperor queried the AOK, "when we fight so *badly*?"[30] Conrad's answer was the one he was resorting to with depressing regularity of late: the threat of resignation. Once again, an uncertain Franz Joseph backed down.

Desperate to demonstrate his ability after the Lodz fiasco, Conrad ordered Boroevic to attack toward Sanok in southeastern Poland and sent Archduke Joseph Ferdinand's Fourth Army to attack Evert's Fourth Army, which was wandering again toward Upper Silesia. Russian shortages of everything—shells, guns, rifles, bullets, uniforms, boots, food—and their inability to mass numbers around Conrad gave some cause for hope. The archduke's Fourth Army collided with Evert near Cracow, while Boroevic's Third Army attacked Sanok, which overlooked the San River and was a road and rail hub.[31] Evert and the Austrians jabbed ineffectually at each other until Radko-Dimitriev's Third Army, detained outside Przemysl until mid-November, came up to support Evert, having been replaced at Przemysl by yet another Russian army: Selivanov's Eleventh.

Now the Austrians were forced back on Cracow again. Thousands of despairing Habsburg troops feigned cholera symptoms to escape combat. The Austrian army commands advertised daily for the return of deserters: "Partyka, born in Matawicz in 1888, black hair, brown eyes, speaks Polish, 1.62 meters tall: if found, arrest and forward to the I Corps tribunal."[32] Archduke Friedrich had just been promoted from general to field marshal, but there was no cause anywhere for celebration; what little he and Conrad could discover about the reality of the front from their cozy headquarters far behind the lines suggested that their armies were not even fighting. On December 2, Conrad instructed his army commanders to decimate (shoot every tenth man) in units that retreated before the enemy.[33]

Conrad trumpeted some local victories, but they were short-lived. The Russian Ninth Army hurled Archduke Joseph Ferdinand's Fourth Army back south of Cracow. The Russian Third and Eighth Armies threw Boroevic's eight divisions back from Sanok and pummeled the seven divisions of General Karl von Pflanzer-Baltin's Armeegruppe in Bukovina. Green flags with the white half-moon and star hoisted over Austro-Hungarian trenches to announce an Ottoman-sponsored holy war against the tsar and deter attacks by Russian Muslim units did not deter. A yawning seventy-mile gap opened between Boroevic and the eleven divisions of the Fourth Army in the foothills of the Carpathians. The Russians were poised to push through this hole and into the Uzsok, Dukla, Lupkov, and Tylicz passes, which would carry them into Hungary and Moravia—the heart of the Habsburg monarchy.

On the Austrian right, Boroevic struggled weakly against the Russian Eighth and Eleventh Armies. The Austrian position was all the more untenable because of the facility with which Russian operatives—men and officers dressed in peasant clothes or Austro-Hungarian uniforms—drifted in and out of the Austrian camps and trenches, spying and scattering vouchers that promised "Slavic troops" cash rewards and special treatment if they would desert to the Russians. Three thousand miles to the east, working on a road crew with other Austro-Hungarian prisoners in Turkmenistan, a captured Austrian officer could verify that this was so. "The Russians divided us by nationality," he observed in late 1914. "The Slavs got the best barracks, the Germans, Hungarians, and Jews the worst. We also had to work longer hours than the Slavs, and take all of the dirty jobs." They all received the same meager rations—beet soup and buckwheat porridge—because the Russian camp commandant pocketed half of the men's daily food allowance, and the guards and kitchen staff took most of the rest, but the Slavs were always allowed to eat first and were encouraged to mock and kick the Germans and Hungarians in line behind them.[34]

The Russians also received ample intelligence on Austrian strength and intentions from captured Austrian officers, who, in Archduke Friedrich's words, displayed "senselessness and garrulousness" in captivity.[35] Austro-Hungarian peasants, many of whom sympathized more with the Russians than with their own army, were another fertile source of intelligence. Archduke Joseph Ferdinand, a scion of this tottering House of Austria, ordered his troops to proceed pitilessly against any Austrian village that aided the Russians: "There is no need to consult a magistrate in such matters; simply take and kill hostages, burn villages to the ground, and hang any suspects on the spot."[36] And this was *Austrian* territory. Clearly the monarchy was at the end of its rope. Only Ludendorff's loan of some German reserve divisions, combined with Russian sluggishness, sufficed to arrest the Russian onslaught. Ruzski, as usual, was for resting and resupplying, and the Russians were down to about ten shells per gun per day.

The Austrians had their backs to the wall and were in danger of being flung through the Carpathians and into the Hungarian plain. They were now deployed in a thin gray line, a weak Second Army on the left, lying along the German border north of Cracow, the First Army northwest of the city (its rear area a place called Auschwitz), the Fourth Army in Cracow, and the Third Army straggling southeast of the city, from Neu Sandez down to Czernowitz.

To save Cracow, Austria's last foothold east of the Carpathians, Conrad ordered an attack across the Vistula. The Austrian Fourth Army and a German division beat the Russian Third Army to a standstill near Cracow at Limanowa in the first two weeks of December. Southeast of Cracow, facing west, the Russians had made themselves vulnerable to a flanking attack, which Archduke Joseph Ferdinand delivered. Using the rails around Cracow and forced marches, he cut into the Russian flank with the Fourth Army. The two sodden, shivering armies fought savagely for two weeks, like troglodytes. The Austrian cavalry, still outfitted with shakos and sabers according to ancient tradition, were especially vulnerable: "Our cavalry fought hand-to-hand at Limanowa, without bayonets! We found hundreds of them dead with their skulls bashed in. It's a crime the way we equip our cavalry," an Austrian general staff colonel morosely recorded.[37]

Though hitting a Russian flank, the Austrians persisted in attacking frontally in many sectors without adequate artillery support. The artillery failed to prepare the attacks, shoot them through, or cover the inevitable retreats, prompting the by-now predictable scolding from Archduke Friedrich: "Honor and the ancient traditions of the Austrian artillery *demand* that you stick to your guns without regard for casualties, to facilitate an orderly retreat by the infantry."[38] The Austrian guns responded by shelling their own men.[39]

The Russians too seemed to be fading, Austria's 6th *Jäger* Battalion taking a thousand Russian prisoners—including a relieved-looking general—in a single day of fighting.[40] Inspecting two hundred such Russian POWs, a German officer remarked upon their misery: "They pressed against the cage like hungry animals wherever anyone from the street held out a piece of bread. They climbed on top of each other, up the iron bars, screamed with bulging eyes, stretched-out hands, in greedy, hoarse voices, each one seeking to draw attention to his own hunger." The Russians reminded him of a Goya painting, horrors like *The Madhouse* or *Saturn Devouring His Son*.[41]

After the Battle of Limanowa, which drove the Russians back thirty-five miles, Conrad boasted that his army alone had held back "half of Asia," broken Russia's momentum, and "pushed them back along the entire front."[42] This stretched the truth considerably. Limanowa had yielded twenty-three thousand Russian prisoners, saved Cracow, and prevented the Russians from thrusting between the Austrian Third and Fourth Armies and pushing them through the Carpathians, but it could not be converted into anything decisive because of the arrival of ample Russian reinforcements, which marched in from Neu Sandez to threaten the flank and rear of Fourth Army, forcing it to yield the ground it had just won at the cost of another twelve thousand casualties.[43] The

Russians jogged forward to reoccupy their temporarily abandoned trenches on the east bank of the Dunajec, making Limanowa yet another Pyrrhic Austrian victory, at best.

It was indeed as if Limanowa had never happened. Writing Bolfras from Berlin, Conrad admitted that nothing "decisive" had been achieved at Limanowa or anywhere; "the Russians are able to paralyze our every stroke with fresh forces." Just as the Russians had used the San to separate the Germans and Austrians, they now used the Dunajec for the same purpose. "They are nailed to one bank and we are nailed to the other," Conrad grumbled.[44] But most of his divisions were now down to a few thousand men or less. The 6th *Jäger* Battalion discovered that of the nineteen hundred men and officers that it had been infused with since July, eleven hundred had been killed, wounded, or captured by December.[45] Touring the battlefield in the rain on December 17, an Austrian staff officer recorded its desolation: "Trenches running off in all directions, filled with water. The field is littered with everything: shell and bullet casings, broken rifles, backpacks, bayonets, caps, helmets, shirts, potatoes, wooden doors that had been torn off their hinges and used as cover, burnt houses, sobbing peasants, corpses floating in the trenches and lying all over the roads, graves marked with wooden crosses, dead horses, fields trampled by thousands of boots, telegraph poles knocked down, barns torn open by shells with the hay sticking out—a picture of misery and chaos."[46]

By year's end the Austrians remained stuck on the line of the Dunajec (just thirty-five miles from Cracow) and, further south, the Carpathians. The war had frozen in place, staff officers scribbling "*Wie gestern*—the same as yesterday" on their daily situation reports. The men too were freezing in place, provided with nothing but sheets of paper ("tissue paper when available," Dankl punctiliously minuted) to wrap their frostbitten feet.[47] The Second Army's 32nd Division was so worn down that Conrad had to grant it a two-week break, but the division commander expressed no gratitude on his return to the line. "We spent our leave under canvas," he noted, "alternately pelted with rain and snow, and afflicted with cholera. Really the leave was illusory; it weakened more than strengthened us."[48]

The Russians stared dully across at their tortured enemy. "Our souls were like hedgehogs, rolled in a ball inside us; outwardly nothing shocked us, inwardly we hibernated," a Russian officer wrote.[49] Austria's best units, like Vienna's 4th Deutschmeister Regiment, held together and even attacked, but with invariably tragic results. Posted at Wodowice, a Deutschmeister battalion stormed the Russian trenches opposite, the men actually obeying the order to fix bayonets and charge. They crossed two hundred yards of fire-swept ground—"Lieutenant Altrichter mortally wounded, Lieutenant Friedrich shot in the chest," the battalion commander dolefully reported—and tumbled into the Russian trenches, where they scuffled briefly with the three hundred occupants before grasping that they lay squarely in the sights of another Russian trench, just beyond the one they'd taken at such dreadful cost. "We could neither attack the new one nor remain in the old one, so we withdrew," their report conceded, "confident that we had done our part to wring some success from that day."[50]

But what success, and to what end? Most units behaved more rationally than this. One general replacing another in command of the Austro-Hungarian 19th Division issued a stern divisional order to his officers—"Some Observations"—that described an army that was literally falling apart, with filthy uniforms, rusty rifles, no saluting, malingering at every opportunity, and profound indiscipline and lack of initiative.[51] That Austro-Hungarian division would eventually be given to the Germans, to flesh out their *Südarmee*, a new army authorized by Falkenhayn to stiffen the wilting Austrians. On Christmas Day 1914, Archduke Friedrich received his own a gift—another retreat, which drove the Habsburg army's back up against the wall of the Carpathians. The First Army and the Fourth Army remained in the Dunajec-Biala position before Cracow and Neu Sandez, but the rest of them fell back to the mountains: the Third Army arrayed on both sides of the Dukla Pass with its headquarters in Kaschau (Kosice), the Second Army around Ungvár (Uzhhorod), *Südarmee* headquarters at Munkacs (Mukachevo), and Pflanzer-Baltin's Army Group at Maramaros-Sziget (Sighetu Marmatiei).

The Habsburg army, in other words, was slowly backing into Hungary, which was entirely the wrong direction. They were supposed to be advancing into Russia. Deeply embarrassed by their lengthening string of defeats, Fritzl and Conrad did what they'd done at Lemberg. They blamed their troops for "failing to execute well-planned operations that *should* have been successful." Conrad refused even to hear the litany of excuses emanating from the front: "AOK cannot understand how our troops, who for days have been apprised of the exact situation, allowed themselves to be surprised and overrun in the fog by the Russians instead of themselves using the fog to surprise and overrun the enemy."[52] The troops understood; they had had enough. Every Austrian soldier was suspect now, whether of cowardice, malingering, or espionage. Regular bulletins from the AOK warned of Russian secret agents circulating freely behind the Austrian lines: "Some have a fish tattooed under their left armpit, others have a Russian cross stamped on their neck, still others have one uniform button with 'Vasil Sergei' engraved on the back." Troops were told to be on the lookout for phantasmal figures: "a captain of the Russian general staff named Lubunoff; he drives around in a car, dark-haired, handsome, well-built, usually in civilian clothes," or "a Russian who speaks fluent Polish, with a pale intelligent face, blue eyes, blond hair, wears a scarf and a black coat; believed to be in the vicinity of our XI Corps."[53]

Archduke Friedrich scored his generals for their inactivity behind the lines while the infantry were being slaughtered at the front. "Divisional commanders *must* be present on the battlefield . . . not far in the rear using the telephone to communicate with their subordinate officers," he railed. Austro-Hungarian troops, Fritzl pleaded, "should never feel that they are being left to their fate by commanders residing safely in the rear areas." He ordered generals to lead from the front, organize flanking attacks, and stop suicidal frontal assaults before they jumped off.[54]

He ordered in vain: of the thirty-two hundred Austro-Hungarian officers killed in the first five months of the war, only thirty-nine were colonels or generals.[55] Neglected by their remote leadership, Austro-Hungarian troops were sometimes succored by the Russians. An Austrian soldier who was shot twice while digging a trench recalled his rescue: "I lay wounded for two hours until found by a Russian infantryman, who hurriedly dressed [my wound] and put me out of firing range on a horse blanket in an old trench."[56] Other Russians were not so kind. Passing a barefoot Russian soldier and a Jewish villager near the Carpathians, a Cossack demanded that the villager remove his "Jew boots" and give them to the soldier. When the villager objected, the Cossack ordered the soldier to lower his trousers, then turned back to the villager: "Kiss his ass now, and consider yourself lucky to be alive." The villager complied. Moments later, the three separated, the Cossack laughing, the Russian soldier admiring his fine

Galician Jews fleeing before the Russian advance in late 1914. Jews were persecuted in the Russian Empire and routinely mistreated by Russian troops, hence their flight away from the oncoming Russians with whatever they could carry. "The shadow of pogroms fell everywhere we operated," a Russian officer noted.
CREDIT: Heeresgeschichtliches Museum, Wien

While the Austro-Hungarian army suffered at the front, Archduke Friedrich (l.) and Conrad (r.) maintained a luxurious headquarters in Friedrich's own Silesian palace in Teschen. Officers noted the essentially civilian routines of the two commanders (naps, long lunches, walks, hours spent reading the newspapers) while the Habsburg army crumbled seventy-five miles to the east.
CREDIT: Heeresgeschichtliches Museum, Wien

new boots, and the Jewish villager barefoot. "The shadow of pogroms," a Russian officer who witnessed the episode wrote, fell everywhere the Russians operated. "People might say that these are just 'anecdotes.' But they're much more than that; they are monuments to our modern history."[57]

Conrad had assiduously avoided the privations of the front, and now he shifted his headquarters from Neu Sandez further west to Teschen in Austrian Silesia, where he settled into Archduke Friedrich's family palace and the neighboring Albrecht High School. This complex would remain his plush headquarters, with stables, tennis courts, coffeehouses, and lavish meals, until his dismissal in March 1917. Conrad used the geography classroom as his office, studied the maps, and gave Fritzl two briefings a day; otherwise the archduke had no role. The heir apparent, Archduke Karl, had even less to do.[58] Officers at the front noted these essentially civilian routines at the AOK: "Our army commanders know how to administer, but not how to *lead*," a major with the Fourth Army wrote. "An army commander has to exhibit will and character, his chief of staff brains." Both were lacking at Teschen.[59]

There was no shortage of good food or wines in Teschen, where Fritzl was rather unpatriotically billing everything, including Conrad's use of his palace, to the War Ministry. But in the land Fritzl and Conrad abandoned, food had become so scarce that Austro-Hungarian officers reporting to units in Galicia and the Carpathians were bringing their own food. Conrad created a "war press headquarters" in Teschen, whose job was to burnish his reputation with puff pieces like *Unser Conrad* (Our Conrad) and *Unsere Dynastie im Felde* (Our Dynasty in the Field). Writers including Rilke and Zweig, photographers, filmmakers, and sculptors were put on the payroll to create the impression of resurgence, with paintings like *Russenjagd* (Russian Hunt) or hopeful pamphlets like *Vom Dunajec zum San* (From the Dunajec to the San).[60] No one was fooled. Conrad's German liaison, General Hugo von Freytag-Loringhoven, reported to Falkenhayn that Conrad's army would most charitably be described as a "brittle instrument." Austrian divisions were down to five thousand men or less, companies to just fifty. The mass slaughter of experienced Austrian officers was a "calamity." The Russians boasted that they held tens of thousands of Austro-Hungarian prisoners (compared with only two thousand Germans). Taking stock of this broken army, Hindenburg complained to the kaiser that he was being compelled to rely on "an indecisive, inferior Austrian army."[61]

In Vienna, Bolfras heard from Conrad that nothing more could be expected in the east. In a Red Cross hospital nearby, a journalist sadly watched the demise of an Austrian soldier just returned from Poland. With green pus weeping from a thigh wound, the soldier lay helplessly as the surgeon slit the infected area and drained it: "The patient first pants, then moans, then a hoarse cry, and then, as he lost hold of himself completely, he began a hideous sort of sharp yelping, like a dog."[62] Jaded army surgeons were now referring to troops as "pus tanks," and the Russians had a three-to-one advantage in this indispensable commodity, with 120 Russian divisions—each consisting of sixteen battalions—against 60 Austro-Hungarian and German divisions of just a dozen battalions each.

Shuttered in his villa in Teschen, Conrad became weirdly obsessed with protocol. He refused to enter any situation in which he might appear subordinate to a German. Invited to Berlin by Falkenhayn to discuss strategy, Conrad begged off, citing his duties in Teschen, and sent a major in his place, a pointed insult that was taken as such by the Germans. At German great headquarters in Mézières, the Austrian liaison, Stürgkh, was aghast: "I began to see in this behavior of Conrad's a great danger to the good relations that were needed to maintain the German alliance as well as the interests of the monarchy." Stürgkh wrote Bolfras, who promised to undertake the damage control that was now becoming necessary each time Conrad expressed himself. When Conrad had journeyed to Breslau to meet the kaiser during his ten-day visit to the Eastern Front, he had refused to talk shop with Falkenhayn there too, explaining to the disbelieving Germans that he was there merely to function as a part of the archduke's entourage, not as Austro-Hungarian chief of staff.[63]

Conrad shouldn't have hidden himself in Fritzl's *Hoflager* when he should have been firming up plans with the Germans, but it was hard to see how better relations between the two headquarters were going to do much to improve the combat effectiveness of the Austro-Hungarian army. Berchtold worried that there was no more common cause for the Germans and Austrians anyway. Vienna was fighting the Russians and Berlin was fighting the British, pouring disproportionate resources into the Ypres salient and even contemplating a naval and air invasion of England. The Germans had killed, wounded, or captured a third of the three-hundred-thousand-man British Expeditionary Force by November 1914, and calculated that London would soon break under the pressure.[64] Austrian diplomats were not so sure, and spoke of an irrational *Britenhass* (hatred of Britain) in German headquarters and a *Tirpitz-Krieg* (a land and naval war structured by Grand Admiral Alfred Tirpitz) that would divert scarce reserves from the Eastern Front to the west.[65] The monstrous war the Germans and Austrians had welcomed in July was spinning out of control, and the Central Powers, hardly on speaking terms, were in grave danger of losing it.

CHAPTER 13

Serbian Jubilee

It was hard to say what was worse: the strategic impact of Austria-Hungary's string of defeats or the political humiliation. Strategically, the Habsburg monarchy was a shambles, gouged open and bleeding everywhere it had engaged an enemy. Thanks to the continued activity of the Serbian army, Austria-Hungary's southeastern border remained embattled and its land connection to the allied Ottoman Empire stopped on the opposite bank of the Danube. Vienna's continuing fecklessness made it harder to coax neutrals into the German camp. If Serbia remained in play, Italy would be tempted to open a third front against Austria. Rumania and Greece, tilting toward the Entente, would tilt even further. Why would Bulgaria, a natural Austrian ally because of its losses to Serbia in the Second Balkan War, risk joining the Central Powers if big Austria could not even beat little Serbia?[1]

A map discovered by Austrian troops in an abandoned Semlin (Zemun) bookshop during Potiorek's September invasion of Serbia hinted at the fate that awaited Austria-Hungary if it did not find ways to strike down Russia and Serbia. The map, titled "The New Division of Europe," had been reproduced from a Russian newspaper and widely sold in Serbia; it depicted Germany broken into northern and southern confederations and Austria-Hungary abolished, its eastern provinces given to Russia, Rumania, the Czechs, and the Hungarians and its southern provinces to the Serbs and the Italians, the Serbs harvesting the lion's share: everything from the Greek border north to southern Hungary and westward to the Adriatic.[2]

To avert this fate, Emperor Franz Joseph had wearily authorized a third invasion of Serbia. In mid-October, the Austrians gathered another two hundred thousand troops at the now familiar bend of the Sava and Drina and thrust again into Serbia. Potiorek brimmed with confidence: "Soldiers of the Fifth and Sixth Armies," he proclaimed, "the goal of this war is nearly attained—the complete defeat of the enemy." He deftly elided the bungled invasions of August and September into this more promising one, and predicted that "the three-month campaign is almost over; we must only break the enemy's last resistance before the onset of winter."[3]

This was a serious invasion, if only because the Serbs—fighting their third war in as many years—had finally exhausted their shell stocks and had little hope of resupply from their allies, who could find no easy way to ship munitions or anything else to landlocked Serbia. All of Serbia's combat units had been halved by the nonstop fighting. On October 27, the commander of the Serbian Second Army looked helplessly at the advancing Austrians and wired Putnik: "We have yet to receive shells; the enemy is bombarding our trenches and we have nothing to fire back; my men are dying under this fire and I have no reserves to replace them with, and no shells to limit the casualties; I thus feel incapable and powerless, and request removal from this command." Putnik denied the request but ordered all of his units to hold as long as they could and then retreat, a process that was far harder now than it would have been in summer because the autumn rains had turned the dirt roads to quagmires that would swallow up any guns and wagons.[4]

In Vienna and Sarajevo, Austro-Hungarian officials took victory for granted and planned major changes. Belgrade would be occupied, and Serbia would be used as plunder to expand Austria and bribe the Balkan neutrals. The Rumanians would get northeastern Serbia around Timok; the Bulgarians would get the southeast corner of the kingdom, while the Austrians would absorb everything west of the Morava as well as Scutari (Shkodër) and

Durazzo (Durrës), taking care to break up "all compact masses of the Serbian element." Those "compact masses"—the Serbian population—would be removed or thinned by Austrian "colonists" *(Colonisten),* who would "change the psychology" of the region, "making Serbia more Habsburg" and less Serbian in outlook. Ludwig Thallóczy, the Finance Ministry section chief who effectively ran Bosnia-Herzegovina, wrote Potiorek in late October to recommend "the West Europeanization of the Serbs with a strong hand" the moment the kingdom was defeated in battle.[5]

Potiorek's plan to defeat the kingdom in battle was the usual: converging attacks from north and west aimed at the city of Nis, which had been Serbia's capital since July and a crucial transportation hub for the army. Potiorek's left-hand group, the Fifth Army, would drive for Valjevo and the line of the Kolubara River, while his right-hand group, the Sixth Army, would thrust again into the Jagodna heights and outflank the Kolubara line from the south. Sited in the Morava Valley, Nis was a principal station on the Orient Express to Constantinople and a vital intersection for Serbian units moving north and south. Nis also served as a clearinghouse for Serbian munitions from the nearby arsenal at Kragujevac. If it fell, the Austrians would cut the kingdom in two and effectively disarm the scattered Serbian army. "Educate the troops about the goal of this campaign," Austrian general Claudius Czibulka told his officers on November 9. "And educate them *before* they go into battle."[6] The Austrians were trying to keep morale up despite the repeated failures and worsening weather. Interrogations of Serbian POWs taken in the September offensive suggested that Serbian morale was also slipping. Serbian enlisted men complained that they had not been fed or paid adequately, and that tax collectors had "taken the last cow from their stalls at home." They ridiculed Prime Minister Pasic for leading the country into war, and spoke of regular abuse by their "brutal officers."[7] This was music to Potiorek's ears and seemed to confirm his optimism.

Rain had swamped the valleys and covered the mountains in snow since early October. Waiting in reserve on the north bank of the Sava, Prince Felix Schwarzenberg pitied the troops on the other side. "At least we get to sleep under a roof; the poor troops in Serbia are sleeping in the open, sitting in the cold and muck, in wet uniforms. It must be awful."[8] It was perhaps most awful for the wounded, who could not be evacuated to hospitals on the muddy roads. They were left on straw in peasant huts, writhing in pain, thousands of them, all over the backroads of Serbia, wherever a battle had flared. Typhus, carried into Serbia in the belly of some Austro-Hungarian trooper, would end up killing one-third of the population of Serbia. For now, it bloomed through the army, and these casualties were also left behind. Even when space on wagons was available, the typhoid cases were not loaded, for fear that they'd infect the healthy men and supplies.[9]

Running low on everything—troops, guns, ammunition, and food—General Putnik now disclosed that "all of my strategy consists in placing the Serbian national mud between the enemy's fighting line and his supplies."[10] The Austrians plunged eagerly into the morass, making the kind of early progress that they had only dreamed of in August and September. Sabac fell, as did Ljesnica and Loznica. None of it was easy, not least because Austrian commanders were ordered to be "extremely frugal with shells so that all supplies of this commodity can be sent to the North Army."[11] The 29th Division had to fight its way into Sabac and then through the town, absorbing hundreds of casualties as they drove with the bayonet at Serbs lying prone and firing from behind the town's railway embankment. Habsburg infantry officers were strictly forbidden to order artillery fire: "Because of the shell shortage, only artillery officers are empowered to decide whether or not to fire."[12] But the Fifth Army did at least get across the Sava and Drina and begin tramping south and east.

The Hofburg was pleased, Bolfras writing Potiorek that he expected the Serbs to break once they came "beak to beak" with the Austrians again.[13] When the largely Croatian 16th Regiment did come beak to beak with a Serbian unit on November 1, the Serbian infantry were ordered to attack, and refused. "Why don't *you* attack?" mutinous Serbs were overheard calling to their officers.[14] Austro-Hungarian intelligence brimmed with these good tidings: the Serbs were down to their last two hundred thousand men; Serbian troops had mutinied in Nis; units had embodied their last reserves; the army was out of rifle ammunition; sixty-year-olds were being called to the colors; all the younger Serbs had been killed or wounded.[15]

Frank's VIII Corps pushed into Serbia from the elbow of the Sava and the Drina. His XIII Corps crossed the Drina at Loznica and took Mount Cer and its commanding plateau from a Serbian rearguard, while the XV and XVI Corps of the Sixth Army crossed the Drina further south and ascended the Jagodna heights. Here the fighting was as desperate and vicious as in September.

Determined to attrite the Austrians as much as possible, the Serbs defended good trenches with artillery and machine guns, and then, when the fighting climaxed on November 8, they rolled down logs and boulders as well, flung rocks and grenades, and even fired their flare pistols at the Austrians.[16] The attacking Austrian troops suffered as many wounds from blasted shards of rock as from shell splinters.

Krupanj and Rozhan, which had taken a terrible toll earlier, fell in the first week of November. The Austrian 78th Regiment took the heavily defended Gucevo heights on November 6. It was the key point of Putnik's defense line, and the Serbs had held the Austrians there for forty-nine days. Employing tactical surprise, an Austrian "storm company" of two hundred men infiltrated the Serbian trenches in the predawn darkness, subdued them with grenades, then called up the line infantry, which beat the Serbian reserves in a race to the trenches and then drove them off the height, taking a rare bag of prisoners as well: six officers, six hundred men, a cannon, and three machine guns. A grateful Emperor Franz Joseph, relieved to have something to celebrate, showered the unit with 334 medals for bravery, and paid each of the storm company survivors a fifty-crown bonus.[17]

At long last, the war with Serbia seemed to be turning in Austria's favor. Meeting with Regent Alexander and Prime Minister Pasic, General Putnik described the Serbian army's situation as dire, and even mentioned the possibility of a separate peace with the Austrians.[18] The Serbs yielded Valjevo, the main communications hub of western Serbia, on November 15. Potiorek, who had planned to trap and annihilate the Serbs there, nevertheless celebrated in a communiqué that was broadcast across the empire: "After a violent nine-day battle that followed nine days of marching through mountains, swamps, rain, snow and cold, the brave troops of the Fifth and Sixth Armies have taken the line of the Kolubara and put the enemy to flight."[19]

With the Serbs retreating toward Kragujevac, Potiorek straddled the Kolubara River at Valjevo and attributed the South Army's surprising success to his own "relentless pursuit." He fancied himself a modern-day Murat, riding the Serbs into the ground with his saber in their back. Potiorek now invited the press corps, which he'd prudently confined to Austrian territory, to enter Serbia and "bear witness to the decisive battle." Crossing the Macva to reach the fronts around Valjevo and Belgrade, the journalists were shocked by what they saw. William Shepheard of New York's *Evening Sun* reported eighteen scorched, abandoned towns overseen by pitiless Habsburg officers: "They do not admit that they have killed women, but they do admit that they have killed hundreds of civilians. One Hungarian officer proudly showed me a six-foot rake that he used to perform the executions."[20] Quibbles from Austro-Hungarian officers seemed to confirm the worst: "Our goal," General Franz Daniel reminded his troops in late October, "is the destruction of the enemy armed forces, not the destruction of the entire enemy population." He called for an end to rapes, plunder, the desecration of enemy corpses, and the mistreatment of enemy wounded.[21]

Putnik, meanwhile, was raking together his last reserves and still giving ground, hoping to overstretch the Austrians. For once the Austrians gathered in enemy prisoners, hundreds of them, many dressed in civilian clothes, "the better to sneak off to their homes," as Potiorek jeered in a letter to Bolfras.[22] Putnik instructed Serbian officers to keep their men in trenches as much as possible; once on the move, they would desert.[23] Potiorek spent the next dozen days bringing units across the Kolubara and fighting around Ljig. New Austrian shells showed a distressing tendency not to explode—sometimes as many as half of them—but that problem remained manageable because by now the Serbs had so little effective artillery themselves.[24] Potiorek's pontoon bridges lagged far behind and needed to be manhandled through the mud and slush to the front. The Serbs took advantage of the respite to withdraw toward Kragujevac and Arangjelovac, digging new defensive positions in the hills between the Kolubara and Morava valleys.

As the Austrians pushed their trenches closer, they began to notice that Serbian peasants were marking their positions for the Serbian artillery. To indicate infantry, Serbian shepherds would herd sheep and goats onto the open ground before the Austro-Hungarian trenches. To indicate artillery, they would drive cattle into the space. Others would indicate the Austrian strength with flags, waved side to side to indicate infantry (one wave per battalion) or up and down to indicate artillery (one wave per battery). Observing this from their trenches, Austro-Hungarian troops hollowed out the tips of their bullets to create dum-dums whose hideous wounds might deter where warnings hadn't.[25]

The Habsburg army continued to struggle with the question of civilians. Units were ordered to "drive all Serbs before the front; not a single Serb can be allowed to remain behind the lines." If any village signaled the approach of Austrians, troops were ordered "to burn the whole village down." *Komitadjis* were to be shot on sight. Yet virtually every Serbian regular could by now be judged a *komitadji* because none of them had proper uniforms. An American journalist who had just arrived in Austrian-occupied Serbia from Przemysl described the "bestiality" of the Serbian war. Compared with the Russian front, atrocities were common here, and far worse than the ones committed by the Germans in Belgium, which he had also witnessed. The American ascribed it to "the unique Austrian hatred of Serbia." He was particularly struck by the Austrian treatment of Serbian civilians and dead combatants: the former were routinely harassed and murdered, while the latter were heaved without burial or ceremony into open ditches and left to rot.[26]

Sweeping in on the right, the Austrian 4th Mountain Brigade took Uzice without resistance and captured three hundred cases of rifle ammunition, stacks of shells, and hundreds of rifles.[27] When a Serbian runner blundered into an Austrian trench in the fog, he expressed relief: "Thank God, I was late anyway, and they're shooting us for being late."[28] Other Serbian prisoners expressed pessimism about the kingdom's chances: men, guns, and food were running out. Artillery batteries were down to six shells per gun. Serbian troops had been ordered to plunder their own villages to feed themselves and deny provisions to the oncoming Austrians. In those settlements, every second house was decked in mourning, and two-thirds of the women were dressed in widow's weeds. It seemed that in the course of three Austrian invasions nearly the entire nation had been killed.[29]

"Austro-Hungarian troops are landing heavy blows; they have pushed the Serbs off the Drina and deep into the interior," Berlin's *Norddeutsche Allgemeine Zeitung* exulted on November 21. "Our Austrian brothers are winning everywhere," the *Lokalanzeiger* crowed; "one-third of the Serbian army has been destroyed."[30] The rare Austrian aviator who appeared over these battlefields in late November would have seen a continuous line of muddy pike gray from Obrenovac in the north all the way south to Uzice, as the Austrians pressed forward. Arangjelovac was the hinge between the Austrian armies, as it was between the Serbian forces: the Austrian Fifth Army and the Serbian Second Army north of the city, the Austrian Sixth Army and Serbian Third and First Armies south of it. The Russians, French, and British, having moved their legations from Belgrade to Nis, now moved them out of Serbia altogether, to Sofia. There Russian diplomats begged the Bulgarians to join the war against Austria, to which the Bulgarians marvelously replied: "But we fought the Turks for you in 1912, and our reward was to see Macedonia given to Serbia and Greece."[31]

Serbia was utterly isolated; thinking the campaign all but over, Emperor Franz Joseph named General Stefan Sarkotic governor of Serbia on November 24.[32] The general, formerly the Croatian commandant of Zagreb's military district, could be counted on to repress Serbian nationalism with an iron hand: arrest nationalists, ban the Serbian flag, end the religious autonomy of the Orthodox Church, close the monasteries, and secularize *(verstaatlichen)* the Orthodox schools (but certainly not the Catholic ones).[33] Berchtold rejoiced that the capture of Valjevo meant that "a major turning-point had been reached in our war with Serbia."[34] Enjoying his success, Potiorek called for a great Austro-Hungarian summit conference to decide how to divide and administer his "Serbian conquests."[35] Needless to say, the South Army commander was taking his eye off the ball at the worst possible moment. Already planning to encircle the Serbs on the Kolubara, he foolishly swung the already overextended left wing of the Fifth Army wide to seize the Serbian capital as well. Potiorek yearned to "lay the town and fortress of Belgrade at His Majesty's feet" on December 2, the sixty-sixth anniversary of the old emperor's coronation. "My intention is to seize Belgrade with Fifth Army while Sixth Army binds the enemy main force," Potiorek wrote his generals on November 19.[36]

Potiorek should have heeded his Clausewitz, concentrated his entire army against the Serbian "main force," and left Belgrade alone. His units were being ground down by disease and battle, battalions reporting their progress through the mountains thus: "We began the assault with 424 men; after three days we took the hill, but lost half our troops doing so."[37] But Potiorek was always a prickly, insecure man, and he now craved the plaudits that only Belgrade could provide. Potiorek described "panic" in the exiled Serbian government, and rising resistance to Pasic and the Radicals. The roads were full of refugees, and demoralized Serbian troops were deserting in growing numbers, or so Potiorek claimed. An Austrian agent in Nis reported that Serbian troops were cold and miserable, their only winter uniforms "bloodstained German and Austrian rags collected on the Eastern Front" and forwarded to the Serbs by the Russians.[38]

The first Austrian troops into Belgrade, Croats of the 6th Regiment, were shelled by their own artillery, which had not expected Austrian troops so soon. The Croats sent a squad into the Kalemegdan citadel to snatch down the Serbian flag and—an Austrian banner not being available—run up a white one. In this less-than-thrilling way the conquest was complete, the officers of the 6th rather dubiously assuring their superiors that "the streets rang with shouts of 'Zivio Franjo Joszepo!'"—"Hail Franz Joseph!"[39] Vienna celebrated the capture of Belgrade with flags, concerts, parades, illuminations, and a great placard in the city center that read: "The capital of enemy Serbia is in our hands!"

The cities of Germany celebrated too, Austria's minister in Munich reporting jubilant crowds in front of the Habsburg legation and the appearance beneath his window of groups of Bavarian schoolchildren sweetly singing Ich hatt' einen Kameraden. "For the fourth time in history Habsburg's victorious banner flies over Belgrade," the Austrian diplomat cheered. "Military circles and the press here are most impressed by the strategic significance of this: Belgrade as Austria's Antwerp—as both a defensive bastion and a base for future operations by an entire army." The door to Salonika and Constantinople, closed by Serbian resistance, was finally swinging open.[40] Indeed, Vienna envisioned permanent control of Belgrade after the war: a modern fort, command of the Danube, an Austrian-run Orient Express to the Middle East, and a rebuilt city. This last aim was essential because Belgrade lay in ruins, its quays on the Danube burned out and its principal buildings reduced to rubble by Austrian shelling.[41]

Potiorek basked in the attention. He boasted that he had killed at least thirty thousand Serbs and that there could be "no more than 80,000 left."[42] His troops were not only killing the combatants but were slaughtering noncombatants as well, the German-born Serbian general Paul Jurisic Sturm registering Austro-Hungarian atrocities everywhere he went: men, women, and children roped together, disfigured, and then "horribly massacred," women skinned alive or with their breasts lopped off. "Peasants say such sights are to be seen everywhere," a shocked Jurisic-Sturm wrote to headquarters. Serbian officers in Ljesnica reported little boys hanged or shot, and women raped and dragged into slavery.[43] In Britain, R. W. Seton-Watson, who had exposed the evils of Magyarization before the war, now began a collection for the Serbian people, his agents roaming the streets and trams of British towns to collect coins for a Serbian Relief Fund amid all the other horrors of this war.[44]

Potiorek's rise to fame coincided with Conrad's fall from grace, and the Balkan commander was relishing every minute of it. The emperor sent Potiorek a personal letter of thanks and a medal; the city fathers of Sarajevo named a street for him, and even the unfailingly fractious Budapest parliament proclaimed him Hungary's savior. Bolfras' deputy, General Ferdinand Marterer, was dispatched from the Hofburg to note down Potiorek's soaring plans with a new deference. "We must decide now," Potiorek lectured Marterer, "which pieces of Serbia the monarchy will annex when peace is dictated." Potiorek wanted to take "Belgrade, Sabac, all of the Macva, as well as the commanding heights on the Serbian banks of the Drina, the lower Sava and the Danube from Belgrade to Orsova." Marterer took down Potiorek's thoughts and carried them back to the Hofburg.[45]

But Putnik was toying with Potiorek, who after the conquest of Belgrade continued to press into Serbia with an already overextended force. His men stumbled ahead in their threadbare uniforms through deepening fog, mud, and snow. Potiorek's "relentless pursuit," *fliessendes Vormarsch,* meant that his men never had time to rest, dry their boots, or even eat a hot meal.[46] "Our count of sick men is rising," the 9th Division reported. "We urgently need coats and *Baschliks,"* the last a reference to the felt hoods introduced by the Cossacks one hundred years earlier while chasing Napoleon's invaders through the Russian snows. There would be no *Baschliks,* however, or even many coats. The monarchy was running out of textiles along with everything else, and could only provide the troops paper undershirts and paper socks—"service life two days to one week." Austrian officers were unchivalrously ordered to strip Serbian prisoners of their coats and give them to the shivering Habsburg troops. Soldiers were told to wrap their shoes in straw or burlap sacks to keep the cold out. Many Austrian units complained that they were marching barefoot (their shoes had disintegrated), sleeping in the rough, and unable even to light fires to cook or warm up.[47]

"Situation unchanged," the Hungarians of the 69th Regiment reported on November 24 from their trenches east of Bajna Basha. "We fired all night and they fired back; it keeps raining hard; it is very cold."[48] Some units had to be marched off the hills and into the valleys to warm up. Austrian rear echelons, stumbling along in their straw-wrapped shoes, found that men in front were abandoning machine guns, shells, and ammunition so as not to have to lug them through the mud and snow. An Austrian private in VIII Corps described despair in the ranks: "The terrain is horrible; we have no reserves; the soldiers are contemplating suicide."[49] Mud in the valleys and snow on the heights meant that critical supplies were not arriving. Horses died as the fodder ran out, which made it even harder to haul food, ammunition, and guns to the front lines. "There are no supplies and there is nothing to buy," one officer after another lamented from their hilltop deserts. "The situation [of the 9th Division] is appalling," a general wrote on November 25. "One encounters a parade of horribles: wounded men covered in blood, stinking carcasses, broken-down wagons, mud-encrusted troops. How much longer can this continue?" Half of the Austro-Hungarian cavalry fought on foot because their horses had perished.[50]

A new category appeared on Austrian casualty lists: *marod, dienstuntauglich* (broken, unusable). Soon this category began to outnumber killed, wounded, and missing. Austrian prisoners interviewed by an American diplomat in Nis revealed that they had eaten nothing but plums and water in the days before their capture. "The army leadership is killing us," one Austrian officer scribbled. "We've been in nonstop action for a month, barefoot, without bread, living on horsemeat."[51] With their wagons and caissons stuck in the mud, troops were being forced to carry their usual loads plus shells and other supplies on their backs.

Potiorek was unfazed. He had moved closer to the front—to the five-star hotel in the Koviljaca spa near Loznica—and taken the stirring code name "Max-Olymp" for the end game. He had no patience with troop commanders requesting rest or blankets. He now sketched a war-ending stroke in the comfort of his office by a warm stove. He would send the XV and XIII Corps across the upper Ljig, seize Lazarevac, and trap what remained of the Serbian army. When Krauss explained that his men could not go on because they were sick, exhausted, and hungry, Potiorek coldly shot back: *"Da sind sie immer!* Aren't they always?"[52]

Max-Olymp finally conceded the Sixth Army four rest days on November 30, but only because he wanted to pause to complete the occupation of Belgrade in time for the emperor's jubilee. That simple task had turned into a grinding, vicious two-week battle. From Vienna, Berchtold congratulated Potiorek for his "outstanding achievements and glittering results," but from faraway Teschen, Conrad and Archduke Friedrich criticized the pace of Potiorek's operations: "Higher commanders are not displaying sufficient energy and courage, which is weakening our overall situation."[53]

Nested in warm winter quarters like Potiorek's, Conrad shared the South Army commander's ignorance as to the real condition of the Austro-Hungarian army, which was exhibiting as little "energy" in Serbia as it was on its last little patch of Galicia. Indeed, Potiorek's victory was about to unravel. As the Sixth Army gratefully stacked its rifles on the Kolubara and scrounged for food, firewood, and ammunition, King Peter Karageorgevic mounted the heights of Rudnik to inspire the army, and Putnik began a vast counterattack with two hundred thousand troops on December 2. The three divisions of the Serbian First Army converged with the three divisions of the Serbian Third Army on Valjevo, hammering the Austrian Sixth Army and the Fifth Army's XIII Corps out of Razana and Valjevo. The four divisions of the Serbian Second Army closed from Obrenovac on the right and Lazarevac on the left around the Fifth Army's VIII Corps. Putnik had finally been resupplied with shells and bullets and had brought up all of the reserves that were left in the kingdom: police, gendarmes, and troops that had been detached to the Bulgarian and Greek borders. He also knew, from indiscreet Austrian prisoners, the extent of Austria's suffering and demoralization.[54] Austro-Hungarian POWs had volunteered far more information on Potiorek's order of battle than was necessary in their chats with Serbian interrogators. They described the near collapse of the Habsburg army: Austrian companies were at half strength or less, and there were few officers left to manage the men. They described Potiorek's haste and how it had spread his men on a broad front, without reserves, to widen the pursuit and add Belgrade to the list of trophies. The Austrians, in short, were vulnerable everywhere to counterattacks; if the Serbs punched through anywhere, they might rout the entire exhausted, frozen army.[55]

The morale of the Serbs, meanwhile, remained surprisingly solid despite the long retreat and the dire prognostications of the Austro-Hungarian general staff. They had just been resupplied with Russian and French munitions—lugged across the Greek and Montenegrin borders—and were operating on shorter supply lines than the Austrians, close to their principal railway and depots. Hatred of Austria-Hungary was the glue that held them together. Serbian babies were famously greeted by their mothers with the words "Hail, little avenger of Kosovo"—a reference to the defeat of 1389 that had only properly been avenged in 1912—and, as truant boys, were scolded thus: "You won't liberate Macedonia *that* way!"[56] As men, they continued this patriotic education. Sifting through captured papers in late October, Austrian staff officers found a Serbian *Soldier's Primer*, which amounted to "a catechism of hate against Austria-Hungary." The booklet contained a dozen injunctions, including: "You should hate no one so much as the Austrian," "Bosnia-Herzegovina lives under slavery and must be liberated from Austrian rule," "Dedicate your life to raising the Serbian flag in Sarajevo and Mostar," and "We must hate the Austrians the way our fathers hated the Turks."[57]

The fortitude of wounded Serbs treated in Austro-Hungarian hospitals astonished everyone. "They came in covered with mud and with fractures done up with twigs—just as they'd been dressed on the field. Sometimes a fractured hip would be bound with a limb from a tree, reaching from a man's feet to his waist."[58] On the field, Serbian cold-bloodedness was no less remarkable; they entrenched everywhere in beautifully wrought trench lines with flanking positions and they lay in them perfectly still, without noise, light, or movement, until the Austrians walked right into them, to be mown down at point-blank range.[59]

Stunned by Putnik's counteroffensive, Potiorek planned at the very least to hold the line of the Kolubara as Conrad's army in the east was holding the Dunajec, but even that diminished ambition proved too much. Serbia's First and Third Armies struck toward Valjevo and the Second Army toward Belgrade, their combined might crashing into the Austrian positions all at once. The battle would last for ten days, but it was effectively decided in the first day or two. "Forward, heroes!" Serbian officers cried as they scrambled over the top. "With faith in God!" The attack commenced all along the front at 7:00 a.m. on the third as the Serbs appeared like ghosts out of the fog, first startling the Austrians, then panicking them.[60] The First Army pushed the Austrians out of strong positions with surprising ease, taking 410 prisoners, four howitzers, a machine gun, and a thousand shells.[61] Having knocked the Austrians over the Lim on the third, the Serbians received orders to drive them over the Kolubara on the fourth, which they did.

While his attackers overran the Austrian front lines, Putnik pushed Serbian reserves and artillery closer to the front. General Adolf von Rhemen's XIII Corps was down to a combined strength of just seventeen thousand men spread along ten miles of front near Arangjelovac, and was blown to pieces by two Serbian divisions. A pair of Serbian divisions sufficed to rout the Austro-Hungarian VIII Corps as well; hit hard, the Austrian corps quickly ran out of ammo and called for more, only to discover that their ammunition columns were empty. As the desperate troops flung up the lids on one empty caisson after another looking for shells and bullets, they were told that the ammunition was in Valjevo, where it had been sent by rail but not carried up to the men in time.[62]

Potiorek, holed up in Koviljaca spa, fell silent for an entire week. He raged at the weather; it had slowed his pursuit with rain, snow, fog, and mud, yet had suddenly brightened. The sun came out on December 4, dispelling the fog, drying the ground, and facilitating the Serbian bombardments, attacks, and pursuit.[63] King Peter traveled with the Second Army over the hills of Sibnica and Rogaca, urging the men forward. Potiorek's press corps, which had been picking its way across the desolate land between the Sava and the Kolubara to witness "the decisive battle," was abruptly and without explanation hustled back across the Austro-Hungarian border before the journalists could witness and report the worst of the developing rout.[64]

In the hills around Valjevo, the Serbs hit the Austrians with everything they had, thrusting into the gaps between tired Austrian units and ripping them apart—or themselves. The Serbs were attacking and taking ground so quickly that they lacked sufficient telephone wire to connect the racing infantry to the artillery behind, which was confused by the fog in the hills and frequently fired into attacking Serbian units instead of retreating Austrian ones.[65] Each Serbian army reported taking hundreds of unwounded Austrian prisoners every day. "We've taken lots of booty and many prisoners; the enemy is panicking," the First Army reported on December 5.[66] Terrified Austrians stumbled into disused trenches from the fighting in October and November and lay there until they too were overrun and captured.[67] A disbelieving

The Serbian counteroffensive in December 1914 shattered Potiorek's South Army. Here two Austro-Hungarian soldiers huddle in a trench under Serbian fire.
CREDIT: Heeresgeschichtliches Museum, Wien

Potiorek commanded from his spa hotel that the men hold on. He ordered XIII Corps to hold the line at Lazarevac, connect the Sixth and Fifth Armies on its wings, and prepare a counterstroke toward Arangjelovac.[68]

Potiorek, never much of a commander, had clearly lost his grip on reality. Perhaps under the influence of the healing waters of Koviljaca, reputed to reverse pessimism, he now complained that the "unexpected retreat" of the Sixth Army had exposed the flank of the Fifth Army "at the very moment when the Fifth Army was preparing to deliver a war-ending blow to the Serbs."[69] But only the Serbs were delivering blows by this time. Just how weak the Austrians were was attested to by the ease with which the Serbs, racing out in front of their supplies and ammunition and attacking Austrians who were being pressed back on theirs, were able to knock the Austrians out of prepared positions and out of Serbia altogether.

This whirlwind of action would later be dated December 3–13 and named the Battle of Arangjelovac, which was the town on which the two Austrian armies had been converging. In real time it was a confusing melée, as divisions of the Serbian First and Third Armies hammered Potiorek's Sixth Army out of their trenches and wrested the critical high ground between the Kolubara and the Western Morava from the Austrians.[70] Austrian battalions, many reduced to company strength, had nothing left to give and fled before the Serbs. "No sign of friendly troops, no orders received, my men shattered," one officer scribbled as he led his battalion out of Serbia.[71]

On December 9, Potiorek finally divulged to an incredulous Hofburg that all was lost. He had been thrashed again. Putnik pronounced the Austrians "effectively annihilated on the left and the center." He marveled at the number of Austro-Hungarian prisoners and the count of abandoned artillery, machine guns, and rifles, which littered the ground everywhere. So did the Austrian wounded, who had been left to their fate by retreating comrades. The word *"Panik"* recurred in every Serbian report on the Austrians.[72]

Putnik's Second Army then struck at Rhemen's XIII Corps on the Kolubara around Lazarevac, which was now the hinge connecting the two Austro-Hungarian armies. These Serbian troops then fanned northward to drive the rest of the eighty thousand Austrians of the Fifth Army out of Belgrade. The First Army swarmed over the hills above Valjevo, taking five thousand prisoners, and one of its divisions looped into the city, cutting the Sixth Army's main line of supply and retreat.

The Croats of the 42nd Honvéd Division were flung off the heights north of Grabovica. As they retreated on December 7, trying to keep a connection with the 36th Division on their left, they began crossing the Ljig on a single bridge, which collapsed under the weight of the troops, trains, and guns. Serbs appeared and began firing into the forlorn mass, detonating a panic that spread from unit to unit. Men of the Polish and Ukrainian 30th Landwehr Regiment, lined up behind the Croats, scattered in all directions, abandoning their artillery, machine guns, trains, and ammunition to the Serbs.[73]

Nowhere did the Austrians launch an effective counterattack; their daily situation reports, intended to juxtapose their strength (in blue) with the enemy's (in red), calculated their shrinking strength well enough but depicted the enemy's with nothing more than red question marks. They had utterly lost their grip on events. Entrenched at Lazarevac, the Austro-Hungarian 52nd Regiment reported itself "struck with vehement, astoundingly accurate artillery fire." The unit of Slovaks and Hungarians completely dissolved, overrunning its brigade headquarters in a panicky flight to the rear. The stampeded headquarters failed to stem the rout and ordered the neighboring 78th Regiment to fill in the gap, but no one could find it either. "They too had abandoned their positions," an officer wrote.[74]

Potiorek's entire army was racing in a *sauve qui peut* toward the Drina and Sava crossings, or up to the bridgehead at Belgrade, which was still in Austrian hands. The 42nd Honvéd Division, a Croatian unit, crossed the Kolubara near Lazarevac and paused to improvise a rearguard with the neighboring 40th Honvéd Division, but the 40th—Hungarians all—hurried past without stopping, their officers curiously insisting that they had "strict orders to retreat," not fight. The 42nd followed up muddy roads under a cold rain toward Belgrade. Their horses were too weak to pull the divisional artillery or trains, which were abandoned to the Serbs, who crossed the Ljig below the Croats and struck into their flank and rear. Deployed nearby, the 4th Honvéd Regiment was also routed. Observing the Serbs busily digging up to their front and around their flanks, they simultaneously observed the withdrawal of the German and Czech units on their right and left and decided to withdraw themselves, throwing away their packs, blankets, and cartridge pouches to speed their flight. When they reached the Sava, the regiment counted just nine hundred survivors. Seventy percent of its strength was listed as "missing."

Sabac was flooded with fugitives trying to flee the Serbian pursuit. Ordered to cover the escape across the Sava of the Czech 102nd Regiment, the 6th Honvéd (Serbs recruited in southern Hungary) picked their way down a road blocked by abandoned guns and trains. First they encountered a party of Serbian officers who appeared out of the darkness to talk them into surrendering; "we shot two of them," an Austrian officer recalled. Then they proceeded to the rescue of the floundering 102nd. The Honvéd officers warned their men not to speak Serbian to one another during the march, but they did, and the terrified Czechs of the 102nd Regiment, hearing their approach, opened fire and wouldn't stop. The Honvéds actually had to dig trenches to protect themselves from the friendly fire, which continued through the night.[75]

Hurrying to cross the river at Belgrade, William Shepheard of the *Evening Sun* reported "masses of wounded and panicky men, a total rout." An Austrian junior officer confirmed that the mingling of three frightened Habsburg corps there led to "total and indescribable confusion: orders were not transmitted, rear guards were abandoned, as was everything else—artillery, ammunition, wagons, food, ambulances, wounded, in short, everything."[76] Falling snow blocked the roads, and Shepheard witnessed "many officers literally going mad." With its low budgets and small peacetime strength, the Austro-Hungarian army had relied since the 1880s on "reserve officers"—middle-class students or professionals with just one year of military service—and these greenhorns cracked under the strain of this awful campaign. Shepheard watched as an Austrian major rode past a wounded lieutenant sprawled on the side of the road; the lieutenant shouted something at the major, who furiously drew his pistol and shot the lieutenant several times (succeeding only in hitting him in the foot).[77]

Closing in from the flanks, the Serbs shot better, and raked in guns, shells, and so many unwounded prisoners that escorts for them could not be spared. Austro-Hungarian POWs were simply pointed south or east and told to "follow the telegraph wires until you come to Lazarevac"; cold, wet, and hungry, they dully complied. Austro-Hungarian after-action reports marveled at the alacrity with which their own troops surrendered: "How is it that entire *units* went into enemy captivity without a struggle?" General Schön scribbled from his office in Hungary. "Serbian prisoners confirm that this happened—that this-or-that unit of ours viewed surrender to the enemy as the obvious, natural solution to its predicament." Surely "there is nothing lower or more ignoble than to go unwounded and without a fight into enemy captivity." Schön vowed to investigate all returning Austrian prisoners after the war "to determine the extent of their complicity in their own capture."[78] Many of them, however, planned not to return after the war. Ten thousand Czechs surrendered in Serbia and would shortly join a "Czechoslovak Legion" for service with the Entente against the Central Powers.[79]

Potiorek, who had seemed on the cusp of victory, had instead lost the best part of *another* army: 28,000 dead, 122,000 wounded, and 40,000 missing. Thousand-man Austrian battalions were down to a hundred men or less. The 36th Division had lost half of its officers and 60 percent of its men. The 1st Division's brigades counted barely three hundred men each. Across the board, Austrian survivors of the debacle were judged *Kampfmüde—* battle-fatigued—and useless for further operations.[80] Many Austrian troops tramped past signs, daubed in the Slavic languages of the monarchy and then nailed to fences, trees, and huts along their march routes: "Soldiers of the already defeated Austro-Hungarian monarchy! Give yourselves up! Stop fighting against your own brothers for the benefit of your German masters!"[81]

On December 9, the Serbs punched a hole between the Fifth Army, huddled around Belgrade, and the Sixth Army, which was crowding up to the Drina and Sava crossings. Reflecting on the defeat, the Austrian general Heinrich Pongracz concluded that this one, like all the others, stemmed from the fact that Austro-Hungarian troops still viewed themselves as "dumb parts of a mass instead of thinking, responsible individuals." They refused to patrol aggressively, retreated too easily, never coordinated artillery and infantry attacks, and permitted their rear areas to fill up with shirkers, deserters, or thieves, like Lieutenant Arthur Fischer, who received five years in the brig for rustling dozens of geese and pigs from despairing peasants and breaking into churches along the line of retreat to steal icons, chalices, candlesticks, and furniture.[82]

With the Serbian pursuit biting deep, Potiorek finally authorized a shambolic retreat. Commanders were permitted to abandon their supply trains and focus on evacuating their men. Taking care to call this rout a mere "backward maneuver" *(rückgängige Bewegung),* Potiorek pulled both armies back across the Danube, Sava, and Drina with the loss of most of their equipment and dozens of guns. It was like Dunkirk, only more hopeless: the demoralized, infighting Austro-Hungarians would have a hard time recovering from this defeat. Like Conrad, Potiorek spouted excuses ("We've been in uninterrupted combat for a month") and shifted blame ("We were crippled by the lack of fresh reserve troops and ammunition").[83]

On December 15, Serbian troops retook Belgrade just a day after General Sarkotic's new military government had seated itself there. Potiorek, still at Koviljaca, had grandly ordered his troops to "hold Belgrade or die fighting," but the men retreated instead. Orders went out to arrest telegraph operators who transmitted retreat orders, but that didn't stop the flight either.[84] ("Potiorek would be shot if he appeared among his own troops," one officer scoffed.)[85] In his last throes, Potiorek reminded one of an old Napoleonic maxim: "In war, it is the man, not men, who counts." Potiorek howled that his troops had become criminals: "deserters, cowards, rapists, murderers, arsonists, thieves, bullies, plunderers and cheats." In a calmer moment, he asserted that the loss of Belgrade must not be interpreted as a "Serbian military victory, but instead as a mere symptom of Austrian exhaustion."[86]

Franz Joseph, who had enjoyed Potiorek's jubilee gift of Belgrade for less than a fortnight, did not appreciate the distinction. Bolfras wrote Potiorek that "His Majesty is not pleased," which—in the decorous language of the Hofburg—really meant, "His Majesty is furious."[87] The Germans were furious too. "People here are asking how the so-called backward maneuver out of Serbia could have followed so quickly on the so-called conquest of Belgrade," Austria's minister in Dresden wrote Berchtold. Kaiser Wilhelm II, flattened by flu and bronchitis contracted during his visit to the Eastern Front in November, was "shattered" by the news and confined to bed.[88] The latest losses in Serbia were so monstrous that the Fifth and Sixth Armies had now to be compacted into a single army of just 95,000 rifles. Had the Serbs themselves not been devastated—22,000 killed, 91,000 wounded, 19,000 captured or missing—they might have pursued across the rivers and into Austria-Hungary.[89]

Conrad von Hötzendorf now saw that his name would not, as Karl Kraus had quipped before the war, "be linked with a famous battle on the Drina in the mind of every Austrian schoolboy."[90] Conrad deplored this latest "thunderbolt" from the Balkans, which destroyed the last of the Habsburg army's credibility. The thunderbolt was all the more shocking because Potiorek—a château general who never got closer than seventy miles to the action—continued to peddle excuses for his own witless operations, now blaming them on "desertions among our troops of Slavic nationality."[91] Potiorek even wrote Bolfras on December 12, pleading for another army and another chance: "I'm convinced that I can make everything right; just give me men, rifles and ammunition!" In four weeks he'd be ready to invade again. The Serbs would have "exhausted their means" and would not survive a *fourth* invasion.[92]

But Bolfras and the emperor had heard this song before, and Conrad finally had the club he needed to beat his rival to death. "Now is not the time," Conrad wrote Bolfras with feigned forbearance, "to try to solve the mystery of what happened there." Instead, "we must deal with the facts—an undeniable defeat suffered—and the consequences: not a single man could be spared from the Russian theater" to reinforce the Balkans. If Potiorek could not pull his shrunken force together, the Austrians might have to retreat all the way back to the Danube at Budapest, ceding everything in between to the Serbs.[93] Potiorek's leadership, Conrad said, was "a puzzle." How could so much have been lost so quickly?[94] Conrad had earlier counseled Potiorek to "take the offensive into the heartland of the enemy," but now he pretended that he hadn't. The "present surprising turn of events is a mystery to the AOK," Conrad lied.[95] At German great headquarters in Mézières, Falkenhayn deplored the inevitable impact of Potiorek's defeat on the other fronts and coldly asked Stürgkh: "How on earth did *this* general attain such a dazzling reputation in your army?"[96]

This time even the Hofburg had lost faith in Potiorek, who had expended three hundred thousand men in his three botched invasions. Heartened by this latest defeat, the Italians were inching closer to intervention against Austria-Hungary. They held back for political and economic reasons—there was little popular support for war and the kingdom lacked everything from steel and iron to ammunition, chemicals, lumber, and rubber—but support was building, impelled in part by a demagogue named Benito Mussolini, who had formed a "revolutionary interventionist *fascio*" in Milan and was calling for pro-war demonstrations in every Italian city. Prime Minister Antonio Salandra gave speeches in parliament demanding war to "fulfill Italy's territorial and maritime aspirations" at Austria's expense.[97]

"All of the advantages we'd wrung from the Serbs at such a bloody cost have been squandered," Bolfras chided Potiorek. "All of your errors are now visible to the public, which holds the supreme leadership responsible." To spare the crown further embarrassment, Potiorek was bundled into retirement on December 22, along with General Frank. Recalled to Vienna for an exit interview with the emperor, Potiorek was met on the railway platform by imperial adjutants and told to continue on to his home in Klagenfurt. The meeting with the emperor "was indefinitely postponed," and indeed it would never happen. Potiorek did not miss the rebuke and compared himself with the disgraced commander of 1866. "Like Benedek, I must go quietly to my grave," he jotted, with wilting bombast.[98]

Conrad met with Foreign Minister Berchtold just before Christmas to describe the ruin of the Habsburg army: the best officers, NCOs, and troops had "either died or been removed from service" by wounds, illness, or capture. The old Austro-Hungarian army had been decapitated and gutted by 957,000 casualties in all theaters: 189,000 dead, 490,000 wounded, and 278,000 prisoners. What remained, as General Adolf von Rhemen put it, was "fantastically undisciplined." Officers wrote directly to their commanders demanding awards for bravery; troops plundered their own civilians, shambled around in ragged uniforms, and scowled menacingly at their officers.[99]

With many regiments completely wiped out, the Habsburg army was increasingly reliant on very young and very old conscripts.[100] The Austrian draft brought in eight hundred thousand new recruits in late 1914, and the 2.3 million men who had been deemed unfit for service in the decade before the war were called back for another look. Training was perfunctory at best—just shooting, digging, attacking, and exposure to platitudes like this one: "Victorious men become brave men; a happy soldier is worth double" (Leute siegen, mutizieren lassen; ein lustiger Soldat ist doppelwert).[101] Now only the physically disabled, war industry workers, priests, and civil servants were exempted from service. So many howitzers, field guns, shells, and rifles had been left on the battlefields in Galicia and Serbia that Austria's industry could hardly fill the gaps. But with just 303,000 effectives left on the Eastern Front and fewer than 100,000 around Serbia, Austria-Hungary's material needs were far lighter than normal. Some of Austria's cavalry regiments had to be dismounted and reclassified as "foot cavalry" for the duration of the war because the loss of 150,000 horses in 1914 could not be made good. German officers at Teschen remarked on Conrad's paranoia, "fatalism," and "loss of confidence." He was now blaming everything on the Germans, whom he called Austria's "secret enemy."[102]

While Potiorek had been losing on the Balkan Front, the situation on the Eastern Front had only gotten worse. Russia had by now built to a breathtaking strength of 170 divisions, which were spread across fifty-three corps and sixteen armies of a quarter million men each.[103] Against this eastern horde, the Central Powers had just sixty divisions in twenty-eight corps. Limply, Stuttgart's Neue Tagblatt pretended that the defeat in Serbia didn't matter all that much because the ruin of yet another Habsburg army merely meant that what remained would finally be turned against Russia: "The episode in Serbia conforms to the highest principle of strategy: concentrate all forces on that spot where you wish to seek a decision."[104] Unfortunately for the survivors of this blundering campaign, who would shortly be packed off to the Eastern Front, the "spot" chosen by Conrad for a decision in the east would be even more desolate and hopeless than the one they were leaving.

CHAPTER 14

Snowmen

THE SCANDAL OF THE LATEST AUSTRIAN DEFEAT rippled across
Europe. Serbia had somehow repulsed a third Austro-Hungarian
invasion. The German plan to "win on the Bug by winning on
the Seine" lay in ruins, and indeed the armies of the Central Powers had failed to reach either the Seine or the Bug. The Habsburg
Empire looked fatally weakened by its relentless defeats and million casualties. Outnumbered on the Russian front and crushed
in Serbia, the Austrians were plainly on their last legs. If the Dual
Monarchy collapsed, the Germans would probably go under too.
Unable thus far to win in the west, how would Berlin wage a two-
front war without Austro-Hungarian manpower? The Germans
would have to defend their western and eastern borders alone,
break the tightening British naval blockade, and fend off yet another great-power army, which—taking stock of the Austrian
defeats—was poised to enter the fray.

The Italians now began preparing in earnest for war, and
the Germans rushed the sixty-five-year-old Prince Bernhard von
Bülow, who'd been the kaiser's chancellor until 1909, to Rome as
their new ambassador to twist arms and forestall Italian intervention. In Vienna, Berchtold took for granted that Bülow would try
to trade Austro-Hungarian territory to Rome in return for continued Italian neutrality. In Teschen, Conrad spoke the obvious:

Austria-Hungary could not bear the addition of an Italian front to its Russian and Serbian fronts. It may have been his only sensible observation in the entire war.

Count István Burián, Tisza's candidate to replace an increasingly distraught Berchtold at the Foreign Ministry, traveled to German great headquarters in Mézières to quash arguments from the kaiser and Falkenhayn that Austria immediately cede Trieste, South Tyrol, or Dalmatia to the Italians to keep them out of the war. It was a sad predicament for a monarchy that still liked to call itself the "Wall of the Germans" *(Vormauer des Germantums)* in the east.[1] "Austria-Hungary has often been humbled, but never like *this*," the *Times* of London observed. "Beaten in Serbia, all Galicia lost, Austria's political and military future is in Germany's hands and Austria's generals may soon be replaced with Germans."[2] In fact, by the beginning of 1915 Austria-Hungary had been reduced to German vassalage by the defeats of 1914. The emperor sent Archduke Karl to Falkenhayn's headquarters in France in January to reassure the Germans that the Habsburg army was not really falling apart.[3] The Germans thought otherwise. "When," the German foreign secretary wrote his ambassador in Austria, "will Vienna awaken to the fact that its arrogance and pretensions are not sustainable at a time when even the lowly Serbs can inflict such awful blows?"[4]

The Russians too took heart from the latest Austrian defeat. With little to fear from the Habsburg army, the Russians planned to attack the Germans in 1915—to invade Silesia, occupy Breslau, aim again for Berlin, and take pressure off the Western Front. To secure both flanks for the push, Grand Duke Nikolai advanced his right toward East Prussia, and with his left pushed into the Carpathians, striving to secure the passes and drive the Austrians down into the Hungarian plain, where they would be helpless to interfere with a Russian invasion of Germany. Falkenhayn had hoped to shift eight to ten corps from east to west in 1915 to break the stalemate there, but now he realized that he couldn't, because of the Austro-Hungarian defeats in Serbia, Galicia, and Poland. The Germans were trapped in an increasingly hopeless war of attrition.[5]

Conrad, who was taking delivery of the shattered remnants of Potiorek's South Army, pleaded for real (i.e., German) reinforcements but was rebuffed. Falkenhayn—who met in Berlin with Conrad on New Year's Day 1915—protested that nothing could be spared for the east because already he "was outnumbered two to one in the west." The meeting, in the German War Ministry, exposed all of the rancor dividing the two allies. "Your Third Army," Falkenhayn said, "it advanced well to begin the war, but now keeps retreating, it's gone back *another* 50 kilometers." Falkenhayn and his staff insisted that Conrad "hold his current positions, face east," and stop giving ground. "There just can't be *that* many Russians facing you," Falkenhayn added, to which Conrad replied that indeed there were.

Even worse, Conrad added, the Russians had replaced their casualties and brought units back to full strength with fresh reserves. "You need to do what we do," Falkenhayn said, "bring your units back up to full strength with sick and lightly wounded men." That's "our practice too," Conrad countered, "but we've been fighting for five months with enormous casualties: the number of badly wounded, dead and severely sick troops has ripped huge holes in our army."

Falkenhayn was unsympathetic; the retreating, he repeated, had to stop, to which Conrad peevishly replied: "Didn't *your* army begin the war in the west with its own great retreat, all the way back to the Meuse?" That, Falkenhayn objected, was an error ordered by his predecessor. "But a retreat is a retreat," Conrad jeered. "If you really could have held, then you wouldn't have retreated!" They parted in a foul mood. "Nothing came of the meeting," Conrad recorded. "We both stuck to our original positions; I have a feeling that they've got nothing to give us. He said he's going to speak with Ludendorff before making a final decision."[6]

That afternoon, Conrad and Falkenhayn met again for two and a half hours. This time Ludendorff joined them. Falkenhayn reiterated that he had no troops to spare for the Austrians or anyone else; he had already dispatched critical replacements to the east, and was only holding off an enemy "twice as large" in the west by "every sort of finesse, including a wall of barbed wire and other obstacles that were keeping the French at bay." Germany's first new trained formations, four corps, would be available in February. The generals argued over the best use for them, Ludendorff and Falkenhayn agreeing that the Central Powers were far more vulnerable to a long war of attrition than the maritime Entente. "Because of the power of the neutrals and England, we have to break out; we cannot lie passively behind barbed wire. We have to strike a blow *somewhere*," Falkenhayn insisted.

But Conrad, Ludendorff, and Falkenhayn couldn't agree on where to land the blow. France and Flanders were killing grounds. East Prussia was too remote from the Galician front. Poland lacked roads and a reliable path across the heavily defended Vistula. The Carpathians were too steep, cold, and snowy. "We've already spilled so much German blood," Ludendorff grumbled, "and still no breakthroughs." Conrad seethed; "I felt like saying," he later complained, "that *our* blood is worth just as much as *yours*." After much haggling, Ludendorff offered three divisions to aid Conrad. Ludendorff then used that small concession to Conrad to justify a demand to Falkenhayn for Germany's four new corps, proposing a joint Austro-German offensive in the east to make use of the manpower. Falkenhayn countered that nothing substantial could be gained in the winter snows; however, having failed to win the war in France, his clout with the kaiser was waning. Thus, Ludendorff's *Ostheer* successfully wrung the four corps from the Western Front with the argument—unassailable in view of Austrian rottenness—that Conrad's last-ditch counteroffensive in the Carpathians needed support on its northern flank.

Hindenburg and Ludendorff vowed to finish off the Russians before the spring thaw unfroze the White Sea and permitted the delivery of American supplies and munitions to Russia. With the Baltic and Black Sea ports blockaded, Russia had to rely on what little matériel it could import through Archangel, which was never ice-free for more than half the year. "Russia," General Nikolai Golovine observed, "became a sort of barred house, which could be entered only through the chimney."[7] Everything was in ludicrously short supply. The British military attaché reported from

Petrograd in 1915 the incredible fact that the entire Russian army—five million men, deployed from Estonia to Ukraine— possessed just 650,000 rifles. Others estimated the number of Russian rifles at just over 1 million. Whatever the actual number, millions of Russian troops were standing around more or less uselessly, waiting for comrades to be struck down by wounds or disease in order to have their rifles.

Golovine, quartermaster general of the Russian Ninth Army, recalled that rifles were so scarce that Southwest Front headquarters had directed him to arm his infantry with long-handled axes and call them "halberdiers."[8] The halberdiers wouldn't even have the benefit of artillery. A Russian artillery officer in the Carpathians reported that divisional headquarters had sent his battery the following command: "Report immediately upon whose authority you fired twelve shrapnel rounds the other day."[9] Russia's dire shortage of everything explains the survival of Austria-Hungary into 1915 more than any other single factor. Had the Russians ever been fully armed and supplied, they would easily have knocked Austria out of the war. But they weren't, and Ludendorff glimpsed hope—not in Austria's powers but in Russia's weaknesses. Just as the Germans had brought on the war to "save" Austria-Hungary, they now intensified it to revive the monarchy, Ludendorff warning Falkenhayn in January 1915 that "Austria's emergency is our great incalculable."[10] It had to be fixed.

Conrad mixed the German divisions loaned by Ludendorff with an equal number of Austrians and formed the *deutsche Südarmee*, or German South Army, in the middle Carpathians. Austro-Hungarian ineptitude having been amply demonstrated, the *Südarmee* was placed under a German commander, General Alexander von Linsingen. With big Austrian armies on either flank, it would drive out of the mountains to the relief of Przemysl. Ludendorff would support the operation by striking out of East Prussia with the four new corps brought from France (General Hermann von Eichhorn's Tenth Army) as well as the Eighth Army (now entrusted to General Otto von Below) and Mackensen's Ninth Army.

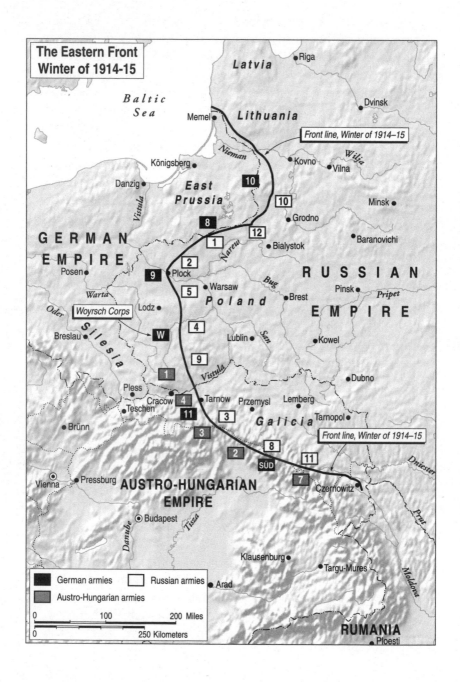

The Eastern Front
Winter of 1914-15

The Russians had eighteen corps on the Vistula, but their plans were divided as usual. Ivanov and Alekseev continued to insist that the shortest road to Berlin lay on the Southwest Front, over the carcass of Austria-Hungary. Przemysl could be taken, the neutral states won for the Entente, and Hungary invaded, wrenching it and its food supplies away from Austria and collapsing the Central Powers from the flank. Ruzski's Northwest Front, buttressed by Danilov in the Stavka, pushed back, insisting that truly decisive results could only be attained against the Germans in East Prussia. Central Poland, the Northwest Front advocates asserted, was barred by German fortifications, and the Carpathians in winter were a natural fortress. Ruzski's new chief of staff, General Gulevich, added little to the debates, according to the British military attaché. He "was a gross, fat man, who had put on much flesh since the war started, for he rested in bed daily from two till five p.m."[11]

Once more, Grand Duke Nikolai permitted his own gross, fat strength to be frittered away by the opposing commands. Ivanov got thirty-one divisions in the Carpathians and eighteen more divisions—the Fourth and Ninth Armies—in the central plains along the Vistula. Ruzski got fifteen and a half divisions in East Prussia and twenty-three and a half divisions (the First, Second, and Fifth Armies) around Lodz.[12]

None of these armies had the resources to deal a fatal blow. Russian troops were still hungry and poorly equipped, and ammunition remained a constant worry. The chief of the War Ministry's Artillery Department, General Kuzmin Karavaev, had broken down and wept in a meeting with Sukhomlinov, begging the influential war minister "to make peace, owing to the shortage of artillery ammunition." The grand duke, who was in only theoretical command of the army, knew none of this; the byzantine regulations of the Russian army meant that requests for equipment, ordnance, and other supply went directly from the fronts to the sixty-six-year-old Sukhomlinov in Petrograd, and Sukhomlinov shared none of this information. He was notoriously venal, increasing his personal fortune tenfold as minister of war, and was taking a cut from every army contract, or just sequestering public funds for future embezzlement. As the ammunition crisis bit, Sukhomlinov was sitting—unbeknownst to anyone outside his entourage—on two hundred million unspent gold rubles that had been appropriated for shells and bullets.[13]

If the ill-equipped Russians could batter their way through the Carpathians and into the Hungarian plain, they would seize the granary of the Central Powers at the very moment that food shortages caused by the Entente blockade were beginning to be felt in Germany and Austria-Hungary. It was, however, a big if. With the large detachments to East Prussia and Central Poland, the Russians arrayed just forty-five divisions along the Carpathians, against fifty-two reconstituted Austrian and German divisions.[14]

Russian efforts to punch through the Carpathians were slowed by terrain and weather, a Russian artillery officer recalling a night in December 1914 when his battery had required four hours to climb a half mile, and that was with twelve horses pulling each gun and a dozen men pushing. With the Austrians entrenched, the Russians attacked as witlessly in the Carpathians as the Austrians had in Galicia. Giving fire support to one such attack, a Russian artillery officer wonderingly recorded the scene: "The gray-haired regimental commander sat on a stump in the trench with the telephone in his hand and delivered his orders: one company was to attack *'frontal.'* He said this knowing full well that within twenty-five minutes every man in the company would be dead or mutilated; he ordered the other companies to go forward in reserve, which merely meant that they would be killed later, not immediately."

From his battery position on a cliff overhead, the Russian officer watched the attack. The first company was shot down, then a second: "We saw 500 men killed in less than an hour on the green-brown slopes." By late December, the Russians were pulling back, retreating over the same difficult ground they had so recently conquered. "The retreat was tough," Lieutenant Fedor Stepun recalled. "Austrians all around us and two other terrible enemies: the utter incompetence of our generals and the weather—icy roads and muddy quagmires wore out our horses; they would just stop in their tracks and refuse to go on." Pausing in a mountain village

The Russians attacked as witlessly in the Carpathians as the Austrians had in Galicia. Here entrenched Austrian infantry shoot down a Russian assault in December 1914. CREDIT: Heeresgeschichtliches Museum, Wien

to rest, Stepun's column was taken under accurate fire by an Austrian battery. Looking up, they saw an Austrian soldier and a civilian directing fire from the church steeple. As the civilian was led away, Stepun looked him over: "He was an old Jew, ancient old, and he knew that he was about to die; as he passed I glanced at his face and had to look away immediately—I have never in my life seen such an expression of terror and despair in the eyes of a man." Arriving on the San River, having retreated for five days out of the mountains, Stepun's battery was crossing back to the east bank on a pontoon bridge when an iceberg struck the bridge and heaved the entire unit—men, horses, guns, and ammunition wagons—into the frigid water below. "Even the weather," Stepun remarked, "seems to have turned against us."[15]

To throw the Russian army out of the Carpathians and reestablish a solid foothold in Galicia, Conrad counterattacked, sending three armies forward on January 23. One Austro-Hungarian army, Boroevic's Third, would take the passes of the western Carpathians; Linsingen's *Südarmee* would seize the central passes, and further east General Karl von Pflanzer-Baltin's Army Group (which would shortly be renamed the Seventh Army) would attack through the Bukovina to strike the Russian flank. As Falken-hayn had predicted, nothing substantial could be expected in this ice-bound wilderness, even the usually exculpatory Austrian general staff history judging the counteroffensive toward Prze-mysl—directed by Conrad from his comfortable headquarters in Teschen—"a cruel folly." Without Franz Ferdinand to boss him around, Conrad was finally coming into his own as a Wallenstein, Bolfras bitterly complaining in early 1915 that "we are being ruled by the AOK."[16]

With Przemysl well into its second siege and projected to ex-haust its supplies by mid-March, Boroevic battered against the Russian trenches. Having lost control of the Uzsok Pass and its mile-long railroad tunnel to the Russians on New Year's Day, Boroevic now lost half his strength in the struggle to recover it, which he accomplished on January 23. On January 26, the *Südar-mee* attacked, but barely advanced the length of a football field that day, and each successive one. As one German officer put it: "Hannibal, it's true, in the end crossed the Alps, but the Romans were not sitting there. We, on the other hand, must not only cross the mountains but drive the Russians out at the same time."[17]

The whole operation was flawed, the Austrians and Germans massing just 175,000 troops with a thousand artillery pieces for a sequence of suicidal assaults on entrenched Russian positions.[18] Officers in the Austro-Hungarian 19th Division tried to interest the men in the slaughter by charging them with the "defense of Hungary," but most of these troops cared even less for Hungary than they did for Austria. Wallowing uphill through knee-deep snow, they launched daily attacks against Russian infantry and artillery on the high ground at Ökörmezö. They battled succes-sively for tactical key points with fanciful names like Hohe Gor-gon and Zalom, and took them only to be repulsed. They resumed the attack five days later, assaulting the same three-thousand-foot Russian-held heights they had stormed, taken, and lost the previ-ous week. Snow that had been knee deep a few days earlier was waist deep now. Companies were down to a handful of men. By the end of January, the 6th *Jäger* Battalion, which had numbered 1,069 men on New Year's Eve, had only 100 left. Even the fabled

Jägergeist—the Spirit of the Huntsman—could not bear this blood, snow, ice, wind, and death forever. An alarming number of officers broke under the strain, sent home with only this explanation: *zusammengebrochen,* "shattered."[19]

March companies of recruits and reservists arrived to flesh out the devastated Austro-Hungarian formations and looked in horror at the battlefield and their unimaginative officers, who continued to attack the heavily defended ridges. The *Südarmee* took the Kalinowce after three days of vicious battle in mid-February, but then lost it to Russian counterattacks on the fourth day. Efforts to attack under cover of darkness went no better; crossing snow, ice and frozen tarns, the troops made too much noise. "The sound of cracking ice betrayed us as we advanced toward the Russian wire," a battalion of the Austrian 5th Division reported. "The enemy illuminated us as we got near and hit us from three sides," killing or wounding fifty-one and generating seventy-four more "missing," which the division—concerned for its reputation— assured corps were the honorably dead, but were probably just cold, tired men who lay up in the Russian wire until the shooting stopped, then surrendered.[20] "The most puzzling thing about this war," a Russian officer wrote his mother on January 21, "is that we don't come to hate the enemy . . . I think it's because we're united by a common bond; we've all been forced to do the thing most alien to human nature: kill our fellow man."[21]

General Joseph von Stürgkh, Austria's military liaison on the Western Front, traveled to Teschen in February to visit the AOK, and was stunned by his reception. "So," Conrad drawled, "what's going on with our in-house enemy—the Germans—and what's the latest thinking of the Comedian—the German kaiser?" Conrad then treated Stürgkh to a long tirade about the sins of German officers attached to the AOK: they "sniffed around," meddled in his affairs, spied on him, denounced him in the press, spread malicious rumors, and threw a bureaucratic net over him to cramp his activity. Stürgkh left the meeting doubting Conrad's sanity, writing, "He hated the Germans, and was nervous and overwrought, suffering from paranoia." He was also a roaring hypocrite, writing Bolfras that he couldn't understand why the contest between

Falkenhayn and Ludendorff for the kaiser's ear was so ferocious: "I personally believe that in times as serious as these, all personal ambitions must be put aside."[22]

Conrad's adjutant, Major Rudolf Kundmann, increasingly did the work of a babysitter. When Bolfras wrote Conrad requesting a report on the general staff chief's visit to Berlin, Conrad ignored the request. Kundmann told him that he had to comply—it was the emperor asking, after all—and Conrad still refused. "He always says no first," Kundmann wrote in his diary, "and only later realizes that others are right." Conrad's adjutant was suffering pangs of guilt at the predicament of their men in the mountains. "More cold and rain, we've deployed the troops in this filth for fourteen days at a time—they must be at the end of their resistance." Conrad was too; he had the flu and assured Kundmann that he was "at death's door." Kundmann was nauseated by the spectacle: "He's always exaggerating; others around here have had the flu; he's not the only one, but of course whatever afflicts him is always an emergency; nothing else matters to him." He paused, then added in English: "Egoist."[23]

Buffeted in the Carpathians, Boroevic had far more than the flu to worry about. Having expressed doubts about the wisdom of Conrad's attacks, he had half his front taken and given to General Eduard von Böhm-Ermolli, who had missed much of the war thanks to his wanderings between Serbia and Galicia and could be counted on to be less leery of reality on this front than the long-suffering Boroevic.[24] Reality soon intruded. Böhm-Ermolli's renewed push with the Second Army jumped off on February 17 and went nowhere in the snow and ice. Austrian shells would fall in the soft snow and fail to detonate. The infantry gained no ground and lost half its strength, forty thousand men, to cold and wounds. "You must imagine snow waist deep, the heights furrowed with trenches, the frosty balsam stillness split with screaming shells and shrapnel and the rat-tat-tat of machine guns," a correspondent wrote.[25]

Generals would awake to discover that hundreds of their men and officers had frozen to death in their sleep. Hundreds more deserted, the German representative at Teschen worriedly noting that thousands of Austrians were "going into Russian captivity

"You must imagine snow waist deep, the heights furrowed with trenches, the frosty balsam stillness split with screaming shells and shrapnel." Here cold Austrian troops stand to in the Carpathians, awaiting a Russian attack.
CREDIT: Heeresgeschichtliches Museum, Wien

without firing a shot." The worst offenders were the Czechs and Rumanians. One Czech regiment lost 1,850 of 2,000 men to desertion in a single night. Rumanian march battalions had their oath to the emperor covertly revoked by priests, who would urge them to desert to the Russians at the first opportunity.[26]

The object of the campaign—to seize the Carpathian passes, liberate the fortress of Przemysl, and deter Italian and Rumanian intervention in the war—seemed a cruel joke. Weapons had to be thawed before every operation.[27] Troops simply stopped fighting. Officers could not locate them on horseback, because horses could not traverse the ice and drifted snow, and the apathetic, frozen men refused to march or fight anyway. A German officer sent to the headquarters of the Austrian 19th Division to request sketches of projected Austrian operations was unimpressed: "The operation sketches give a picture of great dissipation and splintering of forces . . . weak little pushes that lead nowhere. . . . The entire division has dissolved into bands of guerrillas."[28]

Habsburg officer reports were at least as gloomy, because the men would not do anything without physical coercion. Troops passing a stuck wagon would refuse to push it out of the snow; asked directions by a mounted courier, they would gape silently. Ordered to help load wounded comrades into ambulances, they would shrug and walk on. Ordered to unload supply or ammunition wagons, they would vanish. Directed to clear a path of obstacles, they would slouch away. So many officers and NCOs had fallen dead or ill that control of any sort became difficult.[29]

The winter campaign in hilly country seemed even more futile than usual, for the moment trenches were finished they came under flanking fire from the ridges to right and left. A German liaison officer found the Austrian troops "exhausted and rotten," the Slavic units "unreliable."[30] An Austrian general deplored the "prowling and creeping around of his men," who "no longer saluted, cleaned their rifles, shaved or cut their hair. . . . They wear dirty, ripped and mismatched uniforms. Don't bother teaching them to fight," he instructed his officers, "they learn that in battle; teach them to *obey*."[31]

With their deep reservoirs of manpower, the Russians kept attacking, and the shriveling Habsburg army struggled to mount a defense. The 42nd Honvéd Division, which had experienced the worst of Serbia in the three invasions of 1914, now found itself moved with the XIII Corps to this front. General Johann Salis' evaluation of the 42nd Honvéd on March 3 was calculated to lower expectations: "Only the divisional artillery and cavalry can be described as battle-capable. The value of the infantry has plummeted to a level where they're good for nothing." The men had been killed and replaced too many times; the march companies of newcomers were scattered around as needed, ruining what little ésprit de corps remained. Two of the division's regiments, the 27th (Germans) and 28th (Czechs), had already been decimated (every tenth man shot) for yielding their positions without a fight—and they, not surprisingly, were no better after the experience than before it. "Really just a mob of demoralized men," their commander noted.[32] At Kobila in March and April 1915, the Czechs of the Austrian 81st Regiment described relentless attacks by "massed, howling Russian storm columns." Entrenched on heights, the 81st recalled that "there wasn't a day or night when the Russians didn't try to surround us with their superior numbers. There were always more of them, and each attack was stronger than the last."[33]

The butcher's bill mounted, with no deterrent effect on the Russians. "The Russian soldier is stupid and spineless," an Austrian manual reminded the troops, "which makes him excellent material in the hands of his despotic officers. Human life means nothing to them."[34] One Russian lieutenant, who stopped to chat with his platoon in the Carpathians, was struck not by their stupidity but by their by their complexity. "Children," he said in the paternal way of the Russian officer, "why don't you dig yourselves in?" "Your Honor," the troops replied, "why should we? If we want trenches, we beat the Austrians and take theirs, because they're so good at digging. And anyway, it's hard to attack from a deep trench; from our shallow ones it's so much easier." Gauging their tone, which was half serious and half mocking, the Russian officer concluded: "Here you see just how these men combine irony, laziness and piety."[35] Such a blasé approach to battle surely helped to offset its horror. On March 31, after a typical Russian onslaught, the officers of the Austrian 81st Regiment counted four hundred dead Russians on the ground in front of their trenches. The Russians were carelessly losing this many men every day in this single sector, among hundreds like it—yet they kept coming.

The misery of Austrian units in the Carpathians was clearly only exceeded by that of Russian units, who were being driven into the Austrian guns like cattle. "Don't worry about flanks and the rear, just worry about the front, that's where the enemy will be," Brusilov liked to intone, and the Russian officers seemed to have followed this advice literally, as one Austrian battalion commander's record of the fighting confirmed: "March 18: Repelled frontal attack by two Russian companies, counted 50 Russian corpses on the parapet. March 19: Repelled strong enemy frontal attack, about 200 corpses on the parapet."[36]

When the ground began to thaw, both sides pushed their trenches forward; this furious digging brought the front lines to within thirty feet of each other in some sectors. Clashes ensued: "For two hours we fired and threw grenades at each other from a range of [15 feet]." Issued hand grenades for the first time, many Austro-Hungarians accidentally blew themselves up, necessitating a redesign of the grenade in March.[37] Men slunk away from this madness; in the minor engagement with hand grenades, four hundred unwounded Russians and five of their officers surrendered, and seventy-eight Austrians did too.[38]

Now and then the Russians would break through and tear apart neighboring Austrian units, forcing them out of their trenches and into the open. On one such day, April 2, an Austrian regiment was forced back on a village behind it. They lost fourteen officers and 802 men in the retreat, a third of their dwindling strength.[39] Behind the lines, the Russians were devouring the occupied territory of Austria-Hungary. "Lately I've been requisitioning," a Russian officer wrote on April 15, "which means taking the last cow from Galicians in trade for paper scrip, which is really just stealing. The Galician wife weeps, screams and kisses my hand, and when my men lead her cow away, she bites theirs."[40]

The agony of Galicia seems not to have affected Conrad. His calendar at Teschen was peppered with entries like "The chief's in the coffeehouse" or "The chief spent the morning reading the newspapers."[41] His mistress, Gina, came for a four-day visit in January, which drew hoots of abhorrence from Vienna and the army. The Austrian media, guided by the army's press headquarters in the bucolic Vienna suburb of Rodaun, also carried on as if nothing were amiss. Jaunty stories of Austrian and German heroism and resourcefulness alternated with tales of Russian, Polish, and Ukrainian haplessness. There were cartoons of frightened Russian soldiers dressed in diapers trying to crawl past grinning Austrian infantry, with the caption "Masters of disguise." There were cartoons of fish leaping out of the lakes and rivers of Poland and Galicia because of all the Russians who had fled and drowned in the water: "We're pulling out," one jolly fish says to its fellow as it alights on dry land, "because this water has become too polluted." The cartoonists made light of the horrors at the front. "Internal enemy, reports from the northern theater of war" showed a poor Austrian soldier scratching at lice in three frames and then stripping to his shorts and flinging his uniform away in the fourth: "our energetic attack finally forced the defender to yield his position." But the reality was that these Habsburg troops were not only lousy; they were nasty. The Austrian press bureau reported the following story as light comedy: An Austrian and German patrol was looking for food "somewhere in southern Poland." Every peasant turned them away with the same doleful explanation: *"Njima panje! Njima! Moskal schätzko sabralle!"* "Nothing, nothing at all, sir. The Russians have eaten everything." This being southern Poland, the German was suddenly overcome with diarrhea, and he asked to use the toilet. The peasant stared, uncomprehending, and then answered, "No, sir! The Russians have eaten that too!" These eastern peasants were, in short, nearly as oafish as the shit-eating Russians: dim-witted, wide-eyed, unhygienic, so unlike the clean, orderly Germans and Austrians in their midst.[42]

Russian propaganda was no better. It exhorted the troops and the home front to keep going in "the War for the Hagia Sophia"— the great Orthodox basilica-turned-mosque in Constantinople, which must have seemed as remote from these blasted places as the moon. Reading Russian papers delivered to his dugout in Galicia in early 1915, a Russian officer was struck by the headline: "This war has indissolubly joined Russian, Pole, and Jew in a common struggle." Laying the paper aside, the Russian pondered: "Let me tell you how it *really* is; we're in Galicia, the first spring day, gorgeous weather, and clumping along the dirt track comes a battered old sleigh. Reclining in the sleigh is a young Cossack, his ponytail neatly arranged under his fur cap. Dragging the sleigh over the rocks and dirt is a mare so starved and skinny that her ribs are sticking out like busted springs from a mattress; astride the mare—face frozen with fear—is an old 'Jew boy.' Every now and then the Cossack lazily hits the Jew across the back with his knout, which is the signal for the Jew to whip the horse."[43]

Having lost a million troops in Galicia and Serbia in the first four months of fighting, the Austrians lost another eight hundred thousand in the Carpathians—three-quarters of them from illnesses that would have been avoided in winter quarters. A winter war that had been justified in Vienna and Teschen by the need to relieve the garrison at Przemysl was about to lose that garrison along with the manpower equivalent of a half dozen additional Przemysl garrisons trying (and failing) to rescue them.[44]

The Second Army alone lost forty thousand men to frostbite in the first days of March. Indeed, on daily casualty reports, losses from freezing *(Erfrierung)* far outnumbered battle casualties.[45] The *Südarmee* had lost two-thirds of its strength. The Third Army was a wreck, and all of this at a time when Italy was on the verge of adding its weight to the war against Austria-Hungary.[46] Russian probes into the passes in March and April were hardly resisted, forcing Conrad to appeal again for German troops.

Conrad's position was becoming preposterous. "His awareness that our weaknesses could not be fixed without lavish German aid gnawed at his heart like a worm," Stürgkh observed on a visit to the AOK. "He knew that Germany—providing this aid—would demand influence over Austrian leadership in return, and this fact demoralized him, and made him unsympathetic as an ally." Conrad spent his days asserting "parity" with the Germans in his headquarters, snubbing them, sending their routine coalition paperwork back for revision, and insisting on an increasingly illusory Austrian independence.[47] Ludendorff, who by now had developed a robust contempt for Conrad and the Austrians, nevertheless rode to the rescue again, dispatching the *Beskidenkorps*—troops from Ludendorff's front as well as two and a half divisions from the *Südarmee*—to stem the Russian advance.

Przemysl fell back into Russian hands on March 22, 1915.[48] This capped the fatuity of the Carpathian winter campaign, in which 800,000 men had been sacrificed to rescue the 150,000 famished inhabitants of a fortress, who now ran up the white flag and went into Russian captivity. A British witness to the Austrian surrender wrote that the garrison looked "half-starved . . . a more hopeless, dejected crowd I have never seen." Their officers had clearly not shared the privations of the enlisted men; they had "a prosperous and well-fed look, and, according to the inhabitants, had lived in every luxury."[49] American correspondent Stanley Washburn crossed the ninety miles from Lemberg to Przemysl— "the road deep in mud and blocked with prisoners being evacuated"—and was also struck by the contrasts inside the fortress. The officers looked healthy and untroubled by defeat. "To observe them chatting gaily on streets . . . it was hard to realize that their horses were eaten or their troopers were Russian prisoners."

Those troopers were faint with hunger. In the course of the siege, the Austro-Hungarians had eaten up the food stocks, then begun on the transport horses, then eaten the cavalry horses, and finally every dog and cat in the city. Austrian officers had withheld (and fed) their personal horses until just ten hours before the surrender, when they too were all slaughtered, not to feed the starving enlisted men, but to keep the horses out of Russian hands. One of the first Russian officers to enter Przemysl after the capitulation described "the most horrible sight I've ever seen in war . . . the Hungarian soldiers, crazed for want of food, their hands and faces smeared with blood as they devoured the raw and dripping bits of flesh, gouged with their knives and fingers from the dead bodies of newly-killed horses."[50]

An even greater scandal played out in Vienna, where one of the monarchy's ancient regiments—the 28th, recruited in the region of Prague—was formally dissolved in April 1915 by order of the emperor. The entire regiment, which was largely Czech, had left its place in the line in the Carpathians to surrender to the Russians, only to discover that the trench they thought was full of Russians was actually full of German infantry. Fifty officers and men were put on trial for high treason; eight were hung, the rest sentenced to hard labor. The troops of the line were first decimated, with every tenth man shot, and then dispersed to other units.[51]

Here was the crisis of the monarchy. The Austro-Hungarian army had suffered two million casualties and achieved nothing.

Four Habsburg armies of forty-two divisions had been transported into the Carpathians and destroyed, more by Austria's own inept hand than anyone else's.[52] There were no more than a quarter of a million intact troops anywhere in the Habsburg monarchy. Russia had absorbed 1.9 million casualties in the war thus far, yet still had 6.3 million troops in the field. "Mother Russia has sons enough," the proverb went. The tsar's reserves appeared infinite, an appearance ruthlessly confirmed by Russia's general staff chief in March 1915: "Even if we continue for two more years at the present rate of 'wastage,' we will have no difficulty finding the men."

There were difficulties, of course. Russian wastage in the first year of the war was so high—three hundred to four hundred thousand men a month—that the army actually exhausted the supply of men who could legally be called to arms. But that just meant that the tsar began drafting men illegally: youngsters who had not yet reached military age, police, men with deferments that had once seemed ironclad, and the twenty million non-Russian peoples of the empire, who had not been liable for military service before the war but now abruptly were. The Duma, which might have been expected to protest the slaughter and crimp the supply of cannon fodder, fed it instead, offering the army all the exempt and non-exempt peoples it wanted.[53] And so, by fair means and foul, the Russian brown overcoats were filled with beating hearts and sent shuffling into the Austrian guns.

Passing a line of Russian prisoners in May 1915, General Stürgkh was surprised at how well they looked; while Austria was already scraping up its dregs, these Russians looked "strong, healthy, well-fed, of optimal age, very well-dressed and shod. They looked in no way defeated . . . just happy to be out of the trenches."[54] Only the inability of the Russians to tap their full potential (a notional army of seventeen million) and capitalize on their successes ("they do not get effectively driven back, but they cannot get forward either," as one contemporary put it) bought the Austrians a respite. The dueling Russian generals—Ruzski in the north versus Ivanov in the south—could not agree on which front to emphasize, and Ruzski eventually simply ignored the grand duke's order to emphasize the south. Thus, two-thirds of Russia's strength remained north of the Pripet marshes when Ivanov struck into the Carpathians in April, taking the Dukla Pass. Russia's industrial base and infrastructure remained woefully inadequate, producing too few shells and only seventy thousand rifles for the 1.4 million recruits who entered service in 1915.[55]

But what could the hapless Austrians conceivably do with these advantages? The veteran Habsburg army was gone, replaced with an unseasoned militia army. Even the veterans were not particularly formidable. Conrad circulated a questionnaire to his troop commanders in March 1915, asking for their impressions of the fighting thus far, and the submissions were discouraging, to say the least. The men were demoralized; they hated their uniforms (too bright) and their backpacks (too heavy, and "crammed with useless things"). Massive casualties had still not cured the officers of their preference for "deep formations and broad fronts," which, by massing clumps of bright blue-gray uniforms, attracted enemy fire. But those company columns in closed platoons seemed to be the only way to move these refractory men forward, "to retain maneuverability," as one officer put it. They were also the only way to make the men shoot, because they would not actually fire their weapons without an officer or NCO standing over them. They would just bury their faces in the dirt and pray for deliverance. "The addiction of the men to their spades must be broken," a *Jäger* officer submitted. "When the men are ordered to attack, they take a few steps forward and then start digging in immediately, so far away from the enemy that they cannot even reach him with their rifles." Their trenches reflected this (justified) pessimism. "The men spend all of their time improving their dugouts, parapets and shrapnel protection and no time fashioning ways to shoot out of the trench." An apparently formidable Austro-Hungarian trench line was thus anything but, instead merely "isolated groups of blind, covered, walled-in men."

Shirking *(Drückebergerei)* had become the Austrian rule, not the exception. Even ancient ethnically German regiments reported "heightened shirking and indiscipline." Troops in every regiment would attempt to desert, and when captured they would claim that they had been among the "missing" in a recent skirmish or battle. When a man was struck during an attack, everyone around him would stop attacking, gather him up, and carry him back to an aid station. Conrad was advised to form "mounted military police" to patrol ceaselessly wherever Austro-Hungarian units were deployed, to stop straggling and desertion.

The officer corps had its own morale problems. Auffenberg, who had been hustled off the stage after his victory at Komarów for criticizing Archduke Peter Ferdinand, was arrested at his home in Vienna in April 1915, jailed for thirty-six days, and then put on trial for the scandal that had forced him out of the War Ministry in 1912. A scandal that had seemed unimportant to the emperor then—insider trading on the shares of Skoda just before Auffenberg announced a big purchase of artillery—now seemed hugely important. Auffenberg's name was deleted from schoolbook accounts of Komarów, and he was accused of endangering national security by selling stock tips to foreign investors. The whole affair—never entirely substantiated—reeked of payback and pettiness.[56]

Officers less exalted than Auffenberg were bitterly divided between the careerists—*Lebenskünstler* or survival artists—and the less fortunate new cadres called up at the start of the war. Most of the one-year volunteer officers, students and professionals who had taken reserve officer status to avoid conscription, now found themselves at the front. They lacked *Protektion* in Vienna and access to what were called "bulletproof assignments" *(kugelsicheren Posten)*. Most bulletproof of all were the Hungarians, for any officer with any connection to the Hungarian Parliament, whether deputy, page, aide or analyst, could take leave for the duration of its legislative sessions. This was just the latest of Franz Joseph's divisive concessions to the Magyars, but the fact that it had been conceded in November 1914—when the Habsburg army needed every man it could get—was cause for even more frustration in Vienna than usual.[57]

The new arrivals on Austria's front lines found a situation unlike anything they had (briefly) trained for. The already lightly gunned Austro-Hungarian artillery had lost a thousand cannon in the first six months of the war but had succeeded only

By early 1915, the Habsburg officer corps was bitterly divided between career officers, who often had the contacts to secure "bulletproof" assignments away from the front, and the hastily mobilized volunteer officers, who toiled in the trenches. This captured group of Austro-Hungarian officers looks relieved to be out of combat.
CREDIT: Heeresgeschichtliches Museum, Wien

in manufacturing 278 replacements. Shell production hovered at around one-eighth of monthly requirements.[58] No wonder the troops had lost all faith in their artillery. "They attribute our horrible casualties to the lack of artillery preparation and support . . . and the lack of heavy guns," one officer wrote.[59] They were right. Asked to comment on their cooperation with heavy artillery units in Conrad's questionnaire, most division commanders answered simply, "This division never had the use of heavy artillery."[60] The old army, in which officers would have attempted to explain this shortcoming to the men in their own languages, was drowned in the mud of Serbia and Galicia and the snow of the Carpathians. So many Austrian field-grade officers were killed or disabled in the first months of the campaign that they had to be hastily replaced with largely German or Hungarian reserve officers who had neither the time nor the inclination to learn the "regimental languages" of their men.

The survivors were inconsolable anyway, in any language. Austrian officers who had scoffed at Freud before the war now developed a psychiatric vocabulary to describe what was happening to their troops. They were *nervenzerrüttenden* (nerve-wrecked) or *nervenzersetzenden* (nerve-dissolved). They had lost their *Selbst-Kontrolle* (self-control) and suffered *Sinnesverwirrung* (confusion of the senses), *Nervenstörungen* (disturbances of the nerves), or total *Nervenzusammenbrechen* (nervous collapse). Everyone, it seemed, suffered a degree of *Nervenschok* (nerve shock). Men were administered sodium bromide as a tranquilizer, but it never dispelled the central horror: the sight of so many of their comrades mashed into a bloody pulp by enemy fire. Observing these stricken men in an army hospital, a war correspondent wrote: "For a week or so after they come in, lots of them are dazed. They just lie there scarcely stirring from the shock to their nerves."[61]

The Austro-Hungarian draft, which took men between nineteen and forty-two, was quietly adjusted to take all men between eighteen and fifty. Gypsies, formerly classed as useless, were made liable for military service for the first time in Habsburg history. More than two million men who had been written off as mentally or physically "unfit for service" in prior years were deemed fit by the stroke of a pen.[62] With the Italians arming to what was rumored to be a strength of thirty corps and 1.3 million troops along the Trento and the Isonzo, the Austro-Hungarians pondered throwing in the towel altogether.[63] Conrad told Bolfras in March 1915 that the jig was up; the Habsburg army was broken and the Germans would have to be blackmailed into rescuing it again. "We can always threaten a separate peace with Russia, as a counterweight," he darkly minuted. In April, Conrad voiced the same threat to Falkenhayn: Austria-Hungary would sooner part with Galicia (to Russia) than Trieste (to Italy), so take your pick.

Convinced that Austria was on the brink of collapse, Falkenhayn sent Stürgkh first to Teschen and then on to Vienna to persuade Conrad and the emperor to make the concessions that would keep Italy out of the war. In both places, Stürgkh got nowhere. Conrad and Tisza had just succeeded in firing Berchtold (in January 1915) for daring to suggest that Italy be bought off with Habsburg Trentino and Austria's share of Albania. They had placed Count István Burián in the Foreign Ministry with instructions to concede nothing. "What does Falkenhayn want *now?*" Conrad sniffed on Stürgkh's arrival in Teschen. He then sent the general to Vienna, explaining that foreign policy was not his area. It always had been; it just wasn't anymore.

In Vienna, Stürgkh saw the old emperor for the last time and was drowsily informed that "territorial concessions *won't* be made" to the Italians or anyone else. Hundreds of thousands more would be killed and wounded on the Italian front to appease this old man's idea of honor and empire. In his meeting with Stürgkh, Burián averred that he might push for concessions if he knew the Italians really meant business: "If someone points an unloaded pistol at me, I won't give him my wallet until I see if the pistol is loaded, and only then make my decision." But how would a victim know if the pistol was loaded until the thief pulled the trigger? And the process of loading the pistol would increase the risk of violence, as the mobilizations of 1914 had proven. Stürgkh departed unimpressed by Burián or anyone else in official Vienna. The Germans, he wrote, were more alive to the threat of Italian intervention than the more directly threatened Austrians. Prince Bülow relayed another unofficial offer from Rome: Italy would remain neutral in return for the South Tyrol. It was a fair offer, and welcome after the defeats in Serbia and the Carpathians, the fall of Przemysl, and the collapse of the army, but Emperor Franz Joseph rejected it again out of hand. Having already lost on two fronts, he seemed untroubled by the prospect of defeat on a third.[64]

Vienna's detachment from the realities of this awful war had never been more painfully apparent. Touring an Austro-Hungarian hospital in Budapest—engulfed in the reek of steam, disinfectant, and putrefying wounds—a war correspondent named Arthur Ruhl was struck by the reality. "Only those who have seen what modern guns can do know how much to fear them," he wrote. He was sickened by the contrast between these broken men and the troop trains, covered in green branches and flowers for luck, that passed under the windows of the hospital with yet more cannon fodder for the Eastern Front. The men looking down from their hospital beds were not so lucky, gouged as they were by shells and bullets. One had a cut in his neck the width of a hand, so deep that Ruhl could see the carotid artery pulsing behind a thin film of tissue. He studied X-ray pictures of shrapnel and bullet wounds, seeing "bone splintered by rifle bullets and shot through the surrounding flesh as if they had been exploded." The number of amputees from the Carpathian front was no less striking: many of them were "battle casualties, but also sentries left twenty-four hours or more without relief in winter, their feet frozen and cut off at the ankle." He walked through the wards, counting (and smelling) "thousands of frozen feet and hands," most of them "black, and rotting away."[65]

For Austria-Hungary, the whole bungled war was rotting away. The rest of it would be a delegation of the Austrian war effort to Germany, a pathetic end to a conflict that decision makers in Vienna had believed might halt the decline of Austria-Hungary and revive the imperial idea. Austria had had its chance in Galicia and Serbia—more chances, on better terms, than it might have expected. But even with German help, the monarchy had squandered every opportunity, until its army lay shattered on a line that wended from Poland along the crests of the Carpathians and all the way south to Bosnia. The very meaning of Austria had been shattered too. Beaten too many times to count, the Dual Monarchy had lost whatever respect it had commanded from its subjects and neighbors, and lost any semblance of cohesion or, for that matter, sovereignty. Its days on the earth were numbered.

Epilogue

IN MARCH 1915, as the snow softened in the Carpathians, Conrad ordered the Austro-Hungarian generals to reeducate their troops on the purpose of the war. The men, it seemed, "had preposterously divergent views of the conflict," and this state of affairs had to be "clarified and unified." Conrad's new narrative was this: after years of careful preparation, the enemies of Austria-Hungary and Germany, "peaceful central Europe," had lunged at these helpless victims, "from the deepest peace." The "bandits" of Paris, London, and Petrograd had launched a desolating "war of adventure," the French to find new fields of investment, the British to rule the world, the Russians to "enslave" yet more peoples with "fire, sword, and Siberia" under the entirely hypocritical banner of pan-Slavism, "as if Russia," the point paper chuckled, "were a land of freedom."

Austro-Hungarian troops were to be told by their officers that they were embarked on a new Thirty Years War and must defend central Europe from the ravages of the Entente. If not, the results could only exceed the horrors of the 1600s, when—a nod to the mutinous Czechs—"only a quarter of the population of Bohemia survived the conflict." In sum, Austrian troops were told that they were fighting because England, France, and Russia had conspired to make Germany and Austria-Hungary "slave peoples." The greatest slave driver of the three was Russia, "a rich, backward land—ruled by soldiers and bureaucrats, where corruption finds a home everywhere and the masses live in poverty and ignorance."

367

The Russians had caused this war, Conrad explained, to distract their revolutionary intelligentsia (dangerous men like Lenin and Trotsky) from Russia's internal problems and fire them instead with a crusading pan-Slavism. Russia—"hordes of Asiatic and half-Asiatic barbarians, outnumbering us four to one"—sought Constantinople, but also the Balkans, as a market for Russian exports, and to wield the Balkan nations against Austria-Hungary, "a peaceful empire of the peoples." The choice was plain: fight on, or suffer the "fate of the Balkans," which was to be defeated, colonized, and left in "hunger and misery." This, the circular enjoined Austrian troops, "is what you should be thinking about in those hours when you're thoroughly exhausted: the need for victory. Surely *all* of your fresh dreams of youth cannot have been extinguished by the travails of this war."[1]

But Austria's imperial dreams had been extinguished, all of them. No one believed these fictions, least of all their authors. The Austro-Hungarian war ministry waged a parallel campaign to try to understand the reasons—besides the lack of artillery—for the military's poor performance. Another questionnaire was sent to commanders in early 1915, this one marked *Verschluss*, top secret. "Were national-chauvinistic or other destructive tendencies apparent in our officers? Did our officers really speak the languages of their men well enough to lead and inspire them? Do we need to make sure that officers are of the same nationality as the men under their command?" As for the troops, "why so many examples on all fronts of insufficient toughness or total collapse?" Was the seed of "ethnic and anti-military agitation" inside the Austro-Hungarian regiments planted by the active-duty troops present before the war even started, or was it imported by the reservists summoned in the mobilization?

The romantic nonsense of a happy empire of united peoples that had undergirded the army in peacetime had dissolved entirely under the stress of war. Potiorek had warned in 1912 that a third of Austria-Hungary's soldiers would refuse to fight in a great war, and events were proving him right. The fact that troops reported for duty was less important than their lack of engagement once in uniform.[2] The army was falling apart, in large part because no one believed any longer in the multinational "Austrian mission," which, to Austria's Slavs at least, seemed to be nothing more than shoveling poorly equipped Austro-Hungarians into the German war machine.[3]

The Germans briskly and contemptuously took over the Austrian war effort. The Austrian liaison on the Western Front noted in mid-1915 that Conrad had already been reduced to insignificance by "German staffs and commands" at Mézières and Pless, the German great headquarters in west and east, respectively.[4] For the remainder of the war, every time the Austrians were hard pressed, the Germans would ride to the rescue. They intervened in Galicia in 1914–1915, in Serbia in 1915, in Bukovina and Galicia again (after the shattering Brusilov Offensive) in 1916, and again in Galicia in 1917 after the first Kerensky Offensive. Caporetto in 1917, a feat of German and Austrian arms, was undertaken, as Ludendorff put it, as much "to prevent the collapse of Austria-Hungary"—weakened by eleven fruitless battles on the Isonzo River—as to knock out the Italians.[5]

By 1915, the Germans had taken over the Austro-Hungarian war effort. Here VII Corps commander Archduke Joseph poses with German general Hans von Seeckt and their staffs in the Carpathians.
CREDIT: Heeresgeschichtliches Museum, Wien

Some of these German rescues, to be sure, gave fleeting cause for hope. In the Gorlice-Tarnów Offensive in May 1915, the Germans and Austrians took back in a week what the Russians had required six months to take. They killed and wounded 1.4 million Russians and captured a million more. It was shocking what a little artillery could do. The German Eleventh Army deployed four hundred guns—nearly half of them heavy trench busters—with a stockpile of three hundred thousand shells.[6] Strung out in the rather relaxed way they had become accustomed to against the low-caliber Austrians, the Russians were stunned by the apparition of the Germans on the flank of their Carpathian positions. It was Russia's Caporetto—"this severe trial would have been fatal to most armies," Britain's attaché wrote from the Stavka—and the Russians survived only because the Germans were so distracted by other threats and the Austrians so unrelievedly weak.[7]

With their center ruptured and their army broken in two halves—one in Galicia, the other in Poland—the Russians ran so fast in the spring of 1915 that some units retreated forty-five miles a day.[8] But all of the problems revealed by the guns of August remained. General August von Mackensen's vaunted *Durchbruchsschlacht* (breakthrough battle), fortuitously timed for the moment when Russia's "shell crisis" all but disarmed the Russian artillery, was entirely a German victory. Its key methods could not even be attempted by the low-tech Austrians absent an industrial and military revolution.

General Nikolai Golovine compared the German methods at Gorlice-Tarnów to the approach of "some huge beast" that would sneak its infantry close to the Russian trenches, then "draw its tail, the heavy artillery, toward the trenches," but just beyond the range of the inferior Russian guns. The beast would then shatter the Russian trenches with "drumfire" *(Trommelfeuer)*, artillery fire so thick and fast that it sounded like the continuous beating of a drum. The Germans—or their Austro-Hungarian auxiliaries— would then lope forward to occupy the desolated Russian trenches. If Russian reserves counterattacked, the German artillery would kill them too; any survivors would be shot down by German infantry opportunistically sheltering in captured trenches or shell

Better organized, armed, and led than the Austrians, the Germans—seen resting here on the march in May 1915—routed the Russians again in the Gorlice-Tarnów offensive. CREDIT: National Archives

holes. "The beast would then draw up its tail again, and its heavy guns would start their methodical hammering of the *next* Russian line of defense."[9]

The Germans tempered the cruelty of war by shielding their troops with expensive technology; the Austro-Hungarians economized—before and during the war—and threw their infantry away like trash. "The Germans expend metal, we expend life," a Russian general confessed in 1915, and the same could be said of the Austrians. Speeding through Poland with his German unit in June 1915, Lieutenant Harry Kessler paused to examine the wreckage of an Austro-Hungarian attack: "millions of flies and a thick, humid atmosphere . . . the forest thickly sown with corpses. All Austrian. The faces all completely black, like Negroes, already half rotted, covered with filth and dirt. There's one at almost every tree. . . . It was one of the bloodiest affairs of this war and completely without point or consequence."[10] As Kessler's anecdote suggested, Gorlice-Tarnów was more of a breakthrough for the Germans than for the Austrians. Despite the fact that whole Russian artillery regiments were limited to just ten shells a day by this date, Austro-Hungarian battle reports spoke of yet more fruitless and costly attacks and limited gains.[11]

Serbia was finally beaten in October 1915. Fresh from his Gorlice success, Mackensen was entrusted with an army group comprising Max von Gallwitz' German Eleventh Army and Hermann von Kövess' Austrian Third Army. They attacked south across the Danube while two Bulgarian armies attacked west, and Serbia—out of men and ammunition—succumbed. A Habsburg diplomat vowed that this campaign would "tip the balance in the war in the east." It would open a line of supply to Asia and infuse the Central Powers with much-needed oil, metals, and other materials. "The collapse of the Serbian barrier will finally give us control of this vital strategic line, as well as the path of the Danube," the Austrian diplomat wrote Foreign Minister Burián in late October.[12] The Bulgarians took Nis on November 8 and Bitola (Monastir) on November 24. Gallwitz thrust down the Morava valley against light resistance, splitting Serbia from the inside out. By mid-December, Gallwitz had advanced all the way to Kumanova in Macedonia, just a hundred miles from Salonika. Aerenthal and Franz Ferdinand had only dreamed of Salonika; now the Germans were poised to live the dream, as part of a larger strategy to take Salonika, known as "Britain's second Gibraltar," and then Suez, "the gateway to three worlds." Mackensen would lead the charge.[13]

But the Germans were capable only of prolonging the war, not of winning it. They destroyed the British Expeditionary Force at Mons and Ypres only to discover the twenty-five corps of Kitchener's "new armies" forming behind the dead men and the five-hundred-ship Royal Navy strangling the German people. The Germans killed, wounded, or captured hordes of Russians in 1914, only to confront an even bigger army the next year. General Erich Ludendorff, who took over the German war effort from 1916 to the end, made a statement that encapsulated his strategic failings. "Tactics," he wrote, "have to be considered before purely strategic objects, which are futile to pursue unless tactical success is possible." That much was true—the strategic plans of the Entente and Central Powers generally failed because assaulting trenches could not achieve them—but Ludendorff's conceit was to believe that by refining his tactics he could overcome the insuperable strategic challenge of the war: how would an Austro-German alliance of 120 million defeat an Entente alliance of 260 million that wielded more troops, more ships, and 60 percent more national income than the Central Powers?[14] Superb at tactics, the Germans were appalling at strategy, avoiding the frank net assessments of themselves and the Austrians that would have led them to seek a diplomatic solution, not war, in July 1914.

Instead of distancing themselves from the increasingly reckless Germans, the Austro-Hungarians squirmed into their embrace. This was not a foregone conclusion. After eighty-six-year-old Emperor Franz Joseph finally gave up the ghost at Schönbrunn Palace in November 1916, Archduke Karl (now Emperor Karl I) sought conditions for a separate peace with the French and Russians through his brother-in-law Prince Sixtus, an officer in the Belgian army. The ensuing Sixtus Affair came to a head in March 1917 and was Austria's last chance to escape the German-directed war with a hope of survival. The Allied terms conveyed to Austria by Sixtus demanded the surrender of Alsace-Lorraine, the restoration of Serbian and Belgian independence, and Austrian "disinterest" in Russian claims to Constantinople.

In view of all of the disasters that had already afflicted Austria-Hungary, Emperor Karl was pleasantly surprised by the mildness of the terms, and expressed himself eager to proceed.[15] Unfortunately, he expressed himself eager in writing, and proceeded slowly. When the Germans got wind of the affair a year later, after Karl's letters were published by Clemenceau to divide the Central Powers, Ludendorff summoned Karl to German great headquarters in May 1918 and jerked him back into line. Emperor Karl first lied (the letters were "forgeries"), then blamed his foreign minister (who threatened suicide if the emperor persisted), and finally threw himself upon the mercy of the Germans, declaring himself "as innocent as a newborn child." The terms the Germans demanded of the prodigal son were harsh: strict military and economic subservience to Berlin for the duration of the war.

It was a pivotal moment. Woodrow Wilson's outline of America's goals in Europe—summarized in his Fourteen Points of January

The Sixtus Affair of March 1917 was Austria's last chance to escape the war. When the German kaiser (l.) got wind of it, he summoned Austria's new emperor, Karl I (r.), to German great headquarters and jerked him back into line. Karl declared himself "as innocent as a newborn child" and meekly succumbed to all German demands.
CREDIT: National Archives

1918, ten months after America entered the war—had called only for the reorganization of Austria-Hungary, not its dissolution. France and Britain were still keen to see a reformed Austria-Hungary installed as a barrier against German or Soviet expansion after the war. If Emperor Karl was going to bolt, he had to bolt now; the Russians had been knocked out of the war and the Italians nearly so at Caporetto. He would never have as much leverage as he briefly enjoyed at the start of 1918. The Germans were readying a massive offensive on the Western Front with troops pulled from

Russia. Conrad, in his last turn as a general, was about to give back (in June 1918) most of what had been gained at Caporetto by losing another three hundred thousand soldiers in the witless Battle of the Piave. The Hungarians, who enfranchised only 7 percent of their citizens and rejected American-style "autonomous development" for their Slavs and Rumanians, were not the sort of partner likely to survive a second look from Woodrow Wilson.[16]

Time, in other words, was of the essence, but instead of defecting from the Central Powers, which would have bought him some support from the war-weary Entente, Karl weakly bowed to German pressure, accepting German command of everything in Austria-Hungary—troops, roads, railways, munitions, and factories—and going so far as to vow that henceforth Austria-Hungary would fight as doggedly for Strasbourg as for Trieste.[17] President Wilson, initially willing to work with the Austrians, now turned disgustedly away from that "vassal of the German government" and recognized in September 1918 the Czechoslovak and Yugoslav "national committees" that would commence the dismemberment of Austria-Hungary.[18]

The war began with Austria-Hungary dependent on German arms, and that's how it ended. The Germans planned a great spring and summer offensive on the Western Front in 1918 with the troops that they had extracted from Russia, and when the offensive failed, the German and Austrian Empires failed with it. Too late, Emperor Karl issued a manifesto to his peoples in October 1918 promising change and a new "ministry of nationalities," but by then the monarchy's Czechs, Poles, and Hungarians had already declared independence and Karl could do little else but go into exile. The monarchy that had come in with a bang—vanquishing the Turks and saving Christendom—went out with a whimper.

Historians often cite the Habsburg monarchy's survival until 1918 as evidence of its essential toughness or legitimacy, but this is a hard claim to credit. The monarchy was a cruel, bone-crushing machine. It ran through its prime draft classes in 1914 in the most careless fashion, and thereafter relied on "poorly nourished children and aging men," as Archduke Friedrich wearily put it in 1915.[19] Using records submitted by the Russians, Italians, and Serbs, the French estimated in 1916 that—thanks to the near annihilation of the Habsburg army in 1914 and the average monthly loss of 120,000 men since—Austria-Hungary had already "consumed" most of the men available to it.[20] The estimated 650,000 Austrians still unconsumed would have looked queasily at a future in the service of *this* army. Their numbers were fleshed out with "third-revision men," conscripts who had already been evaluated and rejected twice as being physically or mentally unfit to bear arms. What kind of army was this?[21] An anonymous letter delivered to the doors of the Hofburg in 1916 drilled through the nostalgia to the truth: "Majesty, if you want to experience the reality of this war, you don't need to send your war minister all the way to the front, just send him to the reserve depots, where men with severe tuberculosis are being conscripted, where fifty-year-old men with heart problems are being marched around till they collapse, where men who declare themselves ill are locked up in jail for fourteen days."[22] Men like this had no place on the battlefield, where they died in droves. On the Eastern Front alone, one million Austrians died, half of them from infection and diseases. When the war switched from maneuver to trench warfare in the fall of 1914, the Habsburg army didn't get any better; it just got easier to police. But whenever Austro-Hungarian troops found themselves in the open, committed to new attacks, they usually fought badly or deserted. Thus, the AOK sent a withering top-secret memo to corps and divisional commanders in October 1915 wanting to know why the Russians fought so much better "despite having even lower-quality reserve troops and officers than us, and even less ammunition"; how two hundred thousand Austro-Hungarians had been able to "vanish so quickly and completely" during operations in Galicia; and why "so many attacks—even those against a numerically inferior enemy—had fallen apart."

Everyone who had been anywhere near the front knew the answers: the Austrian troops didn't care, and they had lost the will to endure life on the march and in the trenches. They were civilians through and through. When released from their trenches and ordered to march, legions of them simply sat down by the side of the road and waited to be captured. Archduke Friedrich called for a triage—the "relative best material" to the front, old men and other weaklings to the rear. It was a testimony to just how thoroughly shirking had penetrated the Habsburg army, with the best men using what connections they had to get a safe billet in the rear, that the archduke had to accompany this suggestion with the threat of an audit, "to make sure that this instruction is being strictly enforced to raise our combat power."[23]

Regimental pride was becoming a thing of the past already in 1914. The conversion of men from soldiers to cannon fodder was palpable, as the regiment—traditional repository of history, pomp, and circumstance—was withering away in the heat of war. Brünn (Brno) was the scene of scandal in December 1914, when a company of the 8th Regiment was entrained and departing for the front. As the train gathered speed, an infantryman leaped out of his wagon in full battle dress, landed on the platform, and ran for his life; cornered in the station square, he was clubbed to the ground by MPs, while three hundred onlookers stared in amazement.[24] Poles of the Habsburg 30th Regiment, picking up replacements from Graz in April 1915, beat them savagely, called them "German pigs," ripped open their packs, and stole their food.[25] Those Polish bullies in Graz would have drawn some corporate pride from the fact that they belonged to a regiment founded in Lemberg in 1725, but none from their new fate: independent battalions randomly slotted into ad hoc *Gruppen* that were used to sweep up the viable residue of shattered units and get them back to the front, where they too could be killed.[26]

Everywhere the trench war was hellish. A war correspondent reported the sight of frostbite cases and amputees from the Carpathians in a Budapest hospital in 1915, "the doctors boasting of their facility at finding a good flap of healthy tissue and making a proper stump while their peasant victims grinned and scowled by turns."[27] Another correspondent watched in horror as the mingled corpses of Austrians and Russians were dumped in open ditches like so many "bits of pig iron." This was not the fate, as he put it, imagined "by the girls in Vienna, when they cheered these strong youths in the flush of early manhood." It was not even the fate imagined by the Austro-Hungarian war ministry, which had pledged to "bury the men—six to a coffin—on heights easily viewed from afar, to show the heroic soldiers the piety and gratitude felt by the Fatherland." Instead the anonymous men were dumped in mass graves and strewn with quicklime.[28]

Conrad in 1916 set the insouciant tone of the high command in one of his blimpish communiqués: assure the men that as long as they "dig in three meters underground, they will be safe. Even a direct hit on such a trench will hardly affect the men, only some concussion and shaking, but the troops will be fine."[29] He and Archduke Friedrich were not nearly so complacent when it came to finding bombproof quarters for themselves and salvaging their tattered reputations. Conrad and Fritzl fought like dogs through 1916 to quash an inquiry into their leadership of the two Battles of Lemberg requested by the disgraced General Brudermann, a Hofburg favorite. "AOK," Conrad nervously harrumphed in July 1916, "is not in the position to respond to every grievance, memorandum, battle report, etc. submitted by generals relieved of their command in war."

Though he loathed the Germans, Conrad now insisted that Brudermann observe "the guiding principle of the German army: that a general once relieved of command will never get another, and will never remonstrate against his removal." Such *omertà* certainly suited Conrad, whose entire postwar career, scribbling tendentious memoirs, was an act of self-justifying remonstrance. His 1916 backstabbing of Brudermann would run to twenty-five typed, single-spaced pages, and it was like the first draft of his memoir, portraying himself as the innocent victim of a foolhardy subordinate. "In the interest of discipline, I must urge His Majesty's Military Chancery to reject this inquiry along with Brudermann's request for rehabilitation," he wrote. In August, after some thought, General Bolfras and the emperor folded again, rejecting both inquiry and rehabilitation.[30]

The troops were never appeased by Conrad's assurance that they'd be fine in the trenches. They weren't—the whole army was shaken and concussed. It wanted no more. By the end of the war, the Habsburg army had been divided into two factions: a small "assault mass" (young, motivated men) and a large "defense mass" (the bulk of the army). The assault mass—well fed, well paid, well equipped storm troops on the German model—undertook all attacks, and the defense mass took on an entirely passive role for the duration of the war, digging and repairing trenches and defending them.[31]

Scenes from the Brusilov Offensive in 1916 shocked even jaded Austrians and showed just how little stomach most of the monarchy's soldiers had for the war. General Karl von Pflanzer-Baltin spoke of his "ruined army," and eyewitnesses watched in wonderment as a vast (and unexpected) Austro-Hungarian counterattack proved, in actual fact, to be a mass surrender, as thousands of Habsburg troops cast away their rifles and ran at the Russian lines with their hands in the air.[32] No fewer than 350,000 Austrians surrendered to the Russians in this way, and Brusilov recovered everything lost in 1915, marching all the way back to the Carpathian passes. The Brusilov Offensive destroyed what little offensive capability the Austrians retained, and forced them to accept German commanders for the duration of the war.[33]

Conrad's headquarters underwent a paroxysm of vindictive activity in 1916, as every Austrian corps and division was ordered to get to the bottom of the problem (again) and solve it. General Tersztyánszky, who had passed from one disaster to the next since his defeat at Sabac two years earlier, accosted his army thus: "The fact that Fourth Army was turned out of its strong positions by an enemy, whose strength was not overwhelming, and driven far back with enormous losses of troops and matériel, and that the painstakingly constructed bridgehead and Styr position was not defended, demands an explanation!" Officers were ordered to investigate their units and discover who had organized the mass desertions and who had acceded to the surrender of so many cannon and machine guns, and to punish "pitilessly" any miscreants who remained.[34]

But what could constitute a more pitiless punishment than continued service in this army and this misguided war? By 1917, the Habsburg army was hardly an army at all. As many men had been killed, wounded, or captured—3.5 million—as remained under arms.[35] With the Entente armies doggedly increasing their quantities of artillery, shell, and machine guns, no Habsburg trooper doubted that he would soon pass from the second category (the quick) to the first (the dead), and thus many began to vote with their feet. A shocking 1.7 million Austro-Hungarian troops were in Russian captivity at the beginning of 1917 (compared with a tenth as many Germans).[36] The Russian Kerensky Offensive in June 1917 rather too easily ripped a thirty-mile gap between the corps of the Austro-Hungarian Third Army and took thousands more prisoners. Had the Russian army itself not been so rotted by disappointment and Bolshevik propaganda, the end for Austria-Hungary almost certainly would have come that year.[37]

On the Italian front, in the Val Sugana, a storied gash in the Alps that had connected the Holy Roman Empire to the Adriatic for centuries, the entire leadership of an Austrian regiment—a Slovenian colonel, four Czech officers, and three Czech NCOs—crossed to the Italian trenches at Carzano and led enemy troops back through their wire and into their trenches to take everyone prisoner. The Austro-Hungarian authorities professed to be scandalized, but this problem had been bubbling since 1914 and was only getting worse.[38] Mass desertions became commonplace; on a single day in October 1918, 1,451 men of the Hungarian 65th Regiment deserted. By then the monarchy was shoveling skilled war workers, boys, and pensioners into its war machine. Graybeards born in the years between Solferino and Königgrätz were called up in 1916 and forced to serve until the end of the war.[39]

From beginning to end, the war lacked logic for Austria-Hungary, nowhere better highlighted than in the sensational defeat and dismemberment of Russia in 1917. Having seized power in November 1917, Lenin's Bolsheviks had abruptly exited the war, granting the Germans the Baltics, Belarus, Poland, and Ukraine at the Treaty of Brest-Litovsk in March 1918. Russia's collapse, which ought to have solidified the Central Powers, deepened their differences instead. German commentators spoke of feeling "swindled" by Austria-Hungary. The Habsburgs fought badly, relied throughout the war on German support, and then, as Russia sank, attempted to secure a share of the massive annexations in Poland and Ukraine. Yet had the Habsburgs actually managed to take

Poland and place it under an archduke, as they tried to do, the imbalance of Slavs to Germans in the monarchy would have increased ruinously. "The 10 million Germans of Austria will *drown in a sea of seventy million or more Slavs*," an analyst wrote in late 1917. Fattened on Poland, Austria-Hungary would have doubled in size and become even more Slavic and Catholic in outlook, all but ensuring a future rift with its ally Germany. That prognostication was anything but far-fetched, the Germans viewing Poland in 1917 not as a land to annex outright, but as a space *(Raum)* first to empty of its Polish inhabitants and then to resettle with Germans. That vision, made possible by Russia's withdrawal from the Great War, would lead to a German campaign of ethnic cleansing and genocide during the next world war.[40]

Russia's defeat gave the Austro-German war effort a second wind, but the Austrians had never solved the problem of Russian manpower, beautifully summarized by the American author (and Russia hand) John Reed: "the paradox of a beaten army that gathers strength, a retreating host whose very withdrawal is fatal to the conquerors." After watching endless columns of Russian infantry marching off to their field kitchens in Lemberg in 1915, Reed wrote: "Now through all the streets poured rivers of soldiers singing. . . . This was the inexhaustible strength of Russia, the powerful blood of her veins spilled carelessly from her bottomless fountains of manhood, wasted, lavished."[41] Reed loved his Russians and romanticized them. In truth, the Russians killed their men as callously as the Austrians did, and the Russian *muzhiks,* no fools, took precautions, either by surrendering to the Austrians without a struggle or deserting. They had mobilized willingly in 1914 but a year later were deserting in large numbers.

Throughout the war, ordinary Russians were struck by the number of soldiers who could be seen, as the tsar's minister of agriculture put it in 1915, "wandering about in the cities, villages, on the railroads and all over Russia." Few of them were on leave—a privilege rarely extended to enlisted men. Russian troop trains carrying reinforcements to the front sometimes arrived at their destination to discover that every soldier on the train had jumped off and run away. Russian march battalions suffered an average 25 percent desertion rate.[42] Whereas by 1916 the French had gotten their monthly casualties down to half the rate of 1914, the casualty rate was undiminished or even rising in Russia. The Russians ran through all of their territorial reserves of the first class in 1914, and had exhausted the entire second class by 1916. Like the Austrians, they began drafting everyone they could lay their hands on, and a Duma committee in 1916 blasted the army for its profligacy: without enough "lead, steel, and explosives," Russian generals thought nothing of "opening the road to victory with human blood." By 1917, the Russians were contemplating the exhaustion of everything, a situation they were grappling with when the revolution began to flare in February. The Provisional Government's determination to continue the war to "final victory" doomed them in the eyes of a people that had become convinced of the war's suicidal futility. The casualties were just too hard to bear: 1.3 million killed, 4.2 million wounded, 2.4 million captured, for a total of nearly 8 million.[43] The Bolsheviks would oust the Provisional Government in November with no more concrete platform than this: Lenin would end the war.

But even the collapse of the Russian bear couldn't save Austria. The Habsburg monarchy divided into "national committees" succored by the Entente that were invited to make their various claims for national independence at the Paris Peace Conference. While Germany was famously punished with the Treaty of Versailles, the Austro-Hungarians learned their fate in the Treaties of St. Germain and Trianon, which formally broke up the Habsburg Empire in 1919 and created the new states of Poland, Czechoslovakia, and Hungary and beefed up the borders of existing ones like Rumania. Serbia absorbed Vienna's old South Slavic lands into a new state called Yugoslavia. The little scrap of Habsburg territory that remained when all of the other peoples had bolted—the German region between Vienna and Innsbruck—sourly grouped itself into a Republic of Austria that was forbidden by treaty to join itself to the much larger German state to the north.

The legacy of the Austro-Hungarian downfall was no small one. Germany was only superficially weakened by the Treaty of Versailles, which detached territory and reparations and imposed strict limitations on the German army and navy. Practically speaking, Germany was strengthened by the new order created at Paris in 1919. Soviet Russia had retreated into civil war and isolation, and the "successor states" carved from Austria-Hungary in central Europe would prove too weak to defend themselves against German (or Soviet) encroachments. They thus allied with the French and British in the interwar period. Paris and London viewed the new states as potential makeweights against a resurgent Germany or Russia. These defense pacts—invoked to fill the vacuum left by the Habsburgs—eventually triggered the Second World War, when the Germans, having bluffly absorbed Austria and helped themselves to Czechoslovakia in 1938, tried encroaching on Poland in 1939. As in 1914, the western powers reluctantly trooped off to war to settle disputes emanating from east-central Europe.

Our historical picture of the lone figure who presided over this unfolding human catastrophe has never been substantially revised. Emperor Franz Joseph remains the bewhiskered old father of the empire whose heart was in the right place. How can this be? As a supreme commander, he was a butcher. As a strategist, he was a knight errant. As a statesman, whose longevity might have allowed him to fix or temper Austria-Hungary's enfeebling problems, he was absent. If the story is true that, when given the news that Italy had declared war on Austria in 1915, the old emperor smiled fondly and whispered, "Finally, war with Italy, now I can be happy," then we must conclude that this man became something in old age that he had never been in his unassertive youth: ferocious.[44]

Overall, we must reconsider the origins of the First World War and carve out a new place for the Austrians. Austria-Hungary wasn't the essentially decent but charmingly slipshod power that muddled into and through the war. It was a desperately conflicted power that thought nothing of throwing all of Europe into the flames to preserve its ancient rights to lands like Bohemia and Hungary—lands that had lost all interest in the Habsburg connection and were trying to break away. Austria's Great War was built on the reckless gamble that the monarchy's internal problems could be fixed by war. They couldn't.[45] This wasn't exactly a postwar revelation. Well before the events of 1914, Prime Minister Casimir Badeni had made

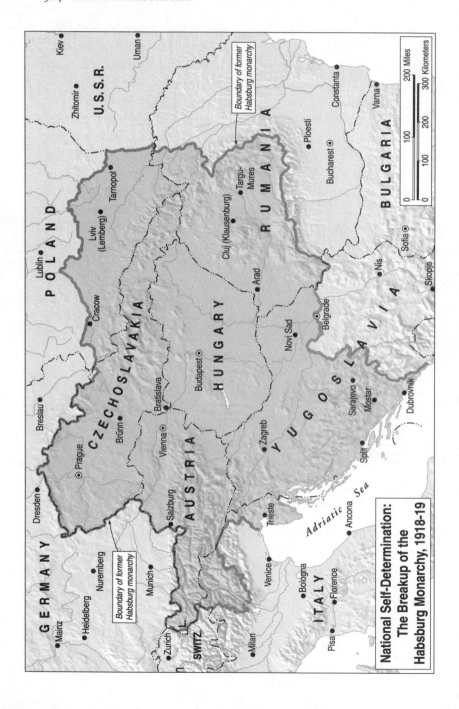

National Self-Determination:
The Breakup of the
Habsburg Monarchy, 1918-19

the obvious connection between Austria-Hungary's frustrated peoples and the military security of the empire: "A country of nationalities cannot wage war without danger to *itself*."[46] And yet it did, the empire's last foreign minister, Count Ottokar Czernin, rather too blithely observing that "we were bound to die; we were at liberty to choose the manner of our death and we chose the most terrible."[47] The troops at the front, exposed to the most terrible conditions in a terrible war, would certainly have agreed with Czernin—author of the stillborn Sixtus Affair—and regretted his inability to forestall or terminate the war.

In July 1914, the old emperor drew his sword for the last time, only to watch, horrified, as the blade was parried, reversed, and driven back into his own gut. The Habsburgs had no business going to war in 1914, yet they did, killing off their own people in poorly prepared offensives before settling into a war of attrition that ensured the already weak monarchy's collapse. Of the many errors and miscalculations in this uniquely catastrophic war, Austro-Hungarian decision-making in 1914 was arguably the most senseless—and the most reprehensible. The Great War has justly earned a dark place on our historical map, and Vienna, no less than Berlin, was the heart of darkness.

Notes

FOREWORD

1. Winston S. Churchill, *The World Crisis: The Eastern Front* (London: Thornton Butterworth, 1931), 32.
2. Ibid., 32.

INTRODUCTION

1. Service Historique de l'Armée de Terre, Vincennes (SHAT), EMA, 7N 1128, Autriche, June 2, 1902, 2ème Bureau, "Magyarisme et pangermanisme."
2. A. J. P. Taylor, *The Habsburg Monarchy 1809–1918* (London: Penguin, 1948), 140.
3. Ibid., 142.
4. SHAT, AAT, 7N 1129, Vienna, March 29, 1905, "La langue de commandement dans les troupes hongroises."
5. SHAT, AAT, 7N 1129, Vienna, Feb. 8, 1905, "La politique hongroise et l'Armée."
6. Norman Stone, *World War One: A Short History* (New York: Basic Books, 2009), 50.
7. James Stone, *The War Scare of 1875* (Stuttgart: Franz Steiner Verlag, 2010), 184–185.
8. Taylor, *Habsburg Monarchy*, 140–141.
9. SHAT, AAT, EMA, 7N 1128, Vienna, April 22, 1902, "Le Ministère des Affaires Etrangères Austro-Hongrois"; Taylor, *Habsburg Monarchy*, 137.
10. David G. Herrmann, *The Arming of Europe and the Making of the First World War* (Princeton: Princeton University Press, 1996), 178.
11. Österreichische Rundschau, June 15, 1914, Politicus, "Imperialismus."

CHAPTER 1: THE SICK MAN OF EUROPE

1. "Der Schlemihl," *Die Zeit*, Feb. 6, 1913; R. J. W. Evans, *The Making of the Habsburg Monarchy 1550–1700: An Interpretation* (Oxford: Oxford University Press, 1984).
2. Winston S. Churchill, *The World Crisis: The Eastern Front* (London: Thornton Butterworth, 1931), 24.
3. Arthur Ruhl, *Antwerp to Gallipoli: A Year of the War on Many Fronts—and Behind Them* (New York: Scribner's, 1916), 232.
4. Service Historique de l'Armée de Terre, Vincennes (SHAT), 7N 1127, Vienna, Oct. 1, 1889, "La question des nationalités dans l'armée Austro-Hongroise."

5. Geoffrey Wawro, *The Franco-Prussian War* (Cambridge: Cambridge University Press, 2003), 305–306.

6. Geoffrey Wawro, *The Austro-Prussian War* (Cambridge: Cambridge University Press, 1996), 281.

7. SHAT, 7N 1124, Vienna, Aug. 20, 1878, Cdt. Tour de Pin, "Aperçu politique."

8. SHAT, 7N 1124, Vienna, Mar. 1878, Capt. de Berghes, "Composition et recrutement du corps d'officiers dans l'Armée Austro-Hongroise."

9. Kriegsarchiv, Vienna (KA), Militärkanzlei Franz Ferdinand (MKFF) 206, Sarajevo, Feb. 7, 1914, FZM Potiorek to Archduke Franz Ferdinand.

10. SHAT, 7N 1123, Vienna, July 15, 1875, Capt. Brunet, "Voyage tactique de l'infanterie en Bohème."

11. SHAT, 7N 1123, Vienna, May 28, 1873, Col. de Valzy.

12. SHAT, AAT, EMA, 7N 851, Vienna, Jan. 1923, Gaston Bodart, "Etude sur organisation générale, politique et administrative."

13. Gunther E. Rothenberg, *The Army of Francis Joseph* (West Lafayette, IN: Purdue University Press, 1976), 109.

14. Ibid., 141–142.

15. SHAT, AAT, EMA, 7N 1129, Austria, Feb. 8, 1904, "Les scandales de la Cour de Vienne."

16. SHAT, EMA, 7N 1128, Vienna, Oct. 14, 1897, Cdt. Berckheim, "Notes sur le haut commandement en Autriche."

17. Otto Pflanze, *Bismarck and the Development of Germany*, vol. 2, *The Period of Consolidation, 1871–1880*, 2nd ed. (Princeton: Princeton University Press, 1990), 376.

18. Christopher Clark, *The Sleepwalkers: How Europe Went to War in 1914* (New York: Harper, 2013), 66–73; Lothar Höbelt, "'Well-Tempered Discontent': Austrian Domestic Politics," in Mark Cornwall, ed., *The Last Years of Austria-Hungary* (Exeter: Exeter University Press, 2002), 48; A. J. P. Taylor, *The Habsburg Monarchy 1809–1918* (London: Penguin, 1948), 157.

19. SHAT, AAT, EMA, 7N 1128, Austria, April 30, 1902, "Les allemands d'Autriche."

20. SHAT, AAT, EMA, 7N 1128, Vienna, May 20, July 14 and 30, 1897, Cdt. Berckheim to Minister of War.

21. Rothenberg, *Army of Francis Joseph*, 121.

22. Carl E. Schorske, *Fin-de-Siècle Vienna: Politics and Culture* (New York: Vintage, 1981), 128–140.

23. National Archives and Records Administration, Washington, DC (NARA), M695, roll 22, Vienna, Sept. 10, 1924, Carol Foster, "The Culture of Austria."

24. *Die Judenfrage* (1908), 5–22.

25. Rothenberg, *Army of Francis Joseph*, 128.

26. Ibid., 78, 85.

27. *Der "Militarismus" in Österreich-Ungarn* (Vienna, Seidel, 1902), 9.

28. Norman Stone, "Army and Society in the Habsburg Monarchy, 1900–1914," *Past and Present* 33, no. 1 (1966): 96–97.

29. Rothenberg, *Army of Francis Joseph*, 132–136, 162; KA, B/677:0-10, 4 (Auffenberg), Sarajevo, Nov. 1910, "Stellung und Aufgaben eines nächsten Kriegsministers"; SHAT, EMA, 7N 1129, Austria-Hungary, Dec. 22, 1903, "L'armée austro-hongroise: indications relatives à sa force de cohesion et à sa fidélité."

30. SHAT, AAT, EMA, 7N 1129, Autriche, 2ème Bureau, July 18 and Aug. 14, 1903, "L'Autriche et le conflit hongrois."

31. KA, B/232, Karton 514, "Baron Pitreich und die Armee."

32. KA, B/677:0-10, 4 (Auffenberg), Sarajevo, Nov. 1910, "Stellung und Aufgabeneinesnächsten Kriegsministers"; Carl Freiherr von Bardolff, *Soldat im alten Österreich: Erinnerungen aus meinem Leben* (Jena: Eugen Diederichs, 1938), 93.

33. SHAT, EMA, 7N 1129, Autriche-Hongrie, 2ème Bureau, "Le victoire du parti politique hongrois—Sa répercussion en Autriche"; Samuel R. Williamson Jr., *Austria-Hungary and the Origins of the First World War* (New York: St. Martin's, 1991), 46–47, 52; Rothenberg, *Army of Francis Joseph*, 130, 150; Stone, "Army and Society in the Habsburg Monarchy," 103–104.

34. *Das Vaterland*, Nov. 18, 1910.

35. British National Archives, Kew (BNA), Foreign Office (FO) 371/1899, Vienna, Mar. 26, 1914, Bunsen to Grey.

36. NARA, M 862, roll 568, Vienna, June 22, 1907, Charles Francis to Root.

37. SHAT, EMA, 7N 1128, Vienna, Dec. 20, 1898, Cdt. Berckheim, "Attitude de l'Armée en Bohème."

38. NARA, M 862, roll 568, Vienna, Nov. 17, 1908, Rives to Root; Dec. 3, 1908, Francis to Root. Also, roll 942, Vienna, Sept. 23, 1908, Rives to Root, "Racial Riots in Austria"; Reichenberg, Sept. 26, 1908, Harris to Asst. Sec. of State, "Demonstrations of Germans Against Bohemians in Reichenberg"; Prague, Oct. 21, 1908, Joseph Brittain to Asst. Sec. of State. Also, Rothenberg, *Army of Francis Joseph*, 130; Robert Musil, *The Man Without Qualities* (New York: Vintage, 1996 [1930–1933]), 2:730.

39. Manfried Rauchensteiner, *Der Tod des Doppeladlers: Österreich-Ungarn und der Erste Weltkrieg* (Graz: Verlag Styria, 1993), 28–33.

40. Musil, *Man Without Qualities*, 2:730.

41. In 1913, 770 million crowns were spent in Cisleithania alone for internal administration. *Salzburger Volksblatt*, Jan. 23, 1914; Österreichische-Ungarische Heeres-Zeitung, Feb. 1, 1913, "Der Moloch Staatsbeamtentum"; KA, B/677:0-10 (Auffenberg), Sarajevo, July 1910, "Geist und innere Verfassung der Armee 1910"; SHAT, 7N 1131, Vienna, Jan. 2, 1912, "Les delegations austro-hongroises."

42. BNA, FO 120/907, Vienna, Aug. 9, 1913, Cuninghame to Cartwright, F C v H, Boer, 7; Moritz Freiherr von Auffenberg-Komarów, *Aus Osterreichs Hohe und Niedergang: Eine Lebensschilderung* (Munich: Drei Masken Verlag, 1921).

43. SHAT, 7N 1127, Vienna, Oct. 1, 1889, "La question des nationalités dans l'armée austro-hongroise"; Josef Pfeiffer, *Slovenische Militär-Sprache: Ein Handbuch* (Vienna: Seidel, 1896).

44. SHAT, EMA, 7N 1129, Vienna, Nov. 18, 1903, "La pénurie d'officiers hongrois pour l'encadrement de l'armée hongroise—les causes de cette pénurie."

45. *Fremden-Blatt*, Dec. 18 and 19, 1913, "Österreich ohne die Nationalitäten nicht Österreich wäre."

46. *Wien Zukunft*, Oct. 1, 1913; *Die Zeit*, Oct. 28, 1910.

47. SHAT, EMA, 7N 846, 2ème Bureau, Rome, April 13, 1916, Col. François, "Cohesion de l'armée austro-hongroise"; 7N 1124, Vienna, Mar. 1878, Capt. De Berghes, "Composition et recrutement du corps d'officiers dans l'armée austro-hongroise."

48. The queue of officer aspirants was so long and promotion so slow that Auffenberg in 1912 recommended creation of a new rank in the army, *Majorleutnant* or *Vizemajor*, i.e., a senior captain. KA, B/677:0-10, 4 (Auffenberg), Vienna, Jan. 1, 1913, "Memorandum nach meiner Demission als Kriegsminister."

49. KA, B/677:0-10 (Auffenberg), Sarajevo, July 1910, "Geist und innere Verfassung der Armee 1910."

50. Bardolff, *Soldat im alten Österreich*, 72.

51. Ibid., 88–89.

52. Franz Conrad von Hötzendorf, *Aus Meiner Dienstzeit 1906–1918* (Vienna: Rikola, 1921–1923), 1:37–38.
53. SHAT, EMA, 7N 1129, Vienna, June 28, 1903, Cdt. Laguiche; Rudolf Jerabek, *Potiorek* (Graz: Verlag Styria, 1991), 27–45.
54. KA, MKFF 199, "Generalstab und Beförderungsvorschrift von einem Truppenoffizier."
55. KA, B/677:0-10, 4 (Auffenberg), Sarajevo, Nov. 1910, "Stellung und Aufgaben eines nächsten Kriegsministers."
56. KA, B/677:0-10 (Auffenberg), Bozen, Dec. 9, 1913, Brosch to Auffenberg.
57. KA, B/677:0-10 (Auffenberg), Bozen, Oct. 28, and Dec. 9, 1913, Brosch to Auffenberg: " . . . die gut dotierte Stelle."
58. NARA, M 862, roll 568, Vienna, Sept. 8 and Nov. 16, 1908, Rives to Root.
59. SHAT, AAT, EMA, 7N 1129, July 18 and Aug. 14, 1903, "La politique austro-hongroise"; "L'Autriche et le conflit hongrois"; Williamson, *Austria-Hungary and the Origins of the First World War,* 14.
60. KA, MKFF 199, copies of *La rivincita di Lissa,* an illustrated Italian weekly; KA, B/677:0-10, 4 (Auffenberg), Vienna, Jan. 1, 1913, "Memorandum nach meiner Demission als Kriegsminister."
61. NARA, M 862, roll 940, Vienna, Oct. 7, 1908, Rives to Root.
62. KA, B/1503:3 (Potiorek), 1913, "Regelung der Amts-und Unterrichtssprache Bosnien und der Herzegovina."
63. KA, B/1503:4, Sarajevo, Nov. 20, 1914, Ein hoher bosnischer Funktionär, "Promemoria über die actuelle Behandlung der serbischen Frage in Bosnien"; Vladimir Dedijer, *The Road to Sarajevo* (London: MacGibbon and Kee, 1967), 127–130.
64. Dedijer, *Road to Sarajevo,* 129.
65. SHAT, AAT, EMA, 7N 1124, Vienna, Oct. 22, 1878, Tour de Pin; Williamson, *Austria-Hungary and the Origins of the First World War,* 14.
66. SHAT, AAT, EMA, 7N 1128, Vienna, May 15, 1902, 2ème Bureau, "L'Hongrie et la dynastie."
67. Matthias Schulz, "Diary Rediscovered: Franz Ferdinand's Journey Around the World," *Spiegel Online,* Mar. 1, 2013; SHAT, AAT, 7N 1129, Autriche-Hongrie, May 1, 1905, "Nouvel aspect du problème de la Succession"; Dedijer, *Road to Sarajevo,* 98–99.
68. Clark, *Sleepwalkers,* 107–108; Auffenberg-Komarów, *Aus Osterreichs,* 228–229.
69. SHAT, AAT, EMA, 7N 852, "Organisation politique et administrative de l'Autriche-Hongrie"; Rothenberg, *Army of Francis Joseph,* 141; Auffenberg-Komarów, *Aus Osterreichs,* 226–227.
70. Dedijer, *Road to Sarajevo,* 121.
71. KA, B/232:119-22, Karton 516, "Programmfür den Thronwechsel, 1911."
72. "Franz Ferdinand und die Talente," *Die Fackel* 7, no. 400 (July 10, 1914): 1–4; Dedijer, *Road to Sarajevo,* 124; Stone, "Army and Society in the Habsburg Monarchy," 108.
73. *Deutsche-Tageszeitung* (Berlin), Sept. 22, 1913; *Vorwärts* (Berlin), Sept. 28, 1913; KA, MKFF 206/19, Jan. 12, 1909, "Bericht der k.u.k. Militäratttché in London über Unterredung Graf Mensdorff mit Mr. Noel Buxton."
74. SHAT, 7N 1131, Vienna, Feb. 2, 1913, "Le commandement des corps d'armée en Autriche-Hongrie."
75. SHAT, 7N 1128, 2ème Bureau, Autriche-Hongrie, Aug. 2, 1902, "L'empereur d'Autriche et l'heritier présomptif du trone."
76. Williamson, *Austria-Hungary and the Origins of the First World War,* 21; Rothenberg, *Army of Francis Joseph,* 142.

77. Williamson, *Austria-Hungary and the Origins of the First World War*, 37, 46.
78. KA, B/677:0-10, 4 (Auffenberg), Sarajevo, Nov. 1910, "Stellung und Aufgaben eines nächsten Kriegsministers."
79. Hötzendorf, *Aus Meiner Dienstzeit*, 1:43; Rothenberg, *Army of Francis Joseph*, 142–143; Dedijer, *Road to Sarajevo*, 122–123.
80. Rothenberg, *Army of Francis Joseph*, 129.
81. Norman Stone, "Moltke-Conrad: Relations Between the Austro-Hungarian and German General Staffs 1909–1914," *Historical Journal* 9, no. 2 (1966): 211; Hotzendorf, *Aus Meiner Dienstzeit*, 1:13–15, 53; Williamson, *Austria-Hungary and the Origins of the First World War*, 50–51.

CHAPTER 2: BETWEEN BLUNDER AND STUPIDITY

1. Sean McMeekin, *The Russian Origins of the First World War* (Cambridge, MA: Belknap Press, 2011), 6–23; William C. Fuller Jr., *Strategy and Power in Russia 1600–1914* (New York: Free Press, 1992), 432–451; Bruce W. Menning, *Bayonets Before Bullets: The Imperial Russian Army 1861–1914* (Bloomington: Indiana University Press, 1992), 222–227.
2. Charles Emmerson, *1913* (New York: Public Affairs, 2013), 93.
3. Geoffrey Wawro, *Warfare and Society in Europe 1792–1914* (London: Routledge, 2000), 212.
4. Service Historique de l'Armée de Terre, Vincennes (SHAT), EMA 7N 1128, Vienna, Feb. 25, 1897, Cdt de Berckheim, "Péninsule Balkanique"; Barbara Jelavich, *History of the Balkans* (Cambridge: Cambridge University Press, 1983), 2:109–110.
5. National Archives and Records Administration, Washington, DC (NARA), M 862, roll 940, Oct. 11, 1914, "Interview with Prince Lazarevich-Hraselianovic"; Andre Mitrovic, *Serbia's Great War 1914–1918* (West Lafayette, IN: Purdue University Press, 2007), 59–60.
6. Mitrovic, *Serbia's Great War*, 62–63.
7. Hugo Hantsch, *Leopold Graf Berchtold* (Graz: Verlag Styria, 1963), 2:17–18.
8. Karl Kraus, "Franz Ferdinand und die Talente," *Die Fackel* 7, no. 400 (1914): 2: "Politik ist das, was man macht, um nicht zu zeigen was man ist."
9. *Reichspost*, Jan. 9, 1913.
10. NARA, M 862, roll 940, Mar. 1909, Robert Lansing, "Nationality and the Present Balkan Situation"; M 862, roll 940, Oct. 11, 1914, "Interview with Prince Lazarevich-Hraselianovic."
11. Norman Stone, "Army and Society in the Habsburg Monarchy, 1900–1914," *Past and Present* 33, no. 1 (1966): 107.
12. Georg von Alten, *Handbuch für Heer und Flotte* (Berlin: Deutsches Verlagshaus, 1909–1914), 6:639.
13. Ibid., 6:639–640.
14. Michael Stephenson, *The Last Full Measure: How Soldiers Die in Battle* (New York: Crown, 2012), 234–235.
15. Georg Markus, *Der Fall Redl* (Vienna: Amalthea Verlag, 1984), 43.
16. Gunther E. Rothenberg, *The Army of Francis Joseph* (West Lafayette, IN: Purdue University Press, 125–127); Franz Conrad von Hötzendorf, *Infanteristische Fragen und die Erscheinungen des Boerenkrieges* (Vienna: Seidel, 1903), 4.
17. Kurt Peball, "Der Feldzug gegen Serbien und Montenegro im Jahre 1914," *Österreichische Militärische Zeitschrift* Sonderheft I (1965): 20; Samuel R. Williamson Jr., *Austria-Hungary and the Origins of the First World War* (New York: St. Martin's, 1991), 63.

18. NARA, M 862, roll 940, Vienna, Oct. 4, 1908, O'Shaughnessy to Root, and Mar. 1909, Robert Lansing, "Nationality and the Present Balkan Situation"; *Boston Herald,* Oct. 9, 1908.

19. Kriegsarchiv, Vienna (KA), B/1503:4, Sarajevo, Oct. 19, 1914, Theodor Zurunic, "Promemoria."

20. KA, B/232:11, Sarajevo, Feb. 23, 1909, FML Appel to Ob. Brosch; British National Archives, Kew (BNA), FO 120/907, Vienna, Oct. 28, 1913.

21. Norman Stone, *The Eastern Front 1914–1917* (London: Penguin, 1998 [1975]), 122; Williamson, *Austria-Hungary and the Origins,* 44; Gunther E. Rothenberg, "The Austro-Hungarian Campaign Against Serbia in 1914," *Journal of Military History,* Apr. 1989, 128–129; Conrad, *Infanteristische,* 4–5; SHAT, 7N 1125, Vienna, July 1, 1882, Capt. Blanche, Vienna, Jan. 1914, 7N 846, 2ème Bureau, Paris, Mar. 29, 1913, Cdt. Girard, "L'Armée Austro-Hongroise"; Franz Conrad von Hötzendorf, *Aus Meiner Dienstzeit 1906–1918* (Vienna: Rikola, 1921–1923), 1:39–40.

22. KA, B/677:0-10, 4 (Auffenberg), Vienna, Jan. 1, 1913, "Memorandum nach meiner Demission als Kriegsminister."

23. Stone, *Eastern Front,* 123; Rothenberg, *Army of Francis Joseph,* 111.

24. KA, B/677:0-10 (Auffenberg), Sarajevo, July 1910, "Geist und innere Verfassung der Armee 1910"; BNA, FO 120/906, Vienna, Jan. 16 and Mar. 14, 1913, Maj. Thomas Cuninghame to Cartwright.

25. Wawro, *Warfare and Society,* 205–209; Lawrence Sondhaus, *Franz Conrad von Hötzendorf: Architect of the Apocalypse* (Boston: Humanities Press, 2000), 61–77.

26. Felix Prinz zu Schwarzenberg, *Briefe aus dem Felde 1914–18* (Vienna: Schwarzenbergisches Administration, 1953), 17.

27. Alfred Krauss, *Die Ursachen unserer Niederlage: Erinnerungen und Urteile aus den Weltkrieg,* 3rd ed. (Munich, 1923), 96–99.

28. Hötzendorf, *Infanteristische,* 1–3, 6, 14, 57–58, 89–90; BNA, FO 120/906, Vienna, Jan. 16 and Mar. 14, 1913, Maj. Thomas Cuninghame to Cartwright.

29. NARA, M 862, roll 940, Pera, Jan. 12, 1909, Rives to Root.

30. NARA, M 862, roll 940, Vienna, Oct. 4, 1908, O'Shaughnessy to Root.

31. NARA, M 862, roll 940, Bucharest, Mar. 12 and 17, 1909, Hutchinson to Bacon; Vienna, Apr. 3, 1909, Francis to Knox; Budapest, Oct. 5, 1908, translation of letter from Franz Joseph to Aerenthal.

32. NARA, M 862, roll 940, Bucharest, Mar. 17, 1909, Hutchinson to Bacon.

33. NARA, M 862, roll 940, Vienna, Oct. 4, 1908, O'Shaughnessy to Root; *Boston Herald,* Oct. 9, 1908.

34. NARA, M 862, roll 940, Paris, Mar. 26, 1909, White to Knox; Vienna, Apr. 3, 1909, Francis to Knox.

35. Christopher Clark, *The Sleepwalkers* (New York: Harper, 2013), 85–87; McMeekin, *Russian Origins,* 28–29, 36; Rothenberg, *Army of Francis Joseph,* 156; Winston S. Churchill, *The World Crisis: The Eastern Front* (London: Thornton Butterworth, 1931), 39–40.

36. Churchill, *World Crisis,* 28–29.

37. KA, B/232:11, Sarajevo, Feb. 18, 1909, GdI Appel to Col. Brosch.

38. NARA, M 862, roll 940, Vienna, Oct. 24, 1908, Rives to Root; Bucharest, Apr. 1, 1909, Hutchinson to Knox; M 862, roll 568, Vienna, Aug. 18, 1909, Rives to Knox; Williamson, *Austria-Hungary and the Origins,* 71.

39. Annika Mombauer, *Helmuth von Moltke and the Origins of the First World War* (Cambridge: Cambridge University Press, 2001), 118.

40. Norman Stone, "Moltke-Conrad: Relations Between the Austro-Hungarian and German General Staffs 1909–1914," *Historical Journal* 9, no. 2 (1966): 202–203; Mombauer, *Helmuth von Moltke*, 75–76; Rothenberg, *Army of Francis Joseph*, 157–158.

41. Wawro, *Warfare and Society*, 145–146; Rothenberg, *Army of Francis Joseph*, 143.

42. *Danzer's Armee Zeitung*, May 28, 1914, "Eine Lanze für das Bajonett."

43. Timothy C. Dowling, *The Brusilov Offensive* (Bloomington: Indiana University Press, 2008), 8–9.

44. Haus-, Hof- und Staatsarchiv, Vienna (HHSA), PA I, 810, Int. LXX/I, Belgrade, July 6, 1914, Storck to Berchtold, "Aktuelles über die *Narodna Odbrana*."

45. "Dies Österreich, es ist ein gutes Land," *Die Fackel* 5, 293 (Jan. 4, 1910) and 5, 368 (Feb. 5, 1913).

46. Vladimir Dedijer, *The Road to Sarajevo* (London: MacGibbon and Kee, 1967), 20; Jelavich, *History of the Balkans*, 2:111.

47. NARA, M 862, roll 940, Budapest, Oct. 5, 1908, trans. of letter from Franz Joseph to Burian; NARA, M 862, roll 940, Mar. 1909, Robert Lansing, "Nationality and the Present Balkan Situation."

48. Williamson, *Austria-Hungary and the Origins*, 73–74, 105.

49. Mitrovic, *Serbia's Great War*, 57–58.

50. NARA, M862, roll 940, Vienna, Feb. 27, 1909, Francis to Bacon; BNA, FO 120/906, Vienna, Jan. 1, 1913, Maj. Thomas Cuninghame to Sir Fairfax Cartwright.

51. NARA, M 862, roll 940, Vienna, Oct. 16, 1908, Rives to Root.

52. Ibid.

53. *Die Industrie*, Apr. 30, 1910, "Quo vadis, Austria?"; NARA, M 862, roll 933, Vienna, Sept. 2, 1908, Rives to Root.

54. NARA, M 862, roll 940, Vienna, Oct. 7, 1908, Rives to Root; Williamson, *Austria-Hungary and the Origins*, 78–79; *Reichspost*, Jan. 9 and 23, 1913; BNA, FO 120/906, Vienna, Jan. 16, 1913, Cartwright to Grey; Churchill, *World Crisis*, 49–53.

55. Moritz Freiherr von Auffenberg-Komarów, *Aus Österreichs Höhe und Niedergang: Eine Lebensschilderung* (Munich: Drei Masken Verlag, 1921), 170–174; Rothenberg, *Army of Francis Joseph*, 145, 152.

56. Sondhaus, *Franz Conrad von Hötzendorf*, 107.

57. SHAT, 7N 1131, Vienna, Jan. 16, 1912, "Le Général Schemua," and Vienna, Apr. 25, 1912, "Notes sur la politique balkanique austro-hongroise"; Sondhaus, *Franz Conrad von Hötzendorf*, 104–107.

58. Sondhaus, *Franz Conrad von Hötzendorf*, 117.

59. NARA, M 862, roll 940, Mar. 1909, Robert Lansing, "Nationality and the Present Balkan Situation."

CHAPTER 3: THE BALKAN WARS

1. National Archives and Records Administration, Washington, DC (NARA), M 862, roll 940, Constantinople, Nov. 10, 1908, Lewis Einstein, "Report on the Present Situation in the Near East."

2. *Die Zeit*, Nov. 15, 1912 and Apr. 17, 1913, "Dilettanten-Vorstellung."

3. *Neue Freie Presse*, Nov. 21, 1912, "Die Zukunft des Fez."

4. FML Otto Gerstner, "Albanien und die Balkan-Frage," *Neue Freie Presse*, Nov. 9, 1912.

5. Haus-, Hof- und Staatsarchiv, Vienna (HHSA), Politisches Archiv (PA) I 872, The Hague, May 19, 1915, Giskra to Burián; Kriegsarchiv, Vienna (KA), B/232:11, Sarajevo, Dec. 2, 1912, FML Appel to Col. Brosch.

6. Service Historique de l'Armée de Terre, Vincennes (SHAT), 7N 1131, Vienna, Jan. 25, 1912, Cdt. Levesque; Hugo Hantsch, *Leopold Graf Berchtold* (Graz: Verlag Styria, 1963), 1:7.

7. British National Archives, Kew (BNA), Foreign Office (FO) 120/907, Vienna, Aug. 26, 1913, Cartwright to Grey.

8. Winston S. Churchill, *The World Crisis: The Eastern Front* (London: Thornton Butterworth, 1931), 57.

9. KA, Armeeoberkommando (AOK), 1912, Chf d GS Ev.B. 3462, Vienna, Dec. 6 and 17, 1912, "Tagesbericht"; Christopher Clark, *The Sleepwalkers* (New York: Harper, 2013), 266–272; Samuel R. Williamson Jr., *Austria-Hungary and the Origins of the First World War* (New York: St. Martin's, 1991), 124, 128; Gunther E. Rothenberg, *The Army of Francis Joseph* (West Lafayette, IN: Purdue University Press, 1976), 166–167.

10. *Neue Freie Presse,* Nov. 21, 1912, and *Wiener Sonn-und Montagszeitung,* Jan. 6, 1913.

11. *Fremden-Blatt,* Dec. 16 and 18, 1913.

12. *Südslawische Revue,* Feb. 1913, 189.

13. KA, B/232:11, Sarajevo, Dec. 2, 1912, FML Appel to Col. Brosch.

14. KA, Militärkanzlei Franz Ferdinand (MKFF) 196, *Berliner Tagblatt,* Sept. 20, 1912, "Deutschland, England, Europa."

15. KA, B/677:0-10 (Auffenberg), Bozen, Oct. 28, 1913, Brosch to Auffenberg; SHAT, 7N 1131, Vienna, Mar. 16, 1912, "Le conflit militaire austro-hongrois"; Lawrence Sondhaus, *Franz Conrad von Hötzendorf: Architect of the Apocalypse* (Boston: Humanities Press, 2000), 120.

16. SHAT, 7N 1131, Vienna, Mar. 16, 1912, "Le conflit militaire austro-hongrois."

17. Rudolf Kiszling, "Alexander Freiherr von Krobatin," in *Neue Österreichische Biographie, 1815–1918* (Vienna: Amalthea, 1923–1987), 17:202–206.

18. Horst Brettner-Messler, "Die Balkanpolitik Conrad von Hötzendorfs von seiner Wiederernennung zum Chef des Generalstabes bis zum Oktober-Ultimatum 1913," *Mitteilungen des österreichischen Staatsarchivs* 20 (1967), 180–182.

19. *Reichspost,* Feb. 22, 1913; *Die Zeit,* Feb. 13, 1914, "Ein neues 1864"; Rothenberg, *Army of Francis Joseph,* 164.

20. Rothenberg, *Army of Francis Joseph,* 165, 168.

21. Moritz Freiherr von Auffenberg-Komarów, *Aus Österreichs Höhe und Niedergang: Eine Lebensschilderung* (Munich: Drei Masken Verlag, 1921), 250.

22. David Fromkin, *Europe's Last Summer* (New York: Vintage, 2005), 90–93; Fritz Fischer, *War of Illusions* (London: Chatto and Windus, 1975), 161–164.

23. Annika Mombauer, *Helmuth von Moltke and the Origins of the First World War* (Cambridge: Cambridge University Press, 2001), 138–144.

24. *Neue Freie Presse,* Nov. 26–Dec. 17, 1912.

25. "Wenn der Kaiser von Österreich reiten lassen will, wird geritten." KA, B/1503:5, Sarajevo, Dec. 21, 1912, Potiorek to Conrad.

26. SHAT, 7N 1131, Vienna, Feb. 23, 1913, "Notes sur la situation"; BNA, FO 120/907, Vienna, Aug. 9, 1913, Chung to Cartwright; *Neue Freie Presse,* Dec. 12 and 13, 1912, "Weltkrieg wegen des Korridors nach Durazzo?"

27. *Neue Freie Presse,* Dec. 14, 1912; Josef Ullreich, "Mortiz von Auffenberg-Komarów: Leben und Wirken," phil. diss., Vienna, 1961, 148–170.

28. Williamson, *Austria-Hungary and the Origins,* 132, 139; SHAT, AAT, 7N 1131, V, Dec. 18, 1912, "Situation militaire"; *Allgemeine Zeitung* (Munich), Jan. 25, 1913, "Politischer Morphinismus."

29. Clark, *Sleepwalkers,* 266–272; *Reichspost,* Jan. 10, 1913.

30. *Neue Freie Presse*, Dec. 12, 1912.

31. *Reichspost*, Jan. 27, 1913; *Neue Freie Presse*, Feb. 7, 1913.

32. *Österreichische Rundschau* 39 (1914), June 15, 1914, Politicus, "Imperialismus."

33. KA, B/677:0-10 (Auffenberg), Bozen, Nov. 1913, Brosch to Auffenberg.

34. KA, B/1503:5, Sarajevo, Dec. 21, 1912, Potiorek to Conrad.

35. Sean McMeekin, *The Russian Origins of the First World War* (Cambridge: Belknap, 2011), 21–22.

36. *Berliner Zeitung am Mittag*, Feb. 4, 1913; *Das neue Deutschland*, Jan. 7, 1913; *Tagespost* (Graz), Feb. 1, 1913.

37. Williamson, *Austria-Hungary and the Origins*, 134; BNA, FO 120/906, Vienna, Feb. 11, 1913, Cartwright to Grey; Mombauer, *Helmuth von Moltke*, 135–136.

38. *Neuen Wiener Journal*, May 30, 1913.

39. SHAT, 7N 1131, Vienna, June 1, 1912, "Le premier dreadnought autrichien inutilisable," and June 6, 1912, "Le dreadnought autrichien."

40. Clark, *Sleepwalkers*, 116; BNA, FO 120/906, Vienna, Apr. 18, 1913, Maj. Thos. Cuninghame to Cartwright; Sondhaus, *Franz Conrad von Hötzendorf*, 128.

41. *Neue Freie Presse*, May 26, 1913.

42. *Neuen Wiener Journal*, May 29, 1913.

43. Ibid., May 30, 1913.

44. *Neue Freie Presse*, May 30, 1914.

45. Georg Markus, *Der Fall Redl* (Vienna: Amalthea Verlag, 1984), 33–53.

46. Ibid., 188, 200–201.

47. *Arbeiter Zeitung*, May 29, 1913.

48. BNA, FO 120/906, Vienna, Apr. 18 and June 4, 1913, Maj. Thos. Cuninghame to Cartwright. Conrad's son had been implicated in the Jandric Affair in April, possibly as a spy, and certainly as a gullible enabler. Markus, *Der Fall Redl*, 75; István Deák, *Beyond Nationalism* (Oxford: Oxford University Press, 1990), 145.

49. *Fromden-Blatt*, May 30, 1913; *Neue Freie Presse*, May 31, 1913; *Wiener Mittagszeitung*, May 31, 1913; Sondhaus, *Franz Conrad von Hötzendorf*, 125; Markus, *Der Fall Redl*, 128–129; BNA, FO 120/906, Vienna, June 5, 1913, Maj. Cuninghame to Cartwright; Graydon Tunstall, *Planning for War Against Russia and Serbia: Austro-Hungarian and German Military Strategies 1871–1914* (New York: Columbia University Press, 1993), 106–107.

50. *Arbeiter Zeitung*, May 30, 1913, "Der Generalstabsobert als Spion"; *Die Zeit*, June 6, 1913.

51. *Neue Freie Presse*, May 31, 1913; *Reichspost*, May 31, 1913; *Arbeiter Zeitung*, May 31 and June 1, 1913; Markus, *Der Fall Redl*, 268.

52. SHAT, 7N 1131, Vienna, May 29 and June 12, 1913, "L'affaire du Col. Redl." Markus, *Der Fall Redl*, 75, 152.

53. BNA, FO 120/907, Vienna, Aug. 30, 1913, Maj. Cuninghame to Cartwright.

54. Moritz Freiherr von Auffenberg-Komarów, *Aus Österreichs Höhe und Niedergang: Eine Lebensschilderung* (Munich: Drei Masken Verlag, 1921), 232, 241–242; FML Johann Cvitkovic in the *Neue Freie Presse*, May 31, 1913.

55. *Budapester Tagblatt*, June 1, 1913.

56. Brettner-Messler, "Die Balkanpolitik," 213.

57. SHAT, Vienna, Feb. 25, 1897, Cdt de Berckheim, "Péninsule Balkanique."

58. Arthur Ruhl, *Antwerp to Gallipoli: A Year of the War on Many Fronts—and Behind Them* (New York: Scribner's, 1916), 153–155; Norman Stone, "Moltke-Conrad: Relations Between the Austro-Hungarian and German General Staffs 1909–1914," *Historical Journal* 9, no. 2 (1966): 212–213.

59. NARA, M 862, roll 940, Mar. 1909, Robert Lansing, "Nationality and the Present Balkan Situation"; *Budapest Hirlap*, Mar. 23, 1913.

60. Rudolf Jerabek, *Potiorek* (Graz: Verlag Styria, 1991), 75.

61. BNA, FO 120/906 and FO 120/907, Vienna, Mar. 14, 1913, Cuninghame to Cartwright, and Vienna August 9, 1913, Cuninghame to Cartwright; *Fremden-Blatt*, Dec. 13–14, 1913; Clark, *Sleepwalkers*, 99.

62. KA, MKFF 196, Dec. 22, 1912, "Übersetzung aus der 'Review of Reviews.'"

63. "Der Chef des Generalstabes," *Freudenthaler Zeitung*, Oct. 4, 1913; KA, B/677:0-10 (Auffenberg), Bozen, Nov. 1913, Brosch to Auffenberg.

64. *Wiener Sonn-und-Montagszeitung*, Sept. 21, 1913, "Die Lehren der Armee-Manöver."

65. BNA, FO 120/907, Vienna, Dec. 8, 1913, Maj. Thos. Cuninghame to Sir Maurice de Bunsen; Georg von Alten, *Handbuch für Heer und Flotte* (Berlin: Deutsches Verlagshaus, 1909–1914), 6:318–319.

66. Churchill, *World Crisis*, 30.

67. *Die Zeit*, Sept. 24, 1913; *Pester Lloyd*, Sept. 27, 1913; *Vorwärts* (Berlin), Sept. 28, 1913.

68. Sondhaus, *Franz Conrad von Hötzendorf*, 133.

69. KA, MKFF 198, Budapest, Sept. 30, 1913.

70. KA, B/677:0-10 (Auffenberg), Bozen, Oct. 28, 1913, Brosch to Auffenberg.

71. BNA, FO 120/907, Vienna, Oct. 29, 1913, Cartwright to Grey.

72. KA, MKFF 197, *Wiener Sonntag-und-Montagszeitung*, Jan. 6, 1913; Williamson, *Austria-Hungary and the Origins*, 154–155.

73. KA, B/677:0-10 (Auffenberg), Bozen, Dec. 9, 1913, "Der Dumme hats Glück!"

74. BNA, FO 120/907, Vienna, Oct. 28, 1913, Cartwright to Grey.

75. BNA, FO 120/906, Vienna, Jan. 1, 1913, Maj. Thomas Cuninghame to Cartwright; Sondhaus, *Franz Conrad von Hötzendorf*, 135.

76. Williamson, *Austria-Hungary and the Origins*, 186–187.

77. SHAT, 7N 1129, Vienna, Mar. 29, 1905, "La situation politique de la Croatie"; Vladimir Dedijer, *The Road to Sarajevo* (London: MacGibbon and Kee, 1967), 132–134.

78. KA, MKFF 202, Vienna, Winter 1910–1911, Brosch, Untertänigstes Referat.

79. Williamson, *Austria-Hungary and the Origins*, 181–182.

80. Mombauer, *Helmuth von Moltke*, 77; Gerhard Ritter, *The Schlieffen Plan* (Westport, CT: Greenwood Press, 1979), 74; Timothy C. Dowling, *The Brusilov Offensive* (Bloomington: Indiana University Press, 2008), 4–5. A Russian corps had 108 field guns in 1914, an Austrian corps 96.

81. KA, MKFF 196, Dec. 22, 1912, "Übersetzung aus der 'Review of Reviews.'"

CHAPTER 4: MURDER IN SARAJEVO

1. Barbara Jelavich, *History of the Balkans* (Cambridge: Cambridge University Press, 1983), 2:110.

2. Kriegsarchiv, Vienna (KA), B/677:0-10 (Auffenberg), Bozen, Oct. 28 and Nov. 1913, Brosch to Auffenberg; Rudolf Jerabek, *Potiorek* (Graz: Verlag Styria, 1991), 77–78; Lawrence Sondhaus, *Franz Conrad von Hötzendorf: Architect of the Apocalypse* (Boston: Humanities Press, 2000), 133.

3. *Wien Zukunft*, Oct. 1, 1913; *Neue Freie Presse*, Oct. 3, 1913.

4. Österreichischen Bundesministerium für Heereswesen und vom Kriegsarchiv, *Österreich-Ungarns Letzter Krieg 1914–18*, ed. Edmund Glaise von Horstenau (Vienna: Verlag Militätwissenschaftlichen Mitteilungen, 1931–1938), 1:6–7; Jerabek, *Potiorek*, 98.

5. Graydon Tunstall, *Planning for War Against Russia and Serbia: Austro-Hungarian and German Military Strategies 1871–1914* (New York: Columbia University Press, 1993), 106.

6. KA, Neue Feld Akten (NFA) 2115, 36 I.D., Vienna, July 20, 1914, "Einiges über höhere Kommandos und Personalien der serbischen Armee."

7. Jerabek, *Potiorek*, 99–105.

8. KA, Militärkanzlei Franz Ferdinand (MKFF) 202, "Studie Sommer 1907: Operationen gegen Serbien."

9. Jelavich, *History of the Balkans*, 2:111.

10. Jerabek, *Potiorek*, 90.

11. Vladimir Dedijer, *The Road to Sarajevo* (London: MacGibbon and Kee, 1967), 9–10.

12. Jerabek, *Potiorek*, 84; Winston S. Churchill, *The World Crisis: The Eastern Front* (London: Thornton Butterworth, 1931), 64.

13. Christopher Clark, *The Sleepwalkers* (New York: Harper, 2013), 367–376; Sean McMeekin, *July 1914* (New York: Basic Books, 2013), 1–20; Dedijer, *The Road to Sarajevo*, 14–16.

14. Carl Freiherr von Bardolff, *Soldat im alten Österreich: Erinnerungen aus meinem Leben* (Jena: Eugen Diederichs, 1938): 90.

15. *Die Fackel* 7, no. 400 (July 10, 1914): 1–4, "Franz Ferdinand und die Talente."

16. Jerabek, *Potiorek*, 95.

17. KA, B/1503:5, Vienna, July 9, 1914, Conrad to Potiorek, *sehr geheim*; Clark, *Sleepwalkers*, 392.

18. KA, B/1503:6, Vienna, July 27, 1914, FZM Krobatin to FZM Potiorek.

19. KA, B/232:11, Karton 15, Sarajevo, July 25, 1914, GdI Appel to Col. Brosch-Aarenau.

20. Andre Mitrovic, *Serbia's Great War 1914–1918* (West Lafayette, IN: Purdue University Press, 2007), 17, 64.

21. Haus-, Hof- und Staatsarchiv, Vienna (HHSA), Politisches Archiv (PA) I, 810, Int. LXX/1, Belgrade, June 30, 1914, Storck to Berchtold.

22. McMeekin, *July 1914*, 109–116; Samuel R. Williamson Jr., *Austria-Hungary and the Origins of the First World War* (New York: St. Martin's, 1991), 192.

23. Annika Mombauer, *Helmuth von Moltke and the Origins of the First World War* (Cambridge: Cambridge University Press, 2001), 151–152; Gunther E. Rothenberg, *The Army of Francis Joseph* (West Lafayette, IN: Purdue University Press, 1976), 168.

24. Clark, *Sleepwalkers*, 381–403; Dedijer, *The Road to Sarajevo*, 289–291; Williamson, *Austria-Hungary and the Origins*, 193; Mitrovic, *Serbia's Great War*, 5–6.

25. HHSA, PA I, 810, Int. LXX/1, Vienna, July 7, 1914, GdI Conrad to Berchtold.

26. David Fromkin, *Europe's Last Summer* (New York: Vintage, 2005), 155.

27. Mitrovic, *Serbia's Great War*, 10.

28. Ibid., 11.

29. Norman Stone, "Hungary and the Crisis of July 1914," *Journal of Contemporary History* 1, no. 3 (1966): 161; Churchill, *World Crisis*, 53.

30. Mitrovic, *Serbia's Great War*, 10. Fromkin, *Europe's Last Summer*, 157.

31. Fromkin, *Europe's Last Summer*, 157.

32. Sean McMeekin, *The Russian Origins of the First World War* (Cambridge, MA: Belknap Press, 2011), 42–46; McMeekin, *July 1914*, 393–394; Churchill, *World Crisis*, 77.

33. David G. Herrmann, *The Arming of Europe and the Making of the First World War* (Princeton: Princeton University Press, 1996), 221.

34. Moritz Freiherr von Auffenberg-Komarów, *Aus Österreichs Höhe und Nieder-gang: Eine Lebensschilderung* (Munich: Drei Masken Verlag, 1921), 256.

35. Mombauer, *Helmuth von Moltke*, 194.

36. Churchill, *World Crisis*, 65.

37. Mitrovic, *Serbia's Great War*, 4.

38. Mombauer, *Helmuth von Moltke*, 191–192.

39. Clark, *Sleepwalkers*, 517; Fromkin, *Europe's Last Summer*, 156; Williamson, *Austria-Hungary and the Origins*, 195; Mombauer, *Helmuth von Moltke*, 103.

40. Service Historique de l'Armée de Terre, Vincennes (SHAT), AAT, EMA, 7N 847, Marseille, Mar. 22, 1917, 2ème Bureau, "2ème Bureau analysé des cahiers de notes d'un officier hongrois prisonnier de guerre."

41. Williamson, *Austria-Hungary and the Origins*, 198–199.

42. Stone, "Hungary and the Crisis of July 1914," 163.

43. HHSA, PA I, 810, LXX/1, Belgrade, July 8, 1914, Wilhelm Storck to Berchtold.

44. Auffenberg-Komarów, *Aus Österreichs*, 257.

45. Williamson, *Austria-Hungary and the Origins*, 203.

46. HHSA, PA I, 810, LXX/1, Vienna, July 20, 1914, Berchtold to Giesl; Stone, "Hungary and the Crisis of July 1914," 166.

47. KA, B/232:11, Karton 15, Sarajevo, July 25, 1914, GdI Appel to Col. Brosch-Aarenau.

48. McMeekin, *July 1914*, 181; Williamson, *Austria-Hungary and the Origins*, 203.

49. HHSA, PA I, 811, LXX/2, July 25 and 27, 1914, "Antwortnote"; Clark, *Sleep-walkers*, 423–430, 457–469.

50. Auffenberg-Komarów, *Aus Österreichs*, 259–260.

51. British National Archives, Kew (BNA), Foreign Office (FO) 371/1900, London, Sept. 1, 1914, Bunsen to Grey.

52. KA, Armeeoberkommando (AOK) 1914, Evidenzbureau (EVB) 3506, Vienna, Aug. 4, 1914; Kurt Peball, "Der Feldzug gegen Serbien und Montenegro im Jahre 1914," *Österreichische Militärische Zeitschrift* Sonderheft I (1965): 20–21; Jerabek, *Potiorek*, 22.

53. KA, MKFF 202, "Studie Sommer 1907: Operationen gegen Serbien"; General Jo-sef von Stürgkh, *Im Deutschen Grossen Hauptquartier* (Leipzig: Paul List, 1921), 158.

54. István Burián, *Austria in Dissolution 1915–18* (New York: George Doran, 1925), 8–9.

55. Norman Stone, "Moltke-Conrad: Relations Between the Austro-Hungarian and German General Staffs 1909–1914," *Historical Journal* 9, no. 2 (1966): 215.

56. McMeekin, *July 1914*, 252–255.

57. HHSA, PA I, 810, Int. LXX/1, Vienna, July 7, 1914, GdI Conrad to Berchtold.

58. *Österreich-Ungarns Letzter Krieg 1914–18*, 1:24.

59. Auffenberg-Komarów, *Aus Österreichs*, 262.

60. Stone, "Moltke-Conrad," 216–217.

61. Auffenberg-Komarów, *Aus Österreichs*, 264–265.

62. BNA, FO 371/1900, London, Sept. 1, 1914, Bunsen to Grey.

63. Herrmann, *Arming of Europe*, 214.

64. Capt. B. H. Liddell Hart, *The Real War 1914–1918* (Boston: Little, Brown, 1963), 31–2; Patricia Clough, "Found: The Secret of World War I," *Sunday Times*, Aug. 14, 1994; Jerabek, *Potiorek*, 108; Mombauer, *Helmuth von Moltke*, 106–107; Herrmann, *Arming of Europe*, 205–206, 217–218.

65. Geoffrey Wawro, *Warfare and Society in Europe 1792–1914* (London: Rout-ledge, 2000), 200–211; Herrmann, *Arming of Europe*, 200–201, 212; Mombauer, *Helmuth von Moltke*, 172.

66. HHSA, PA I, 837, Munich, Aug. 14, 1914, Vélics to Berchtold.

67. HHSA, PA III, 171, Berlin, May 16, 1914, Szögenyi to Berchtold; PA I, 842, Berlin, Oct. 6, 1915, Hohenlohe to Burián; PA I, 837, Munich, Aug. 5, 1914, Vélics to Berchtold.

68. Herrmann, *Arming of Europe*, 218.

69. BNA, FO 371/1900, London, Sept. 1, 1914, Bunsen to Grey; HHSA, PA I, 819, Vienna, Aug. 2, 1914, Tisza to Berchtold; KA, B/1503:6, Vienna, Aug. 6, 1914, GdI Arthur Bolfras to FZM Potiorek.

CHAPTER 5: THE STEAMROLLER

1. Gunther E. Rothenberg, *The Army of Francis Joseph* (West Lafayette, IN: Purdue University Press, 1976), 177.

2. Charles Emmerson, *1913* (New York: Public Affairs, 2013), 115.

3. Alfred Knox, *With the Russian Army 1914–17* (London: Hutchinson, 1921), 1:xvii.

4. Service Historique de l'Armée de Terre, Vincennes (SHAT), EMA, 7N 846, 2ème Bureau, Rome, April 13, 1916, Col. François, "Cohesion de l'Armée Austro-Hongroise."

5. Georg Markus, *Der Fall Redl* (Vienna: Amalthea Verlag, 1984), 43.

6. SHAT, EMA, 7N 846, May 14, 1917, "Armée Autrichienne"; Rothenberg, *Army of Francis Joseph*, 113–114, 173–174, 182; Alfred Krauss, *Die Ursachen unserer Niederlage: Erinnerungen und Urteile aus den Weltkrieg*, 3rd ed. (Munich, 1923), 90–91.

7. Rothenberg, *Army of Francis Joseph*, 159.

8. Kriegsarchiv, Vienna (KA), Militärkanzlei Franz Ferdinand (MKFF) 202, Vienna, Winter 1910–1911, Brosch, Untertänigstes Referat; Österreichischen Bundesministerium für Heereswesen und vom Kriegsarchiv, *Österreich-Ungarns Letzter Krieg 1914–18*, ed. Edmund Glaise von Horstenau (Vienna: Verlag Militärwissenschaftlichen Mitteilungen, 1931–1938), 1:173; Nikolai N. Golovine, *The Russian Army in the World War* (New Haven: Yale University Press, 1931), 34.

9. Rothenberg, *Army of Francis Joseph*, 159.

10. Annika Mombauer, *Helmuth von Moltke and the Origins of the First World War* (Cambridge: Cambridge University Press, 2001), 114.

11. Scott W. Lackey, *The Rebirth of the Habsburg Army* (Westport, CT: Greenwood, 1995), 152; Rudolf Jerabek, *Potiorek* (Graz: Verlag Styria, 1991), 100–101; Rothenberg, *Army of Francis Joseph*, 158; Mombauer, *Helmuth von Moltke*, 81.

12. Norman Stone, "Moltke-Conrad: Relations between the Austro-Hungarian and German General Staffs 1909–1914," *Historical Journal* 9, no. 2 (1966): 205–208.

13. Graydon Tunstall, *Blood on the Snow: The Carpathian Winter War of 1915* (Lawrence: University Press of Kansas, 2010), 15; General Josef von Stürgkh, *Im Deutschen Grossen Hauptquartier* (Leipzig: Paul List, 1921), 23, 159.

14. Graydon Tunstall, *Planning for War Against Russia and Serbia: Austro-Hungarian and German Military Strategies 1871–1914* (New York: Columbia University Press, 1993), 148, 170, 174; Lawrence Sondhaus, *Franz Conrad von Hötzendorf: Architect of the Apocalypse* (Boston: Humanities Press, 2000), 145–146.

15. Winston S. Churchill, *The World Crisis: The Eastern Front* (London: Thornton Butterworth, 1931), 137.

16. "Eisenbahntechnisch nicht durchzuführen." Stone, "Moltke-Conrad," 219; Mombauer, *Helmuth von Moltke*, 102–103.

17. Norman Stone, "Hungary and the Crisis of July 1914," *Journal of Contemporary History* 1, no. 3 (1966): 163–164; Stone, "Moltke-Conrad," 217; Rothenberg, *Army of Francis Joseph*, 173.

18. *Österreich-Ungarns Letzter Krieg 1914–18*, 1:12–13.

19. Norman Stone, *The Eastern Front 1914–1917* (London: Penguin, 1998 [1975]), 76–77; Norman Stone, "Die *Mobilmachung* der österreichisch-ungarischen Armee 1914," *Militärgeschichtliche Mitteilung*, 1974, 70–71.

20. Graydon Tunstall, "The Habsburg Command Conspiracy: The Austrian Falsification of Historiography on the Outbreak of World War I," *Austrian History Yearbook* 27 (1996): 192–193.

21. Rothenberg, *Army of Francis Joseph*, 179.

22. KA, B/3 (Dankl): 5/1, Tagebuch (1), Aug. 2, 1914.

23. Moritz Freiherr von Auffenberg-Komarów, *Aus Österreichs Höhe und Niedergang: Eine Lebensschilderung* (Munich: Drei Masken Verlag, 1921), 265; Tunstall, *Planning for War*, 176–177; Sondhaus, *Franz Conrad von Hötzendorf*, 135.

24. Sondhaus, *Franz Conrad von Hötzendorf*, 147; Rothenberg, *Army of Francis Joseph*, 179.

25. KA, B/1503:6, Aug. 12, 1914, Sarajevo, Potiorek to Conrad.

26. Stone, *Eastern Front*, 77.

27. SHAT, AAT, EMA, 7N 846, Paris, March 1914, "Organisation de l'armée austro-hongroise sur le pied de guerre."

28. KA, Neue Feld Akten (NFA) 528, 9 ID, "Intendanz der k.u.k. 9. I-T-D, 26 Juli-8 Dez. 1914."

29. Stone, *Eastern Front*, 78–79.

30. Sondhaus, *Franz Conrad von Hötzendorf*, 152; Josef Redlich, *Schicksalsjahre Österreichs 1908–19: Das politische Tagebuch Josef Redlichs* (Graz: Verlag Böhlau, 1953), 1:247.

31. Redlich, *Schicksalsjahre Österreichs*, 1:247.

32. KA, B/1503:6, Sarajevo, Aug. 8, 1914, Potiorek to GdI Emil Woinovich.

33. James M. B. Lyon, "'A Peasant Mob': The Serbian Army on the Eve of the Great War," *Journal of Military History* 61 (July 1997): 483–484; Hew Strachan, *The First World War*, vol. 1, *To Arms* (Oxford: Oxford University Press, 2001), 343; Joseph Schön, *Sabac!* (Reichenberg: Heimatsöhne, 1928), 12–13.

34. Lyon, "Peasant Mob," 501.

35. KA, B/3 (Dankl): 5/1, Tagebuch (1), Aug. 10, 1914.

36. KA, NFA 1372, 11. Korps Kdo, Lemberg, Aug. 14, 1914, "Abschiebung unverlässlicher Elemente."

37. Haus-, Hof-, und Staatsarchiv, Vienna (HHSA), Politisches Archiv (PA) I, 837, Munich, Aug. 19 and Oct. 8, 1914, Vélics to Berchtold.

38. HHSA, PA I, 837, Munich, Oct. 8, 1914, Vélics to Berchtold.

39. Sean McMeekin, *The Russian Origins of the First World War* (Cambridge, MA: Belknap Press, 2011), 22; Knox, *With the Russian Army*, 1:43–45.

CHAPTER 6: MISFITS

1. Service Historique de l'Armée de Terre, Vincennes (SHAT), EMA, 7N 1128, Vienna, Oct. 14, 1897, Cdt. Berckheim, "Notes sur le haut commandement en Autriche."

2. Rudolf Jerabek, *Potiorek* (Graz: Verlag Styria, 1991), 110; Moritz Freiherr von Auffenberg-Komarów, *Aus Österreichs Höhe und Niedergang: Eine Lebensschilderung* (Munich: Drei Masken Verlag, 1921), 232.

3. R. G. D. Laffan, *The Serbs* (New York: Dorset Press, 1989 [1917]), 190.

4. Jaroslav Hasek, *The Good Soldier Svejk and His Fortunes in the World War*, trans. Cecil Parrott (London: Penguin, 1985 [1923], 433).

5. Kriegsarchiv, Vienna (KA), Neue Feld Akten (NFA) 529, Bijelina, August 9, 1914, 9; ITD, FML Scheuchenstuel; Hew Strachan, *The First World War*, vol. 1, *To Arms*

(Oxford: Oxford University Press, 2001), 336; Jerabek, *Potiorek*, 108–111; Manfried Rauchensteiner, *Der Tod des Doppeladlers: Österreich-Ungarn und der Erste Weltkrieg* (Graz: Verlag Styria, 1993), 128.

6. Carl Freiherr von Bardolff, *Soldat im alten Österreich: Erinnerungen aus meinem Leben* (Jena: Eugen Diederichs, 1938), 72.

7. SIIAT, 7N 1127, Vienna, March 10, 1889, Capt de Pange.

8. Strachan, *First World War*, 341.

9. Gunther E. Rothenberg, *The Army of Francis Joseph* (West Lafayette, IN: Purdue University Press, 1976), 175.

10. Jerabek, *Potiorek*, 114.

11. Ibid., 9–45, 69–70.

12. KA, NFA 2115, 36 ID, 5 Armee Kommando to 36 ID, Brcko, Aug. 2, 1914, Op. Nr. 15; Rothenberg, *Army of Francis Joseph*, 103.

13. Kurt Peball, "Der Feldzug gegen Serbien und Montenegro im Jahre 1914," *Österreichische Militärische Zeitschrift Sonderheft* I (1965): 20; Jerabek, *Potiorek*, 116–117; Moritz Freiherr von Auffenberg-Komarów, *Aus Österreichs Höhe und Niedergang: Eine Lebensschilderung* (Munich: Drei Masken Verlag, 1921), 264.

14. James M. B. Lyon, "'A Peasant Mob': The Serbian Army on the Eve of the Great War," *Journal of Military History* 61 (July 1997): 486–478.

15. Ibid., 495–498.

16. Ibid., 499–500.

17. Groszen Generalstab, Serbien, *Der Grosze Krieg Serbiens zur Befreiung und Vereinigung der Serben, Kroaten und Slovenen* (Belgrade: Buchdruckerei des Ministeriums für Krieg und Marine, 1924–26), 1:32–34.

18. Lyon, "Peasant Mob," 491.

19. KA, Gefechtsberichte (GB) 24, 483 c/2, k.u.k. Warasdiner I.R. 16, "Gefechtsbericht Kurtovica am 12. August 1914"; Groszen Generalstab, Serbien, *Grosze Krieg*, 49–50.

20. KA, NFA 935, k.u.k. 72, Infanterie-Brigade-Kommando, Tagebuch, 13 Aug. 1914; NFA 1795, 8. KpsKdo, GdK Giesl, "Gefechtsbericht über die Zeit vom 12 bis 20 August."

21. Karl Kraus, ed., *Die Fackel* (Munich: Kösel-Verlag, 1968–76), "Die letzten Tage der Menschheit," 35 (1. Szene, 1. Akt).

22. Rothenberg, *Army of Francis Joseph*, 150; Krauss, "Bekleidung," 33–35.

23. KA, NFA 935, k.u.k. 72, Infanterie-Brigade-Kommando, GM Haustein, "Bericht über das Gefecht am 14 Aug. bei Dobric."

24. KA, GB 24, 484 b/5, I.R. 16, Col. Budiner, "Gefechtsbericht über das Gefecht von Kozjak und Dobric am 14. Aug. 1914."

25. KA, GB 24, 483 c/2, k.u.k. Warasdiner I.R. 16, "Gefechtsbericht Kurtovica am 12. August 1914"; Joseph Schön, *Sabac!* (Reichenberg: Heimatsöhne, 1928), 144.

26. KA, GB 24, 36 ITD, GM Haustein, "Bericht über das Gefecht am 14. Aug. bei Dobric," "Gefechtsbericht über das Gefecht auf Vk. Gradac und bei Jarebicka crvka am 16. Aug 1914."

27. Groszen Generalstab, Serbien, *Grosze Krieg*, 1:107, 172–173.

28. KA, NFA 1795, 8. KpsKdo, GdK Giesl, "Gefechtsbericht über die Zeit vom 12 bis 20 August."

29. KA, NFA 529, Vienna, Aug. 13, 1914, GM Kanik, Etappen-Oberkommando-Befehl Nr. 1.

30. KA, NFA 170, 17 Brig., GdK Giesl, Aug. 25, 1914, "Wahrnehmungen während der letzten Gefechte"; NFA 935, 72 Inf. Brig., Kosjak, Aug. 15, 1914, Ord. Off. Goriany to GM von Haustein.

31. Haus-, Hof- und Staatsarchiv, Vienna (HHSA), Politisches Archiv (PA) I, 819, Vienna, Aug. 15, 1914, Berchtold to Tarnowski.

32. Schön, *Sabac*, 127.

33. KA, Armeeoberkommando (AOK) 1914, Evidenzbureau (EVB) 3506, Evidenzbüro des Generalstabes B. Nr. 57./I.

34. Groszen Generalstab, Serbien, *Grosze Kriege*, 1:102–104.

35. Ibid., 1:139–142.

36. Schön, *Sabac*, 29, 131.

37. KA, B/1503:6, Sarajevo, Aug. 14, 1914, k.u.k. Armee-Kommando Op. 248; SHAT, EMA 7N 1129, Vienna, June 28, 1903, Cdt. Laguiche.

38. Groszen Generalstab, Serbien, *Grosze Krieg*, 1:320.

39. Schön, *Sabac*, 20.

40. Ibid., 133; Groszen Generalstab, Serbien, *Grosze Krieg*, 1:142–143.

41. Groszen Generalstab, Serbien, *Grosze Krieg*, 1:320–321.

42. KA, GB 17 (k.k. 21 LITD), Tellovica, Aug. 15, 1914, Landwehr I.R. 6, Capt. Rudolf Kalhous, "Gefechtsbericht über den Angriff und Einnhahme der Cer-Höhe am 14. August 1914"; Schön, *Sabac*, 99–100; Groszen Generalstab, Serbien, *Grosze Krieg*, 1:107–108.

43. KA, NFA 489, 42 Sch. Brig., Aug. 16, 1914, "Tagebuch"; NFA 170, 17 Brig., 5 Armee, Op. 402/15, Brcko, Aug. 22, 1914, GdI Frank; NFA 528, "9. ITD Abfertigung am 21. Aug. 1914"; GB 17, 21 LITD, Kdo. Op. Nr. 75/1 Bijelina, Aug. 22, 1914, FML Przyborski, "Bericht über das Gefecht am 16. Aug. 1914."

44. *Le Figaro*, Aug. 14, 1914.

45. Schön, *Sabac*, 25–26.

46. KA, B/1503:4, Sarajevo, Aug. 16, 1914, Potiorek to Bilinksi.

47. KA, NFA 528, 9 ITD, "Kurzer Gefechtsbericht für die Zeit vom 12. bis 20. August 1914"; KA, NFA 935, k.u.k. 72 Infanterie-Brigade-Kommando, Tagebuch, 13 Aug. 1914.

48. KA, NFA 528, 9 ITD, "Intendanz."

49. KA, NFA, 529, Aug. 21, 1914, 9 ITD, nr. 170, k.u.k. 5 Armee-Kommando, GdI Frank; Jerabek, *Potiorek*, 160.

50. KA, NFA 2115, 36 ID, 4 Baon to I.R. 16 Commando, Kozjak, Aug. 15, 1914.

51. Jerabek, *Potiorek*, 121.

52. KA, NFA 2159, Sarajevo, Aug. 13, 1914, 6 Armee-Kommando, FZM Potiorek.

53. Alfred Krauss, *Die Ursachen unserer Niederlage: Erinnerungen und Urteile aus den Weltkrieg*, 3rd ed. (Munich, 1923), 33–34; KA, NFA 528, "9. ITD Abfertigung am 21. Aug. 1914."

54. Jerabek, *Potiorek*, 121.

55. KA, B/1503:4, Sarajevo, Aug. 19, 1914, Potiorek to Bilinksi.

56. Krauss, *Die Ursachen unserer Niederlage*, 94–98; KA, GB 86, 1914–15, "Erfahrungen über den Kampf um befestigte Stellungen: Vorgang der Deutschen"; Felix Prinz zu Schwarzenberg, *Briefe aus dem Felde 1914–18* (Vienna: Schwarzenbergisches Administration, 1953), 17.

57. Schön, *Sabac*, 146.

58. Ströer, 15.

59. KA, NFA 1850, k.u.k. BH IR Nr. 3, Grabovci, Aug. 22, 1914, Obstlt. Panic.

60. Ströer, 18.

61. KA, G-B 21, 31 ITD, Aug. 29, 1914, FML Eh. Josef, "Gefechtsbericht über die Gefechte am 18. u. 19. August bei Sabac und Pricinovic"; GB 21, Op. no. 15/22, 31 ITD, Aug. 15, 1914, Maj. Wilhelm Jeskowski, "Bericht über meine Eindrucke in Sabac"; Schön, *Sabac*, 78–81; Groszen Generalstab, Serbien, *Grosze Krieg*, 1:214–215.

62. KA, NFA 2115, 36 ID, GdI Frank, Op. Nr. 403/20.

63. KA, NFA 528, G-B 21, 32. ITD, Op. Nr. 29/4, "Gefechtsbericht über das Gefecht sö Sabac am 18. Aug. 1914."

64. KA, NFA 1842, 32 ID, Aug. 25, 1914, Op. 27/3, "Verluste"; Groszen Generalstab, Serbien, *Grosze Krieg*, 1:208.

65. Groszen Generalstab, Serbien, *Grosze Krieg*, 1:323.

66. KA, NFA 1046, 32 ID, Aug. 19, 1914, "Tagebuch"; GB 21, 32 ITD, Op. 29/4, FML Griessler, "Gefechtsbericht über das Gefecht bei Cerovac am 19. Aug. 1914"; Schön, *Sabac*, 97; Groszen Generalstab, Serbien, *Grosze Krieg*, 1:208.

67. KA, NFA 1794, 4. Korpskdo, Sept. 5, 1914, GdK Tersztyánszky, "Bericht über die Kämpfe bei Sabac."

68. KA, GB 21, 31 ITD, Aug. 29, 1914, FML Eh. Josef, "Gefechtsbericht über die Gefechte am 18. u. 19. August bei Sabac und Pricinovic."

69. KA, NFA 1813, FML Eh Joseph, Aug. 29, 1914, "Gefechtsbericht über den Kampf bei Sabac am 23. Aug."

70. KA, B/1503:6, Sarajevo, Aug. 20, 1914, Potiorek to Bolfras; NFA 935, 36 ITD, Aug. 19, 1914, Col. Budiner to 36 ITD-Kommando.

71. KA, NFA 1787, Sambor, Sept. 4, 1914, 4 Korps-Kommando to 31 Infanterie-Truppen Division; Rothenberg, *Army of Francis Joseph*, 142; KA, NFA 1794, 4 Korpskdo, Sept. 5, 1914, GdK Tersztyánszky, "Bericht über die Kämpfe bei Sabac."

72. Jerabek, *Potiorek*, 125

73. KA, GB 42, Han Glasinac, Aug. 27, 1914, Col. Konopicky, 4 Geb. Brig.

74. Schön, *Sabac*, 26.

75. KA, NFA 2116, 36 ID, Op. Nr. 77, Brcko, Aug. 5, 1914.

76. KA, GB 42, Han Glasinac, Aug. 27, 1914, Col. Konopicky, 4 Geb. Brig.; NFA 2159, Han Gromile, Aug. 27, 1914, 4 Geb. Brig., Abfertigung.

77. KA, GB 42, 7 Geb. Brig., "Gefechts-Bericht über den Angriff auf die Höhe Panos am 20. Aug. 1914"; NFA 2159, Han Glasinac, Aug. 27, 1914, k.u.k. 4 Gebirgsbrigade-Kommando, "Resumée der Auszeichgsanträge."

78. KA, GB 24, 36 ITD, "Gefechtsbericht über das Gefecht bei Zavlaka-Marjanovica am 18–21 Aug. 1914"; GB 74, k.u.k. 42 HID, Op. 200/I, Patkovaca, Sept. 3, 1914, "Gefechtsbericht über das Gefecht von Krupanj, 16. Aug. 1914."

79. KA, B/1503:7, Vienna, Sept. 26, 1914, Bolfras to Potiorek; NFA 2159, 18 ITD, 220/10, Aug. 20, 1914, FML Ignaz Trollmann, "Äussere Abfertigung."

80. Schön, *Sabac*, 25; Schwarzenberg, *Briefe aus dem Felde*, 15.

81. KA, NFA 2115, k.u.k. 13 Korps-Kommando, Op. Nr. 194/56.

82. Andre Mitrovic, *Serbia's Great War 1914–1918* (West Lafayette, IN: Purdue University Press, 2007), 67–68.

83. KA, MFA 528, 9 ID, "ITD Abfertigung am 21. Aug. 1914"; NFA 2159, 18 ITD, 220/10, Aug. 20, 1914, FML Ignaz Trollmann, "Äussere Abfertigung"; NFA 2115, 36 ID, k.u.k. XIII Korps Kommando to 36 ID, Dugopolje, Aug. 13, 1914.

84. R. A. Reiss, *Report on the Atrocities Committed by Austro-Hungarian Forces* (London, 1916); Jonathan Gumz, *The Resurrection and Collapse of Empire in Habsburg Serbia 1914–1918* (Cambridge: Cambridge University Press, 2009), 54–55; Laffan, *The Serbs*, 191–195.

85. Groszen Generalstab, Serbien, *Grosze Krieg*, 1:218–219.

86. Ibid., 1:245.

87. KA, GB 74, k.u.k. 42 HID, Op. 200/III, Patkovaca, Sept. 4, 1914, "Gefechtsbwericht über das Gefecht bei Bela-crvka 18. Aug. 1914."

88. KA, NFA 475, 41 Sch. Brig., Aug. 22 and 27, 1914, FML Przyborski.

89. KA, NFA, GB 12, k.u.k. 9 ITD Kdo Op. Nr. 221, "Kurze Gefechtsbericht für die Zeit vom 12. bis 20. Aug. 1914"; Peball, "Der Feldzug," 25.

90. Holger H. Herwig, *The First World War: Germany and Austria-Hungary 1914–1918* (London: Edw. Arnold, 1997), 88–89.

91. KA, GB 21, 32 ITD, Op. 29/4, FML Griessler, "Gefechtsbericht über das Gefecht bei Jevremovac am 23. Aug. 1914"; KA, GB 21, 31 ITD, Aug. 29, 1914, FML Eh. Josef, "Gefechtsbericht über den Kampf bei Sabac am 23. August."

92. KA, B/16 (FML Ferdinand Marterer), Tagebuch, Aug. 26, 1914.

93. KA, B/1503:6, Sarajevo, Aug. 20, 1914, Potiorek to Bolfras; Gumz, *Resurrection and Collapse*, 55–58.

94. KA, B/1503:6, Sarajevo, Aug. 13, 1914, Armee-Kommando-Befehl Nr. 1, "Soldaten der 6. Armee!"

95. KA, NFA 170, Pratkovica, Aug. 21, 1914, k.u.k. 17 Infantrie-Brigade-Kommando.

96. KA, B/1503:6, Sarajevo, Aug. 21, 1914, Potiorek to Bolfras.

97. Jerabek, *Potiorek*, 134–135.

98. Ibid., 136.

99. KA, AOK (1914/15) EVB 3510, "Die österreichisch-ungarische Kanaille," Aug. 27, 1914; Jerabek, *Potiorek*, 131.

100. KA, NFA 2115, 36 ID, Brcko, Aug. 31, 1914, 5 Armee Oberkommando to VIII and XIII Corps.

101. HHSA, PA I, 819, Sofia, Aug. 21, 1914, Tarnowski to Berchtold; Jenikoj, Aug. 22, 1914, Pallavicini to Berchtold; Sinaie, Aug. 23, 1914, Czernin to Berchtold; PA I, 845, Naples, Sept. 1, 1914, Egon Pflügl to Berchtold; Rome, Sept. 8, 1914, Karl Macchio to Berchtold; Milan, Sept. 30, 1914, Györgey to Berchtold.

102. HHSA, PA I, 819, "Communiqué vom 22. Aug. 1914."

103. KA, B/1503:6, Vienna, Aug. 25–26, 1914, Bolfras to Potiorek.

CHAPTER 7: KRÁSNIK

1. Haus-, Hof- und Staatsarchiv, Vienna (HHSA), Politisches Archiv (PA) I, 837, Munich, Aug. 14, 1914, Vélics to Berchtold.

2. Hew Strachan, *The First World War*, vol. 1, *To Arms* (Oxford: Oxford University Press, 2001), 290.

3. R. G. D. Laffan, *The Serbs* (New York: Dorset Press, 1989 [1917]), 195–196.

4. HHSA, PA I, 842, Berlin, Aug. 25, 1914, Prince Gottfried Hohenlohe to Berchtold.

5. Ibid.; Holger H. Herwig, *The First World War: Germany and Austria-Hungary 1914–1918* (London: Edw. Arnold, 1997), 92–93.

6. Österreichischen Bundesministerium für Heereswesen und vom Kriegsarchiv, *Österreich-Ungarns Letzter Krieg 1914–18*, ed. Edmund Glaise von Horstenau (Vienna: Verlag Militätwissenschaftlichen Mitteilungen, 1931–1938), 1:12.

7. Manfried Rauchensteiner, *Der Tod des Doppeladlers: Österreich-Ungarn und der Erste Weltkrieg* (Graz: Verlag Styria, 1993), 140–144.

8. HHSA, PA I 842, Munich, Sept. 8, 1914, Vélics to Berchtold.

9. *Österreich-Ungarns Letzter Krieg*, 1:176; C. R. M. F. Cruttwell, *A History of the Great War 1914–1918* (Chicago: Academy, 2007 [1934]), 52.

10. Gerard Silberstein, *The Troubled Alliance: German and Austrian Relations, 1914–17* (Lexington: University Press of Kentucky, 1970), 278.

11. Ward Rutherford, *The Tsar's Army 1914–1917*, 2nd ed. (Cambridge: Ian Faulkner, 1992), 24; Herwig, *First World War*, 89–90; Rauchensteiner, *Der Tod*, 135–136, 146.

12. Franz Conrad von Hötzendorf, *Mein Anfang* (Berlin: Verlag für Kulturpolitik, 1925), 9–18.

13. Otto Laserz, "Die Feuertaufe von einem Kaiserschützen, der sie August 1914 miterlebte," unpublished manuscript, Kriegsarchiv, Vienna (KA), Handbibliothek.

14. Ibid.

15. KA, Neue Feld Akten (NFA) 1787, 31 ID, Sambor, Sept. 4, 1914, FML Eh. Joseph: "Shooting at planes, whether our own or the enemy's, is strictly forbidden."

16. KA, NFA 909, Aug. 1914, "Instruktion für das Benehmen der Kommandos und Truppengegen über Luftfahrzeugen." Margin note in red: "Über haupt nicht schiessen!"

17. KA, NFA 1372, XI Korps Kdo Lemberg, Aug. 12, "Leistungsfähigkeit der Fliegerkomp."

18. Lawrence Sondhaus, *Franz Conrad von Hötzendorf: Architect of the Apocalypse* (Boston: Humanities Press, 2000),153.

19. Moritz Freiherr von Auffenberg-Komarów, *Aus Österreichs Höhe und Niedergang: Eine Lebensschilderung* (Munich: Drei Masken Verlag, 1921), 280–281.

20. Norman Stone, *The Eastern Front 1914–1917* (London: Penguin, 1998 [1975]), 80; Arthur Ruhl, *Antwerp to Gallipoli: A Year of the War on Many Fronts—and Behind Them* (New York: Scribner's, 1916), 283–284; *Österreich-Ungarns Letzter Krieg 1914–18*, 1:66, 168.

21. *Österreich-Ungarns Letzter Krieg 1914–18*, 1:168–169; Rutherford, *Tsar's Army*, 46.

22. General A. A. Broussilov, *Mémoires du General Broussilov: Guerre 1914–18* (Paris: Hachette, 1929), 51.

23. KA, NFA 1372, 11 Korps Kdo, Lemberg, Aug. 23, 1914, "Flieger Aufklärung."

24. Graydon Tunstall, *Planning for War Against Russia and Serbia: Austro-Hungarian and German Military Strategies 1871–1914* (New York: Columbia University Press, 1993), 228–234.

25. Sondhaus, *Franz Conrad von Hötzendorf*, 153.

26. Moritz Freiherr von Auffenberg-Komarów, *Aus Österreichs Höhe und Niedergang: Eine Lebensschilderung* (Munich: Drei Masken Verlag, 1921), 278, 283–284.

27. Alfred Knox, *With the Russian Army 1914–17* (London: Hutchinson, 1921), 1:97; Herwig, *First World War*, 90–91.

28. Auffenberg-Komarów, *Aus Österreichs*, 286, 288; Silberstein, *Troubled Alliance*, 253–256.

29. KA, B/3 (Dankl): 5/1, Tagebuch (1), Aug. 2, 1914; NFA 909, k.u.k. 4. Armeekommado, Aug. 11, 1914, Gdl Auffenberg; Auffenberg-Komarów, *Aus Österreichs*, 265.

30. KA, B/3:14, Vienna, Jan. 24, 1914, Conrad, Generalbesprechung 1914.

31. Stone, *Eastern Front*, 26; Nikolai N. Golovina, *The Russian Army in the World War* (New Haven: Yale University Press, 1931), 11–13.

32. Rutherford, *Tsar's Army*, 31, 34–35.

33. Ibid., 27–28, 47.

34. *Österreich-Ungarns Letzter Krieg 1914–18*, 1:175.

35. Knox, *With the Russian Army*, 1:50.

36. Cruttwell, *History of the Great War*, 50; Stone, *Eastern Front*, 94; Rutherford, *Tsar's Army*, 25–26.

37. Stone, *Eastern Front*, 82–83.

38. Rutherford, *Tsar's Army*, 53; *Österreich-Ungarns Letzter Krieg 1914–18*, 1:177.

39. *Österreich-Ungarns Letzter Krieg 1914–18*, 1:177.

40. Timothy C. Dowling, *The Brusilov Offensive* (Bloomington: Indiana University Press, 2008), 8; Rutherford, *Tsar's Army*, 23.

41. Knox, *With the Russian Army*, 1:97–98.

42. Stone, *Eastern Front*, 82, 84–85.

43. KA, NFA 1840, k.u.k. IR Nr. 4, Tarnawatka, Aug. 24, 1914, Maj. Nauheim, "Gefechtsbericht über das am 15. August nördlich Podlesina stattgefundene Gefecht"; Auffenberg-Komarów, *Aus Österreichs*, 271–272.

44. *Österreich-Ungarns Letzter Krieg 1914–18*, 1:166–167.

45. KA, B/3 (Dankl): 5/1, Tagebuch (1), Aug. 13, 1914.

46. Auffenberg-Komarów, *Aus Österreichs*, 288.

47. *Österreich-Ungarns Letzter Krieg 1914–18*, 1:168–171.

48. Kasper Blond, *Ein Unbekannter Krieg: Erlebnisse eines Arztes während des Weltkrieges* (Leipzig: Anzengruber-Verlag, 1931), 8–9.

49. KA, NFA 1836, Wislowa, Aug. 28, 1914, GM Peteani, "Tätigkeit der 1. KTD in der Zeit vom 15 Aug bis 27 Aug 1914."

50. KA, B/3 (Dankl): 5/1, Tagebuch (1), Aug. 23, 1914.

51. KA, NFA 909, Przemysl, Aug. 19, 1914, GdI Eh. Friedrich.

52. KA, NFA 1845/2, Gefechts-Berichte der k.u.k. Infanterie-Regimenter Nr. 80–83, Sibiu, Dec. 1930, GM Leopold Hofbauer, "Erinnerungen an meine Regimentskommando-Führung beim k.u.k. I.R. Nr. 83."

53. KA, B/3 (Dankl): 5/1, Tagebuch (1), Aug. 23, 1914.

54. KA, NFA 1866, k.u. 74 Inf. Brig. Kdo, GM Cvrcek, "Aus führlicher Gefechtsbericht über das Gefechtzw. Andrrzejow und Wierzchowiska der 74. LW Inf. Brig. am 24. Aug. 1914."

55. KA, B/3 (Dankl): 5/1, Tagebuch (1), Aug. 24, 1914.

56. KA, NFA 1845/1, Gefechts-Berichte der k.u.k. Infanterie-Regimenter Nr. 71–79, Aug. 31, 1914, Col. Boeri, "Gefechtsbericht über das Gefecht bei Polichna am 23.8.1914."

57. KA, NFA 1845/1, Gefechts-Berichte der k.u.k. Infanterie-Regimenter Nr. 71–79, Sept. 2, 1914, Col. Felzer, "Gefechtsbericht betreffend das Gefecht bei Polichna am 23.8.1914."

58. *Österreich-Ungarns Letzter Krieg 1914–18*, 1:182–183.

59. KA, NFA 1845/2, Gefechts-Berichte der k.u.k. Infanterie-Regimenter Nr. 80–83, Sibiu, Dec. 1930, GM Leopold Hofbauer, "Erinnerungen an meine Regimentskommando-Führung beim k.u.k. I.R. Nr. 83."

60. Herwig, *First World War*, 91; Gunther E. Rothenberg, *The Army of Francis Joseph* (West Lafayette, IN: Purdue University Press, 1976), 107–108; KA, NFA 2115, 36 ID, Armeeoberkommando (AOK) Etappenoberkommando, Przemysl, Aug. 23, 1914, GM Kanik, "Grosser Verbrauch von Pneumatics."

61. KA, NFA 1845/2, Gefechts-Berichte der k.u.k. Infanterie-Regimenter Nr. 80–83, Sibiu, Dec. 1930, GM Leopold Hofbauer, "Erinnerungen an meine Regimentskommando-Führung beim k.u.k. I.R. Nr. 83."

62. KA, B/3 (Dankl): 5/1, Tagebuch (1), Aug. 24, 1914.

63. KA, Gefechtsberichte (GB) 86, Generalstab Nr. 8,069, "Kriegserfahrungen"; Stone, *Eastern Front*, 86.

CHAPTER 8: KOMARÓW

1. Kriegsarchiv, Vienna (KA), Neue Feld Akten (NFA) 1877, Sept. 28, 1914, GdI Eh. Friedrich, "Erfahrungen aus den bisherigen Kämpfen."

2. KA, NFA 1868, GM Stipek, Bozen, Oct. 7, 1914, "Gefechtsbericht u. Belohnungsanträge über das Gefecht am 28. Aug. 1914."

3. KA, NFA 1868, Johann Komaromi, "Damals bei Budynin."

4. KA, Gefechtsberichte (GB) 86, Generalstab Nr. 8069, "Kriegserfahrungen, Taktik der Feinde," n.d.; Timothy C. Dowling, *The Brusilov Offensive* (Bloomington:

Indiana University Press, 2008), 7; Nikolai N. Golovine, *The Russian Army in the World War* (New Haven, CT: Yale University Press, 1931), 132.

5. Golovine, *Russian Army*, 126; Dowling, *Brusilov Offensive*, 6; Ward Rutherford, *The Tsar's Army 1914–1917*, 2nd ed. (Cambridge: Ian Faulkner, 1992), 24.

6. KA, NFA 1878, k.u.k. 2 Korps Kdo, Jan. 21, 1915, "Kriegserfahrung."

7. KA, NFA 1845/2, Gefechts-Berichte der k.u.k. Infanterie-Regimenter Nr. 80–83, Sibiu, Dec. 1930, GM Leopold Hofbauer, "Erinnerungen an meine Regimentskommando-Führung beim k.u.k. I.R. Nr. 83"; NFA 909, Aug. 17, 1914, "Einfetten der Wasserjacke vorgeschrieben."

8. KA, NFA 1845/2, Gefechts-Berichte der k.u.k. Infanterie-Regimenter Nr. 80–83, Sibiu, Dec. 1930, GM Leopold Hofbauer, "Erinnerungen an meine Regimentskommando-Führung beim k.u.k. I.R. Nr. 83."

9. KA, B/1438:18–28 (Paic), Beilage zum Aufmarschbefehl: "Russland—Charakteristik einiger Generale."

10. Österreichischen Bundesministerium für Heereswesen und vom Kriegsarchiv, *Österreich-Ungarns Letzter Krieg 1914–18* (Vienna: Verlag der militärwissenschaftlichen Mitteilungen, 1930–1938), 1:184.

11. KA, B/3:14 (Dankl), Karl Paumgartten, "Das Lied vom General Dankl."

12. *Österreich-Ungarns Letzter Krieg 1914–18*, 1:12–13.

13. Dennis E. Showalter, *Tannenberg: Clash of Empires* (North Haven, CT: Archon, 1991), 318–326; Arthur Ruhl, *Antwerp to Gallipoli: A Year of the War on Many Fronts—and Behind Them* (New York: Scribner's, 1916), 106–107.

14. KA, NFA 1807, 15 ID, Gefechtsberichte, k.u.k. 15 ITD Kdo, "Gefecht bei Pukarczow am 27. U. 28. Aug. 1914."

15. KA, NFA 1845/2, Gefechts-Berichte der k.u.k. Infanterie-Regimenter Nr. 80–83 Sibiu, Dec. 1930, GM Leopold Hofbauer, "Erinnerungen an meine Regimentskommando-Führung beim k.u.k. I.R. Nr. 83."

16. FML Rudolf Pfeffer, *Zum 10. Jahrestage der Schlachten von Zlocsow und Przemyslany, 26–30 August 1914* (Vienna: Selbstverlag, 1924), 42; *Österreich-Ungarns Letzter Krieg 1914–18*, 1:186.

17. Pfeffer, *Zum 10. Jahrestage*, 43.

18. *Österreich-Ungarns Letzter Krieg 1914–18*, vol. 1, 190; Moritz Freiherr von Auffenberg-Komarów, *Aus Österreichs Höhe und Niedergang: Eine Lebensschilderung* (Munich: Drei Masken Verlag, 1921), 293.

19. Josef Redlich, *Schicksalsjahre Österreichs 1908–19: Das politische Tagebuch Josef Redlichs* (Graz: Verlag Böhlau, 1953), 1:254, 259.

20. Auffenberg-Komarów, *Aus Österreichs*, 295–296.

21. KA, NFA 1840, k.u.k. IR Nr 5, Innsbruck, May 10, 1915, Maj. Koch, "Gefechtsbericht: Ereignisse vom 26–29 August 1914."

22. KA, NFA 1850, k.u.k. bh IR Nr. 1, Vienna, Oct. 30, 1914, "Gefechtsbericht," Capt. Nikolaus von Ribicey; Vienna, Oct. 25, 1914, Oberlt. Anton Viditz, "Gehorsamste Bitte."

23. KA, NFA 1850, Vienna, Dec. 6, 1914, Capt. Bruno Brelic, "Gefechtsbericht."

24. KA, Militärkanzlei Seiner Majestät (MKSM), MKSM-SR 95, Aug. 30, 1914, AOK to MKSM.

25. KA, NFA 1807, 15 ID, Gefechtsberichte, k.u.k. 15 ITD Kdo, "Gefecht bei Pukarczow am 27 und 28. Aug. 1914."

26. Ibid.; KA, NFA 909, 6. Korpskommando, Stubienko, Aug. 19, 1914, "Disposition"; NFA 909, Oleszyce, Aug. 28, 1914, GM Krauss.

27. Auffenberg-Komarów, *Aus Österreichs*, 296–297.

28. KA, NFA 1878, "Unzulänglichkeit unserer Friedenskader des Heeres."

29. KA, B/1438:29–37 (Paic), GM Paic, "Auszug aus dem Tagebuche des XIV. Korpskommandos für die Zeit vom 26. August bis 14. September 1914"; Österreich-Ungarns Letzter Krieg 1914–18, 1:199.

30. KA, B/677:11–22, June 1918, "Den Verlauf der Schlacht von Komarów."

31. Auffenberg-Komarów, Aus Österreichs, 295–297.

32. KA, MKSM-SR 95, Aug. 30, 1914, AOK to MKSM; Österreich-Ungarns Letzter Krieg 1914–18, 1:200.

33. KA, NFA 1868, Johann Komaromi, "Damals bei Budynin."

34. Auffenberg-Komarów, Aus Österreichs, 298.

35. Winston S. Churchill, The World Crisis: The Eastern Front (London: Thornton Butterworth, 1931), 29.

36. KA, B/677:11–22, June 1918, "Den Verlauf der Schlacht von Komarów"; Auffenberg-Komarów, Aus Österreichs, 301.

37. KA, NFA 1807, 15 ID, Gefechtsberichte, k.u.k. 15 ITD Kdo, "Gefecht bei Pukarczow am 27. und 28. Aug. 1914."

38. Churchill, World Crisis, 161.

39. C. R. M. F. Cruttwell, A History of the Great War 1914–1918 (Chicago: Academy, 2007 [1934]), 40; Norman Stone, The Eastern Front 1914–1917 (London: Penguin, 1998 [1975]), 85–86; Rutherford, Tsar's Army, 25–26.

40. KA, B/677:11–22, June 1918, "Den Verlauf der Schlacht von Komarów."

41. Rudolf Jerabek, "Die Brussilowoffensive 1916: Ein Wendepunkt der Koalitionskriegführung der Mittelmächte," dissertation, Vienna, 1982, 13.

42. KA, NFA 1868, Lt. Karl Popper, "Das Feldjaegerbattalion Nr. 6 im Weltkrieg 1914."

43. KA, NFA 1845/2, Gefechts-Berichte der k.u.k. Infanterie-Regimenter Nr. 80–83 Sibiu, Dec. 1930, GM Leopold Hofbauer, "Erinnerungen an meine Regimentskommando-Führung beim k.u.k. I.R. Nr. 83."

44. KA, NFA 909, Vienna, Aug. 25, 1914, FZM Krobatin, "Mitteilungen über Kriegsereignisse."

45. Stone, Eastern Front, 88; Auffenberg-Komarów, Aus Österreichs, 299.

46. KA, NFA 1372, 3. Armeekdo, Sambor, Aug. 20, 1914, GdK Brudermann, to corps, "Festigung der Disziplin"; Lemberg, Aug. 22, 1914, GdK Brudermann to corps, "Verbreitung unwahrer Gerüchte."

47. KA, NFA 1842, Przemysl, Aug. 30, 1914, Op. 1962, GdI Conrad.

48. KA, B/1438:18-28 (Paic), Beilage zum Aufmarschbefehl: "Russland—Charakteristik einiger Generale."

49. KA, B/677:11-22 (Auffenberg), n.d., Auffenberg, "Verlauf der Schlacht von Komarów"; Auffenberg, 314–316; Golovine, Russian Army, 143.

50. KA, B/677:11-22, June 1918, "Den Verlauf der Schlacht von Komarów."

51. KA, B/677:11-22 (Auffenberg), n.d., Auffenberg, untitled draft, Vienna, Dec. 1916, "Skizze aus den letzten drei Jahren meiner 43-jährigen Dienstzeit."

CHAPTER 9: LEMBERG AND RAWA-RUSKA

1. Österreichischen Bundesministerium für Heereswesen und vom Kriegsarchiv, Österreich-Ungarns Letzter Krieg 1914–18 (Vienna: Verlag Militätwissenschaftlichen Mitteilungen, 1931–1938), 1:187.

2. Otto Laserz, "Die Feuertaufe von einem Kaiserschützen, der sie August 1914 miterlebte," unpublished manuscript, Kriegsarchiv (KA) Handbibliothek, n.d.

3. KA, Neue Feld Akten (NFA) 1803, 6. ITD, "Gefechtsbericht über die Gefechte bei Gologory und Turkocin in der Zeit vom 26 bis 31. Aug. 1914."

4. KA, NFA 1795, Lemberg, Aug. 29, 1914, GdK Kolossváry, "Bericht über das Gefecht am 26 und 27. Aug. 1914."

5. KA, NFA 1367, k.u.k. 3 Armeekommando, Lemberg, Aug. 26, 1914, GdK Brudermann to corps and division commands.

6. KA, NFA 1795, 11 Korps Kdo, Lemberg, Aug. 29, 1914, GdK Kolossváry, "Bericht über das Gefecht am 26 und 27. Aug. 1914."

7. KA, NFA 1372, k.k. österreichische Staatsbahndirektion, Lemberg, Aug. 28, 1914.

8. KA, NFA 1794, 3 Korpskdo, "Gefechtsbericht über die Gefechte vom 26 bis 31 Aug. 1914."

9. Ibid.; NFA 529, 9 ID, AOK Op. Nr. 1996, Sept. 16, 1914; KA, NFA 1842, Sept. 7, 1914, AOK to 32 ID.

10. KA, NFA 1794, 3 Korpskdo, "Gefechtsbericht über die Gefechte vom 26 bis 31 Aug. 1914," Fortsetzung des Angriffes.

11. KA, NFA 1367, Lemberg, Aug. 27, 1914, GdK Brudermann to corps and division commanders; Rudolf Pfeffer, *Zum 10. Jahrestage der Schlachten von Zlocsow und Przemyslany, 26–30 August 1914* (Vienna: Selbstverlag, 1924), 47–49.

12. KA, NFA 1803, 6 ITDskdo, "Gefechtsbericht über die Gefechte bei Gologory und Turkocin in der Zeit vom 26 bis 31. Aug. 1914."

13. KA, NFA 1794, 3. Korpskdo, "Gefechtsbericht über die Gefechte vom 26 bis 31 Aug. 1914."

14. Pfeffer, *Zum 10. Jahrestage*, 64; Franz Conrad von Conrad Hötzendorf, *Aus Meiner Dienstzeit 1906–1918* (Vienna: Rikola, 1921–23), 4:540–542.

15. Alfred Krauss, *Die Ursachen unserer Niederlage: Erinnerungen und Urteile aus den Weltkrieg*, 3rd ed. (Munich: 1923), 99–101.

16. KA, NFA 1795, Lemberg, Aug. 29, 1914, GdK Kolossváry, "Bericht über das Gefecht am 26 und 27. Aug. 1914."

17. KA, NFA 1795, Vienna, Nov. 14, 1914, GdI Meixner, "Die Tätigkeit des VII Korps."

18. Pfeffer, *Zum 10. Jahrestage*, 70, 89.

19. Ibid., 50.

20. General A. A. Broussilov, *Mémoires du General Broussilov: Guerre 1914–18* (Paris: Hachette, 1929), 55.

21. KA, NFA 1367, Lemberg, Aug. 30, 1914, GdK Brudermann to corps and division commanders.

22. KA, NFA 1842, Sept. 7, 1914, k.u.k. AOK to 32 ID, "Kampfweise der Russen."

23. KA, NFA 1877, Sept. 28, 1914, GdI Eh. Friedrich, "Erfahrungen aus den bisherigen Kämpfen."

24. KA, NFA 1845/2, Gefechts-Berichte der k.u.k. Infanterie-Regimenter Nr. 80–83, Sibiu, Dec. 1930, GM Leopold Hofbauer, "Erinnerungen an meine Regimentskommando-Führung beim k.u.k. I.R. Nr. 83."

25. KA, NFA 911, 4. Armeekommando, Dec. 14, 1914, GdI Eh. Joseph Ferdinand, "Protokoll aufgenommen am 11. Nov. 1914, Gefangennahme und Flucht des Zugsführers Josef Erlsbacher."

26. KA, NFA 1367, 3. Armee Kdo, Grodek, Aug. 31, 1914, GdK Brudermann to corps commanders; Pfeffer, *Zum 10. Jahrestage*, 92.

27. Broussilov, *Mémoires*, 56.

28. KA, NFA 1372, 3. Armeekdo, Sept. 4, 1914, GdK Brudermann to corps.

29. Pfeffer, *Zum 10. Jahrestage*, 76, 95.

30. Stanley Washburn, *On the Russian Front in World War I: Memoirs of an American War Correspondent* (New York: Robert Speller, 1982), 48–49.

31. Pfeffer, *Zum 10. Jahrestage*, 58–9; Hötzendorf, *Aus Meiner Dienstzeit*, 4:533.

32. Moritz Freiherr von Auffenberg-Komarów, *Aus Österreichs Höhe und Niedergang: Eine Lebensschilderung* (Munich: Drei Masken Verlag, 1921), 272, 304–305.

33. Holger H. Herwig, *The First World War: Germany and Austria-Hungary 1914–1918* (London: Edw. Arnold, 1997), 91; General Josef von Stürgkh, *Im Deutschen Grossen Hauptquartier* (Leipzig: Paul List, 1921), 40.

34. Stürgkh, *Im Deutschen Grossen Hauptquartier*, 40–41.

35. Gunther E. Rothenberg, *The Army of Francis Joseph* (West Lafayette, IN: Purdue University Press, 1976), 177; Stanley Washburn, *Field Notes from the Russian Front* (London: Andrew Melrose, 1915), 61.

36. KA, Militärkanzlei Franz Ferdinand (MKFF) 202, "Die Minimalkriegsfälle Winter 1910/11": "Zu viel und zu wenig! Es muss nicht immer wie 1866 sein! Dass man gleich den ganzen Aufmarsch auf eine unglückliche Politik basirt, das ist zu dumm!"

37. Fedor Stepun, *Wie war es möglich: Briefe eines russischen Offiziers* (Munich: Carl Hanser Verlag, 1929), 18–19.

38. KA, Militärkanzlei Seiner Majestät (MKSM-SR) 95, Lemberg, Sept. 6, 1914, Statthalter Galizien to Stürkgh. NFA 909, 4. Armeekommando, "Nationalitäten Galiziens"; NFA 1877, Sept. 28, 1914, GdI Eh. Friedrich, "Erfahrungen aus den bisherigen Kämpfen."

39. National Archives and Records Administration, Washington, DC (NARA), M 865, roll 22, Vienna, Sept. 10, 1924, Carol Foster, "The Culture of Austria."

40. Norman Stone, *The Eastern Front 1914–1917* (London: Penguin, 1998 [1975]), 89; Karl Kraus, ed. *Die Fackel* (Munich: Kösel-Verlag, 1968–1976), 6:3, "Wenn die Trompete statt der Kanone los ging, er könnte noch immer der tüchtigste Feldherr sein" (*Fackel* 366, Jan. 1913).

41. KA, NFA 909, k.u.k. 6. Korpskommando, Sept. 3, 1914, GdI Boroevic, "Alle drei Divisione."

42. KA, NFA 1367, 3. Armeekdo, Mosciska, Sept. 3, 1914, GdK Brudermann to corps. Auffenberg-Komarów, *Aus Österreichs*, 339.

43. KA, NFA 1868, Lt. Karl Popper, "Das Feldjägerbattalion Nr. 6 im Weltkrieg 1914."

44. KA, B/1438:29–37 (Paic), GM Paic, "Auszug aus dem Tagebuche des XIV. Korpskommandos für die Zeit vom 26. August bis 14. September 1914."

45. KA, B/1438:29–37 (Paic), July 31, 1929, "Die Armeegruppe Erzherzog Joseph Ferdinand während der Schlacht bei Rawa-Ruska-Lemberg."

46. Auffenberg-Komarów, *Aus Österreichs*, 307.

47. KA, B/677:11–22 (Auffenberg), Vienna, December 1916, "Skizze aus den letzten drei Jahren meiner 43 jährigen Dienstzeit"; NFA 909, 4. Armeekommando, Zakliczyn, Sept. 25, 1914, Armeebefehl. Auffenberg-Komarów, *Aus Österreichs*, 313.

48. KA, B/1438:29–37 (Paic), July 31, 1929, "Die Armeegruppe Erzherzog Joseph Ferdinand während der Schlacht bei Rawa-Ruska-Lemberg."

49. KA, NFA 1842, 32 ID, k.u.k. 2. Armee-Kdo, Dobromil, Sept. 13, 1914, GdK Böhm-Ermolli.

50. Auffenberg-Komarów, *Aus Österreichs*, 338.

51. KA, MKSM-SR 95, Tagesberichte AOK 1914.

52. KA, NFA 1367, 3. Armee Kdo, Mosciska, Sept. 4, 1914, GdK Brudermann to corps.

53. Service Historique de l'Armée de Terre, Vincennes (SHAT), EMA, 7N 1128, Vienna, Oct. 14, 1897, Cdt. Berckheim, "Notes sur le haut commandement en Autriche."

54. KA, B/96:3a (Brudermann), "Brief Sr. Kais. Hoheit des AOK GdI Eh. Friedrich an Se. Majestät Kaiser Franz Josef I."

55. Auffenberg-Komarów, *Aus Österreichs*, 344.

56. KA, MKSM-SR 95, Sept. 6, 1914, AOK to MKSM; Herwig, *First World War*, 94.

57. KA, NFA 1367, 3. Armeekdo, Oct. 2, 1914, "Folgende Beobachtungen und Erfahrungen aus der Front in den bisherigen Kämpfen."

58. KA, Gefechtsberichte (GB) 86, Generalstab Nr. 8069, "Kriegserfahrungen, Taktik der Feinde," n.d.

59. KA, NFA 1845/2, Gefechts-Berichte der k.u.k. Infanterie-Regimenter Nr. 80–83 Sibiu, Dec. 1930, GM Leopold Hofbauer, "Erinnerungen an meine Regimentskommando-Führung beim k.u.k. I.R. Nr. 83."

60. KA, NFA 1367, 3 Armee Kdo, Mosciska, Sept. 9, 1914, GdI Boroevic to corps.

61. Josef Redlich, *Schicksalsjahre Österreichs 1908–19: Das politische Tagebuch Josef Redlichs* (Graz: Verlag Böhlau, 1953), 1:270, Sept. 9, 1914.

62. Lawrence Sondhaus, *Franz Conrad von Hötzendorf: Architect of the Apocalypse* (Boston: Humanities Press, 2000), 159.

63. KA, NFA 1838, 15 Drag. Regt., Sept. 15, 1914, "Gefechtsbericht über das Gefecht am 8/9 bei M.H. Czana östl. Rzyczki;" SHAT, AAT, EMA 7N 848, 2ème Bureau, Section Russe, "Die Stärkeverhältnisse in den bedeutendsten Schlachten des Weltkrieges: Deutschland und Österreich-Ungarn."

64. KA, B/1438 (Paic): 29–37, GM Josef von Paic, "Die Kämpfe des 2. Regiments der Tiroler Kaiserjäger am 6. u. 7. September 1914." Most of this exposé has been destroyed or lost—only a few suggestive pages remain. Auffenberg-Komarów, *Aus Österreichs*, 339–341.

65. KA, NFA 1868, March 2, 1916, Maj. Beck, "Ereignisse am 6. u. 7. Sept. 1914"; Plesna, Sept. 28, 1914, "Bericht über das Gefecht bei Michalovko am 7. Sept. 1914."

66. KA, NFA 1868, Lt. Karl Popper, "Das Feldjaegerbattalion Nr. 6 im Weltkrieg 1914."

67. KA, B/1438:29–37 (Paic), GM Paic, "Auszug aus dem Tagebuche des XIV. Korpskommandos für die Zeit vom 26. August bis 14. September 1914."

68. KA, Armeeoberkommando (AOK) 1914/15, Evidenzbureau (EVB) 3510, Cracow, Dec. 17, 1914.

69. KA, NFA 911, 4. Armeekommando, Dec. 14, 1914, GdI Eh. Joseph Ferdinand, "Protokoll aufgenommen am 11. Nov. 1914, Gefangennahme und Flucht des Zugsführers Josef Erlsbacher"; Sondhaus, *Franz Conrad von Hötzendorf*, 75–76.

70. KA, NFA 1372, 3. Armeekdo, Moswiska, Sept. 6, 1914, GdK Brudermann to corps.

71. Broussilov, *Mémoires*, 58.

72. KA, NFA 909, k.u.k. AOK, Sept. 7, 1914, "Kampfweise der Russen."

73. KA, NFA 1813, 30 ITD, Gorlice, Oct. 3, 1914, FML Kaiser, "Gefechtsbericht über die Zeit vom 6–12 Sept. 1914."

74. KA, B/1438:29–37 (Paic), GM Paic, "Auszug aus dem Tagebuche des XIV. Korpskommandos für die Zeit vom 26. August bis 14. September 1914."

75. Sondhaus, *Franz Conrad von Hötzendorf*, 155.

76. Auffenberg-Komarów, *Aus Österreichs*, 358.

77. Ibid., 359.

78. KA, B/1438:29–37 (Paic), GM Paic, "Auszug aus dem Tagebuche des XIV. Korpskommandos für die Zeit vom 26. August bis 14. September 1914."

79. Auffenberg-Komarów, *Aus Österreichs*, 363.

80. Washburn, *On the Russian Front*, 51.

81. Arthur Ruhl, *Antwerp to Gallipoli: A Year of the War on Many Fronts—and Behind Them* (New York: Scribner's, 1916), 231; Washburn, *On the Russian Front*, 51.

82. KA, NFA 1367, 3. Armee Kdo, Mosciska, Sept. 11, 1914, GdI Boroevic to corps.

83. KA, NFA 1367, Przemysl, Sept. 13, 1914, Przemysl, GdI Boroevic to corps; Auffenberg-Komarów, *Aus Österreichs,* 364.

84. Timothy C. Dowling, *The Brusilov Offensive* (Bloomington: Indiana University Press, 2008), 14–16.

85. KA, B/1438:18–28 (Paic), "Der Fall Auffenberg."

86. Haus-, Hof- und Staatsarchiv, Vienna (HHSA), Politisches Archiv (PA) I, 842, Berlin, Aug. 25, 1914, Prince Gottfried Hohenlohe to Berchtold; Herwig, *First World War,* 92–93.

87. HHSA, PA I, 842, Berlin, Aug. 25, 1914, Hohenlohe to Berchtold, Sept. 7, 1914.

88. KA, NFA 909, 4. Armeekommando, Sept. 15, 1914, "Orientierung von Offizieren und Mannschaft über Aufgabe."

89. Washburn, *Field Notes,* 65.

90. KA, NFA 910, AOK, Oct. 15, 1914, GdI Eh Friedrich, "Versprengte—Massnahmen gegen dieselben"; NFA 1367, 3. Armeekdo, Przemysl, Sept. 15, 1914, GM Boog to corps.

91. KA, NFA 1367, 3. Armeekdo, Przemysl, Sept. 15, 1914, GM Boog to corps.

92. Auffenberg-Komarów, *Aus Österreichs,* 369.

93. KA, NFA 1367, 3. Armeekdo, Krosno, Sept. 20 and 21, 1914, GdI Boroevic to corps.

94. Auffenberg-Komarów, *Aus Österreichs,* 370.

95. Ibid., 374.

96. C. R. M. F. Cruttwell, *A History of the Great War 1914–1918* (Chicago: Academy, 2007 [1934]), 52; KA, MKFF 189, "Ein Bankerott."

97. Auffenberg-Komarów, *Aus Österreichs,* 377–378.

98. Ibid., 366–367.

99. KA, B/677:11–22, Berlin, n.d., Freiherr von Schönthan zu Pernwaldt, "Erinnerungen an den Sieger von 'Komarow'"; Auffenberg-Komarów, *Aus Österreichs,* 380, 389.

100. KA, NFA 910, 4. Armee Kdo, Zakliczyn, Oct. 2, 1914, GdI Auffenberg, "Offiziere und Soldaten der 4. Armee!"

101. I. S. Bloch, *The Future of War* (Boston: Ginn, 1897), 45.

102. KA, NFA 1367, 3. Armeekdo, Oct. 2, 1914, "Folgende Beobachtungen und Erfahrungen aus der Front in den bisherigen Kämpfen."

103. KA, B/677:11–22, Berlin, n.d., "Erinnerungen an den Sieger von 'Komarów'"; Winston S. Churchill, *The World Crisis: The Eastern Front* (London: Thornton Butterworth, 1931), 220.

104. Herwig, *First World War,* 75, 95.

105. KA, NFA 909, k.u.k. Kriegsministerium, Kriegsfürsorgeamt, Vienna, Sept. 20, 1914, FML Löbl, "Aufruf."

106. Herwig, *First World War,* 90.

107. KA, NFA 1367, 3. Armeekdo, Oct. 2, 1914, GdI Boroevic to corps. B/677:11–22, Berlin, n.d., "Erinnerungen an den Sieger von 'Komarów.'"

108. Washburn, 59; Ruhl, *Antwerp to Gallipoli,* 231.

109. KA, MKSM-SR 95, Sept. 29, 1914, AOK to MKSM.

CHAPTER 10: DEATH ON THE DRINA

1. Rudolf Jerabek, *Potiorek* (Graz: Verlag Styria, 1991), 138–139, 151, 160–161.

2. Kriegsarchiv, Vienna (KA), B/1503:7, FZM Potiorek to Armeeoberkommando (AOK) and Militärkanzlei Seiner Majestät (MKSM), "Resüme der serbischen Truppenverteilung 31. August."

3. KA, B/1503:7, Sept. 2, 1914, Conrad to Potiorek; Jerabek, *Potiorek,* 136, 142.

4. KA, B/1503:6, Vienna, Aug. 14, 22, and 25, 1914 and B/1503:7, Vienna, Aug. 29, 1914, Bolfras to Potiorek; Jerabek, *Potiorek*, 133–134.

5. Jerabek, *Potiorek,* 137.

6. KA, AOK 1914, Evidenzbureau (EVB) 3506, k.u.k. 6 Armee-Kommando, Sarajevo, Aug. 25 and 26 and Sept. 1 and 3, 1914, Potiorek to MKSM; NFA 2115, 416/28, 5 Armee, Sept. 6, 1914, "Resumé über feindliche Lage"; James M. B. Lyon, "'A Peasant Mob': The Serbian Army on the Eve of the Great War," *Journal of Military History* 61 (July 1997): 492.

7. KA, Neue Feld Akten (NFA) 2115, 13. Korps-Kommando, Bijelina, Sept. 3, 1914, GdI Rhemen.

8. KA, NFA 2115, 36 ID, Bijelina, Sept. 3, 1914, GdI Rhemen, "Bermerkungen."

9. KA, NFA 475, 41 Sch. Brig., Seliste, Sept. 9, 1914, GdK Giesl.

10. KA, NFA 475, 41 Sch. Br., Jarak, Sept. 24, 1914, FML Krauss to GM Panesch. Op. Nr. 195/40, FML Krauss, "Direktiven für die nächsten Kämpfe."

11. KA, NFA 475, 41 Sch. Br., Jarak, Sept. 21, 1914, FML Krauss.

12. KA, MKSM-SR 95, Sarajevo, Sept. 7, 1914, Präsidialbureau Bosnien-Herzegovina to Potiorek.

13. Jerabek, *Potiorek*, 140–142; KA, B/1503:6, Op. Nr. 453, Sarajevo, Aug. 29, 1914, "Fliegermeldung"; KA, B/1503:7, Doboj, Sept. 3, 1914, Potiorek to Bolfras; Sept. 4, 1914, AOK to Potiorek.

14. Felix Prinz zu Schwarzenberg, *Briefe aus dem Felde 1914–18* (Vienna: Schwarzenbergisches Administration, 1953), 23.

15. KA, NFA 528, 9 ID, "Tagebuch II, 21. Aug-8-Okt. 1914"; GB 30, k.u.k. 17. Inf-Brig-Kdo, Vehino selo, Sept. 11, 1914, GM Daniel, "Gefechtsbericht über die Kämpfe an der Drina am 8. bis 9. Sept. 1914."

16. KA, NFA 2115, 5. Armee-Kommando, Brcko, Aug. 31, 1914, Frank to 36 ITD.

17. KA, Gefechtsberichte (GB) 24, 36 ITD, "Gefechtsbericht über Drinaforzierung von Megjasi am 8. Sept. 1914"; NFA 2115, 36 ID, I.R. Nr. 79, Col. Schöbl, "Gefechtsbericht für den 8. Sept. 1914"; GB 1, Jamena, Sept. 13, 1914, GdI Frank, "Gefechtsbericht Raca und Megjasi."

18. KA, NFA 475, 41 Sch. Brig., Sept. 10, 1914, Oblt. Sappe, "Gefechtsbericht für den 8–9 Sept. 1914"; 8 Korps-Kommando, Op. Nr. 511, Seliste, Sept. 9, 1914, GdK Giesl.

19. KA, NFA 475, 41 Sch. Br., Op. Nr. 195/40, Sept. 1914, FML Krauss, "Direktiven für die nächsten Kämpfe"; NFA 191, 18 Inf-Brig., k.u.k. 18 Inf-Brig-Kdo, Serb. Raca, Sept. 23, 1914.

20. KA, NFA 529, 9 ID, Raca, Oct. 2, 1914.

21. KA, NFA 529, 9 ID, Oct. 10, 1914, GM Daniel.

22. KA, GB 10, k.u.k. 4 Gebirgsbrigadekommando, "Gefechtsbericht 8. und 9. Sept. 1914."

23. Jerabek, *Potiorek*, 150–151.

24. KA, NFA 529, 9 I.D., 8 Korps-Kdo, Seliste, Sept. 4, 1914 and Grk Sept. 17, 1914, GdK Giesl.

25. KA, GB 10, k.u.k. 4 Gebirgsbrigade-Kdo, Debelsosaje, Sept. 26, 1914, "Gefechtsbericht über die Gefechte vom 13–16 Sept. 1914."

26. KA, NFA 170, 17 Brig., k.u.k. 8 Korps-Kdo, Grk, Sept. 18, 1914.

27. KA, GB 10, "Gefechtsbericht Landwehr 37, 8. September"; GB 42, 1 Geb. Brig., Jagodna, Sept. 25, 1914, "Gefechts-Berichte."

28. KA, GB 24, 36 ITD, "Gefechtsbericht über Drinaforzierung von Megjasi am 8. Sept. 1914"; Manfried Rauchensteiner, *Der Tod des Doppeladlers: Österreich-Ungarn und der Erste Weltkrieg* (Graz: Verlag Styria, 1993), 133.

29. Schwarzenberg, *Briefe aus dem Felde*, 19.

30. KA, NFA 2115, 36 ID, Megjasi, Sept. 12, 1914, Capt. Bubin, "Wahrnehmungen bei eigenen Truppen."

31. KA, NFA 475, 41 Sch. Brig., Jarak, Sept. 19 and 24, 1914, FML Krauss, "Abfertigung."

32. Arthur Ruhl, *Antwerp to Gallipoli: A Year of the War on Many Fronts—and Behind Them* (New York: Scribner's, 1916), 251.

33. KA, NFA 475, 41 Sch. Brig., Jarak, Sept. 29, 1914, FML Krauss, "Abfertigung."

34. KA, NFA 2115, 36 ITD-Kommando, "Nachrichten über den Feind."

35. Groszen Generalstab, Serbien, *Der Grosze Krieg Serbiens zur Befreiung und Vereinigung der Serben, Kroaten und Slovenen* (Belgrade: Buchdruckerei des Ministeriums für Krieg und Marine, 1924–1926), 2:261.

36. Haus-, Hof- und Staatsarchiv, Vienna (HHSA), Politisches Archiv (PA) I, 905, Budapest, Sept. 15, 1914, Tisza to Berchtold *per Telefon.*

37. KA, NFA 475, 5 Armee Etappenkommando, Sept. 9, 1914, Col. Ottokar Landwehr; NFA 1787, 2 A.K, Sambor, Sept. 6, 1914, "Beschiessen von Automobilen."

38. KA, NFA 475, 41 Sch. Brig., Sept. 21, 1914, FML Krauss, "Beitrag zur Abfertigung"; NFA 529, 9 ID, 6. Armee-Kommando Op. 601/OK, Sept. 23, 1914.

39. KA, NFA 529, 9 ID, 8 Korps-Kdo, Grk, Sept. 18 and Raca Sept. 27, 1914, GdI Frank.

40. KA, NFA 475, Vienna, Sept. 20, 1914, Kriegsministerium Erlass; GB 42, 6 Gebirgsbrigade-Kommando, Lipnica, Oct. 8, 1914, GM Goisinger, "Bericht über die Kämpfe um Jagodna."

41. KA, B/1503:7, Vienna, Sept. 20 and 26 and Oct. 8, 1914, Bolfras to Potiorek, "Hier gibt es keinen Hofkriegsrat."

42. KA, NFA 2115, 36 ID, Op. 663/OK, "französischer Kriegsschauplatz."

43. Jerabek, *Potiorek*, 155.

44. HHSA, PA I, 905, Sofia, Sept. 26, 1914, Mittag to Berchtold; Athens, Sept. 25, 1914, Szilassy to Berchtold; Jeniköj, Sept. 24, 1914, Pallavicini to Berchtold.

45. C. R. M. F. Cruttwell, *A History of the Great War 1914–1918* (Chicago: Academy, 2007 [1934]), 53; Holger H. Herwig, *The First World War: Germany and Austria-Hungary 1914–1918* (London: Edw. Arnold, 1997), 89.

46. KA, NFA 2115, Oct. 1, 1914, AOK to 13 Korps-Kommando, GdI Eh. Friedrich.

47. Jerabek, *Potiorek*, 156–158.

48. KA, AOK, EVB 3506, 96/B, 108/B, 112B, 115/B, 123/B, 131B. Sept. 12, 20, 21, 23, 25 and Oct. 1, 7, 1914. NFA 2115, 13 Korps-Kdo, Op. Nr. 225/7, Sept. 25, 1914, "Nachrichten über den Feind."

CHAPTER 11: WARSAW

1. General Josef von Stürgkh, *Im Deutschen Grossen Hauptquartier* (Leipzig: Paul List, 1921), 46, 132.

2. Octavian C. Taslauanu, *With the Austrian Army in Galicia* (London: Streffington, 1919), 75.

3. Graydon Tunstall, *Blood on the Snow: The Carpathian Winter War of 1915* (Lawrence: University Press of Kansas, 2010), 10.

4. Kriegsarchiv, Vienna (KA), Gefechtsberichte (GB) 1, "Die Kämpfe der Gruppe Hofmann in den Karpathen im Sept. und Okt. 1914."

5. KA, Neue Feld Akten (NFA) 910, Zakliczyn, Sept. 28, 1914, GM Krauss, "Widerrechtliche Benützung von Krankenzügen"; K.u.k. Kriegsministerium, Abt. 10, Vienna, Nov. 27, 1914, GM Urban, "Transporte, deren Abgehen."

6. Rudolf Jerabek, "Die Brussilowoffensive 1916: Ein Wendepunkt der Koalitionskriegführung der Mittelmächte," dissertation, Vienna, 1982, 12.

7. Holger H. Herwig, *The First World War: Germany and Austria-Hungary 1914– 1918* (London: Edw. Arnold, 1997), 96.

8. Ibid., 95–96.

9. Haus-, Hof- und Staatsarchiv, Vienna (HHSA), Politisches Archiv (PA) I, 837, Munich, Nov. 24 and Dec. 8, 1914, Oct. 11, 1915, Vélics to Berchtold.

10. HHSA, PA I, 837, Munich, Oct. 22, 1915, Vélics to Burián.

11. HHSA, PA I, 837, Munich, Nov. 24, 1915, Vélics to Burián.

12. HHSA, PA I, 842, Berlin, Oct. 6 and Nov. 8, 1914, Hohenlohe to Berchtold.

13. Norman Stone, *The Eastern Front 1914–1917* (London: Penguin, 1998 [1975]), 96; Jerabek, "Brussilowoffensive," 11.

14. Ward Rutherford, *The Tsar's Army 1914–1917*, 2nd ed. (Cambridge: Ian Faulkner, 1992), 72.

15. Stone, *Eastern Front*, 96; Alfred Knox, *With the Russian Army 1914–17* (London: Hutchinson, 1921), 1:139–140; Rutherford, *Tsar's Army*, 75–76.

16. John Morse, *In the Russian Ranks* (New York: Grosset and Dunlap, 1918), 258; Winston S. Churchill, *The World Crisis: The Eastern Front* (London: Thornton Butterworth, 1931), 85.

17. Winston S. Churchill, *The Unknown War* (New York: Scribner, 1931), 76.

18. Fedor Stepun, *Wie war es möglich: Briefe eines russischen Offiziers* (Munich: Carl Hanser Verlag, 1929), 22, 31.

19. Hew Strachan, *The First World War*, vol. 1, *To Arms* (Oxford: Oxford University Press, 2001), 359; Gunther E. Rothenberg, *The Army of Francis Joseph* (West Lafayette, IN: Purdue University Press, 1976), 181.

20. Stone, *Eastern Front*, 93; Knox, *With the Russian Army*, 1:xxix.

21. Manfried Rauchensteiner, *Der Tod des Doppeladlers: Österreich-Ungarn und der Erste Weltkrieg* (Graz: Verlag Styria, 1993), 146–148; Herwig, *First World War*, 107.

22. Jerabek, "Brussilowoffensive," 13–15, 18–22.

23. Annika Mombauer, *Helmuth von Moltke and the Origins of the First World War* (Cambridge: Cambridge University Press, 2001), 147–148.

24. Capt. B. H. Liddell Hart, *The Real War 1914–1918* (Boston: Little, Brown, 1963), 125; Jerabek, "Brussilowoffensive," 24.

25. Stone, *Eastern Front*, 94–97.

26. Harry Kessler, *Journey to the Abyss: The Diaries of Count Harry Kessler, 1880–1918*, ed. and trans. Laird M. Easton (New York: Knopf, 2011), 655.

27. C. R. M. F. Cruttwell, *A History of the Great War 1914–1918* (Chicago: Academy, 2007 [1934]), 80.

28. Rutherford, *Tsar's Army*, 78; Max Hoffmann, *The War of Lost Opportunities* (New York: International, 1925), 150.

29. Kessler, *Journey to the Abyss*, 657.

30. Morse, *In the Russian Ranks*, 118; Knox, *With the Russian Army*, 1:146.

31. Kessler, *Journey to the Abyss*, 653.

32. KA, NFA 1795, 7 KpsKdo, Dobromil, Oct. 31, 1914, GdI Meixner, "Geefechtsbericht über die Kämpfe bei Chyrow und Dobromil von 11 bis 24. Okt. 1914."

33. Rutherford, *Tsar's Army*, 77.

34. Knox, *With the Russian Army*, 1:xxxiii; Rutherford, *Tsar's Army*, 74.

35. KA, NFA 910, Krakau, Nov. 14, 1914, GdI Eh Joseph Ferdinand.

36. Jerabek, "Brussilowoffensive," 1.

37. KA, NFA 1367, 3. Armeekdo, Oct. 29, 1914, GdI Boroevic to corps. Jerabek, "Brussilowoffensive," 1.

38. KA, NFA 1794, 5 Korpskdo, Wachok, Oct. 28, 1914, Maj. Aladar von Kovacs, "Bericht über Situation, Zustand etc. der Truppen des 37. LITD."

39. Kessler, *Journey to the Abyss*, 654.

40. KA, NFA 1794, 1 Korpskdo, Chechlo, Nov. 15, 1914, GdK Kirchbach to GdK Dankl.

41. HHSA, PA I, 842, Dresden, Oct. 29, 1914, Braun to Berchtold.

42. Stürgkh, *Im Deutschen Grossen Hauptquartier*, 132–133.

43. Stone, *Eastern Front*, 101.

44. Stepun, *Wie war es möglich*, 22.

45. Stanley Washburn, *On the Russian Front in World War I: Memoirs of an American War Correspondent* (New York: Robert Speller, 1982), 96–97; Knox, *With the Russian Army*, 1:167.

46. KA, NFA 1868, Lt. Karl Popper, "Das Feldjägerbattalion Nr. 6 im Weltkrieg 1914."

47. KA, NFA 1151, 19. ITD Kdo, Jaroslau, Oct. 28, 1914, Divisionskdobefehl Nr. 10, FML Lukas.

48. Herwig, *First World War*, 108; Stone, *Eastern Front*, 123.

49. KA, NFA 911, AOK, Nov. 16, 1914, "Schilderung der Meldentaten einzelner Truppenkörper und Personen für die Jugend."

50. HHSA, PA I, 842, Berlin, Nov. 12 and 17, 1914, Hohenlohe to Berchtold.

51. Cruttwell, *History of the Great War*, 82; Morse, *In the Russian Ranks*, 130, 155.

52. Liddell Hart, *The Real War*, 109; Max Hoffmann, *War Diaries* (London: Secker, 1929), 1:46.

53. Henry Norman, *All the Russias* (London: William Heinemann, 1902), 3; HHSA, PA I, 837, Munich Dec. 29, 1915, Vélics to Burián; PA I, 842, Berlin, Aug. 11, 1914, Szögeny to Berchtold.

54. HHSA, PA I, 842, Dresden, Oct. 29, 1914, Baron Karl Braun to Berchtold

55. Jerabek, "Brussilowoffensive," 34–35; Cruttwell, *History of the Great War*, 84.

56. Liddell Hart, *The Real War*, 110.

CHAPTER 12: THE THIN GRAY LINE

1. Haus-, Hof- und Staatsarchiv, Vienna (HHSA), Politisches Archiv (PA) I, 837, Munich, Nov. 24 and Dec. 8 and 17, 1914, Vélics to Berchtold.

2. Alfred Knox, *With the Russian Army 1914–1917* (London: Hutchinson, 1921), 1:214.

3. HHSA, PA I, 842, Berlin, Nov. 4, 1914, Braun to Berchtold.

4. John Morse, *In the Russian Ranks* (New York: Grosset and Dunlap, 1918), 93.

5. HHSA, PA I, 837, Munich, Dec. 1, 4, 8, 1914, Vélics to Berchtold; PA I, 842, Berlin, Nov. 30, 1914, Braun to Berchtold.

6. Harry Kessler, *Journey to the Abyss: The Diaries of Count Harry Kessler*, ed. and trans. Laird M. Easton (New York: Knopf, 2011), 673.

7. Österreichischen Bundesministerium für Heereswesen und vom Kriegsarchiv, *Österreich-Ungarns Letzter Krieg 1914–18* (Vienna: Verlag Militätwissenschaftlichen Mitteilungen, 1931–1938), 1:173–174.

8. Timothy C. Dowling, *The Brusilov Offensive* (Bloomington: Indiana University Press, 2008), 6–7; Knox, *With the Russian Army*, 1:196, 217.

9. Knox, *With the Russian Army*, 1:xxxiii, 218.

10. HHSA, PA I, 837, Munich, Nov. 24 and Dec. 1, 8, 17, 20, 1914, Vélics to Berchtold, "Mannschaften vorwärts, Munition zurückhalten."

11. Knox, *With the Russian Army*, 1:229.

12. C. R. M. F. Cruttwell, *A History of the Great War 1914–1918* (Chicago: Academy, 2007 [1934]), 87.

13. Ward Rutherford, *The Tsar's Army 1914–1917*, 2nd ed. (Cambridge: Ian Faulkner, 1992), 75.

14. Kriegsarchiv, Vienna (KA), Neue Feld Akten (NFA) 911, k.u.k. 4. Armeekommando, Nov. 29, 1914, GdI Eh Joseph Ferdinand.

15. Fedor Stepun, *Wie war es möglich: Briefe eines russischen Offiziers* (Munich: Carl Hanser Verlag, 1929), 31–33.

16. Josef von Stürgkh, *Im Deutschen Grossen Hauptquartier* (Leipzig: Paul List, 1921), 100.

17. KA, NFA 911, 6 KK, "Abfertigung am 29/11"; K.u.k. Festungskommando in Krakau, Krakau, Nov. 27, 1914, "bürgerliches Wohnungsschutzkomite"; "Ganz besonderes wird über die ungarische Honvéd geklagt"; 1. Op.-Armeekdo, Dec. 1, 1914, "Requirierung-Plünderung und Standrecht"; KA, NFA 1868, Lt. Karl Popper, "Das Feldjägerbattalion Nr. 6 im Weltkrieg 1914."

18. Morse, *In the Russian Ranks*, 222.

19. Ibid., 219.

20. Rutherford, *Tsar's Army*, 87.

21. HHSA, PA I, 842, Berlin, Nov. 25, 1914, Braun to Berchtold; Holger H. Herwig, *The First World War: Germany and Austria-Hungary 1914–1918* (London: Edw. Arnold, 1997), 111.

22. Stürgkh, *Im Deutschen Grossen Hauptquartier*, 134.

23. John Reed, *Eastern Europe at War* (London: Pluto, 1994 [1916]), 98.

24. Knox, *With the Russian Army*, 1:181, 220.

25. Kessler, *Journey to the Abyss*, 666–667.

26. Morse, *In the Russian Ranks*, 223–224.

27. Herwig, *First World War*, 109–110; Cruttwell, *History of the Great War*, 86.

28. Rutherford, *Tsar's Army*, 88.

29. HHSA, PA I, 842, Berlin, Nov. 30, 1914, Braun to Berchtold.

30. Herwig, *First World War*, 108.

31. Graydon Tunstall, *Blood on the Snow: The Carpathian Winter War of 1915.* (Lawrence: University Press of Kansas, 2010), 7.

32. KA, NFA 911, k.u.k. 1. Op.-Armeekdo, Nov. 29, 1914, "Strafsache Partyka und Pawlina."

33. KA, NFA 911, k.u.k. 1. Op.-Armeekdo, "Erinnerung an Standrechtskundmachung"; "Choleraverdächtige"; KA, Armeeoberkommando (AOK) 1914/15, Evidenzbureau (EVB) 3510, 2 Armee-Kommando, k. Nr. 311, Sanok, Nov. 4, 1914, Col. Bardolff; AOK EVB Nr. 2674, Dec. 16, 1914.

34. Kasper Blond, *Ein Unbekannter Krieg: Erlebnisse eines Arztes während des Weltkrieges* (Leipzig: Anzengruber-Verlag, 1931), 22–24.

35. KA, NFA 911, AOK, Dec. 14, 1914, FM Eh Friedrich, "Verhalten höherer Kommandanten und Kriegsgefangener"; "einer solchen Gesinnungslosigkeit oder . . . Geschwätzigkeit."

36. KA, NFA 911, k.u.k. 4. Armeekdo, Dec. 11, 1914, GM Mecenseffy; Dec. 7, 1914, GdI Eh Joseph Ferdinand.

37. KA, B/1438:18–28 (Paic), Col. Theodor von Zeynek, "Aus meinen Tagebuch Notizen 1914."

38. KA, NFA 911, AOK, Dec. 9, 1914, "Gefechtsleitung, Zusammenwirken von Infanterie und Artillerie im Gefecht."

39. KA, NFA 911, Dec. 17, 1914, "1. Meldung."

40. KA, NFA 1868, Lt. Karl Popper, "Das Feldjägerbattalion Nr. 6 im Weltkrieg 1914."

41. Kessler, *Journey to the Abyss*, 664.

42. KA, NFA 170, k.u.k. 5 Armee-Kdo Nr. 602, Dec. 19, 1914, "Nachrichten"; Herwig, *First World War*, 110.

43. KA, B/1438:29–37 (Paic), GM Paic, untitled, undated study of Erzherzog Joseph Ferdinand.

44. KA, B/1450:124–125 (Conrad), Col. Rudolf Kundmann, Tagebuch Nr. 11, Berlin, Jan. 1, 1915; letter, Conrad to Bolfras.

45. KA, NFA 1868, Lt. Karl Popper, "Das Feldjaegerbattalion Nr. 6 im Weltkrieg 1914."

46. KA, B/1438:18–28 (Paic), Col. Theodor von Zeynek, "Aus meinen Tagebuch Notizen 1914."

47. KA, NFA 911, k.u.k. 1. Op-Armeekdo, Dec. 1, 1914, "Ausfassung von papierenen Fusslappen."

48. KA, NFA 1813, 32 ITD, Feb. 3, 1915, Unewel, GM Goiginer, "Gefechtsbericht über die Kämpfe bei Starasol von 10 Oct–6 Nov. 1914."

49. Stepun, *Wie war es möglich*, 20.

50. KA, NFA 1840, k.u.k. Inf Reg Nr. 4, 1 Feldbaon, Standort, Nov. 18, 1914.

51. KA, NFA 1151, 19 ITDKdo, Zaborow, Dec. 27, 1914, Divisionskdobefehl Nr. 13.

52. KA, NFA 911, AOK, Dec. 26, 1914, FM Eh. Friedrich, "Bemerkungen über Truppenführung."

53. KA, NFA 911, AOK, Dec. 15, 1914, GM Krauss, "Russische Spionage."

54. KA, NFA 2116, AOK Nr. 5033, Dec. 9, 1914, GdI Eh. Friedrich, "Gefechtleitung, Zusammenwirken von Infanterie und Artillerie im Gefecht."

55. Dowling, *Brusilov Offensive*, 24–25.

56. Arthur Ruhl, *Antwerp to Gallipoli: A Year of the War on Many Fronts—and Behind Them* (New York: Scribner's, 1916), 250.

57. Stepun, *Wie war es möglich*, 116–117.

58. Manfried Rauchensteiner, *Der Tod des Doppeladlers: Österreich-Ungarn und der Erste Weltkrieg* (Graz: Verlag Styria, 1993), 172–173.

59. KA, B/1438:18–28 (Paic), Col. Theodor von Zeynek, "Aus meinen Tagebuch Notizen 1914"; Lawrence Sondhaus, *Franz Conrad von Hötzendorf: Architect of the Apocalypse* (Boston: Humanities Press, 2000), 162–166, 180–182.

60. Service Historique de l'Armée de Terre, Vincennes (SHAT), AAT, EMA, 7N 851, n.d., "La Propagande en Autriche pendant la guerre mondiale."

61. Herwig, *First World War*, 110.

62. Ruhl, *Antwerp to Gallipoli*, 259–260.

63. Holger Afflerbach, *Falkenhayn: Politisches Denken und Handeln im Kaiserreich* (Munich: Oldenbourg, 1994), 249–254; Stürgkh, *Im Deutschen Grossen Hauptquartier*, 102–103.

64. HHSA, PA I, 837, Munich, Nov. 17, 1914, Vélics to Berchtold; "*Westminster Gazette* has called for 'a curtailment of the war'"; B. H. Liddell Hart, *The Real War 1914–1918* (Boston: Little, Brown, 1963), 69.

65. HHSA, PA I, 837, Munich, Nov. 10, 1914, Vélics to Berchtold, "streng vertraulich"; PA I, 842, Vienna, Dec. 3, 1914, Berchtold to Vélics; "Streng vertraulich: über die gefährliche Anglophobie der Stimmung in Deutschland."

CHAPTER 13: SERBIAN JUBILEE

1. C. R. M. F. Cruttwell, *A History of the Great War 1914–1918* (Chicago: Academy, 2007 [1934]), 90.

2. Haus-, Hof- und Staatsarchiv, Vienna (HHSA), Politisches Archiv (PA) I, 819, Tuzla, Oct. 25, 1914, Masirevich to Berchtold.

3. Kriegsarchiv, Vienna (KA), Neue Feld Akten (NFA) 170, 17 Brig., k.u.k. Oberkommando der Balkanstreitkräfte, Nov. 5, 1914, FZM Potiorek.

4. Groszen Generalstab, Serbien, *Der Grosze Krieg Serbiens zur Befreiung und Vereinigung der Serben, Kroaten und Slovenen* (Belgrade: Buchdruckerei des Ministeriums für Krieg und Marine, 1924–1926), 3:256, 6:80.

5. KA, B/1503:4, Sarajevo, Oct. 19, 1914, "Promemoria Sektionschef Theodor Zurunic," with margin notes by Bosnian Sektionschef Ludwig Thallóczy; Vienna, Oct. 22, 1914, Thallóczy to FZM Potiorek; HHSA, PA I, 819, Bern, Nov. 22, 1915, Gagern to Burián.

6. KA, NFA 2116, 36 ITD, Op. Nr. 134/24, Ljesnica, Nov. 9, 1914, FML Czibulka.

7. HHSA, PA I, 819, Tuzla, Oct. 23, 1914, Masirevich to Berchtold.

8. Felix Prinz zu Schwarzenberg, *Briefe aus dem Felde 1914–18* (Vienna: Schwarzenbergisches Administration, 1953), 24.

9. Ibid., 24–25; Joseph Schön, *Sabac!* (Reichenberg: Heimatsöhne, 1928), 83.

10. R. G. D. Laffan, *The Serbs* (New York: Dorset Press, 1989 [1917]), 199.

11. KA, NFA 475, 41 Sch. Br., Jarak, Oct. 24, 1914, FML Krauss.

12. KA, Gefechtsberichte (GB) 21, 29 ITD, Op. Nr. 102/10 and 114/17, "Gefechtsbericht für den 31. Okt. und 1. Nov. 1914" and "Gefechtsbericht für den 3. Nov. 1914"; NFA 475, Op. 199/127, Oct. 1, 1914, FML Krauss.

13. KA, B/1503:7, Vienna, Oct. 8, 1914, Bolfras to Potiorek.

14. KA, NFA 2116, 36 ID, Nov. 1, 1914, Trbusnica, IR 16 to 36 ITD.

15. KA, Armeeoberkommando (AOK) 1914, Evidenzbureau (EVB) 3506, k.u.k. Evidenzbureau des Generalstabs, 123/B, 131/B, 148/B, 158/B, 166/B, 178/B, 179/B, Oct. 1, 7, and 23 and Nov. 2, 10, 22, and 23, 1914.

16. KA, GB 42, 4 GB, "Gefechtsbericht über den 6. bis 16. November 1914."

17. KA, NFA 1845/1, Gefechts-Berichte der k.u.k. Infanterie-Regimenter Nr. 71–79, "Die Erstürmung des Gucevo-Rückens durch das I.R. 78."

18. Andre Mitrovic, *Serbia's Great War 1914–1918* (West Lafayette, IN: Purdue University Press, 2007), 70.

19. KA, NFA 911, AOK, Nov. 17, 1914, Potiorek via GdI Eh Friedrich; Groszen Generalstab, Serbien, *Der Grosze Krieg,* 3:454.

20. HHSA, PA I, 819, 2a, FPA 305, Feb. 12, 1915, FML Krauss to k.u.k. Kriegsüberwachungsamt.

21. KA, NFA 528, 9 I.D., Oct. 20, 1914, GM Daniel.

22. KA, B/1503:7, Tuzla, Nov. 15 and 16, 1914, FZM Potiorek to Bolfras; NFA 528, 9 ID, Nov. 10–13, 1914, "Disposition."

23. Groszen Generalstab, Serbien, *Der Grosze Krieg,* 3:346.

24. KA, NFA 2116, 36 ITD, Moni Bogovagya, Nov. 18, 1914, Col. Müller.

25. KA, NFA 2160, 4 Geb. Brig., Jagodna, Nov. 6, 1914, "Abfertigung"; NFA 170, 17. Brig., k.u.k. 8 Korps-Kommando Res. Nr. 936, Bogatic, Nov. 4, 1914.

26. KA, NFA 2116, 36 ID, Op. Nr. 128/6, Koviljaca, Nov. 3, 1914, FML Czibulka; HHSA, PA I, 819, 2a, FPA 305, Feb. 12, 1915, FML Krauss to k.u.k. Kriegsüberwachungsamt.

27. KA, NFA 2160, 4 Gebirg, Brig., Nov. 29, 1914, "Intendanz."

28. KA, NFA 1840, k.u.k. IR 6, Baon 1, n.d., "Kämpfe um den Gradjenik com 23–25 Nov. 1914."

29. HHSA, PA I, 819, Tuzla, Nov. 12 and Koviljaca, Nov. 28, 1914, Konstantin Masirevich to Berchtold; KA, B/1503:7, Tuzla, Nov. 18–19, 1914, Potiorek to Bolfras; PA I, 819, Teschen, Nov. 25, 1914, Friedrich Wiesner to Berchtold; Laffan, *The Serbs,* 200.

30. KA, NFA 2116, 36 ID, "Zeitungsnachrichten vom 21. Nov. 1914"; NFA 2161, Nov. 10, 1914, "Neuste Nachrichten."

31. HHSA, PA I, 872, Sofia, Nov. 6, 1914, Tarnowski to Berchtold.

32. KA, B/1503:7, Vienna, Nov. 25, 1914, Bolfras to Potiorek.

33. KA, B/1503:4, Sarajevo, Nov. 20, 1914, Ein hoher bosnischer Funktionär, "Promemoria über die actuelle Behandlung der serbischen Frage in Bosnien."

34. HHSA, PA I, 819, Vienna, Nov. 17, 1914, Berchtold to Potiorek.

35. KA, B/1503:7, Tuzla, Nov. 29, 1914, Potiorek to Kriegsminister.

36. KA, B/1503:7, Tuzla, Nov. 19, 1914, FZM Potiorek, Op. Nr. 2529/OK.

37. KA, NFA 1840, k.u.k. IR 6, Baon 1, nd, "Kämpfe um den Gragjenik com 23–25 Nov. 1914."

38. KA, AOK (1914), EVB 3506, k.u.k. Evidenzbureau des Generalstabs, 183/B, 186/B, 189/B, 190/B, 192/B, Nov. 27, 30 and Dec. 3, 4, 6, 1914; HHSA, PA I, 819, Vienna, Dec. 15, 1914, Berchtold to Vladimir Giesl.

39. KA, NFA 1840, k.u.k. IR 6, Baon 1, "Eiziehen der serb. Fahne am 2. Dez. 1914 am Kalimedgan."

40. HHSA, PA I, 819, Munich, Dec. 3, 1914, Ludwig Vélics to Berchtold.

41. HHSA, PA I, 819, Teschen, Nov. 25, 1914, Wiesner to Berchtold.

42. Groszen Generalstab, Serbien, Der Grosze Krieg, 3:424–425.

43. Mitrovic, Serbia's Great War, 73–74.

44. Ibid., xv.

45. KA, B/16, Beilage 2, "Aus den persönlichen Vormerkungen des Generals der Infanterie Oskar Potiorek vom 17. Nov. 1914."

46. Rudolf Jerabek, Potiorek (Graz: Verlag Styria, 1991), 168–170.

47. KA, NFA 529, 9 ID, Nov. 30, 1914, "Abfertigung"; NFA 170, 17 Brig., 5 Armee-Etappen Kommando, Nov. 24, 1914, Col. Ottokar Landwehr, "Verlautbarungen"; Jan. 1915, "Merkblatt über Erfrierung und Kälteschutz"; KA, NFA 2116, 36 ITD, Celije, Nov. 21, 1914, IR 16 to 36 ITD.

48. KA, NFA 2160, 4 Gebirg, Brig., Nov. 24, 1914, "III/69 meldet."

49. Holger H. Herwig, The First World War: Germany and Austria-Hungary 1914–1918 (London: Edw. Arnold, 1997), 111; KA, NFA 170, 17 Brig., Bogatic, Nov. 4, 1914.

50. KA, NFA 2160, 4 Gebirg, Brig., Nov. 29, 1914, "Intendanz"; NFA 2116, 36 ITD, Op. Nr.173, Becinen, Dec. 18, 1914, 36 ITD to 13 Korps-Kdo; Jerabek, Potiorek, 177.

51. HHSA, PA I, 819, Bucharest, Dec. 31, 1914, Szent-Ivany to Berchtold; KA, NFA 2160, 4 Gebirg, Brig., Nov. 25–28, 1914, "Intendanz"; Jerabek, Potiorek, 183.

52. KA, NFA 2160, 4 Gebirg, Brig., Nov. 30, 1914, "Deckadressen"; Kurt Peball, "Der Feldzug gegen Serbien und Montenegro im Jahre 1914," Österreichische Militärische Zeitschrift Sonderheft I (1965): 28; Groszen Generalstab, Serbien, Der Grosze Krieg, 5:2.

53. KA, B/1503:7, Koviljaca, Nov. 30, 1914, FZM Potiorek, Op. Nr. 3068/OK; NFA 2116, 36 ID, k.u.k. AOK Op. Nr. 5102 v. 1914 an das k.u.k. Oberkommando der Balkanstreitkräfte, "Verhalten höherer Kommandandten und Kriegsgefängener"; HHSA, PA I, 819, Vienna, Dec. 2, 1914, Berchtold to Potiorek.

54. Groszen Generalstab, Serbien, Der Grosze Krieg, 6:2–3, 80–83.

55. KA, NFA 2116, 36 ID, k.u.k. AOK Op. Nr. 5102 v. 1914 an das k.u.k. Oberkommando der Balkanstreitkräfte, "Verhalten höherer Kommandandten und Kriegsgefängener."

56. John Reed, Eastern Europe at War (London: Pluto, 1994 [1916]), 22–23.

57. HHSA, PA I, 819, Tuzla, Oct. 25, 1914, Masirevich to Berchtold.

58. Arthur Ruhl, Antwerp to Gallipoli: A Year of the War on Many Fronts—and Behind Them (New York: Scribner's, 1916), 251.

59. KA, GB 86, GM Heinrich Pongracz, k.u.k. 53 ITD, Sept. 19, 1915, Op. 244, "Erfahrungen in diesem Kriege."

60. Groszen Generalstab, Serbien, *Der Grosze Krieg,* 6:86–91.

61. Ibid., 6:103–104.

62. Ibid., 6:152–157.

63. Ibid., 6:157–158.

64. HHSA, PA I, 819, 2a, FPA 305, Feb. 12, 1915, FML Krauss to k.u.k. Kriegsüberwachungsamt.

65. Groszen Generalstab, Serbien, *Der Grosze Krieg,* 6:316.

66. Ibid., 6:321.

67. KA, NFA 1845/1, Gefechts-Berichte der k.u.k. Infanterie-Regimenter Nr. 71–79, GM Stracker, "Gefechtsbericht über das Gefecht den 5. Dez. 1914 südostl. Burovo."

68. Groszen Generalstab, Serbien, *Der Grosze Krieg,* 6:403–404.

69. Ibid., 7:108.

70. Ibid., 6:351.

71. KA, NFA 1840, Inf Baon 1/1 to 1 Geb. Brig., Nikinci, Dec. 8–12 and 15, 1914.

72. Groszen Generalstab, Serbien, *Der Grosze Krieg,* 6:351–352.

73. KA, NFA 1866, 42. k.u. Landwehr Inf Div, "Gefechtsbericht über den Kampf am 7. Dec. 1914."

74. KA, GB 29, k.u.k. 13 IB, Dobrinica, Dec. 28, 1914, GM Karl Stracker, "Gefechtsbericht fur den 5. Dezember."

75. KA, GB 74, Ruma, Jan. 2, 1915, "Gefechtsbericht über den Kampf am 3. Dec. 1914"; GB 67, "Gefechtsbericht für die Zeit von 2. bis 14. Dez. 1914," k.u. I.R. 4 GB 67, Surcin, Dec. 18, 1914, "Gefechtsbericht über die Verwendung k. ung. LS I.R. 6 bei Sabac 8–9 Dez. 1914."

76. Service Historique de l'Armée de Terre, Vincennes (SHAT), AAT, EMA, 7N 847, 2ème Bureau, "Journal de Marche d'un officier autrichien depuis le debut de la guerre jusqu'au 19 Juillet 1915."

77. HHSA, PA I, 819, 2a, FPA 305, Feb. 12, 1915, FML Krauss to k.u.k. Kriegsüberwachungsamt; Gunther E. Rothenberg, *The Army of Francis Joseph* (West Lafayette, IN: Purdue University Press, 1976), 108.

78. KA, NFA 170, 9 ITD, Ó Futak, Jan. 1, 1915, GM Schön; KA, GB 29, k.u.k. 13 IB, Dobrinica, Dec. 31, 1914, GM Karl Stracker, "Gefechtsbericht für den 7 Dezember 1914"; KA, GB 29, k.u.k. 13 IB, Jan. 4, 1915, GM Karl Stracker, "Gefechtsbericht für den 13. Dezember"; Laffan, *The Serbs,* 202.

79. National Archives and Records Administration, Washington, DC (NARA), M 695, roll 21, Chicago, June 14, 1917, D. Fisher and J. Smetanka to Lansing.

80. KA, NFA 2116, 36 ITD, 72 I.B., Zeleznik, Dec. 13, 1914, Col. Lexardo; KA, NFA 2116, 36. ID, Op. Nr. 184/4, Dec. 29, 1914, "Standes-und-Verlust-Nachweisung"; KA, GB 10, 1 ITD, Res. Nr. 349, n.d.; Jerabek, *Potiorek,* 185.

81. HHSA, PA I, 819, Nov. 1914, FML Schleyer to Berchtold.

82. KA, NFA 2162, 4. Gebirgsbrigade, Vlasenica, Dec. 31, 1914, "Frührapport"; NFA 191, 18 IB, 5. Armee Etap-Kdo, Res. Nr. 4987, Dec. 10, 1914; KA, GB 86, GM Heinrich Pongracz, k.u.k. 53 ITD, Sept. 19, 1915, Op. 244, "Erfahrungen in diesem Kriege."

83. KA, B/1503:7, Dec. 9, 1914, FZM Potiorek to MKSM, AOK, KM, LVM; Jerabek, *Potiorek,* 187.

84. KA, NFA 2162, 4. Gebirgsbrigade, Nr. 257/13, Vlasenica, Dec. 27, 1914, GM Konopicky.

85. HHSA, PA I, 819, Teschen, Dec. 13, 1914, Giesl to Berchtold; Jerabek, *Potiorek,* 188, 196.

86. KA, NFA 170, 17 Brig., Dec. 16, 1914, FPA Nr. 305, FZM Potiorek.

87. HHSA, PA I, 819, Peterwardein, Dec. 18, 1914, Kinsky to Berchtold; KA, B/1503:7, Vienna, Dec. 12, 1914, Bolfras to Potiorek.

88. HHSA, PA III, 171, Berlin, Dec. 12, 1914, Hohenlohe to Berchtold.

89. HHSA, PA I, 819, Dresden, Dec. 22, 1914, Braun to Berchtold; Herwig, *First World War*, 112.

90. Karl Kraus, ed., *Die Fackel* (Munich: Kösel-Verlag, 1968–1976), 5:12 (Jan. 4, 1910).

91. KA, AOK (1914), EVB 3506, k.u.k. Evidenzbureau des Generalstabs, 205/B, Dec. 19, 1914.

92. KA, B/16, Beilage 7, Brief Potiorek an Bolfras, Dec. 12, 1914.

93. KA, B/16, Teschen, Dec. 14, 1914, Conrad to Bolfras.

94. KA, B/1503:7, Dec. 14, 1914, GdI Conrad, "Beurteilung der Lage."

95. Gunther E. Rothenberg, "The Austro-Hungarian Campaign Against Serbia in 1914," *Journal of Military History*, April 1989, 144.

96. General Josef von Stürgkh, *Im Deutschen Grossen Hauptquartier* (Leipzig: Paul List, 1921), 110.

97. HHSA, PA I, 845, Milan, Dec. 12, 1914, Ladislaus Györgey to Berchtold; KA, GB 86, 3 Korps Kommando, 1917, "Die kriegswirtschaftliche Lage Italiens."

98. KA, B/1503:7, Vienna, Dec. 20, 1914, Bolfras to Potiorek; Jerabek, *Potiorek*, 40, 201.

99. KA, NFA 2116, 36. ITD, Op. Nr. 320/8, Dec. 20, 1914, GdI Rhemen; NFA 170, 8. Korps-Kdo, Res. Nr. 72, Jan. 11, 1915, FML Scheuch.

100. Herwig, *First World War*, 113.

101. KA, NFA 2116, 36 ID, Op. Nr. 184/9, Kraljevo, Dec. 29, 1914, FML Czibulka, "Ausbildung."

102. Herwig, *First World War*, 129–130.

103. Österreichischen Bundesministerium für Heereswesen und vom Kriegsarchiv, *Österreich-Ungarns Letzter Krieg 1914–18* (Vienna: Verlag Militätwissenschaftlichen Mitteilungen, 1931–1938), 1:762.

104. HHSA, PA I, 837, Munich, Nov. 11, 1914, Vélics to Berchtold; 819, Stuttgart, Dec. 19, 1914, Koziebrodski to Berchtold.

CHAPTER 14: SNOWMEN

1. Kriegsarchiv, Vienna (KA), Armeeoberkommando (AOK) 1914–1915, Evidenz-bureau (EVB) 3510, Dec. 22, 1914, "Italien: Auszüge aus Attache- und Kundschafts-berichten"; Haus, Hof- und Staatsarchiv, Vienna (HHSA), Politisches Archiv (PA) III, 171, Berlin, Dec. 5, 1914, Hohenlohe to Berchtold; Vienna, Dec. 7, 1914, Hoyos to Hohenlohe.

2. HHSA, PA I, 819, Sofia, Dec. 13, 1914, Tarnowski to Berchtold; Pera, Dec. 15, 1914, Pallavicini to Berchtold; *Times* clipping in Copenhagen, Dec. 17, 1914, Szechenyi to Berchtold.

3. General Josef von Stürgkh, *Im Deutschen Grossen Hauptquartier* (Leipzig: Paul List, 1921), 112–113.

4. Rudolf Jerabek, *Potiorek* (Graz: Verlag Styria, 1991), 193.

5. HHSA, PA I, 837, Munich, Feb. 20, 1915, Vélics to Burián.

6. KA, B/1450: 124–125 (Conrad), Col. Rudolf Kundmann, Tagebuch Nr. 11, Berlin, Jan. 1, 1915.

7. Nikolai N. Golovine, *The Russian Army in the World War* (New Haven: Yale University Press, 1931), 37.

8. Ibid., 127–128.

9. HHSA, PA I, 837, Munich, Jan. 25, 1915, Vélics to Burián; Timothy C. Dowling, *The Brusilov Offensive* (Bloomington: Indiana University Press, 2008), 6; Fedor Stepun, *Wie war es möglich: Briefe eines russischen Offiziers* (Munich: Carl Hanser Verlag, 1929), 83.

10. HHSA, PA I, 837, Munich, Dec. 30, 1914, Vélics to Berchtold; Norman Stone, *The Eastern Front 1914–1917* (London: Penguin, 1998 [1975]), 122; B. H. Liddell Hart, *The Real War 1914–1918* (Boston: Little, Brown, 1963), 70.

11. Alfred Knox, *With the Russian Army 1914–17* (London: Hutchinson, 1921), 1:235.

12. Stone, *Eastern Front*, 112.

13. Ward Rutherford, *The Tsar's Army 1914–1917*, 2nd ed. (Cambridge: Ian Faulkner, 1992), 28; Knox, *With the Russian Army*, 1:219–220.

14. Knox, *With the Russian Army*, 1:237.

15. Stepun, *Wie war es möglich*, 35–36, 41–44, 49.

16. Gunther E. Rothenberg, *The Army of Francis Joseph* (West Lafayette, IN: Purdue University Press, 1976), 177; Stone, *Eastern Front*, 42.

17. Harry Kessler, *Journey to the Abyss: The Diaries of Count Harry Kessler, 1880–1918*, ed. and trans. Laird M. Easton (New York: Knopf, 2011), 669.

18. Graydon Tunstall, *Blood on the Snow: The Carpathian Winter War of 1915* (Lawrence: University Press of Kansas, 2010), 11.

19. KA, Neue Feld Akten (NFA) 1868, Lt. Karl Popper, "Das Feldjaegerbattalion Nr. 6 im Weltkrieg 1914."

20. KA, NFA 1803, 5. ITD Kdo, Góry, Jan. 15, 1915, "Gefechtsbericht über die nächtliche Unternehmung gegen Zakrzów."

21. KA, B/1450:124–125 (Conrad), Col. Rudolf Kundmann, Tagebuch Nr. 11, Berlin, Jan. 1, 1915, letter, Conrad to Bolfras; Stepun, *Wie war es möglich*, 43, 65.

22. Stürgkh, *Im Deutschen Grossen Hauptquartier*, 115–116.

23. KA, B/1450:124–125 (Conrad), Maj. Rudolf Kundmann, Tagebuch Nr. 11, Teschen, Feb. 3, 1915.

24. Stone, *Eastern Front*, 114.

25. Arthur Ruhl, *Antwerp to Gallipoli: A Year of the War on Many Fronts—and Behind Them* (New York: Scribner's, 1916), 267.

26. Generalleutnant August von Cramon, *Unser Österreich-Ungarischer Bundesgenosse im Weltkriege* (Berlin: Mittler u. Sohn, 1920), 9.

27. HHSA, PA I, 837, Munich, Feb. 20, 1915, Vélics to Burián; Dowling, *Brusilov Offensive*, 22–24.

28. Kessler, *Journey to the Abyss*, 672.

29. KA, NFA 2116, 36 ID, AOK Nr. 2096, GM Höfer, Dec. 16, 1914; NFA 170, 17 Brig., Etappen-Kdo, Dec. 31, 1914, Ob. Ottokar Landwehr.

30. Stone, *Eastern Front*, 122.

31. KA, NFA 170, k.u.k. 8 Korps-Kdo, Op. Nr. 617/28, Dec. 21, 1914, FML Scheuchenstiel.

32. KA, NFA 1866, 13 Korps Kdo, March 3, 1915, FML Salis, "einen Rudel demoralisierter Mannschaft."

33. KA, NFA 1845/2, Gefechts-Berichte der k.u.k. Infanterie-Regimenter Nr. 80–83, "Die 81er im Osterkampf um die Kobila."

34. KA, NFA 1878, "Kriegserfahrungen," 6 Auflage, "Taktik der Feinde: Russen."

35. Stepun, *Wie war es möglich*, 80–81.

36. KA, NFA 1868, Maj. Lunzer, Amniowa, April 3, 1915, k.u.k. FJ Baon Nr. 9, "Bericht über die Tätigkeit der Gruppe Maj. Von Lunzer vom 2/III bis 29/III"; NFA 1878, AOK, Oct. 15, 1915, "Ursachen und Vermeidung grosser Verluste."

424 – Notes to Epilogue

37. KA, NFA 1878, k.u.k. 1. Armeekdo, March 2, 1915, "Verwendung von Handgranaten."

38. KA, NFA 1868, Sattel 993, May 8, 1915, Maj. Heinich von Lunzer, "Gefechtsbericht über den Angriff auf Jawornik 6./5.1915."

39. NFA 1845/2, Gefechts-Berichte der k.u.k. Infanterie-Regimenter Nr. 80–83 "Die 81er im Osterkampf um die Kobila."

40. Stepun, *Wie war es möglich*, 113.

41. KA, B/1450:124–125 (Conrad), Col. Rudolf Kundmann, Tagebuch Nr. 11.

42. Beiblatt der *"Muskete,"* Vienna, March 11, 1915.

43. Stepun, *Wie war es möglich*, 115.

44. Tunstall, *Blood on the Snow*, 12.

45. KA, NFA 1868, k.u.k. 1 Regt. Der Tiroler Kaiser Jäger, March 13, 1915, Col. Mollinary, "Bericht über das Gefecht von Sekowa am 8. März."

46. Stone, *Eastern Front*, 314.

47. Stürgkh, *Im Deutschen Grossen Hauptquartier*, 116–117.

48. Rudolf Jerabek, "Die Brussilowoffensive 1916: Ein Wendepunkt der Koalitionskriegführung der Mittelmächte," dissertation, Vienna, 1982, 1:6–8.

49. Stone, *Eastern Front*, 114.

50. Stanley Washburn, *On the Russian Front in World War I: Memoirs of an American War Correspondent* (New York: Robert Speller, 1982), 89.

51. HHSA, PA I 842, Leipzig, Dec. 4, 1915. Includes copy of "Die 28er—Armee-Befehl de dato 25 April 1915."

52. Tunstall, *Blood on the Snow*, 12, 20–21.

53. Golovine, *The Russian Army*, 58.

54. Stürgkh, *Im Deutschen Grossen Hauptquartier*, 140; Golovine, *The Russian Army*, 48–54.

55. John Morse, *In the Russian Ranks* (New York: Grosset and Dunlap, 1918), 252; Dowling, *Brusilov Offensive*, 7, 26. Of the 5 million Russians under arms in 1915, only 650,000 to 1.2 million (there were various estimates) actually had a rifle. See Knox, *With the Russian Army*, 1:267–270; Ruhl, *Antwerp to Gallipoli*, 266.

56. KA, B/677:23, Manfred Beer, March 1993, "General von Auffenberg-Komarów nach 70-jährigen Attacken posthum rehabilitiert"; Josef Ullreich, "Moritz von Auffenberg-Komarów: Leben und Wirken," dissertation, Vienna, 1961, 148–150.

57. KA, NFA 911, 4 Armee Kdo, Cracow, Nov. 16, 1914, "Beurlaubung Mitglieder des ungarischen Reichstages."

58. Rothenberg, *Army of Francis Joseph*, 184–185; Stone, *Eastern Front*, 124.

59. Replies to the *Frage-Bogen* and additional *Fragepunkte* here: KA, Gefechtsberichte (GB) 86, Standort der Brigade, Mar. 17, 1915, GM Balberitz; Standort, March 18, 1915, Feld-Jäger Battalion Nr. 17; Standort, Mar. 20, 1915, 50 Inf-Brig. Kommando.

60. KA, NFA 1878, Allgemeine Erfahrungen, 1914–1915. See reports throughout this *Karton*.

61. KA, GB 86, 93 ITD, July 1915, GM Adolf Boog, "Nervenstörungen"; Ruhl, *Antwerp to Gallipoli*, 256.

62. Dowling, *Brusilov Offensive*, 24.

63. HHSA, PA I, 905, Copenhagen, Sept. 30, 1914, Dionys Széchenyi to Berchtold.

64. Stürgkh, *Im Deutschen Grossen Hauptquartier*, 118–120.

65. Ruhl, *Antwerp to Gallipoli*, 244, 248, 252–257.

EPILOGUE

1. Kriegsarchiv, Vienna (KA), Neue Feld Akten (NFA) 1878, Kriegsministerium, March 20, 1915, "Ursachen und Ziele des Weltkrieges 1914/15."

2. KA, B/1503:5, Sarajevo, Dec. 21, 1912, Potiorek to Conrad.

3. KA, NFA 1878, "Fragen die dem Kpskmdo bis 31./1 1915 erschöpfend zu beantworten sind"; A. J. P. Taylor, *The Habsburg Monarchy 1809–1918* (London: Penguin, 1948), 254.

4. General Josef von Stürgkh, *Im Deutschen Grossen Hauptquartier* (Leipzig: Paul List, 1921), 148.

5. B. H. Liddell Hart, *The Real War 1914–1918* (Boston: Little, Brown, 1963), 305.

6. Richard DiNardo, *Breakthrough: The Gorlice-Tarnow Campaign 1915* (Santa Barbara: Praeger, 2010), 48–49.

7. Alfred Knox, *With the Russian Army 1914–17* (London: Hutchinson, 1921), 1:349–350.

8. Fedor Stepun, *Wie war es möglich: Briefe eines russischen Offiziers* (Munich: Carl Hanser Verlag, 1929), 129; Harry Kessler, *Journey to the Abyss: The Diaries of Count Harry Kessler, 1880–1918*, ed. and trans. Laird M. Easton (New York: Knopf, 2011), 685.

9. Nikolai N. Golovine, *The Russian Army in the World War* (New Haven: Yale University Press, 1931), 221.

10. Kessler, *Journey to the Abyss*, 687.

11. Golovine, *Russian Army*, 145.

12. Haus-, Hof- und Staatsarchiv, Vienna (HHSA), Politisches Archiv (PA) I, 837, Munich, Oct. 22 and 28, 1915, Vélics to Burián.

13. HHSA, PA I, 837, Munich, Nov. 30, Dec. 22, 1915, Vélics to Burián.

14. Liddell Hart, *Real War*, 368–369.

15. William de Hevesy, "Postscript to the Sixtus Affair," *Foreign Affairs* 21, no. 3 (April 1943).

16. Taylor, *Habsburg Monarchy*, 254–255; Géza Andreas von Geyr, *Sándor Wekerle* (Munich: Oldenbourg, 1993), 353, 378–379, 396–397.

17. David Stevenson, *Cataclysm* (New York: Basic Books, 2004), 304; Alan Sked, *The Decline and Fall of the Habsburg Empire 1815–1918* (London: Longman, 1989), 259; Holger H. Herwig, *The First World War: Germany and Austria-Hungary 1914–1918* (London: Edw. Arnold, 1997), 369–370.

18. A. Scott Berg, *Wilson* (New York: Putnam, 2013), 538; Sked, *Decline and Fall*, 260; Taylor, *Habsburg Monarchy*, 268–271.

19. KA, NFA 1878, AOK, Oct. 15, 1915, "Ursachen und Vermeidung grosser Verluste." "Jünglinen und alternden Männern."

20. Golovine, *Russian Army*, 48–49.

21. Service Historique de l'Armée de Terre, Vincennes (SHAT), EMA 7N 846, Jan. 30, 1916, "La Situation Militaire: L'état actuel de l'Autriche-Hongrie." Mission Russe, Paris, March 24, 1917, Col. Ignatieff.

22. KA, B/75 (Bolfras), Frühjahr 1916, Anon. letter to Kaiser Franz Joseph I.

23. KA, NFA 1878, AOK, Oct. 15, 1915, "Ursachen und Vermeidung grosser Verluste."

24. HHSA, Allgemeines Verwaltungsarchiv (AVA), MdI Präs., Karton 1733, Prot. Nr. 1511, Jan. 20, 1915, Kriegsüberwachungsamt to Interior Minister.

25. HHSA, AVA, MdI Präs., Karton 1733, Prot. Nr. 8797, Apr. 27, 1915, Statthalter Graz to Interior Minister.

26. KA, Gefechtsberichte (GB) 86, March 17, 1915, GM Balberitz.

27. Arthur Ruhl, *Antwerp to Gallipoli: A Year of the War on Many Fronts—and Behind Them* (New York: Scribner's, 1916), 244.

28. KA, GB 86, 4 Armee Etappenkommando, "Allgemeine Direktiven für die Errichtung von Militärfriedhofen im Felde, Juni 1915"; Stanley Washburn, *On the*

Russian Front in World War I: Memoirs of an American War Correspondent (New York: Robert Speller, 1982), 59.

29. KA, NFA 1877, AOK, Feb. 4, 1916, GO Conrad.

30. KA, B/96:3a, AOK to Militärkanzlei Seiner Majestät, July 26, 1916; Bolfras to Brudermann, Aug. 21, 1916.

31. Geoffrey Wawro, "Morale in the Austro-Hungarian Army," in *Facing Armageddon*, ed. Hugh Cecil and Peter Liddle (London: Leo Cooper, 1996), 399–410; SHAT, EMA 7N 845, Paris, Oct. 13, 1917, "Renseignements sur les 'troupes d'assaut' de l'Armée Austro-Hongroise d'après enquête faite au camp de prisonniers de Bagnaria-Arsa."

32. Rudolf Jerabek, "Die Brussilowoffensive 1916: Ein Wendepunkt der Koalitionskriegführung der Mittelmächte," dissertation, Vienna, 1982, 2:308–9.

33. Timothy C. Dowling, *The Brusilov Offensive* (Bloomington: Indiana University Press, 2008), xv.

34. KA, NFA 1795, 4. Armeekdo, June 26, 1916, GenObst Tersztyánszky to 10 KpsKdo.

35. SHAT, AAT, EMA 7N 846, 2ème Bureau, May 14, 1917, "Armée Autrichienne."

36. Golovine, *Russian Army,* 74.

37. Dowling, *Brusilov Offensive,* xix–xx.

38. KA, GB 1, k.u.k. 10 Armee Korps-Kdo, Oct. 8, 1917, "Gefecht bei Carzano–Verrat am 18. Sept. 1917"; Liddell Hart, *Real War,* 128.

39. SHAT, AAT, EMA 7N 846, 2ème Bureau, Oct. 13, 1918, "Recrutement."

40. Dresden, Sächsiches Kriegsarchiv, Zeitgeschichtliche Sammlung 127, "Zwei politische Aufsätze, 1917."

41. John Reed, *Eastern Europe at War* (London: Pluto, 1994 [1916]), 92.

42. Golovine, *Russian Army,* 122.

43. Ibid., 67, 77, 93.

44. I was told this anecdote by Prof. Lothar Höbelt of the University of Vienna.

45. Norman Stone, "Army and Society in the Habsburg Monarchy, 1900–1914," *Past and Present* 33, no. 1 (1966): 111.

46. Gunther E. Rothenberg, *The Army of Francis Joseph* (West Lafayette, IN: Purdue University Press, 1976), 128.

47. Norman Stone, *World War One: A Short History,* (New York: Basic Books, 2009), 22.

Bibliography

Archives

AUSTRIA
Vienna
HHSA Haus-, Hof- und Staatsarchiv
AVA Allgemeines Verwaltungsarchiv
PA Politisches Archiv
KA Kriegsarchiv
AOK Armeeoberkommando
B Nachlässe
GB Gefechtsberichte
MKFF Militärkanzlei Franz Ferdinand
MKSM Militärkanzlei Seiner Majestät
NFA Neue Feld Akten
EVB Evidenzbureau

FRANCE
Vincennes
SHAT Service Historique de l'Armée de Terre

GERMANY
Dresden
Sächsiches Kriegsarchiv

UNITED KINGDOM
Kew
BNA British National Archives
FO Foreign Office
WO War Office

UNITED STATES
Washington, DC
NARA National Archives and Records Administration

Published Sources

Afflerbach, Holger. *Falkenhayn: Politisches Denken und Handeln im Kaiserreich.* Munich: Oldenbourg, 1994.

Alten, Georg von. *Handbuch für Heer und Flotte.* 6 vols. Berlin: Deutsches Verlagshaus, 1909–1914.

Auffenberg-Komarów, Moritz Freiherr von. *Aus Österreichs Höhe und Niedergang: Eine Lebensschilderung.* Munich: Drei Masken Verlag, 1921.

Bardolff, Carl Freiherr von. *Soldat im alten Österreich: Erinnerungen aus meinem Leben.* Jena: Eugen Diederichs, 1938.

Bloch, I. S. *The Future of War.* Boston: Ginn, 1897.

Blond, Kasper. *Ein Unbekannter Krieg: Erlebnisse eines Arztes während des Weltkrieges.* Leipzig: Anzengruber-Verlag, 1931.

Brettner-Messler, Horst. "Die Balkanpolitik Conrad von Hötzendorfs von seiner Wiederernennung zum Chef des Generalstabes bis zum Oktober-Ultimatum 1913," *Mitteilungen des österreichischen Staatsarchivs* 20 (1967).

Brosch-Aarenau, Alexander von. *Der militärische Ausgleich.* Vienna: k.u.k. Hofbuchdruckerei, 1909.

Broussilov, A. A. *Mémoires du General Broussilov: Guerre 1914–18.* Paris: Hachette, 1929.

Brusilov, A. A. *A Soldier's Notebook.* London: Macmillan, 1930.

Buchanan, Meriel. *The Dissolution of an Empire.* London: Murray, 1932.

Burián, István. *Austria in Dissolution 1915–18.* New York: George Doran, 1925.

Churchill, Winston S. *The World Crisis: The Eastern Front.* London: Thornton Butterworth, 1931.

———. *The Unknown War.* New York: Scribner, 1931.

Clark, Christopher. *The Sleepwalkers.* New York: Harper, 2013.

Cornwall, Mark, ed. *The Last Years of Austria-Hungary.* Exeter: University of Exeter Press, 2002.

Cramon, August von. *Unser Österreich-Ungarischer Bundesgenosse im Weltkriege.* Berlin: Mittler u. Sohn, 1920.

Cruttwell, C. R. M. F. *A History of the Great War 1914–1918.* Chicago: Academy, 2007 [1934].

Danilov, Yuri. *La Russie dans la Guerre Mondiale.* Paris: Payot, 1917.

Deák, István. *Beyond Nationalism.* Oxford: Oxford University Press, 1990.

Dedijer, Vladimir. *The Road to Sarajevo.* London: MacGibbon and Kee, 1967.

Der "Militarismus" in Österreich-Ungarn. Vienna: Seidel, 1902.

DiNardo, Richard. *Breakthrough: The Gorlice-Tarnow Campaign 1915.* Santa Barbara: Praeger, 2010.

Dowling, Timothy C. *The Brusilov Offensive.* Bloomington: Indiana University Press, 2008.

Emmerson, Charles. *1913.* New York: Public Affairs, 2013.

Fischer, Fritz. *Germany's Aims in the First World War.* New York: Norton, 1968.

———. *War of Illusions.* London: Chatto and Windus, 1975.

Fraccaroli, A. *La Serbia nella sua terza Guerra.* Milan, 1915.

Fromkin, David. *Europe's Last Summer.* New York: Vintage, 2005.

Fuller, William C., Jr. *Strategy and Power in Russia 1600–1914.* New York: Free Press, 1992.

Golovine, Nikolai N. *The Russian Army in the World War.* New Haven: Yale University Press, 1931.

Groszen Generalstab, Serbien. *Der Grosze Krieg Serbiens zur Befreiung und Vereinigung der Serben, Kroaten und Slovenen.* 7 vols. Belgrade: Buchdruckerei des Ministeriums für Krieg und Marine, 1924–1926.

Gumz, Jonathan. *The Resurrection and Collapse of Empire in Habsburg Serbia 1914–1918.* Cambridge: Cambridge University Press, 2009.

Hagen, Mark von. *War in a European Borderland: Occupations and Occupation Plans in Galicia and Ukraine 1914–1918.* Seattle: University of Washington Press, 2007.

Hantsch, Hugo. *Leopold Graf Berchtold.* 2 vols. Graz: Verlag Styria, 1963.

Hasek, Jaroslav. *The Good Soldier Svejk and His Fortunes in the World War.* Trans. Cecil Parrott. London: Penguin, 1985 [1923].

Herrmann, David G. *The Arming of Europe and the Making of the First World War.* Princeton: Princeton University Press, 1996.

Herwig, Holger H. *The First World War: Germany and Austria-Hungary 1914–1918.* London: Edw. Arnold, 1997.

Hötzendorf, Franz Conrad von. *Aus Meiner Dienstzeit 1906–1918.* 4 vols. Vienna: Rikola, 1921–1923.

———. *Infanteristische Fragen und die Erscheinungen des Boerenkrieges.* Vienna: Seidel, 1903.

———. *Mein Anfang.* Berlin: Verlag für Kulturpolitik, 1925.

Hoffmann, Max. *The War of Lost Opportunities.* New York: International, 1925.

———. *War Diaries.* 2 vols. London: Secker, 1929.

Jelavich, Barbara. *History of the Balkans.* 2 vols. Cambridge: Cambridge University Press, 1983.

Jerabek, Rudolf. "Die Brussilowoffensive 1916: Ein Wendepunkt der Koalitionskriegführung der Mittelmächte." 2 vols. Dissertation, Vienna, 1982.

———. *Potiorek.* Graz: Verlag Styria, 1991.

Kerensky, A. F. *The Catastrophe.* New York: Appleton, 1927.

Kessler, Harry. *Journey to the Abyss: The Diaries of Count Harry Kessler, 1880–1918.* Ed. and trans. Laird M. Easton. New York: Knopf, 2011.

Knox, Alfred. *With the Russian Army 1914–17.* 2 vols. London: Hutchinson, 1921.

Kraus, Karl, ed. *Die Fackel.* 12 vols. Munich: Kösel-Verlag, 1968–1976.

Krauss, Alfred. *Die Ursachen unserer Niederlage: Erinnerungen und Urteile aus den Weltkrieg.* 3rd ed. Munich 1923.

Lackey, Scott W. *The Rebirth of the Habsburg Army.* Westport: Greenwood, 1995.

Laffan, R. G. D. *The Serbs.* New York: Dorset Press, 1989 [1917].

Liddell Hart, B. H. *The Real War 1914–1918.* Boston: Little, Brown, 1963.

Ludendorff, Erich. *My War Memoirs.* New York: Harper, 1919.

Lyon, James M. B. "'A Peasant Mob': The Serbian Army on the Eve of the Great War." *Journal of Military History* 61 (July 1997): 481–502.

Markus, Georg. *Der Fall Redl.* Vienna: Amalthea Verlag, 1984.

McMeekin, Sean. *July 1914.* New York: Basic Books, 2013.

———. *The Russian Origins of the First World War.* Cambridge, MA: Belknap Press, 2011.

Menning, Bruce W. *Bayonets Before Bullets: The Imperial Russian Army 1861–1914.* Bloomington: Indiana University Press, 1991.

Mitrovic, Andre. *Serbia's Great War 1914–1918.* West Lafayette, IN: Purdue University Press, 2007.

Mombauer, Annika. *Helmuth von Moltke and the Origins of the First World War.* Cambridge: Cambridge University Press, 2001.

Morse, John. *In the Russian Ranks*. New York: Grosset and Dunlap, 1918.

Musil, Robert. *The Man Without Qualities*. 2 vols. New York: Vintage, 1996 [1930–1933].

Neue Österreichische Biographie, 1815–1918. 22 vols. Vienna: Amalthea, 1923–1987.

Norman, Henry. *All the Russias*. London: William Heinemann, 1902.

Österreichischen Bundesministerium für Heereswesen und vom Kriegsarchiv. *Österreich-Ungarns Letzter Krieg 1914–18*. 7 vols. Ed. Edmund Glaise-Horstenau, Rudolf Kiszling, et al. Vienna: Verlag der militärwissenschaftlichen Mitteilungen, 1930–1938.

Paléologue, Maurice. *An Ambassador's Memoirs*. London: Hutchinson, 1933.

Peball, Kurt. "Der Feldzug gegen Serbien und Montenegro im Jahre 1914." Österreichische Militärische Zeitschrift Sonderheft I (1965).

Pfeffer, Rudolf. *Zum 10. Jahrestage der Schlachten von Zlocsow und Przemyslany, 26–30 August 1914*. Vienna: Selbstverlag, 1924.

Pflanze, Otto. *Bismarck and the Development of Germany*. 2nd ed. 3 vols. Princeton: Princeton University Press, 1990.

Rauchensteiner, Manfried. *Der Tod des Doppeladlers: Österreich-Ungarn und der Erste Weltkrieg*. Graz: Verlag Styria, 1993.

Redlich, Josef. *Schicksalsjahre Österreichs 1908–19: Das politische Tagebuch Josef Redlichs*. 2 vols. Graz: Verlag Böhlau, 1953.

Reed. John. *Eastern Europe at War*. London: Pluto, 1994 [1916].

Regele, Oskar. *Feldmarschall Conrad*. Vienna: Herold, 1955.

Reiss, R. A. *Report on the Atrocities Committed by Austro-Hungarian Forces*. London, 1916.

Ritter, Gerhard. *The Schlieffen Plan*. Westport: Greenwood Press, 1979.

Rothenberg, Gunther E. *The Army of Francis Joseph*. West Lafayette, IN: Purdue University Press, 1976.

———. "The Austro-Hungarian Campaign Against Serbia in 1914." *Journal of Military History*, April 1989: 127–146.

Ruhl, Arthur. *Antwerp to Gallipoli: A Year of the War on Many Fronts—and Behind Them*. New York: Scribner's, 1916.

Rutherford, Ward. *The Tsar's Army 1914–1917*. 2nd ed. Cambridge: Ian Faulkner, 1992.

Schorske, Carl E. *Fin-de-Siècle Vienna: Politics and Culture*. New York: Vintage, 1981.

Schwarzenberg, Felix Prinz zu. *Briefe aus dem Felde 1914–18*. Vienna: Schwarzenbergisches Administration, 1953.

Shanafelt, Gary W. *The Secret Enemy: Austria-Hungary and the German Alliance 1914–18*. New York: East European Monographs, 1985.

Schön, Joseph. *Sabac!* Reichenberg: Heimatsöhne, 1928.

Showalter, Dennis E. *Tannenberg: Clash of Empires*. North Haven: Archon, 1991.

Silberstein, Gerard. *The Troubled Alliance: German and Austrian Relations, 1914–17*. Lexington: University Press of Kentucky, 1970.

Sked, Alan. *The Decline and Fall of the Habsburg Empire 1815–1918*. London: Longman, 1989.

Sondhaus, Lawrence. *Franz Conrad von Hötzendorf: Architect of the Apocalypse*. Boston: Humanities Press, 2000.

Stepun, Fedor. *Wie war es möglich: Briefe eines russischen Offiziers*. Munich: Carl Hanser Verlag, 1929.

Stevenson, David. *Armaments and the Coming of War: Europe 1904–14.* Oxford: Clarendon Press, 1996.

———. *Cataclysm.* New York: Basic Books, 2004.

Stone, Norman. "Army and Society in the Habsburg Monarchy, 1900–1914." *Past and Present* 33, no. 1 (1966).

———. *The Eastern Front 1914–1917.* London: Penguin, 1998 [1975].

———. "Hungary and the Crisis of July 1914." *Journal of Contemporary History* 1, no. 3 (1966).

———. "Die *Mobilmachung* der österreichisch-ungarischen Armee 1914." *Militärgeschichtliche Mitteilung,* 1974.

———. "Moltke-Conrad: Relations Between the Austro-Hungarian and German General Staffs 1909–1914." *Historical Journal* 9, no. 2 (1966): 201–28.

———. *World War One: A Short History* (New York: Basic Books, 2009).

Strachan, Hew. *The First World War,* vol. 1, *To Arms.* Oxford: Oxford University Press, 2001.

Stürgkh, General Josef. von. *Im Deutschen Grossen Hauptquartier.* Leipzig: Paul List, 1921.

Taslauanu, Octavian C. *With the Austrian Army in Galicia.* London: Streffington, 1919.

Taylor, A. J. P. *The Habsburg Monarchy 1809–1918.* London: Penguin, 1948.

Tunstall, Graydon. *Blood on the Snow: The Carpathian Winter War of 1915.* Lawrence: University Press of Kansas, 2010.

———. "The Habsburg Command Conspiracy: The Austrian Falsification of Historiography on the Outbreak of World War I." *Austrian History Yearbook* 27 (1996): 181–198.

———. *Planning for War Against Russia and Serbia: Austro-Hungarian and German Military Strategies 1871–1914.* New York: Columbia University Press, 1993.

———. *The Verdun of the East: Fortress Przemysl in World War I.* Bloomington: Indiana University Press, 2011.

Ullreich, Josef. "Moritz von Auffenberg-Komurów: Leben und Wirken." Dissertation. Vienna, 1961.

Washburn, Stanley. *Field Notes from the Russian Front.* London: Andrew Melrose, 1915.

———. *On the Russian Front in World War I: Memoirs of an American War Correspondent.* New York: Robert Speller, 1982.

Wawro, Geoffrey. *The Austro-Prussian War.* Cambridge: Cambridge University Press, 1996.

———. *The Franco-Prussian War.* Cambridge: Cambridge University Press, 2003.

———. *Warfare and Society in Europe 1792–1914.* London: Routledge, 2000.

Wildman, Allan K. *The End of the Russian Imperial Army.* 2 vols. Princeton: Princeton University Press, 1987.

Williamson, Samuel R., Jr. *Austria-Hungary and the Origins of the First World War.* New York: St. Martin's, 1991.

Index